Contracting Freedom

POLITICS AND CULTURE IN MODERN AMERICA

Series Editors: Keisha N. Blain, Margot Canaday,
Matthew Lassiter, Stephen Pitti, Thomas J. Sugrue

Volumes in the series narrate and analyze political and
social change in the broadest dimensions from 1865 to
the present, including ideas about the ways people have
sought and wielded power in the public sphere and the
language and institutions of politics at all levels—local,
national, and transnational. The series is motivated by
a desire to reverse the fragmentation of modern U.S.
history and to encourage synthetic perspectives on
social movements and the state, on gender, race, and
labor, and on intellectual history and popular culture.

CONTRACTING FREEDOM

Race, Empire, and
U.S. Guestworker Programs

Maria L. Quintana

PENN

UNIVERSITY OF PENNSYLVANIA PRESS

PHILADELPHIA

Published by
University of Pennsylvania Press
Philadelphia, Pennsylvania 19104-4112
www.upenn.edu/pennpress

Printed in the United States of America on acid-free paper
10 9 8 7 6 5 4 3 2 1

Hardback ISBN: 9780812253887
Ebook ISBN: 9780812298499

Library of Congress Cataloging-in-Publication Data

Names: Quintana, Maria, author.
Title: Contracting freedom : race, empire, and U.S.
guestworker programs / Maria L. Quintana.
Other titles: Politics and culture in modern America.
Description: Philadelphia : University of Pennsylvania
Press, [2022] | Series: Politics and culture in modern
America | Includes bibliographical references and index.
Identifiers: LCCN 2021052458 | ISBN
9780812253887 (hardcover)
Subjects: LCSH: Seasonal Farm Laborers Program.
| Agricultural laborers, Foreign—United States—
History—20th century. | Foreign workers—United
States—History—20th century. | Contract labor—United
States—History—20th century. | Race relations—History—
20th century. | Imperialism—History—20th century.
Classification: LCC HD1525 .Q65 2022 | DDC
331.5/440973—dc23/eng/20211227
LC record available at https://lccn.loc.gov/2021052458

For Aurelia and Lucía

CONTENTS

ABBREVIATIONS

AACC	Anglo-American Caribbean Commission (later the Caribbean Commission)
AEC	American Emigrant Company
AFL	American Federation of Labor
AFL-CIO	American Federation of Labor and Congress of Industrial Organizations
BBPA	Bahamas Benevolent Protective Association
CPN	Confederación Proletaria Nacional
CPUSA	Communist Party USA
CTM	Confederación de Trabajadores Mexicanos
FSA	Farm Security Administration (formerly the Resettlement Administration)
ILO	International Labor Organization
JPL	Jamaican Progressive League
LULAC	League of United Latin American Citizens
NAACP	National Association for the Advancement of Colored People
NFLU	National Farm Labor Union (later the NAWU)
NIRA	National Industrial Recovery Act
NLRA	National Labor Relations Act
ORIT	Inter-American Regional Organization of Workers
PAU	Pan-American Union (later the Organization of American States)
PNM	People's National Movement (Trinidad and Tobago)
PNP	People's National Party (Jamaica)
PPD	Popular Democratic Party (Puerto Rico)
STFU	Southern Tenant Farmers' Union
WFA	War Food Administration
WMC	War Manpower Commission
WRA	War Relocation Authority

UFW	United Farm Workers, AFL-CIO
USDA	United States Department of Agriculture
USDL	United States Department of Labor
USES	United States Employment Service
UTAVM	Unión de Trabajadores Agrícolas del Valle
WINEC	West Indies National Emergency Committee (later WINC)

Freedom Struggles and the Labor Contract

On September 29, 1942, several hundred Mexican contract workers or "braceros" boarded a train to the Southwestern United States to work in agricultural fields as part of the Allied war effort during World War II. Before their departure, the Mexican secretary of labor, Francisco Trujillo Gurría, said to those on board, "Each of you is to regard himself as a fighter for democracy, even if we cannot give you guns." He continued, "You must not regard this trip to the United States as merely an economic opportunity for yourselves. You go to aid the common cause of our united war." When the workers arrived in places like Stockton, California, and El Paso, Texas, Mexican consuls came out to greet them and pushed them to give their best to produce "food for victory." U.S. radio commentators and newspapers exhorted, "You can do your share by fighting as hard on the food production front as the American soldiers are fighting on the battle fronts of the world."[1] A year later, in 1943, Jamaican, Bahamian, and Puerto Rican workers boarded airplanes in the Caribbean to journey to the Eastern United States, Florida, and the Midwest for the same purpose, with the U.S. War Department lending its planes and ships to transport the workers. As thousands of Bahamian and Jamaican men went to work in rural communities from Iowa to Connecticut, they, too, experienced an enthusiastic welcome from locals, with military bands, invitations to church, access to country clubs, and more community-sponsored parties—also hailed as heroes and fighters in the Allied war effort.[2] This successful labor mobilization campaign resulted in the cyclical migration of over 4.5 million Mexican migrant workers and hundreds of thousands of Caribbean migrant workers to the United States between 1942 and 1964, giving rise to the guestworker importation programs that exist today under new guises and forms.

U.S. guestworker importation expanded and flourished as an instrument of conceptual freedom during World War II, when the U.S. military inducted over 6 million men for the war.[3] Believing a labor shortage threatened food production, U.S. officials proposed a set of hemispheric programs and organizations to manage labor migration that would, according to all the governments involved, produce enough food to ensure that the United States could "win the war against fascism and racism, saving the world from slavery and oppression." On Labor Day in 1942, the U.S. Office of War Information (OWI) promoted these programs with the propaganda theme "free labor will win" to news and other media agencies, contrasting labor in the United States with "unfree" labor in Nazi Germany. The OWI maintained, "Free labor challenges the deluded Axis idea that slave labor can out-produce free labor. With a resounding promise that free labor will win, American labor holds out the hand of hope to the enslaved nations of the world."[4] After the end of World War II, the threat of Communism loomed large, leading U.S. officials to continue to engage a language of "freedom" to protect U.S. capitalism in the world. As President Harry Truman declared in his 1949 inaugural address, the United States should assist "the free peoples of the world, through their own efforts," to create self-sufficiency through economic production in a "worldwide effort for the achievement of peace, plenty, and freedom."[5]

The officials who implemented the Mexican farm labor program, or the bracero program, and the farm labor programs in the British West Indies publicly referred to imported laborers as "guests," "allies," "neighbors," and "friends," journeying to the U.S. in mutual understanding and consent, as propagated through a language of reciprocal international ties and agreement. The individual labor contract each worker signed epitomized this focus on freedom, serving as proof of their voluntary agreement and offering a set of rights, duties, and stipulations designed to ensure the welfare and protection of the workers once in the United States. The workers themselves likewise faithfully recited and articulated a discursive framework of freedom at parties designed to welcome them into U.S. rural communities, proud to sign up and help to produce "vital foods" as their patriotic mission. In May 1945, a group of Mexican contract workers informed President Harry S. Truman, "We dedicate ourselves to the war effort and offer our humble cooperation in the global effort to defend the liberty of individuals and towns."[6]

Other contract workers pointed out the conflict between rhetoric and reality as they experienced the supposed "freedom" of the labor programs on the ground. A contingent of Mexican braceros noted that they "would be happy to stay for work now that the war is over, but only with better salaries and protections, honoring compensation for accidents, edible food, medical attention, etc." These same workers were critical of the bracero program because they were not permitted to put a Mexican flag next to an American flag at the entrance of the camp, as was done in the other camps they had visited. Like their Mexican counterparts, Afro-Caribbean laborers were soon just as disenchanted with the language of freedom offered them. In a letter to President Franklin D. Roosevelt, three Jamaican workers in Hubbardsville, New York, declared, "According to our contract we were told we would start work on arrival. We are now pending for a period of eight days of which conditions are rather imperfect." After a similar wait, six Bahamian workers declared, "We are strong men and willing to work and now we are not doing our part in the war effort situation in helping our boys overseas." Others were more exact: "I have not worked for two weeks and I have a family in the Bahamas to support and I cannot earn $2 a day. . . . How in this world am I to live?" With growers requesting excess contract workers to ensure a surplus of labor and reduce wages, reporters noted that Bahamian workers lived in a "virtual slum" in the camps at Winchester, Virginia, where more than 1,000 congregated in "dingy gray shacks."[7] These were hardly the stories that U.S. government officials publicized, and they reveal the dark underbelly of state programs of labor abuse, estrangement, and racial exclusion. The U.S. government and growers often did not honor the contracts they signed with imported migrant workers, who suffered endless grievances.

Nonetheless, the labor programs with Mexico, the British West Indies, and Puerto Rico served as a paradigm for the value of formal labor contracts, bilateral agreements between nation-states, and equal rights at a time of intensifying pressure on Western democracies. During World War II, civil rights and anticolonial activists began to associate the Nazi genocide of European Jews with racism existing across the world, demonstrating affinities between European fascism, U.S. racial segregation, and British colonial rule, which placed the United States at a diplomatic impasse.[8] U.S. policymakers during this period were deeply concerned about the propaganda strategies pro-German forces throughout the Caribbean and Latin America might use to criticize the United States as a racist state, interrupting U.S. economic affairs in the hemisphere. They were also anxious about raw materials from Latin America and the strategic importance of the Caribbean as a military site during and after World War II. To ensure the United States remained viable as a hegemonic power, U.S. officials asserted the right to self-determination of all peoples and began to consider institutional labor arrangements, national organizations, policies, laws, and legislation that could promote racial equality and end colonial exploitation, including "guestworker" and "contract labor" initiatives.[9]

In the Caribbean, British colonialism was likewiseunder siege, as a
robust labor movement challenged British colonial officials to ponder how
economic and labor crises on the islands might be resolved. Because of the
strategic and economic importance of the Caribbean during the war, President Roosevelt prompted progressive U.S. leaders to investigate the social
and political climate on the islands. Roosevelt's New Deal adviser on the
Caribbean, Charles Taussig, and the U.S. governor of Puerto Rico, Rexford
Tugwell, completed a survey and a series of reports declaring that Great Britain and the United States had a shared interest in the problems of the Caribbean, prompting the formation of the joint Anglo-American Caribbean
Commission (AACC) on March 9, 1942.[10] Influenced by the scholarship of
Afro-Caribbean historian Eric Williams, officials of the AACC promoted
contract farm labor programs between the United States and the British
West Indies as a means to extend liberty and eventual independence to the
Caribbean colonies. Likewise, the Mexican labor advocate and civil rights
activist Dr. Ernesto Galarza, then a member of the Pan-American Union,
embraced the World War II moment to propose a joint organization and
agreement between the U.S. and Mexican governments, to ensure the freedom of historically exploited Mexican labor migrants. Many officials of the
Puerto Rican Popular Democratic Party (PPD) similarly pursued the idea
of a farm labor migration program in Puerto Rico in 1948, arguing for governed labor mobility as a way to uplift working Puerto Ricans and eventually
free the island from the yoke of colonialism.[11]

The idea of state-managed labor mobility appealed to many progressive
officials and labor advocates who genuinely saw the Mexican and Caribbean labor importation programs as a means to politically and economically improve the lives of migrant farm laborers and grant them civil rights.
Inspired by the ideological promise of liberalism as a political philosophy
based on liberty, equality before the law, and the consent of the governed,
federal officials and administrators defended the World War II guestworker
programs as a solution to the rampant discrimination and racism faced by
migrant farmworkers. These officials developed a framework for the labor
programs that portrayed "race" as a contradiction to modern civil society,
rather than as one of its structuring conditions, a contradiction that could
be overcome through proper state intervention. They popularized the labor
contract as a buffer against racial discrimination and advertised the United
States as a welcoming place for Mexican and Caribbean workers, even though
that was hardly the case.[12]

The Co-Constitution of U.S. Guestworker Programs

This book represents the first scholarly attempt to examine the broad geographical dimensions of the World War II U.S. contract farm labor programs together and in sweeping detail. It views these labor programs relationally and in tandem to reveal how they were co-constituted and mutually understood across time and space, producing a liberal consensus during this period that lives on today. By examining debates among government officials, labor leaders, civil rights activists, and agribusiness employers, it explores how the contractual consent and freedom of 1940s guestworker programs legitimated and extended U.S. racial and imperial domination abroad in the post–World War II period. More broadly, *Contracting Freedom* pursues the argument that liberalism, as a normative political idea and practice in the modern world, cannot be divorced from empire. In comparing the labor programs across geographic regions, it demonstrates that a global shift in the ideology of liberalism nurtured race and empire both before and after World War II, as numerous states sought to expand control over laborers through anti-imperial and race-neutral measures.[13]

The particular form of liberalism that officials and labor advocates advanced in proposing the labor importation programs, "racial liberalism," or rights-consciousness liberalism, indicated a new strategy to address inequality and white supremacy through the expansion of federal authority during the New Deal.[14] Yet the New Deal has been left out of most historical analyses of the World War II guestworker programs, with historians tending to agree that it was wartime labor needs, together with conservative growers' lobbying efforts, that produced the programs.[15] Likewise, racial liberalism has been left out of most analyses of the New Deal, as historians tend to emphasize the failure of the New Deal as a whole to actively pursue racial equality.[16] While the New Deal's most enduring achievements, including universal social security and housing loans under the Federal Housing Administration (FHA), were allocated along racial lines, there were many contentious moments when state officials more expansively interpreted the goals of the New Deal. And even though there were many segregationist New Deal officials who did not support civil rights, there were also those who attempted to draw the attention of a growing group of U.S. bureaucrats to the issue of racial inequality. These officials, influenced by the rising global anticolonial and civil rights movements, attempted to make racial liberalism central to broader legislative change in the United States from the 1940s to the 1950s.

In response to the Black civil rights movement's planned March on Washington in 1941, for instance, Roosevelt issued Executive Order 8802, institutionalizing the Fair Employment Practices Commission (FEPC), which required that companies with government defense contracts not discriminate "on the basis of race, creed, color, or national origin." Although Roosevelt reluctantly issued this order, some New Deal officials followed it closely, arguing for imported contract workers to be included as "defense workers." As a result, one of the first stipulations written into all Caribbean and Mexican labor contracts required that workers not be discriminated against "on the basis of race, creed, color, or national origin," with this clause written into the contracts of each labor importation program thereafter.[17] By delineating a series of legal rights to the workers through the contract, including an antidiscrimination clause and the right to the "same guarantees enjoyed by other agricultural workers under the laws of the United States of America," the architects of the labor programs hoped to extend the promise of freedom to Mexican and Caribbean migrant farmworkers.

The ideology of racial liberalism was not a new phenomenon, as it shared congruencies with earlier notions of the cultural melting pot and racial democracy spreading throughout Latin America in the 1920s and 1930s. U.S. intellectuals and U.S. Department of Agriculture officials traveling to and from Mexico at this time became inculcated in the values of Mexican pluralism and racial harmony, with those values shaping their ideas about the state's relationship to its people. The very idea of racial democracy, as fueled by Latin American intellectuals like José Vasconcelos in Mexico and Gilberto Freyre in Brazil, stood in patriotic contrast to the blatant racial divisions and violence taking place in the United States. Finding hope in Mexico's postrevolutionary state for the answers they sought to modern social conflict in the countryside, many U.S. intellectuals and officials began to debate the role of the federal state as a mediator of racial conflict.[18]

Members of Roosevelt's "brain trust," including Secretary of Agriculture (later Vice President) Henry A. Wallace and Undersecretary of Agriculture Rexford Tugwell, as well as U.S. labor leaders and intellectuals, took frequent "goodwill" tours of Mexico throughout the 1930s in an attempt to survey the Mexican government's implementation of agrarian reforms. They saw in the Mexican revolutionary state the possibilities presented in the experimental redistribution of hundreds of thousands of acres of Mexico's most productive acres from large landowners to farmworkers. Interested in merging state regulation with the principles of economic science to forge a more equitable and balanced capitalism in the United States, USDA planners became inspired by Mexico to solve "the agrarian question." They, along with intellectuals at Columbia University including historian of Latin America Frank Tannenbaum, helped formulate the legislation that established the Farm Security Administration (FSA), one of the organizations originally responsible for the management of the farm labor programs during World War II.[19]

The ideas of these New Deal intellectuals and leaders gained credence at this time, as a rising backlash in Latin America against U.S. militarism and Washington's dollar diplomacy had forced the Roosevelt administration to promote a diplomacy of neighborly good intentions and reciprocal intellectual exchanges through the Good Neighbor Policy.[20] As President Roosevelt later confessed, "While it was the prospect of war profits that caused the extension of monopoly and unjustified expansion of industry in Latin America . . . we seek to dominate no other nation. We ask no territorial expansion. We oppose imperialism. We believe in democracy; we believe in freedom; we believe in peace." During an April 1943 joint radio broadcast with the Mexican president Manuel Ávila Camacho in Monterrey, Mexico, as part of a seventeen-day, 7,600-mile wartime inspection tour, Roosevelt made the following statement: "We recognize a mutual interdependence of our joint resources. . . . We know that the day of exploitation of the resources and the people of one country for the benefit of any group in another country is definitely over."[21] With the United States' strategic military and economic connections to Latin America and the Caribbean threatened by the global anticolonial and civil rights movements, officials promoted a purportedly "new" anti-imperialism that provided an opening for those officials and progressives seeking social change in the United States.

In arguing that the wartime expansions of the federal state would eventually move American political subjectivity beyond the color line and beyond imperialism, intellectuals and federal officials reaffirmed U.S. exceptionalism and the promises of liberalism. Their turn to racial liberalism limited the global anticolonial reach of civil rights intellectual discourse, as it made the U.S. federal government the site of productive antiracist social change. As historians Mary Dudziak, Penny Von Eschen, and others have shown, as Black activists pursued a vision of global anticolonial transformation during and after World War II, an increasingly influential discourse of U.S. race relations folded Black political thought back into the liberal nationalist narrative of "freedom."[22] A similar problem emerged with the 1940s labor programs. As progressive and radical intellectuals and officials enacted this transformation toward anti-imperialism and racial equality through state-managed labor importation programs, they likewise folded migrant labor into the

Figure 1. Americans All. This OWI poster publicized the sup-
posed equality of the United States and Mexico as allies during
World War II. Leon Helguera for the Office of War Information,
U.S. Government Printing Office. Courtesy of University of
North Texas Digital Library.

narrative of freedom and made the state the primary vehicle of social change.
This process made illegible the tangible ways the U.S. federal government had
historically served as a mechanism to commodify and coerce labor while also
inflating capitalist profits for private enterprise.

This race-neutral and purportedly anti-imperial political shift in the liberal order during the 1940s limited awareness of global capitalism and the

role that race and empire had played in its development.[23] It not only elided the global history of U.S. colonialism and slavery, it made the labor programs out to be advances beyond Old World empire and its corollary, slavery. In turn, the systematic and sustained mistreatment of contract laborers came to be viewed as a contradiction to liberal ideals, not a logical continuation of empire in a different guise. The very naming of the programs as "guest-worker" or "contract labor" initiatives erased any suggestion of a coercive labor importation scheme, thus obscuring the reality that these workers had few opportunities for economic survival other than to sign a labor contract.[24] In effect, contract labor programs became a sanitized means to expand the U.S. government's power to manage, control, import, and deport laborers in a theoretically postimperial, postslavery context.

The fact that Japanese inmates incarcerated during "Japanese internment" were offered farm labor contracts at the same time begs for an analysis of the language of "freedom" used to construct the labor programs. As with the Mexican and Caribbean labor programs, New Deal officials defended and framed the project of Japanese internment as a race-neutral government project designed to protect and ensure the welfare and "freedom" of Japanese Americans. Upon imprisonment in "internment centers," the War Relocation Authority (WRA) encouraged Japanese Americans to sign labor contracts and enlist voluntarily for farm labor in a mobile "Work Corps." The putative voluntarism of their farm labor contracts obscured the fact that Japanese Americans were prison inmates who had few other options than to "volunteer" for labor contracts. Even further, the farm labor contracts signed by incarcerated Japanese Americans threatened further imprisonment if they chose to leave the work site in the face of harsh living and working conditions, making visible the coercion of their labor contracts. "Freedom," therefore, was a racial project, as well as an effective tool of racialized labor coercion. While some labor leaders and activists had a more inclusive vision of freedom that legitimized the guest worker programs, that vision, in the end, resulted in state-led labor coercion and the continuation of empire.

As much as New Deal state officials as well as civil and labor rights advocates tried to convince themselves and the public of the bilateral, reciprocal, and voluntary or "free" nature of the labor programs, placing the entangled histories of the Japanese American, Mexican Puerto Rican, and British West Indian labor programs together reveals how central the history of colonialism and racial coercion was to their formation. The bilateralism of the Mexican labor agreement and contract, upon which all other labor programs were modeled, cast the labor programs as acts of sovereign and equal nations. However, the island of Puerto Rico had been a colonial possession of the United States since 1898, with U.S. investments in sugar and agriculture undeniably stunting the islands' labor economy. The British West Indies (Jamaica, the Bahamas, British Honduras, and Barbados) were colonies of the British Empire, with the U.S. government importing contract laborers by permission of the British colonial minister. Laborers that the United States recruited from the British West Indies consisted mostly of formerly enslaved Africans and their children, who came to work for U.S. businesses like the United Fruit Company and U.S. state projects like the Panama Canal at the beginning of the twentieth century.[25] The history of slavery and agriculture structured the economies of the Caribbean and led to new forms of labor extraction and coercion throughout the twentieth century. Contextualizing the labor programs within these regional histories contemporaneously illustrates that the labor programs emerged out of a long history of European and U.S. colonialism in the Caribbean, upending the bilateral and anti-imperial framework upon which they were designed.

Many contemporary scholars have referred to the bracero program in particular as "colonial-like" or as a form of "imported colonialism," but the policies and practices surrounding imported contract labor are deeply rooted in the history of colonialism and slavery in the United States and not necessarily "imported" at all.[26] Considering the history of colonialism and enslavement and its foundational role in the labor programs permits us to critique the customary liberal progressive and exceptionalist narrative in the United States that slavery ended with abolition. Since abolition, liberalism has been used innovatively to encourage the circulation of goods and working people, leading to the expansion of ever stronger states required to regulate and govern the movements of "free labor."[27] In turn, the extension of rights and protections to migrant laborers via the labor contract led to new forms of subjection, coercion, administration, and governance. The liberalism that emerged in the 1940s thus ushered in new practices of labor control through state power—even as it simultaneously conjured and elided colonial subjecthood.

Liberalism and Empire

Rather than focusing on how empire should be defined or whether the nation-state should be defined as distinct from empire, this book unveils the processes by which people become subject to state power(s)—an inherently racialized and imperial process. This focus harkens back to the original definition of *empire* in the English language: "that which is subject to imperial rule."[28] When progressive 1940s liberal labor advocates and state officials, employed the tenets of liberalism, including the claim that governments exist to protect and guarantee the rights of the individual, and the discourse of equality, to argue for the expansion of state power to extend certain rights to migrant farm laborers, they made migrant workers subject to state authority or empire. An investigation into the ways liberalism legitimized and organized guestworker labor programs reveals that the abuses that resulted were not about government corruption, nor about government failure to fulfill "the law," nor about governments failing to do what they otherwise *should* be doing. Rather, the abuses of the labor programs were, in part, a result of the liberal implementation and policies of the programs as New Deal officials and labor advocates sought to expand state governance to benefit workers. In other words, the exploitative realities of the labor programs—wage theft, injury, displacement, isolation, and poor living conditions—were not a government failure, but a product of the liberalism by which state power became justified.

The concept of state power discussed in this book is neither monolithic nor static; it is not only a set of bureaucratic agencies, informed by political advocates, but also a particular process of negotiation, force, consent, and contestation through which governance is accomplished. In some ways, the state functions as a mediating body, weighing the priorities of various interest groups with unequal access to power, negotiating compromises between political factions, and incorporating working-class demands into legislation, but on capitalist terms.[29] Liberalism is the philosophical foundation upon which the modern state, as a governing body, has acquired authority, and it has long been predicated upon the differentiation of the world along race-based lines. Liberalism offered an expansion, not an elimination, of race or modalities of race. The European empires that gave rise to liberal modernity facilitated the organization of the world through an imperial gaze defined by the white male subject, a gaze that divided inferior from superior, civilized from uncivilized, and human from inhuman. Therein lies the violence of the liberal state: in the process of deciding who belongs and who does not along race, gender, and foreign/domestic lines, state officials turn human beings into subjects of state power and of violence.[30] That power and violence is structured not simply by the use of physical force but by the shared understandings, norms, and rituals that permeate day-to-day life for officials and community members. For contract workers, even the threat of violence—as in the threat of deportation, the threat of incarceration, or the threat of removing one's ability to earn a wage—were powerful but violent tools used by local, state, and federal officials, by growers, and by local community members to coerce laborers into conforming to the will of the state.[31]

The liberalism that took shape in the 1930s and 1940s was different from nineteenth-century and early twentieth-century liberalism, which had been characterized by a staunch commitment to minimal federal government intervention. Former U.S. contract labor efforts, including the World War I Mexican labor importation program, had allowed employers to privately recruit contract workers with little government interference. Since local government offices lacked power to enforce the labor agreement or the contract, little was achieved by way of the first Mexican labor program in protecting contract workers in the face of exploitative employers and *enganchadores* or *patrones* (private labor contractors).[32] The coercive power of the employer determined contract worker treatment before the 1940s, often without any legal sanction against abuses. Partially in response to this, New Deal officials and labor advocates of the 1930s and 1940s sought to guarantee reasonably paid jobs and decent working conditions to migrants by promoting and expanding the state's role in hiring workers and enforcing the labor contract. If the World War I labor program had failed to ensure the guarantees or protections of Mexican contract workers, New Deal officials believed that the 1940s labor program could be capaciously managed by the liberal state so as to guarantee the welfare of workers. To that end, a slew of "protective" government agencies were created in the 1940s to govern each labor program and protect contract freedom.

Numerous scholars and historians have addressed the twentieth-century growth of state power and violence against Mexican labor migrants, focusing on the exploitation, dispossession, and deportation that arose with increased governmental power over contract workers, without confronting the role of liberalism as the bedrock upon which such state power and violence rests. Kelly Lytle Hernández's book, *Migra!*, importantly shows how the bracero program resulted in the legitimization, professionalization, and exponential growth of the Border Patrol, with the legalization of Mexican migrants through the labor contract ultimately precipitating the expansion of the agency and the increased use of "illegality" as a tool to control and deport Mexican workers. As she notes, with the start of the bracero program in 1942, the Border Patrol's net of surveillance expanded, with interrogations increasing from 473,720 in 1940 to 9,389,551 in 1943—an almost twenty-fold increase. Historian Adam Goodman likewise mentions in his book, *Deportation Machine*, that the Immigration and Naturalization Service (INS) carried out nearly six million expulsions during the period of the bracero program— almost all to Mexico, and roughly six times as many as in the previous half century.[33] In other words, it was only when the U.S. and Mexican governments established a *legal* contract labor program that the focus on worker *illegality* gained wide popular traction in the United States, making the labor contract central to understanding how liberalism fueled the application of state power and violence against migrant workers.

With the contract and worker *legality* so central to the historic expansion of state power and violence against migrant workers, *Contracting Freedom* begins by tracing the history of the labor contract, focusing on the postemancipation period, when U.S. policymakers expanded federal immigration laws to increase distinctions between legal and illegal labor, between foreign and domestic laborers, between *contratados* and U.S. citizens, and between white and nonwhite labor. These distinctions rationalized racial segregation and controlled mobility, normalized the surveillance and deportation of noncitizen workers, and allowed for the exploitation of workers at the hands of a powerful agricultural elite class—all forms of violence.

In highlighting the liberal entanglements of the guestworker labor programs and the processes by which contract workers became subject to state violence, *Contracting Freedom* demonstrates that the labor programs were not merely a product of U.S. state power, but of multiple overlapping state projects. The Mexican and Puerto Rican governments, actively involved in their own liberal New Deal projects not unlike those in the United States, framed new hierarchies and divisions of labor through the labor programs.[34] Mexico had long sought to expand state power over agricultural labor, in attempts to either include peripheral indigenous populations within the centralized claims of the nation-state through landownership, or exclude them through indigenous land expropriation. By the early twentieth century, a discourse of "modernity" justified the claims that the Mexican state made on indigenous land, as it appropriated indigenous land for its own purposes.[35] Government acts forced the mobility of Mexican labor, and later the control of that labor mobility through the bracero program. Similarly, the Puerto Rican labor importation program materialized in 1948 as a product of Governor Luis Muñoz Marín's state-led modernization campaign known as *Manos a la Obra* or Operation Bootstrap, which also resulted in labor mobility, displacement, and management. The liberalism that structured the labor programs fueled the combined aims of state-led modernization and economic development, whether from the perspective of the United States, British, Puerto Rican, or Mexican governments.

The governments of Mexico and Puerto Rico encouraged the enrollment of laborers into guestworker programs as part of a gendered and racial project in liberal state-building, often convincing rural Mexicans and Puerto Ricans of their patriotic and manly duty in the development of Mexico and Puerto Rico, while also persuading them to see themselves as part of the Mexican and Puerto Rican national projects. The fact that Mexicans and Puerto Ricans flocked to recruitment centers to journey to the United States as braceros indicated to many that these were coveted positions that workers sought because they were well-paid and well-treated. By constructing migrant workers as individual liberal subjects capable of signing a contract of their own free will, the contract became a capitulation to narratives of liberal individualism. In the process, government officials also turned migratory workers into heroic subjects making a sacrificial effort to feed their families and patriotically improve their national economies through monetary remittances. Each state government involved thus elided the shared histories of contract workers as peasants, landless people, and the working poor, who had been made vulnerable by government policies, making it nearly impossible to see the larger political and economic forces at work shaping their lives.

Contract workers, as putative "guests," protested the contradictions they experienced as well as the fact that the protections promised in their contracts were not realized. Critiquing the specious and misleading representation of the labor program, many concluded that the contract was a hoax. One bracero stated, "A few of us have read our contracts but we just read them for fun. The contracts do not mean anything in this camp."[36] As they experienced hostility from local communities and employers, they became interpreters and critics of the contracts, calling into question the notion of freedom as put forth by the state and by their labor contracts. While not all read the contract or were aware of its provisions, they criticized their treatment and the promises of both governments involved. While some embraced the vision of freedom the state offered by the contract through the ability to work and earn money in the United States, others saw it as a limited freedom and repeatedly attempted to strike for better wages and working conditions, becoming essential architects in the debates over contract freedom. This book amplifies the insights of 1940s and 1950s contract workers across multiple chapters, bringing to light the subtle ways that workers embraced, rejected, or criticized the liberalism the labor programs espoused.

The way historians have documented the labor programs as separate from one another has obscured their overlapping and mutually constitutive imperial histories. As many historians have observed, American exceptionalism impairs popular recognition of U.S. imperial conduct—but there is more to it than that.[37] As interdisciplinary scholar Lisa Lowe demonstrates, liberalism disaggregates and elides the "intimate connections between the four continents" to reduce them to national histories and to frame them as seemingly discrete and disconnected developments. The only way to change this lies in the struggle to comprehend the "absence of the intimacies of four continents, to engage slavery, genocide, indenture, and liberalism as a conjunction, as an actively acknowledged loss within the present."[38] By doing so, we can reckon with the past in new ways while also being open to alternative epistemologies, beyond political emancipation or citizenship in the state.

Contracting Freedom addresses the intimacies that link the concurrent Mexican, Puerto Rican, and Afro-Caribbean contract labor programs in the mid-twentieth century. It is an attempt to illuminate the historical and cultural processes through which multiple groups of migrant laborers across the Western Hemisphere became subject to state power through a shifting logic of liberalism. This is, therefore, a study at the crossroads of the literature on race and empire, immigration policy, civil rights, and labor migrations.[39] It is an intervention in postcolonial studies, insofar as it suggests that differentiating between nation-states and empires or colonies—whether the British Empire, Mexico, the Puerto Rican "Commonwealth," or the United States—belies the fact that national and colonial power are deeply intertwined. In placing the labor programs within the framework of ethnic studies, labor studies, civil rights history, immigration history, and U.S. and Latin American comparative colonialism, this book aims ultimately to demonstrate the limitations and contradictions of state-centered approaches to social justice and to point to other political possibilities.

The Long Arc of Guestworker Labor and Empire

To expose the shared historical and ideological links driving the programs, each chapter of *Contracting Freedom* places the contemporaneous Mexican and Caribbean U.S. labor importation programs within the context of their formative moments: slavery and indentured servitude in the British Caribbean colonies, the incarceration of Japanese Americans during World War II, and the U.S. labor and civil rights movements. In viewing guestworker programs within these contexts, it reveals continuities with older forms of empire while illustrating how guestworkers and their advocates attempted to compel the state to fulfill the guarantees and rights of the contract during the long civil rights movement. By focusing on their daily struggles, *Contracting Freedom* highlights emerging visions of social justice at a time when liberalism and freedom took on new meanings. This book is therefore about freedom struggles and the critiques of the liberalism that emerged in the 1940s–1960s. In them, we can begin to find glimpses of wider visions of social justice that challenged the mandates of the U.S. liberal state, beyond legalistic "freedom" as it is framed by rights through the state.

Chapter 1 elaborates on the ambiguous contradictions of freedom and coercion, focusing on the interconnected histories of slavery and the labor contract. This chapter provides a genealogy of the labor contract, to show how the U.S. government has historically policed the racialized boundaries of "foreign" and "domestic" through the slave/free dialectic that figures the labor contract. Whether imagined as a form of "slavery" or "freedom," the contract became, in different historical moments, a means to exclude foreign contract laborers from U.S. citizenship, while transforming them into resources or commodities to be transferred from one nation-state (or colony) to another. Instead of turning to the slave/free dialectic to frame and critique the labor programs, this chapter stresses how the logics of that paradigm have sustained the capitalist commodification of racialized labor.

Chapter 2 examines the formation of the bracero program from the perspective of the labor and civil rights activist Dr. Ernesto Galarza. In initially proposing a Mexican labor program in 1940 and 1941 as an official of the Pan-American Union, Galarza took part in forging a particular kind of liberal politics that celebrated a U.S. labor importation program as marking a new hemispheric age of freedom. This chapter demonstrates how an ideology of racial liberalism gained momentum during the formation of the bracero program in the context of the Good Neighbor Policy, the New Deal, and World War II, divulging how Galarza's defense of a labor importation program was not an anomaly but rather part of a broader continuum in state attempts to control labor migrations. Chapter 3 shifts the focus to the U.S. West, to explore the intimate links between the incarceration of Japanese Americans and the importation of Mexican laborers in 1942. Through different congressional committee hearings headed by Representative John H. Tolan (California), this chapter explores how the U.S. entry into World War II shifted New Deal officials' strategies and priorities to finding new sources of labor. As agricultural employers clamored for new workers to fill the wartime labor shortage, Tolan and his colleagues turned their attention to Mexican workers and Japanese Americans, whose incarceration in concentration camps ironically had contributed to the perceived labor shortage in the first place.

Chapter 4 investigates braceros' reactions to the moral language used by government officials and labor advocates, to show how they invented their own terms for understanding the labor programs and the labor contract. Placing the bracero program within the history of the civil rights movement, it then focuses on how Galarza's transnational farm labor unionization efforts and appeals to the state to enforce the rights of the labor contract, along with federal immigration laws, served to fortify and justify divides between citizens and undocumented migrants. Chapter 5 details how Puerto Rican officials, trained in the United States and steeped in New Deal liberalism, configured a U.S. labor importation program in the late 1940s and into the 1950s. Here, the United States and Puerto Rican governments became just as invested in choices as with the Mexican labor program; in the choice of the Puerto Rican government to serve the greater good however it saw fit, and in the choice of the individual worker to serve the Puerto Rican and U.S. nations as an expression of democracy and good will. The new conceptually "postcolonial" model of governance that transpired on the island in the 1950s promised the right to self-determination of all peoples, a legitimizing rhetoric that became necessary for the United States to maintain its hegemony over the island.

Last, Chapter 6 addresses the struggles of British West Indian contract workers within the context of the anticolonial national independence movements in the Caribbean and the Black freedom movement in the United States. This chapter illustrates how the promises of liberal protections and rights through the labor programs expanded the U.S. government's influence over the Caribbean, which some anticolonial activists welcomed as a means to gain national independence for the islands. Once the British colonies gained independence in the 1960s, the labor programs continued—in order to improve local economies and to secure votes for nascent political parties— and served to deepen and legitimize the U.S. presence across the Caribbean.

*   *   *

In 2010, officials and community members commemorated the bracero program with a sixteen-mile stretch of road along California Highway 101 in Monterey County, California. The plaque for Bracero Memorial Highway celebrates the bracero program as "a contribution to making the United States of America the most powerful nation in the world." According to the memorial, "with their strong arms and backs" braceros worked on America's dams, railways, roadways, assembly plants, mines and helped to develop America's agricultural lands. They fought in the U.S. military and helped to feed the Allied forces during the war and the reconstruction that followed, "lifting many nations from rubble and raising the standard of living around the world." The memorial also claims braceros as proud members of "America's Greatest Generation." While activists pushed for the creation of this memorial with the goal of including braceros as part of U.S. history, valued for their contributions to the United States, the memorial also reveals the many ways liberalism still structures how the bracero program is remembered. By insisting on guestworkers' contributions to the United States, the writers of the memorial recreated a notion of the United States as a land of opportunity based on democratic ideals and personal liberty, one that features the inclusion of guestworkers in its unique national history. This vision of "freedom" imagines the bracero program as one more step on the path to equality and inclusion for migrant workers. In contrast, in this book we see that guestworkers imagined alternatives to the type of freedom imposed upon them by the labor contract, since many saw themselves less as "builders of an exceptional nation" and more as dissidents against it, dreaming of a more expansive freedom beyond the contract and beyond borders.

CHAPTER 1

Free or Slave?: A Genealogy of Labor Contract Coercion and Freedom

Labor activists and supporters have long insisted that contract guestworker programs are "close to slavery," if not the epitome of slavery itself. In the 1963 words of Henry Anderson, farm labor union organizer, activist, and apprentice of Mexican American civil rights activist Dr. Ernesto Galarza: "The distinguishing characteristic of the bracero system is that it is a *captive* labor system. . . . [except] we no longer buy slaves; we rent them." Anderson's language mirrored that of the writer Truman E. Moore, who referred to agricultural migrant labor in the United States as a new form of slavery in his 1965 book, *The Slaves We Rent*. And it also influenced Galarza's thinking, when he wondered aloud, "Is this indentured alien—an almost perfect model of the economic man, an 'input factor' stripped of political and social attributes that liberal democracy likes to ascribe to all human beings and ideally—is this *bracero* the production man of the future?"[1] This characterization of guestworker programs as a form of slave labor continues even today with the work of scholars and of civil rights organizations like the Southern Poverty Law Center, an agency that published a report titled *Close to Slavery: Guestworker Programs in the United States*.[2]

Though aiming to evoke sympathy for the workers, the use of slavery and concentration camps as metaphors has had the effect of constructing braceros as a foreign element completely and entirely outside of the U.S. labor force and liberal modernity.[3] It also had the unintended consequence of turning (mostly white) U.S. citizen agricultural workers into "free laborers," producing freedom in the United States much as early nineteenth-century antebellum arguments over slavery and freedom had. In constructing the bracero labor contract as an instrument of unfreedom in the 1960s, Galarza and others produced freedom as a racial project, turning citizens into "free" laborers and noncitizen/non-white workers into potential "slaves."[4] While these pronouncements seem in direct opposition to how U.S. officials originally conceived the World War II labor programs as antiracist and anti-imperial efforts toward freedom, they were part and parcel of a long history of debates over slavery and freedom that demonstrate that the slave/free dialectic has long served as a rhetorical device to maintain the racial boundaries of coercion among workers, whether in the legitimization or prohibition of the labor contract.

The slave/free dialectic that emerged out of slavery has repeatedly been used to resolve tensions in capitalism and recreate coercive systems of labor, in the continued production of people as commodities.[5] The 1940s–1960s debates progressives engaged over the inherent "freedom" or "slavery" of the bracero program were not new, but rested in a specific legal genealogy, arising from slave emancipation and nineteenth-century laws regarding Asian contract labor in the British Caribbean colonies. Since the initial development of Asian contract labor after abolition, a growing faith in the state to regulate labor migration to advance the cause of freedom led to countless laws, agencies, and government hearings that would do the work of connecting migrant labor with slavery or freedom. The importation of contract or indentured labor from Asia to Europe and the Americas gave rise to multiple debates over the inherent free or coercive nature of the labor contract. In the United States, these nineteenth-century debates resulted in the growth of state power over labor regulation, while also contributing to a racial genealogy that categorized nonwhite workers as unfree, as slaves, as "peons," or as "coolies," with the state designated the regulator of freedom.

Arguments about the supposed "freedom" of the labor contract originated during the period of slave emancipation among the Spanish, British, Portuguese, and U.S. governments in the nineteenth century, as these states vacillated between guaranteeing the freedoms and protections of the labor contract and critiquing the labor contract as a new form of enslavement. The opposition between capital and liberalism that manifested during slavery had generated several very real tensions—how could one espouse the liberal ideals of equality and universality of rights along with the state-endorsed labor extraction, exploitation, and racial exclusion that were required for capitalism to function? The fuzziness of what it meant to be "slave" and what it meant to be "free" as overlapping signifiers (and epistemological terms rooted in classical liberalism) made them readily available as linguistic tools to overcome the contradictions that emerged. Whether through the employment of imported contract laborers as an attempt to alleviate labor coercion, or through various U.S. immigration acts in the 1860s through the 1920s designed to protect the nation against "slavery," the slave/free dialectic resolved the dissonance between liberalism and capitalism.[6]

This genealogy is reflected in the U.S. immigration restriction acts from the 1860s to the 1920s, including the Chinese Exclusion Act (1882) and the Foran Act (1885) banning imported contract labor. Each U.S. immigration restriction act during this period framed imported contract and immigrant labor as either "slave" or "free" during a specific moment in the growth of state power over labor regulation. The Foran Act, also known as the Alien Contract Labor Law, specifically prohibited foreign Asian imported contract labor as a form of slavery in 1885. In the 1910s and 1940s, the U.S. government allowed for the importation of Mexican contract workers during the bracero program. More than fifty years after the Foran Act had forbidden foreign contract labor in the United States, a renewed acceptance of the foreign labor contract emerged with the bracero program, revealing a revived faith in the ability of the state to regulate labor migrations for the cause of "freedom."[7] Through numerous laws and agencies, 1940s U.S. federal officials guaranteed that imported contract labor from Mexico and the Caribbean would serve as a form of voluntary—not slave—labor. Nonetheless, contract labor importation programs were the product of the state's increased efforts to control labor migration and regulate its borders, just as the immigration restriction acts had been. What made the 1940s focus on labor contracts different from immigration restriction is that the contract turned the state into a potential regulator of freedom, with the state protecting migrants' rights so as to gain broad political legitimacy.

Placing the U.S. contract labor program agreements within the context of nineteenth-century slavery, indentured servitude, and efforts toward immigration restriction can help us to understand how, by the 1930s and 1940s, the contract came to be (re)interpreted anew by activists, government officials, and laborers in the United States. As much as the architects of the 1940s guestworker programs wished to distance themselves from the colonial origins of the labor contract, the context of slavery and emancipation dictated and guided the discursive shifts that resulted in the labor programs. Underlying each of these shifts was a set of values that assumed the liberal nation-state was the ultimate guarantor of freedom and equality, thus fueling the growth of government regulation over migrant labor in the twentieth century.

Since the 1960s, state officials, labor activists, historians, and scholars have routinely characterized migrant contract labor as a form of voluntary or free labor, as a form of slavery, or as something in between freedom and slavery.[8] Viewing the Mexican and Caribbean labor programs of the twentieth century through the historical lens of the debates over the inherent slavery or freedom of the labor contract can expose how the labor programs were not necessarily a form of "imported colonialism," but rooted in a long history of liberalism and empire. Whether imagined as a form of "slavery" or "freedom," the contract became, in different historical moments, a means to exclude foreign contract laborers from U.S. citizenship, while transforming them into resources or commodities to be transferred from one nation-state (or colony) to another.

This perspective suggests that instead of relying on the slave/free dialectic to renew or critique the labor programs, we should give greater attention to how the logics of that paradigm have sustained and advanced colonial practices into the twentieth century. And, rather than turn to the liberal state to resolve the inequalities created by guestworker labor contracts, we should critique and disrupt the role of the state as an arbiter of freedom. Official debates surrounding "contract" not only deepened and muddled the divide between slavery and freedom, but they also resolved, clarified, and reproduced that divide, with lasting historical implications, as similar debates are used even today to sustain guestworker programs into the twenty-first century.

How "Contract" Was Materially Rooted in the Slave/Free Divide

Today the contract is so prevalent as a binding agreement that it is natural to assume that it has always existed. Yet the notion of a contract was originally tied to the British Empire and only emerged in the context of British colonialism in the eighteenth and nineteenth centuries. The notion of "contract" arose from the political philosophy of liberalism, the catchword of which was "freedom" or "liberty," and was grounded in the notion that all people are born with individual rights. Liberal social contract theory of the late seventeenth century was conceived as a means to justify political authority and the state through the free consent of individuals, creating a new type of political community based on the voluntary actions of individuals during the

Enlightenment.[9] Of their own volition, individuals exchanged autonomy for the protection of the political community by the state, which would ensure their "freedom." This was, according to Locke, the "Social Contract."[10] The ideal of the contract was also modeled on classical political economy's rule of market exchange. A "contract" expressed obligations arrived at through competition between formally equal and autonomous individuals—not dominion and dependence. The contract functioned to impose social order through personal choice as a material emblem of human relations in free-market transactions. As the historian Amy Dru Stanley argues, "In the eyes of most Americans it was the abolition of slavery that assured the ascendance of the contract. Emancipation apocalyptically achieved the transition from status to contract, appearing to destroy all traces of bondage . . . by affording free slaves the right to own themselves and enter into voluntary relations of exchange."[11] The contract stood as the legal paradigm of liberalism, and it became, in the age of slave emancipation, a symbol of freedom.

The notion of contract rights that sprouted out of the liberalism of the Enlightenment was imagined in the context of debates over slavery; slavery did not contradict contract but underwrote its existence. Under classical liberal theory, the individual consented to state authority in exchange for certain rights and freedoms. Property rights were the foundation of the liberal theory of political order, as these rights upheld that human labor was invested in the individual as property-in-oneself, that property rights could be purchased in others (slaves) outright, or that they might enter the labor market themselves and temporarily trade some of their own rights-in-persons for wages. In other words, both slavery and the concept of "rights" included the rights to the labor of oneself and others. Western systems of slavery and freedom thus had the same roots, such that "freedom" implied the freedom to enslave others and the two were co-constitutive.[12]

With British abolition of the slave trade in 1807, slavery had become morally objectionable as the epitome of a lack of self-ownership and property-in-oneself through wages. Adam Smith stated in *The Wealth of Nations*, "A person who can acquire no property can have no other interest but to eat as much and to labour as little as possible." His arguments for free trade and free labor became an article of faith among British abolitionists, as they argued that free laborers doubled the output of slaves and deemed slave laborers in the Caribbean colonies unfit to compete with free laborers.[13] Abolitionists welcomed the end of the slave trade, but as historians have shown, Black workers themselves engaged in a number of slave rebellions that contributed to the end of slavery.[14] Slavery was officially abolished in the British Empire on August 1, 1834, but Caribbean planters continued to command full rights to the labor of ex-slaves, who were bound in a form of apprenticeship for a period of six years. In response to Black workers' resistance to the apprenticeship system, it ended in 1838, around the same time East Indian workers began to be brought into the British West Indies as contract laborers under individual labor contracts. These contract laborers were racially referred to as "coolies." As historian Hugh Tinker has shown, the British government sought to adapt and replace colonial (slave) labor and apprenticeship with migrant (wage) labor via the labor contract in an attempt to create safeguards to prevent the perpetuation of slavery in new forms.[15]

In 1813, Britain had already dissolved its monopoly trading companies in India, moving away from strict mercantilism to expanded worldwide trade, signaling the conversion in Britain from mercantilism to modern "free trade" capitalism and from colonial practices of slavery to new forms of labor governance.[16] What made free trade possible was not deregulation but increased state regulation of "free labor." As the anthropologist Sidney Mintz has observed, so-called free trade emerged simultaneously with the gradual emancipation of enslaved labor and the migration of state-regulated indentured Asian labor. The enjoined logics of free trade and free labor meant an increase in the power of various colonial governments to define and advance freedom, and the power to distinguish between free and unfree.[17] In the case of Britain, when planters desired access to Asians as a new source of labor, the British Colonial Office attempted to reconcile the inequalities resulting from "free labor" and "free trade" through the creation of a state-regulated contract labor importation program between India and the British West Indies. With the labor contract, imported workers rhetorically became the subjects of a regulatory state. European colonial officials used the labor contract to legitimize this new form of state management, marking it as the hallmark of "free labor" through a discourse of regulation, protection, and voluntary consent. Colonial labor became naturalized and extended through the foreign labor contract, refiguring the state regulation of foreign workers as a means to "free labor" even as it expanded the power of states to manage the global structure of colonial labor. Protecting contract laborers provided justification for all governments to intervene at every level of migration, from medical inspections to health and safety provisions on the ship.

When contract labor from India began to be imported by plantation owners in the British Caribbean, the main subject of political debate among British colonial officials was the extent to which government ought to regulate and inspect these new workers, so as to enforce their "freedom." The debates focused on improved ship conditions, measures to ensure all laborers departed willingly, and the assurance that the colonies to which migrants went would be "suitable for free men." There would be a colonial "protector" at the ports where emigration was permitted as well as at the work site, to give advice, listen to worker grievances, and secure the workers' contract rights. In spite of these new regulations, Caribbean plantation owners were able to draw upon a new pool of cheap labor with the minimum restrictions from the 1840s to the 1920s.[18]

While some members of the British colonial state turned the contract into a universal emblem of freedom, labor advocates and colonial officials simultaneously made it a marker for slavery, spurning the wage contract as a form of compulsion.[19] By 1840, critics of the "coolie" labor importation system in the British West Indies considered it a "new system of slavery." As British colonial statesman Lord John Russell stated on February 15, 1840, "I should be unwilling to adopt any measure to favour the transfer of labourers from British India to Guiana. . . . I am not prepared to encounter the possibility of a measure which may lead to a dreadful loss of life on the one hand, or, on the other, to a new system of slavery."[20]

A similar process took place in the United States, where the ability to participate in the marketplace without competition from foreign workers came to define freedom. From the 1850s to the1870s, the labor contract became a means to conspicuously blur the difference between free and unfree labor relations as it was interpreted variously as either the essence of freedom or a vestige of slavery at different moments.[21] U.S. political debates over Chinese "coolies" in the 1850s and 1860s demonstrate this ambiguity, revealing how "contract" could embody both slavery and freedom. Initially, Southern plantation owners introduced Chinese contract labor as "free labor" improvements on slave labor, much as East Indian "coolies" had been introduced in the British Caribbean. In 1852, the *New York Times* depicted coolies as an alternative to African slave labor and a vehicle to free labor: "a medium between forced and voluntary labor." Intense political debates on the need to protect "free labor" in the United States made it such that Chinese contract labor came to embody the backwardness of slavery, with one U.S. diplomat in

China referring to it as "irredeemable slavery under the form of freedom."[22] If the labor contract could be used historically to challenge the divide between freedom and slavery, it could also help to resolve and clarify that divide. Such were the contradictory effects of the labor contract—it had been used in different instances to define and create anew both slavery and freedom.

Such was the power of the liberal rhetoric around freedom and slavery in the constitution of contract labor that the U.S. Congress passed the Anti-Coolie Act, also known as "An Act to Prohibit the 'Coolie Trade' by American Citizens in American Vessels," signed by President Abraham Lincoln on February 19, 1862. The act's emphasis was on the freedom of Chinese workers, as it "did not apply to or affect any free and voluntary emigration of any Chinese subject, or to any vessel carrying such person as a passenger." To be "free and voluntary," a Chinese subject must possess "a permit or certificate signed by the consul or consular agent of the United States . . . setting forth the act of his voluntary emigration."[23] This act marked the culmination of nineteenth-century slave-trade prohibitions, and it was the federal government's last slave-trade law as well as its first immigration restriction law, demonstrating that immigration restriction was at first intended to protect workers' freedoms after abolition.

As debates over Chinese contract labor make clear, the slave/free dialectic played out in the United States both nationally and locally in complex and multifarious ways, with opinion varying among Anglo settlers, members of the Mexican elite, and between those who lived in the North, South, or the southwestern United States.[24] The white labor movement in California explicitly used white supremacy as a guiding principle in its arguments against Chinese contract labor systems as a form of "slavery," demanding U.S. intervention for humanity's sake, to "protect" free domestic labor and national security.[25] After the 1850s, white racial turmoil increased as immigration from China increased, with domestic workers creating Anti-Coolie clubs in California, which sought to create a clear division between white and Chinese workers. White workers emphasized that Chinese coolie labor undercut their wages and was responsible for the destruction of the financial health of the nation.[26] On April 26, 1862, the state of California passed its own Anti-Coolie Act or the Chinese Police Tax Law, imposing a monthly tax on adults of "Mongolian race" who worked in the gold mines. According to the language of the law itself, it was "An Act to Protect Free White Labor Against Competition with Chinese Coolie Labor and to Discourage the Immigration of the Chinese into the State of California." Though the law was declared unconstitutional by the Supreme Court in 1863, it nonetheless serves as an example of how immigration restriction and the prohibition of imported contract labor were structured by white supremacy and designed to ensure "freedom" for white workers alone.

Even though California had been considered a "free state" since 1849, and white male settlers opposed slavery in California, there were slaves there prior to the Civil War, as well as indentured servants. Mexican and Anglo *rancheros* hired Indians in California under a combined system of debt peonage and direct enslavement until the 1880s. Until 1856, white slaveholders were granted continued legal possession of black slaves brought into the state, and sometimes "hired out" their slaves to profit from their wages.[27] In the mid-nineteenth century, the size, capacity, and power of the U.S. government was limited, with competing local authorities and individuals who sought to live beyond the reach of most authority. In California mining districts, for example, Latin American miners hired and imported some 8,000 Chilean peons between 1848 and 1853 using *contratos de palabra* (verbal contracts). As the historian Edward Dallam Melillo has demonstrated, those Californians who begrudged Chinese contract labor similarly resented Chilean contract labor, using the same racist free labor ideology to rhetorically, legally, and physically attack Chilean contract labor.[28] They also resented Italians and other Southern Europeans as contracted "slaves" into the early twentieth century.

When Congress banned the so-called Coolie Trade as a form of unfree labor with the Anti-Coolie Act, it did not end Chinese labor migration or stall the entry of foreign contract labor altogether. After 1862, Chinese laborers began to arrive in California under a "credit-ticket" system, in which labor brokerage companies recruited workers in China and extralegally forced them to work to pay off the cost of their transport in monthly installments. While the credit-ticket system did not differ much from the labor contract system, it was controlled by the Six Companies, a group of Chinese benevolent associations in California, thus allowing the U.S. government to wash its hands of any coercion involved while also maintaining the illusion that Chinese immigrants were voluntary laborers.[29]

Meanwhile, on July 4, 1864, President Lincoln approved "An Act to Encourage Immigration." Also known as the Immigration Act of 1864, it was a contract labor law authorizing the federal government to enforce contracts made on foreign soil in which emigrants pledged up to one year's worth of labor in exchange for transport to the United States. The law provided for the creation of the U.S. Emigration Office and the American Emigrant Company (AEC), simultaneously enlarging state capacity and leaving some enforcement in private hands. A group of Northern bankers, lawyers, railroad presidents, and politicians incorporated the AEC in Hartford, Connecticut, in 1863, as a response to the labor shortage during the Civil War. The AEC was "Chartered for the Purpose of Procuring and Assisting Emigrants from Foreign Countries to Settle in the United States." According to a company statement, the AEC "offers its services to the employers of labor, and proposes, as the handmaid of the new [U.S.] Immigration Bureau . . . to recruit the industrial power of the country." In a *New York Times* editorial, the company stressed the annual value of the labor of each immigrant by the number of years they stayed in the United States, up to the tenth year, emphasizing the permanent settlement of these contract workers. The AEC's overarching goal in recruiting contract labor from Europe was to "perpetuate the history of the United States," to build towns, states, and territories to "spread over the rich prairies of the West" so that this "population has gone on increasing and extending till it has spanned the continent." Fueled by the ideology of Manifest Destiny, the AEC's goal of Western settlement pivoted around whiteness, as the company professed that it "aims at the introduction in large numbers of a superior class of men from Sweden, Norway, Denmark, Belgium, France, Switzerland, as well as Germany, England, Scotland, Ireland, and Wales."[30]

While shrouded in white supremacist racial ideology that indicated what kind of person (white and Northern European) should populate the country, the labor contract again remained inseparable from the logic of slavery and freedom. For one, the U.S. government encouraged the migration of contract workers from Northern Europe to spark the growth of "freedom" westward. Second, employers used these European contract workers as strikebreakers, resulting in U.S. workers across the country condemning this labor importation as another form of "slavery." Nonetheless, national U.S. labor leaders argued against treating white European contract workers as enemies, distinguishing between "U.S. imported labor" and the "importers of labor," while seeking to cooperate with European contract laborers instead of encouraging state intervention to keep them out.[31] National labor leaders' response to the unrest over AEC contract workers demonstrates that the decision to include or exclude immigrants based on their free or slave status was a distinctly racial phenomenon upon which white supremacy flourished.

After the passage of the Thirteenth Amendment on December 6, 1865, abolishing slavery in the United States, federal debates over peonage and contract labor proliferated. Despite the amendment, indentured servitude remained intact throughout the Southwest even though the Anti-Peonage Act (1867) explicitly forbade any person from holding another person to service or labor to pay off a debt. After only four years, in the face of vociferous protest from labor organizations, Congress repealed the 1864 Immigration Act allowing for European contract labor importation, even as the Six Companies continued to recruit laborers from China. While peonage and coolie labor had been banned, politicians still attempted to prove the inherently "free" character of Chinese contract labor. This was seen most directly in the Burlingame-Seward Treaty of 1868, when Republican politicians directly attacked white working-class racial constructions of Chinese labor as "unfree" in California and sought to encourage "free migration" from China.

Signed by U.S. Minister to China Anson Burlingame and Secretary of State William H. Seward, the Burlingame-Seward Treaty was meant to open up markets between the United States and China by offering open or "free" migration between China and the United States. The treaty "cordially recognized the inherent and inalienable right of man to change his home and allegiance, and also the mutual advantage of the *free migration* and emigration of their citizens and subjects respectively from the one country to the other." The treaty also stressed the United States' agreement to pass laws making it a "penal offence" for citizens of the United States to take Chinese subjects *"without their free and voluntary consent."* As abolitionists, Burlingame and Seward both wanted to attract Chinese immigrants to California and to avoid recreating the racial divisions of slavery. As Burlingame proclaimed, "I speak today as in the old time for the equality of men—for the equality of nations." The treaty provided a clear expression of the importance of equality and freedom to harnessing Asian labor power in the development of the western frontier and to securing open markets across the Pacific. It also further stoked "anti-coolie" sentiments throughout the nation. Facing discontent from local workingmen and settlers in California who committed to a race war against Chinese migrants, California politicians began to appeal to the U.S. Congress to repeal the treaty and to enact restrictive immigration laws. Local communities, organized by anti-Chinese activists, also encouraged Chinese workers to deport themselves by making it impossible for them to find work at local businesses.[32]

The California labor movement played a particularly important role in encouraging the federal government's growing capacity to control immigration by law.[33] In the 1870s, the white Workingman's Party focused competitive anxieties on Chinese immigration, protesting competition with Chinese labor and committing violent rampages against Chinese migrants while petitioning the state for intervention to sustain the living standards of white skilled labor so that they should not be made to "live like coolies."[34] They again imagined contract laborers to be a new form of racialized slavery that would replace emancipated Black slaves, and sought an end to slavery to protect the freedom of white workers. The rise in labor union politics and the proliferation of dozens of national trade unions through the 1890s influenced U.S. officials to continue restricting Asian immigration so as to regulate U.S. workers' "freedom."[35]

The American Federation of Labor (AFL), founded in 1881, engaged in a persistent political crusade to deny Chinese and other Asian workers entry into trade unions. Samuel Gompers, president of the AFL, argued that Chinese living standards were incompatible with and destructive to the political and cultural fabric of the United States, mapping racial difference in terms of opposing living standards (slave versus free).[36] These rhetorical framings resulted in the Chinese Exclusion Act of 1882, which restricted Chinese immigration and naturalization whether under contract or not. While the Chinese Exclusion Act never mentioned "coolie" at all, the question of contract labor arose over and over in the congressional debates over the passage of the act, with the debates underscoring the motives for its enactment. In these legislative moments, the state of California and the U.S. federal government stood against "slavery" through immigration restriction, under the assumption that contract laborers or "coolies" were bound laborers, whose "contracts" had served as a mechanism to coerce their labor.[37]

Ongoing anti-Chinese mob violence and expulsions on behalf of local community leaders and labor unions in the West forced the federal government to expand immigration restriction policies, leading up to the Foran Act or the Alien Contract Labor Act of 1885, banning the importation of contract labor. From the 1860s to the 1880s, several anti-Chinese immigration acts, including the Anti-Coolie Act (1862) and the Anti-Peonage Act (1867), had resulted in the growth of federal authority over laborers through federal immigration restriction laws designed to protect "free labor" from slavery. While the 1862 Anti-Coolie Act was ineffective, Congress passed the Page Act on March 3, 1875, which prevented the importation of prostitutes from China and reinstated sections of the "anti-coolie" act, with contract labor from China remaining legal as long as laborers were not "coerced." These anti-Chinese immigration acts extended to the Foran Act, further delineating the contract as a form of slavery in the name of protecting freedom. The law stated, "It shall be unlawful for any person, company, partnership, or corporation, in any manner whatsoever, to prepay the transportation, or in any way assist or encourage the importation or migration of any alien or aliens, any foreigner or foreigners, into the United States, its Territories, or the District of Columbia, under contract or agreement." The Foran Act prohibiting the importation of contract labor, as with other immigration restriction laws, demonstrated that if "freedom" could be proposed to initially justify contract labor importation, "slavery" could be invoked to interdict and exclude it.[38]

The Page Act, the Chinese Exclusion Act, and the Foran Act each proved to be just the beginning of a series of U.S. government policies that pitted slavery against freedom, in the process legitimizing the state's role in attempting to control the movement of people. The Chinese exclusion debates had given state officials the power to racially determine those laborers who were free and those who were unfree in the 1850s through the 1880s, opening the door to a series of racially constructed immigration restriction acts. Putting limitations on "unfree" workers framed U.S. immigration control from the beginning of these debates, as did the underlying assumption that imported contract labor, like slavery, was the antithesis of free labor. From 1862 to 1903, Congress federalized immigration control, legitimized federal deportation laws, and extended border control laws to post-entry social control, solidifying the rise of the state as a protector of U.S. freedom through immigration restriction. As the meanings of contract labor were being worked out during this era, the Supreme Court began to make wide-ranging statements of its support of immigration control, reinforcing the power of the federal government to restrict immigration against the rights claims of noncitizens.

As further examples, the Immigration Act of 1891 and the Geary Law of 1892 extended the deportation powers of the federal government through border control. The Immigration Act of 1891 allowed those apprehended within one year of entry to be deported and subject to future exclusion. The Geary Law required all Chinese to carry a resident permit, without which they could be subject to deportation.[39] Meanwhile, the 1903 Immigration Law increased the list of excluded classes to include "all idiots," "insane persons," and prostitutes, and in 1905, the U.S. Supreme Court ruled in *United States v. Ju Toy* that illegal immigrants could be deported without due process, allowing Congress to deny habeas corpus or right to a trial to noncitizens.

A growing bureaucracy of migration control strengthened the power of the state to exclude and deport, in the name of freedom, any foreign workers considered "unfree," even beyond the racially coded figure of the "coolie." From the 1880s to the 1920s, then, the logic of the state's impulse to regulate freedom through racial immigration restriction was set. While the racial construction of the "coolie" had been behind the initial formation of the unilateral government authority to enforce laws regarding deportation and immigration, the enforcement of these laws could now be applied to other racialized groups, defined in the U.S. Supreme Court case *Chae Chan Ping v. United States* (1889) to be among the "vast hordes of [foreign] people crowding in upon us."[40]

Whether as a regulator of "free" labor through the management of contract labor systems in the mid-nineteenth century, or as a restrictor of "unfree" Asian labor immigration, the U.S. federal government intensified its jurisdiction and power over labor mobility. This resulted in the consolidation of U.S. territorial expansion westward through migrant labor vulnerability by the end of the nineteenth century. Defending and protecting the freedom of workers through contract labor regulation or restriction justified and enabled the project of white western settlement as a moment in the progression of U.S. national history beyond slavery, producing white worker freedom. Even as Chinese contract workers made the accomplishment of western settlement possible through their labor, criticizing their "enslavement" justified their exclusion from the U.S. national project—producing a series of immigration restriction acts that turned them into a vulnerable racial caste of workers whose "slave-like" status marked them as outside the bounds of U.S. national belonging.

From the Foran Act to the Wagner Act

Prior to 1913, the federal government had a very limited degree of regulation and control over working conditions in the United States. This began to change on March 4, 1913, when President William Howard Taft signed a law creating the Department of Labor, giving labor progressives a direct voice in the presidential cabinet. As a product of the Progressive and labor movements, the department aimed "to foster, promote, and develop the welfare of working people, to improve their working conditions, and to enhance their opportunities for profitable employment." Its mandate was "to advise the President with regard to labor problems; to conduct research on employment, wages, cost of living, and working conditions; to handle labor relations and controversies; to enforce labor laws; to administer employment offices and the Federal aspects of Federal-State programs of social security."[41] Through the Department of Labor, progressive officials began to imagine a new function for the state, not only as the protector of freedom through immigration exclusion but as the mediator of freedom through expansive federal authority over workers. Included under the Labor Department's bureaucratic umbrellas were the U.S. Conciliation Service, which mediated labor disputes, and the Bureau of Immigration, Bureau of Naturalization, and Children's Bureau, which were all incorporated into the department to improve working conditions and maintain labor peace.[42]

The entry of the United States into World War I (1917–18) led to the growth of state machinery to ensure adequate war production and improved work conditions, as these factors assumed national importance during the war. The Department of Labor, intent on creating a more efficient labor force and protecting U.S. workers, intensified knowledge production through specialized expertise in labor statistics and labor movements. Although the state apparatus never had the capacity to either weed out slavery or facilitate freedom through the creation of this new bureaucracy, officials nonetheless began to make claims that the state was a guarantor of freedom through the proliferation of progressive government agencies designed to manage the labor supply during World War I. Nonetheless, the regulation of freedom through immigration restriction was still the principal motive of the state such that by 1917, Congress passed the most stringent immigration law to date, the Immigration and Nationality Act.[43]

Growers complained to Congress of a labor shortage as a result of state restrictions on Asian immigration, the mass migration of white and Black Southerners to cities, World War I cutting off European migration to the United States, and the draft removing men from the workforce. The department tried to redistribute labor by relocating workers from areas of labor surplus to areas of labor scarcity and passed "work or fight" ordinances, but neither satisfied growers' demands.[44] As a war security measure, Congress decided to legislate exemptions for the Foran Act of 1885, with the 1917 Immigration and Nationality Act. The 1917 Immigration Act's ninth provision served as a loophole, allowing the U.S. attorney general to waive the entrance requirements of the act when there was an emergency need for foreign labor. The "ninth proviso" went as follows: "The Commissioner General of Immigration with the approval of the Secretary of Labor shall issue rules and prescribe conditions, including exaction of such bonds as may be necessary, to control and regulate the admission and return of otherwise inadmissible aliens applying for temporary admission."[45]

Shortly after the creation of the Department of Labor, the United States, pressured by U.S. growers, organized a unilateral labor program to import Mexican agricultural, railroad, and mining laborers into the United States during World War I, using this proviso. Designed as a security measure, the World War I contract labor importation program (1917–1921) not only waived the thirty-year-old congressional ban on foreign contract labor since the Foran Act of 1885, but it also required that temporary imported laborers sign contracts for the duration of their stay. To prevent an influx of "slave" labor or Chinese contract labor, the secretary of labor established a series of contract stipulations that would require certain standards of wages and housing for admitted Mexican workers that would ensure their "freedom." With this first Mexican contract labor program, the temporary Mexican worker was deemed an individual possessing free will and liberty through the contract. However, the program was not monitored by any central office or administration.[46] The U.S. federal government did not have the capacity to manage the protections in the labor contract, and left it up to private labor contractors and recruiters to hire workers.

The importation of Mexican contract labor into the United States during World War I stood in stark relief to the prohibition of contract labor in the British Empire at the same time. In 1917, the British Empire was forced to halt the emigration of indentured labor from India to the British West Indies, as the anticolonial movement in India moved to end the contract labor system. Mahatma Gandhi, leader of the Indian independence movement against British rule, first began to protest the coolie labor system in 1895, calling the entire system of white-dominated "perpetual indenture" into question.[47] From 1895 to 1915, Gandhi attacked indenture in many writings, arguing that "indenture intensified the 'unnatural relationship' between British and Indians in which racial superiority and inferiority were systematized." He led Indian opinion to oppose Indian labor migrations to British colonies as a form of "temporary slavery." In 1917, several British agencies in India acknowledged the weight of Indian opinion against "coolie" emigration and declared an end to their movements, canceling labor contracts in the colonies.[48] Meanwhile, the United States government sought to recruit Mexican agricultural workers under a new system of contract labor importation.

Whereas Britain had been forced by the anticolonial movements in India to halt the growth of state governance over foreign labor, the United States reconsidered its former exclusion of contract labor in the Foran Act of 1885 and decided to import foreign contract labor during World War I as a means to extend U.S. federal power over the governance of labor and freedom. This is not to say that the exclusion of contract workers via the Foran Act had been successful, as private employers continued to contract Italians and Southern Europeans without government intervention into the early twentieth century. White laborers condemned the "unfree" or "slave-like" conditions of Southern European contract workers, raising the same concerns and anxieties that "coolie" workers had in the prior decades, which again intensified immigration restriction by the 1920s.[49]

Since local government offices lacked power to enforce the labor agreement or the contract, little was achieved in the early twentieth century by way of protecting contract workers, whether from Southern Europe or Mexico. The coercive power of the employer determined contract worker treatment before the 1940s, often without any legal sanction against exploitation. Mexican workers complained about the exploitations of the first Mexican bracero program to the Mexican government, which in 1920 began to compose a model contract that guaranteed Mexican workers certain rights accorded by the Mexican Constitution (1917). In 1920, the U.S. secretary of labor appointed a special committee to investigate the treatment of the workers and found less than ideal wages, working conditions, and housing. Of the approximately 70,000 Mexican workers contracted, nearly one third evaded their contracts due to lack of compliance.[50]

The Mexican government expressed real fears over the outflow of labor with this program, and took a number of measures to reverse the migration trend, including warning would-be emigrants of the hardships they would endure north of the Río Grande, and promoting repatriation for those already in the United States. The Mexican government, angry with the blatant discrimination and exploitation Mexicans experienced as temporary workers in the United States, called an end to the program in 1921, but few Mexicans participating in the program were actually deported or repatriated by the federal government, in large part because it was too expensive and state bureaucracies were not capacious enough to oversee their deportation.[51]

By the 1920s, U.S. government offices began to vacillate between enforcing order through immigration restriction and attempting to sustain labor's

liberty through bureaucratic intervention and the labor contract. Federal officials began to create a small immigration bureaucracy to protect "freedom"
in the United States from Asian "coolies," while also sanctifying racial discrimination and white supremacy in the United States. A small U.S.-Mexico
border police force contingent formed in 1904 to enforce the Chinese Exclusion Acts along the border. During the first labor importation program with
Mexico, the U.S. government nationalized this handful of federal inspectors,
while shifting their focus to regulating the influx and deportation of Mexican
laborers—making their unlawful entry a misdemeanor. As the historian Kelly
Lytle Hernández has shown, this first Mexican labor program provided new
possibilities and demands for the management of "illegal" Mexican laborers
and their deportation from the United States.[52]

Rather than exclude Mexican migrants altogether, the U.S. government
gradually increased its power over immigrants and laborers, establishing
boundaries between who was free and who was not by creating a system of
documentation, contracts, visas, border-crossing cards, and immigration
registration cards for Mexican immigrants. As the historian S. Deborah Kang
notes, by the mid-1920s the regulation of border crossers, rather than the
restriction of immigrants, became a rising concern of the Bureau of Immigration. The emergent regulatory system ensnared Mexicans in a state apparatus
that racialized them not only as indentured "peons" but as undocumented
and illegal. Without the proper identification, the undocumented migrant
became an emblem of slavery because he/she did not have the paperwork and
was therefore not deserving of American "freedom." As "unfree" and "illegal"
subjects of the U.S. federal government, Mexican migrants without appropriate papers were made into official targets of immigration policy, even though
there was no apparatus with the power to carry out or consolidate Mexican
immigration control in the 1920s. Even with the creation of the Border Patrol
(1924) as a mechanism to consolidate immigration control, the flow of laborers from Mexico to the United States remained relatively fluid. Nevertheless,
the National Origins Act or Immigration Act of 1924 gave further meaning
and shape to the idea of the illegal immigrant, placing deportation at the center of U.S. immigration policy and emphasizing the need to patrol the border.
As the historian Mae Ngai has argued, this act placed quotas on nationalities
allowed to enter the United States each year, reshaping the makeup of the
United States by creating new categories of racial difference.[53]

After the Immigration Act of 1924, the Border Patrol began to expel Mexican labor, under the guise of keeping out laborers who were driving down

American standards of freedom. In 1926, a representative from Texas proposed a quota system for immigrants from Mexico to amend the Immigration Act of 1924. This bill would have reduced immigration from Mexico
to 2 percent of the Mexican population of the United States as recorded by
the 1890 Census. When the bill failed to pass due to the lobbying clout of
agribusinessmen who employed Mexican migrant laborers, the State Department moved to restrict Mexican immigration by denying visas to prospective
immigrants through the March 4, 1929, Immigration Act, which made illegal
entry a separate criminal offense and a felony, and dramatically increased
deportations. A frenzy of expulsions culminated in the mass deportations of
Mexican Repatriation (1929 to 1939).[54] By the 1930s, the Great Depression
heightened racist fears of Mexican labor as unemployment levels rose and
wages fell. Although President Herbert Hoover had enthusiastically recruited
Mexican contract laborers as the head of the Food Administration during
World War I, he denounced Mexicans as one of the causes of the Depression
in 1930, claiming "they took jobs away from American citizens," falling back
on the insinuation that Mexican migrants threatened "free" citizen labor,
resulting in Mexican Repatriation.[55]

Meanwhile, U.S. organized labor in the 1930s began to demand a different
sort of state intervention, beyond the immigration restrictions of the 1860s
through 1920s, not simply in the form of protection against "slavery" through
immigration control but through a growing state that could facilitate their
"freedom" by supporting labor's right to unionize. In response, officials created a bureaucratic system to prevent workers from becoming "wage slaves"
as Asian and Mexican immigrants had been perceived to be. With the creation of the labor department in 1913 and its growth into the 1930s, a cluster of influential labor, engineering, managerial, and academic progressives
began to promote and test institutions of collective bargaining.[56] Their rising
knowledge and influence led the New Deal state to privilege the worker and
his agency.

While workers in industry had sustained multiple defeats in 1919 and
refrained from unionism and national politics during the 1920s, changes in
the larger political system, in workers' own orientation, and in the economy,
led workers to unionize more intensely in the 1930s. With the economy in
a state of crisis, U.S. manufacturing production was cut in half, resulting
in mass unemployment. This led to large protests, street riots, and turmoil.
While families had formerly looked to their ethnic institutions and employers
for aid during such times of crisis, during the Great Depression they began to

look to the national government for assistance. Many of these workers were second-generation Europeans and eligible to vote and, for the first time, they realized that the Democratic Party could make a difference in their lives. Many also became increasingly politicized through participation in the Communist Party (CPUSA). Finding a new protector in the state, these workers became involved in electoral politics and the unemployment movement, applying pressure on the federal government to facilitate change within the workplace.[57]

As the legal historian William Forbath has demonstrated, U.S. labor's turn to the state for protection in the 1930s marked a pronounced change from labor politics in the late nineteenth century. The AFL had defined "liberty of contract" in the late nineteenth-century United States as the right of employers and laborers to contract the terms of individual labor relations without the intervention or regulation of the state. Since the judiciary had repeatedly used court injunctions to prevent their meetings, publications, parades, and picketing, the AFL sought to curb the rule of law and its authority. This is not to say that the AFL rejected liberalism or state power, as its leaders became increasingly involved in electioneering and lobbying at both state and national levels, appealing to the First Amendment of the U.S. Constitution to argue against court injunctions so as to restrict the power of the courts over workers. The AFL also turned to the executive branch of the federal government to limit immigration in order to "protect" U.S. workers. Yet just as "liberty of contract" could be used to express a desire to limit state power, it could also be used to invoke state power in order to protect workers' autonomy and ability to unionize. During the New Deal, the state enforcement of labor's rights seemed necessary to assist organized laborers in the mass-production industries.[58] As labor swayed toward the federal government for protection and New Deal attorneys attempted to build a new regulatory state, they placed new pressure on the executive cabinet.

Due to this increased pressure and influence from labor, President Franklin D. Roosevelt began to support labor and the common man over private enterprise, promising to take on the "new industrial dictatorship."[59] In June 1933, Roosevelt signed the National Industrial Recovery Act (NIRA), which contained a labor provision, section 7(a), that granted workers a legal right to organize and bargain collectively. The underlying logic was that a strong labor movement would bring about greater purchasing power among workers, the lack of which was perceived to be the cause of the Great Depression.[60] Workers responded with a surge of social unrest and militancy. The number of unions soared between 1932 and 1933, the number of strikes doubled, and the number of workers participating in work stoppages quadrupled. Workers and New Deal progressives advocated an increased role for the state, even as the Supreme Court declared NIRA unconstitutional in 1935.[61] By the second half of the 1930s, workers were so successful in their efforts that officials began to create legislative acts and government agencies designed to protect workers from "wage slavery." In effect, the rise in influence of organized labor resulted in the creation of an expanded role for the federal government as the facilitator of freedom, through legislative acts that supported organized labor's agency.

Championing their cause was the New Deal senator Robert F. Wagner and his network of political allies. Wagner believed that the government ought to protect U.S. workers from intransigency and instability by securing their agency, and blamed the U.S. government for the economic downturn of the Great Depression because it had not aided workers in their quest for "democracy" in the workplace. His view was not new, but had been influenced by numerous progressive officials who promoted and tested a role for the state in establishing institutions of collective bargaining. In 1933, Senator Wagner sponsored the Wagner-Peyser Act with Representative Theodore A. Peyser of New York, an act President Roosevelt signed to establish a nationwide system of public employment offices, known as the U.S. Employment Service (USES). The result was a system of regional USES offices, which sought to identify industries and geographic regions with labor shortages and surpluses to plan efficient use and transportation of the domestic labor force, linking employers with job seekers. Importantly, the USES later became one of the agencies directly responsible for the management of the Mexican and Caribbean farm labor programs in 1942 and 1943.

After the downfall of the NIRA, Congress, led by Wagner, enacted the National Labor Relations Act (NLRA) of 1935, otherwise known as the Wagner Act. Established under pressure from labor leaders and Democratic legislators, the law eliminated employer interference in unions and established the federal government as the supervisor and arbiter of labor relations. It set up the National Labor Relations Board to protect the right of most workers to organize into unions. When Roosevelt signed the NLRA into law on July 5, 1935, he declared:

A better relationship between labor and management is the high
purpose of this Act. By assuring the employees the right of collective
bargaining it *fosters the development of the employment contract* on
a sound and *equitable basis*. By providing an orderly procedure for
determining who is entitled to represent the employees, it aims to
remove one of the chief causes of wasteful economic strife. By preventing practices which tend to destroy the independence of labor,
it seeks, for every worker within its scope, that *freedom of choice and
action* which is justly his.

In essence, the Wagner Act again molded anew the language of contract, fos-
tering the development of the employment contract as an exemplar of freedom on an "equitable basis," as a device to ensure the freedom and equality
of labor.[62]

The Wagner Act upheld that the federal government would step in to
guarantee that the contract was a form of freedom. Wagner described the
NLRA as "an agency designed for harmony and mutual concessions . . . an
impartial forum, where employers and employees could appear as equals . . .
[and] where they could sign *contracts* of enduring peace rather than mere
articles of uncertain truce."[63] If the NLRA emphasized the freedom of the
labor contract, it also expressed a release of workers from the "bondage" of
the employer. Wagner argued, "There can be no freedom in an atmosphere
of bondage. No organization can be free to represent the workers when it is
the mere creature of the employer."[64] He further stated, "The slave system
of the old South was as tranquil as a summer's day, but that is no reason for
perpetuating in modern industry any of the aspects of a master-servant relationship."[65] Wagner turned to the historic conception of American slavery
to justify the labor contract, renewing the dialectic of slavery and freedom
as an explanation for the value of the labor contract. He equated "liberty of
contract" with state intervention, arguing that the inequality of bargaining
power between the employer and the worker negated the actual liberty of the
contract. At the heart of his argument was a belief in consent through contract, because he believed workers had the right to collectively influence their
contracts through union organization. If the contract was unfree, then the
state would make it free by enforcing workers' collective agency and consent.

Labor's attempt to involve the federal government in ensuring white
worker "freedom" to contract found concrete expression in the Wagner Act.
The contract thus became an instrument by which federal officials organized

the laboring population and regulated the workplace. It also became the norm by which officials reformed employers' conduct to safeguard workers' agency. While U.S. workers had once invoked "liberty of contract" to limit state power over labor, in the 1930s officials and labor advocates invoked liberty of contract to expand state power over labor. During the 1930s, New Deal liberalism became fundamentally intertwined with the expansive use of state power, changing laborers' perspective on the state as a source of bureaucratic protection. The impetus to police the labor contract began to spread across the federal bureaucracy, with vast resources made available for new federal agencies such as the National Labor Relations Board (NLRB), the federal agency established to investigate and resolve complaints under the NLRA.[66]

With this shift, the NLRA guaranteed the basic right of workers to organize into unions and take collective action, but it did not include farmworkers and domestic workers, most of whom were Black, Asian, and Mexican American. This meant that it tended to benefit the white workers who dominated basic industry.[67] Farmworkers were therefore powerless to negotiate their employment status with their agribusiness employers, leading to broader wage gaps between industrial labor and farm labor.

In the context of a robust movement of U.S. labor activists pushing for the expansion of these New Deal protections to cover farmworkers, and as the result of an announced wartime emergency in 1941, New Deal officials began to apply this bureaucratic formula to Mexican and Caribbean workers to fulfill wartime labor needs as part of the "war effort." In the process, they turned the state into a mechanism by which the equality of imported Mexican and Caribbean workers with U.S. workers might be assured—privileging the state's potential to mediate the worker's freedom as a labor contractor. It was the putative goal of "liberty of contract" imagined at this particular stage of liberalism that allowed this vision to take shape. With the goal of state-mandated rights in mind, progressive politicians and leaders invented the figure of the mid-twentieth century contract laborer as one who entered into a contract with one nation-state to legitimately travel to another nation-state temporarily for work. This occurred in the United States as it did in Mexico and other countries in the hemisphere.

The Mexican government did not approve of the way its labor migrants were treated in the United States during the World War I bracero program, when private companies and recruiters governed the hiring and treatment of workers. The rise of the Good Neighbor Policy in combination with the relationships Mexican officials had formed with U.S. diplomats of the New Deal prompted Mexican officials in the 1940s to find an international agreement and labor contract appealing as a means to protect emigrating citizens. With the U.S. government as employer, Mexico and other participating nations became convinced that government could step in as a mediator to ensure workers' rights, protecting them from the capriciousness of capitalism and private enterprise. High-ranking officials within the U.S. Department of State, many of whom were advocates of the New Deal, began to believe that freedom could be attained and extended to Mexican and Caribbean people through the labor contract. This occurred in tandem with the rising popularity of the political philosophy of racial liberalism in the Western Hemisphere, with some officials espousing government intervention to circumvent global and racial inequalities.[68] As a result, state officials in the Caribbean and Latin American eventually aspired to have their laboring populations included as part of the contract labor programs, as well. With the federal government in the role of labor contractor and employer, imported contract labor became a renewed symbol of freedom rather than slavery by 1942.

The Bracero Program Begins

Prior to the enactment of the Wagner Act (1935) and the passage of the NLRA, Senator Robert Wagner supported the Wagner-Peyser Act (1933), an act signed by President Roosevelt to establish the USES. If the Wagner Act made the labor contract a renewed vehicle for freedom, the Wagner-Peyser Act made the state management of contract labor possible, for the USES became one of the organizations directly responsible for recruiting and placing imported contract laborers from Mexico, Puerto Rico, and the British West Indies. At first, the USES published job vacancies and opportunities for the unemployed during the Great Depression, focusing on hiring young men for the Civilian Conservation Corps and other government public works projects. By World War II, it began to focus on hiring young men for jobs in war industries or defense-work projects. As the U.S. government began to perceive agricultural labor to be a national security concern, the USES expanded its focus to placing and recruiting farmworkers, and then imported farmworkers.

On April 30, 1942, a U.S. interagency group comprising the War Manpower Commission, the Department of State, the Department of Labor, the

Department of Justice, and the Office of the Coordinator of Inter-American Affairs, met separately to discuss how a labor program would operate. Their efforts reflected an attempt to resolve the conflicting demands of labor activists who demanded rural social change, growers who demanded workers, and the demands of the Mexican government.[69] On May 28, 1942, Department of Agriculture Secretary Claude Wickard asked Attorney General Francis J. Biddle to waive the contract labor, head tax, and literacy test provisions of the 1917 Immigration Act to permit the temporary entry of Mexican farm workers, to which he agreed. In June, Wickard made an official request for Mexican labor to the Mexican government.

On June 15, 1942, U.S. Ambassador George S. Messersmith, a good friend of Vice President Henry Wallace, met with Mexican Foreign Minister Ezequiel Padilla to seek approval for the migration. Messersmith argued that the need for labor was urgent and would make an important contribution to the war effort.[70] On July 3, 1942, Secretary Wickard attended the second Inter-American Conference on Agriculture at the U.S. Embassy in Mexico City. As head of the American delegation, his purpose was to call a "technical and scientific meeting, not a political one," to convince Mexican authorities to permit the United States government to import Mexican agricultural labor to the United States in order to "raise the standards of rural living" in Mexico. At the conference, Wickard held a meeting with Padilla in which Padilla revealed his misgivings about the proposed undertaking, given the history of discrimination against Mexicans in the United States. Wickard assured Padilla that requests by farmers for workers would not be approved unless an investigation proved that workers were needed. In addition, he claimed that the U.S. government was ready to stand behind the contract of each worker.[71]

They began formal negotiations in Mexico City on July 14, 1942, and then formalized the program via an exchange of diplomatic notes in August. An agreement was reached on the principles governing the program, and Mexican officials decided to consent to a limited emigration on a trial basis. Wallace, as former secretary of the USDA, had a strong interest in Mexican agrarian reform, and followed the negotiations closely. As Messersmith wrote to Wallace in a July 17, 1942, letter, "the conference was quite a success and I believe it was worthwhile. . . . Mr. Wickard was most helpful in the matter of getting Mexican labor for the United States." The Mexican delegation, Foreign Minister Padilla concluded, was satisfied with Wickard's assurances regarding the use of Mexican contract labor and the standards of recruitment. In his letters, Padilla made it clear that his government did not wish the workers to contract directly with American farmers, as had taken place during the first labor program. He proposed that the U.S. government serve as the primary employer and contractor with the farmer and the worker, to shield Mexican contract workers from exploitation. Padilla also refused to allow farmers or their agents to directly recruit workers in Mexico as they had with the World War I labor program, establishing that the Mexican government would be responsible for their recruitment.[72] The binational contract agreement, signed August 4, 1942, covered several general principles and protections, as well as specific problems such as discrimination, transport, wages, deductions, and housing.

In place of the unilateralism of the first Mexican labor program during World War I, U.S. officials applied the tenets of the Good Neighbor Policy to create a binational labor program during World War II. The precedent to suspend the Foran Act had already been set by the first Mexican labor importation program, but this time U.S. officials did so under the premise that the contract would be a means to promote international peace as a reciprocal statement of good-neighborly intentions. According to an amendment of the contract, "The Mexican consuls, assisted by the Mexican Labor Inspectors, recognized as such by the employer will take all measures of protection in the interests of the Mexican workers in all questions affecting them within their corresponding jurisdictions, and will have free access to the places of work of the Mexican workers." While contract workers could not submit complaints to the NLRB, they would nonetheless have access to representation to protect their "freedom," usually in the form of a Mexican consular official, who would then take workers' complaints to the USES office nearest to where the complaint arose. This would ensure that the contract could be used by both the Mexican and U.S. governments to enforce Mexican workers' collective agency and to prevent the racial exploitation that had taken place with the first labor agreement.[73]

In the United States, the Farm Security Administration (FSA) became the leading organization initially responsible for the management of contract workers once in the United States. The FSA (1937) was the direct successor of the Resettlement Administration (RA), which had been created by Wallace's undersecretary of agriculture, Rexford Tugwell. The FSA initially resettled refugees from the Dust Bowl of the Southwest in relief camps in California, but after World War II, began to manage the labor importation programs. As the historian Verónica Martínez-Matsuda carefully details, the FSA labor camps of the 1930s and 1940s were problematic attempts by state officials to advance progressive ideals by working to transform migrants' cultural practices, social behavior, and standard of living. This involved educating citizen and noncitizen families about hygiene, nutrition, child-rearing, and social responsibility, and teaching Mexican contract workers or braceros how to behave as modern subjects. Martínez-Matsuda argues that the FSA farm labor camps in the United States challenged the structural forces in agribusiness and rural society that exploited farmworkers, and provided space for African American, Mexican, and Japanese American farmworkers to push the boundaries and privileges of U.S. citizenship, to demand their civil rights.[74] For the brief time the FSA progressively managed the labor camps of migrant farmworkers (1937–1946) they had a commitment to fulfilling the New Deal's social democratic possibilities while also addressing matters of racial and class injustice. With the FSA initially in control of the bracero program and Caribbean contract programs, it seemed that the U.S. government might fulfill the clauses of the bilateral contract agreement with Mexico.

The bracero program involved several contracts, including the binational government agreement, the contracts that individual Mexican workers initially made with the FSA, and the contracts for groups of workers made by the individual farmers and growers associations with the FSA. Leaders of the U.S. Department of Agriculture (USDA), the War Food Administration (WFA), and the Office for Inter-American Affairs pointed out the benefit of the contracts, specified as an equal partnership whereby the "free" worker exchanged his labor value for "domestic" or "free" wages via the labor contract. This rhetoric justified and legitimized the U.S.-implemented labor programs as a form of negotiation, where two equally autonomous parties could come together of their own volition. The contract enforced the notion that the labor programs were emphatically not a form of enslavement, but a *choice* that Mexican workers made by their own consent, making freedom and equality central to the agreements and the individual labor contracts.

The contract also projected the collective agency of U.S. citizen workers onto Mexican workers by extending the right to elect "spokesmen" to negotiate grievances with their employers, as an accommodation to unionists in the United States and in Mexico. The contract stated, "Groups of workers admitted under this understanding shall elect their own spokesmen to deal with the employer, with the duly authorized representative of the craft or class of employees, or with other interested parties, concerning matters arising out of the interpretation or application of this agreement."[75] With this spokesperson, braceros could voice their collective concerns to the employer, in line with the expansion of U.S. governmental efforts to manage the agency of workers through the labor contract.

The commitment to a new era of international relations made contract labor importation programs very appealing in the 1940s. U.S. officials believed the contract would assure Mexican and Caribbean officials of the United States' anti-imperialism through certain worker guarantees and protections. The Good Neighbor Policy, the development of state infrastructure such as the NLRB, and the intervention of expertise made the state management of immigrant labor in the 1930s and 1940s substantively different from the exclusionary anti-immigration measures taken previously in the 1860s through the 1920s. If it was through U.S. immigration restriction acts that experts established the authority to protect freedom, it was through progressive New Deal government agencies and reforms in the 1930s through the 1940s that the state-centered bureaucracy to mediate freedom was established. By the 1940s, U.S. officials seemed poised to extend the Wagner Act's provisions to noncitizen and nonwhite workers via the binational labor contracts and agreements. Central to this extension of "freedom" to Mexican workers was the budding ideology of racial liberalism, which the labor programs developed and promoted. Racial liberalism became part of a hemispheric creed in the management of labor mobility at this time, as multiple governments grappled with ways to promote equality through state intervention, to foster a new global order purportedly beyond colonialism.

The government-led labor contract, as an instrument of worker protection, became appealing not only to U.S. officials, but to those in Mexico and other countries whose own liberalism prompted them to see the potential of the contract to ensure the welfare of workers. Prior to this, the Mexican government had long sought to prevent Mexican workers from leaving. The historian Ana Raquel Minian has adeptly illustrated how the Mexican government was complicit in criminalizing those Mexican workers who departed without documents, and restricted long-term migration so as to promote economic growth and development in Mexico.[76] During the 1920s–1930s, some Mexican policymakers came to believe that short-term migration improved the productivity of returned workers, modernized Mexico, and created labor peace by reducing rebellions in the countryside—even though this was contentious. Labor contracts established that workers would return to Mexico in a short time and, relatedly, that only men would be contracted—not women, who could reproduce. The labor contract thus facilitated racial and gendered perceptions of workers in both countries, as the contract became linked to

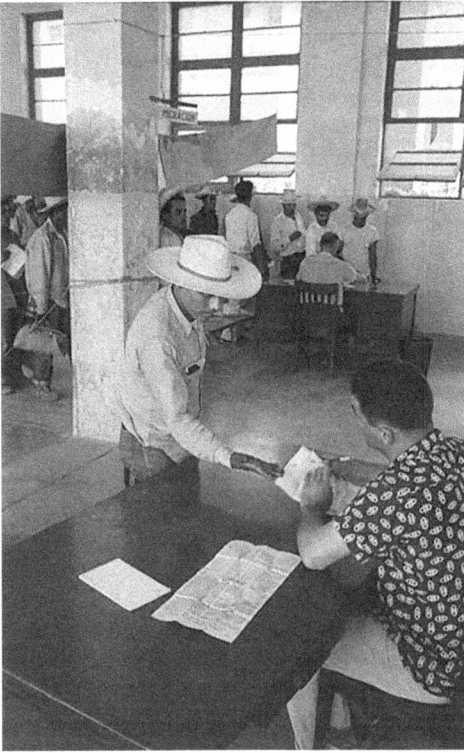

Figure 2. An official reviews
a bracero's documents at the
Monterrey Processing Center,
Mexico, 1956. Leonard Nadel
Photographs and Scrapbooks,
Archives Center, National
Museum of American History.

Mexican men's gendered duty to earn money and return to the family, and
strictly prevented women and families from migrating to the United States.
Return, departure, and affirmation that these contract laborers would not settle down and "reproduce" in the United States was critical to the program's
support both in the United States and Mexico.[77]

Meanwhile, the U.S. government focused on temporary contracts to deflect
anti-Mexican racism, and to reassure the public that the program would not
result in a permanent class of nonwhite workers who might undercut "free"
white Americans. In effect, it was not only expanded government jurisdiction
over contract laborers through the contract, but the short-term nature of the
contract that made the contract an instrument of "freedom."[78] In this way, the
U.S. government freed white workers from concerns over the "hordes" or a
"flood" of immigrant workers settling in their communities, competing with
white workers for jobs, and lowering American wages to "slave standards."
Instead of guaranteeing freedom from discrimination and offering wages

purportedly equal to American workers, the contract's ephemerality made it an apparatus that buttressed white supremacy. Likewise, the Mexican government privileged temporary labor contracts as a means to educate "backwards" rural Mexican workers on "modern" American farming techniques and consumer values, which they could bringback with them to Mexico to improve the economy.[79] In such ways, the U.S.-Mexican labor program served both countries' national narratives of progress, with the contract representing the evolution of the United States' moral character under the Good Neighbor Policy.

In the United States, the federal government, organized labor, and New Deal liberals used the ideal of the labor contract to maintain that U.S. national progress was against slavery and colonialism, and for freedom through an expanded state. In doing so, they ironically and inadvertently masked the new practices by which global divisions of labor were invigorated and innovated via the labor contract. After all, Mexican laborers would be recognized as deserving of state "protection" and of "freedom" only if they had a contract, which meant exercising personal agency through the contract. If they abided by certain standards of self-governance, they could be incorporated into rural populations as legal farmworkers in the United States. These standards included not staying in the United States past the term of their contracts, not joining the U.S. military to fight in the war, and remaining in the agricultural regions of the country so as to be employed solely in agricultural work. As such, the state mandated their exclusion from certain parts of society, and from modern institutions. They were also proclaimed citizen-subjects of Mexico, according to their contracts, not citizen-subjects of the United States. They were entitled, through the contract, to participate in U.S. society, but only to an extent. They were not allowed political participation, nor were they given access to privileges and resources (schools, factories, hospitals, etc.) in the United States. These racial continuities were dismissed and facilitated by the language of contract, based as they were in the long history of the dialectic of slavery and freedom. On the other hand, the Mexican government valued the bracero program as a way to assert its own state presence, to reassure its citizens of Mexico City's control of the emigration system, and to promote economic development, without having to pursue more radical agricultural reforms.[80]

Growers in the United States had their own ideas about the labor importation programs, and balked at the state regulation of farm labor from the inception of the bracero program, fearing unbridled government regulation and socialization of U.S. agriculture. They wanted a program like the

World War I program, where they had recruited workers in Mexico with little government intervention or regulation. For this reason, growers lobbied to dismantle the government agencies charged with administering the program, and the FSA in particular, because of its concern with implementing government protections for destitute farmers.[81] Even as growers in the U.S. West worked on eroding the effectiveness of the FSA and demanded direct access to Mexican labor, growers on the East Coast and in Florida pressured the U.S. government to create their own sort of "bracero program" by importing agricultural laborers from the British Caribbean.

Consonant with Mexican and Asian labor in the West, Bahamian workers had been employed since the 1860s to develop the eastern coast of Florida, until the 1917 Immigration Act slowed their migration. As more and more U.S. farmworkers sought employment in the defense industries, agribusiness leaders demanded that the state give them access to Caribbean workers just as they had given growers in the Southwest access to Mexican workers. They organized their own formidable lobby to write letters, call congressman, march into officials' offices, and testify at hearings, and their efforts eventually proved fruitful. By exchange of diplomatic notes on March 16, 1943, the United States and British colonial governments made an agreement for the importation of temporary contract laborers from the Bahamas to the United States. The agreement was modeled on the Mexican labor agreement, with the same general provisions. Two months later, the United States and British colonial governments made a similar agreement to import Jamaicans onto the sugar plantations of Florida.[82]

*   *   *

The transition in official state discourse over "contract" from the 1800s to the 1930s spurred intensive growth in the governmental regulation of labor and was crucial to the establishment of the Mexican and Caribbean labor importation programs by the 1940s. This heightened state authority over labor demonstrates that while it may seem that slavery and freedom were a contradiction, the two were inherently intertwined and mutually constitutive, used in different ways and in different contexts to encourage state power over the mobility of workers. By characterizing contract labor as "slave" or "free," the U.S. government alternatively banned or encouraged the importation of contract labor. The slave/free dialectic therefore empowered the U.S. government to racially exclude human beings from the benefits of liberal citizenship—whether through the construction of immigration restriction laws or through labor contracts. By the 1940s, the language of freedom again rationalized the movement of contract workers from one country to another, in a process regulated and enforced by the states involved. The debates over freedom therefore fostered the commodification of a racialized caste of labor designed to work almost exclusively in U.S. agriculture, such that as the state became the enforcer of freedom, it also became the enslaver, opening the state up for critique.

The Mexican and Caribbean workers who journeyed to the United States in pursuit of the individual rights and freedoms offered them there, acknowledged the "economic freedom" the labor programs sometimes gave them in granting a chance at gainful employment. Many of the men had no other option than to sign a contract and migrate to the United States as a survival strategy when faced with unemployment or underpaid labor at home. Between 1942 and 1947, 220,000 Mexican contract workers migrated to the United States.[83] Their eagerness to apply for a contract at labor recruitment centers in large numbers was widely publicized in newspapers and media outlets, as all governments involved emphasized the workers' free will and choice in signing labor contracts—rather than their coercion. Yet what they felt upon recruitment was not free will. As one Mexican contract worker, Miguel Jáquez López, detailed, after being medically examined by a government official and signing an unexplained labor contract at the recruitment center, "We would go past the consul and exit outside. And there, where the *patrones* walked, we would each settle and line up like a bunch of sheep, of cattle; there in the pure sun, *chinga!* There, the bosses from each state would arrive."[84] Another Mexican contract worker, Appolonio Venegas, related, "We came here with the interest of working and they treated us as less than human, like animals. Like animals we were sold by the Mexican government."[85] Workers repeatedly mentioned the feeling of being bought and sold as chattel, using the same slave/free dialectic to critique the state that had been used to coax their migrations. However, instead of invoking the slave/free dialectic to expand state power, they invoked it to turn the state into a site of political struggle.

The irony of the labor contract was not lost on the workers, as they learned to reject it in pursuit of their own version of freedom. A Mexican contract worker, Fortino Covarrubias, recalled enlisting in the bracero program at Empalme, Sonora, Mexico, where he suffered greatly during the four months he waited for a contract. Upon crossing into the United States, he, like all braceros, was stripped, medically examined, and deloused "as an animal." He then completed a contract in the fields of California, picking grapes, strawberries, and tomatoes. Covarrubias described the pain of being hunched over for hours at a time, and how he, out of hunger, ate fruits and vegetables from nearby fields while he worked. After his first contract ended, he came without documents to work in the United States, admitting that he had much more freedom without a contract. As he stated, "being here illegally was much more free, easier, and much more beautiful—we just had to be alert when the state came."[86] He spoke with pride and laughter about how he could outrun the authorities—highlighting his lack of fear in the face of the danger and violence imposed by the state. In such ways, contract workers called out the problematic freedoms of the contract by glorifying working without a contract and rejecting the supposed freedom it offered them. They found a means, albeit limited, to escape the constraint and coercion the contract implied while calling out its inherent contradictions, even as new imperial processes materialized around them.

CHAPTER 2

Good Neighbors?: Contract Labor and the
Limits of Freedom During the New Deal

In a 1929 speech, Ernesto Galarza pointedly observed, "From Denver to Los Angeles and from the Imperial Valley to Portland, it is said, an empire has been created largely by the brawn of the humble Mexican, who laid the rails and topped the beets and poured the cubic miles of cement." And yet, he lamented, "These builders of colossal fortunes have done their jobs and gone their ways still clothed in rags." As a former Mexican migrant and a farm labor advocate, Galarza knew that Mexican laborers had become central to the development of the U.S. West and the expansion of the U.S. empire in the nineteenth and early twentieth centuries. If this speech criticized the U.S. empire for not compensating Mexican workers, it also gave Mexican migrant workers a stake in it. After all, he stated, "If it is true that the Mexican has brought to you arms that have fastened a civilization on the Pacific slope, then give him his due." Galarza insisted that the United States should compensate Mexican migrant workers for their efforts toward building the U.S. empire—by making a civic and moral effort to economically and socially ameliorate the inequalities ethnic Mexicans faced. In doing so, he invoked a fundamental principle of U.S. liberalism—that of the freedom to life, liberty, and pursuit of happiness for all. Galarza put forth a plan to bring "order" out of the "chaos" of the seasonal labor supply, to ensure that freedom was secured for Mexican migrant workers, "preferably by government initiative." As he argued, "A bilateral accord with the Mexican government should be sought to iron out the immigration question."[1]

Galarza gave this speech on Mexican migrant labor at the National Conference of Social Work when he was only twenty-four years old. The Great Depression had just started, and this speech was one of Galarza's first attempts to advocate for a Mexican labor program in the face of job shortages. At the social work conference, Galarza publicly defended the rights of Mexican and Mexican American laborers in the United States, suggesting that the inequalities they faced were a product of racial prejudice, lack of jobs, and wage discrimination. Since there were too many workers clamoring for too few jobs, Galarza argued, Mexicans were forced to take the lowest paid and most difficult jobs. While some U.S. officials had reached the conclusion that Mexican immigration should be restricted alongside other nonwhite groups via the 1924 Immigration Act, Galarza instead asked how the state might become involved to resolve the inequalities faced by Mexican Americans in the U.S. labor market. His suggestion for a "bilateral accord" was an attempt to end the control of private businesses over the recruitment of Mexican labor, which had resulted in, as Galarza put it, "too many abuses to be recommended."[2]

Twelve years later, Galarza again proposed this "bilateral accord" when he recommended to U.S. and Mexican officials a contract labor importation program to accomplish the momentous task of social and economic uplift for Mexican workers. In his capacity as chief of the Division of Labor and Social Information of the Pan-American Union (PAU), Galarza stated before the U.S. House of Representatives (1941), "I want to suggest that the time has come for the creation of a joint international agency, composed of representatives of the United States and Mexico, to develop and carry out a long-term program of resettlement, rehabilitation, and regulation of migrants between the two republics." His plan included all working migrants of Latin America and the Caribbean, as he stated, "I believe there is a possibility of setting up a way of approach and of suggesting a solution which will affect the welfare and lift the standard of living, not only of the Mexican in the Southwest, but of the migratory worker in other areas of the Caribbean and of South America."[3] While a leader of the PAU from 1936–1947, Galarza lobbied for "socially progressive international action" on the question of Latin American and Caribbean migrant labor, through international collaboration and joint organization.

While arguing passionately for social welfare and labor rights for workers in the hemisphere, Galarza did not account for the history that had long structured contract labor through the conjoined logic of slavery and freedom. As he stated, "It is a peculiar thing, we have many agreements with the Mexican Government regarding boundaries and practically everything else excepting the flow of human beings from one country to another. As far as I know, there is no treaty or agreement of that kind between two Governments." Galarza viewed the labor program agreement idealistically, as a new policy regime that could replace former lawlessness in labor migrations with beneficent state management. In envisioning the contract agreement as a protector of human freedoms, Galarza's arguments were rooted in the connections between liberal contract theory and the free/slave dialectic that had structured the genealogy of "contract" through the nineteenth century, demonstrated in Chapter 1.[4]

Galarza was an important figure in this formative moment of the labor importation programs, and his proposal for a Mexican labor importation program exemplifies the evolution of the politics of labor management during the early 1940s. Progressive labor and civil rights advocates of the 1940s, nurturing a cultural and ideological shift toward racial liberalism, sought to release liberal freedoms from racial restrictions by extending equal opportunity, possessive individualism, and cultural citizenship to non-white labor migrants. Engaged in this particular moment, Galarza believed that the proper role of the state was to intervene and undo social hierarchies that produced the marginalization of some rather than others. As he and other progressives looked to the state to effect social and economic changes, they persuasively formulated a Mexican labor importation program as an attempt at state-mediated social justice.

In both Mexico and the United States, intellectuals, officials, and social scientists widely debated the role of the state as a mediator of racial conflict, remolding the state's relationship to the distinct peoples of their societies using similar sets of ideas. Racial liberalism and rural reform, in particular, became transnational phenomenon emerging in multiple entangled localities throughout the hemisphere in different moments from the 1920s to the 1950s. The common feature they shared in Latin America and the United States was the centrality of the state as the mediator of racial conflict. As historian Rubén Flores reveals, the interchange of U.S. and Mexican intellectuals and officials during the 1940s led to the formation of U.S. racial liberalism, an ideology inspired by the notion of "racial democracy" in those Latin American nations that attempted, through state intervention, to redefine citizenship around *mestizaje* and mixed-race heritage.[5] Historian Tore Olsson also illustrates how dozens of U.S. New Deal officials took research trips to Mexico in the 1930s and early 1940s to witness the agrarian reforms initiated by the Mexican revolutionary government. They took what they learned from President Lázaro Cárdenas' land redistribution policies and applied it in a U.S. context, seeking to optimistically transform capitalist social relations in the U.S. countryside.[6] Their efforts resulted in the establishment of the Farm Security Administration (FSA) in 1937, which became one of the original agencies responsible for the housing and management of imported contract workers during World War II.

While the labor importation programs were indicative of this shift to race liberal state reform, a deep continuity connected U.S. global ambitions from the eighteenth to the twentieth centuries. The capitalist notions of "free trade" and "free labor" under economic liberalism did not disappear with the shift to racial liberalism, nor did the political notion of universal equality accorded by the nation-state. What made this transformative moment in liberalism so distinctive was the principle that the government could use political administration to produce the "actual" and not merely the theoretical liberty of its people. Through the application of state laws, institutions, organizations, and practices, government officials during the New Deal attempted to make racial equality a reality through the use of expansive government power. They implemented the farm labor importation programs as agrarian reform efforts meant to launch a new race-liberal order. As part of a race-liberal regime, the labor programs limited the possibility of overcoming racism by reinforcing the operation of U.S.-led global capitalism, even as they enabled the normalizing violence of labor coercion, racial exploitation, and deportation.[7]

The adherence to the "freedom" of the labor contract through a framework of racial liberalism and rural social engineering erased the ways that the legacies of colonialism and empire had very much shaped and entrenched the labor force in Latin America and the Caribbean. Through their efforts toward social welfare diplomacy and agrarian reform during the implementation of the Good Neighbor Policy, New Deal reformers, including Galarza, unintentionally disavowed the history of U.S. economic and military interventions in Mexico and the Caribbean as a relic of the past. Yet it was past U.S. imperial efforts, including "free trade" interventions from the 1870s to the 1920s, that had caused a lack of subsistence in Mexico and the Caribbean in the first place, compelling Mexican and Caribbean workers to sell their labor power for a wage and to move to find work, leading to labor arrangements that were more compatible with the imperatives of capitalist industry.[8] It was thus the destruction of local economies through former U.S. and European investments in large business operations in Mexico and the Caribbean that contributed to the creation of a supply of "free wage labor" that seemingly moved of its own free will. Through ostensibly "free" labor mobility, U.S. officials and private corporations in the Caribbean and Mexico obtained workers supposedly without occupation, enslavement, or force.[9] In twentieth-century contract labor arrangements, the contract perpetuated this history, eradicating any sign of coercion involved in the labor migrations of Latin American and Caribbean people to the United States. In celebrating the labor contract as a hallmark of social change and as a vehicle of freedom, New Deal progressives thus inadvertently renewed the United States government's diplomatic stance, conceptually endorsing worker's "free" choice to migrate.

In the process of eliding former histories of colonialism and turning to the state to govern labor migrations, New Deal progressives unknowingly assisted in the reconsolidation of race and empire, even as they were convinced of their own benevolent mission. Their emphasis on the labor contract demonstrated a consistent commitment to the international circulation and recirculation of imperialism as "anti-imperialism," of "coercion" as "freedom," as well as the acceptance of the notion that the regions of Latin America and the Caribbean should be used by the United States as a source of agricultural labor, while also justifying the expansion of state regulation and power over racialized migrant workers. As a result, the labor programs more expansively connected laborers in Mexico and the Caribbean to the United States in a way that earlier U.S. imperial interventions never had.

Ernesto Galarza's Labor Importation Proposal

In the struggle for farm labor freedom, Dr. Ernesto Galarza later became one of the most passionate advocates for braceros, especially during his attempts to unionize braceros as a leader of the National Farm Labor Union (NFLU) in California. His career personifies the different contexts and perspectives on the bracero program that this book explores, making him a recurring figure in the chapters that follow. Without questioning his intentions or his heroic efforts toward social justice for farmworkers, Galarza's political choices and rhetorical strategies are explored in this book to probe the limits and consequences of liberalism as it shifted during the 1940s—especially its promises of state protection through rights and national inclusion through state-administered equality. From proposing a state-sponsored labor program with Mexico to calling for its end, Galarza remained hopeful of the state's capacity to enact and engender freedom, a hope that growing ranks of contract workers from Mexico and the Caribbean slowly recognized as a false promise.

At first glance, Galarza seems the least likely of individuals to have suggested the implementation of the bracero program. As a precursor to the farm labor and civil rights leader César Chavéz in California, he is justly remembered as a civil rights icon for his efforts to document and expose the many program violations. Galarza's views changed soon after the inception of the bracero program, when he began to see it as a new form of slavery. For the next twenty years, he fought against the injustices of the bracero program, critiquing its role in exploiting and abusing Mexican migrant workers. He also published many books on the topic, including *Strangers in Our Fields: Based on a Report Regarding Compliance with the Contractual, Legal, and Civil Rights of Mexican Agricultural Workers in the United States* (1956); *Merchants of Labor: The Mexican Bracero Story, an Account of the Managed Migration of Mexican Farm Workers in California, 1942–1960* (1970); and *Spiders in the House and Workers in the Fields* (1970).[10] After 1947, Galarza focused his efforts on organizing farm laborers in the California fields with the NFLU, in part to ensure that braceros had rights, as stipulated by the contract agreement.

While Galarza's efforts against the injustices of the bracero program have been well documented, his formative role in initially advocating for the bracero program has rarely been noted or even mentioned in the historiography.[11] Galarza himself never acknowledged this role even as its reality shaped his activism and life mission for nearly three decades thereafter. A seeming contradiction, but a closer examination of thought shows that his proposal of a Mexican labor program meshed well with his vision for labor and civil rights as a leader of the Pan-American Union (PAU). His life experiences provide an important window into the historical circumstances that politically shaped Galarza as an activist and intellectual, and explain how it might have been possible for him to initially advocate the establishment of a Mexican labor importation program. His political vision speaks to the seductive power of racial liberalism at the time, and points to some of the central paradoxes and unintended consequences of an ideological commitment to the foundational principles of liberalism. It also demonstrates how it was possible for other labor advocates to subsequently embrace guestworker programs as programs of social uplift into the late 1940s and 1950s.

Even as we know that Galarza promoted a Mexican labor importation program, he alone is not responsible for establishing it. Galarza was one actor among many, influencing the discursive and cultural framework of the program. Nonetheless, he stands as an example of how progressives and civil rights activists, some of whom were fundamentally opposed to imperialism, sought the application of freedom to all under an expansive state, through the extension of rights and protections to migrant workers who were noncitizens. Those progressives in favor of a Mexican labor program took the meanings surrounding "freedom" and applied them to Mexican migrant farm labor, inadvertently making workers' bodies and their production another technology to be manipulated and managed by the state.[12] Galarza's experiences are useful because they illuminate the cultural and political interdependencies that gave meaning to people's lives; he is not part of an abstract category of "imperialists," but he does express an imperial subjectivity. As historian Eric T. Love has shown, instead of characterizing U.S. policymakers as either "imperial" or "anti-imperial," it may be more useful to instead consider policymakers as individuals and complex human beings who do not often fit into simple categories.[13]

A number of personal experiences shaped Galarza's struggle to bring social justice awareness to migrant farm workers. Born to farm laborer parents in the small village of Jalcocotán in the Mexican state of Nayarit, Galarza came to the United States in 1911 as a result of the exodus from Mexico that occurred during the Mexican Revolution. Landing in Sacramento with his mother and uncle at the age of eight, he attended public school in California while picking hops in the San Joaquin Central Valley, earning ten cents an hour. The conditions in the labor camps where his family and most other workers lived were crowded and lacked basic provisions like adequate fresh water and washrooms. Because he had learned English in school, other Mexican migrant workers asked him to speak about the polluted drinking water, providing him with his first experience in organizing and activism. His teachers in Sacramento encouraged him to apply to college, and he earned a scholarship to attend Occidental College in 1923, where he studied the role of the Roman Catholic Church in the political and social history of Mexico.[14]

Galarza then became the first Mexican American in the United States to attend graduate school at Stanford University. Soon after graduating, Galarza expressed concern regarding the plight of Mexican migrant agricultural laborers, which he had experienced firsthand as a child. In 1931, three years after the conference at which he proposed a bilateral program to manage Mexican labor migrations, he published an article entitled "Without Benefit of a Lobby" in *Survey Graphic* magazine that touched on the exploitative conditions faced by Mexican agricultural workers in the Southwest. In this essay, Galarza blamed workers' "squalid" circumstances on their inability to join unions, on the construction of their race as a "degenerate Indian stock," and

on their incapacity to lobby politically.[15] *Survey Graphic* was a magazine produced by the board of directors and editors of Survey Associates, led by Assistant Secretary of State Adolf A. Berle, with the Latin Americanists Ernesto
Galarza, Charles Taussig, and Frank Tannenbaum on its committee.

Upon graduating from Stanford, Galarza married and received a fel-
lowship to pursue a Ph.D. at Columbia University in history and public law.
Moving in the same intellectual circles as Roosevelt's brain trust, a group of
Columbia University academics who helped develop policy recommendations
as part of the New Deal, Galarza advocated for Mexican workers' unionization
and political mobilization, pointing to racism as the central problem faced by
Mexican and Mexican-American workers in the United States. During the
Great Depression, Galarza became concerned with ameliorating the uncertainties of the marketplace and the effects of racist practices in education,
business, and labor. What made Galarza stand out was his internationalist
approach to the New Deal, as well as his attempt to extend progressive reforms
to Mexicans and Mexican Americans in the United States. While most New
Dealers focused on reform in the United States to improve the quality of life
for white working-class Americans, Galarza sought to extend the benefits of
the New Deal across the Western Hemisphere to Latin America and Mexico,
as part of his anti-imperial vision for U.S. diplomacy and Mexican American
civil rights.

One of Galarza's senior colleagues at Columbia University, Frank Tannenbaum, had spent several years in Mexico conducting research on rural education and serving as an adviser to President Lázaro Cárdenas. He undoubtedly
influenced Galarza's intellectual trajectory and interest in agrarian reform in
Mexico and vice versa. Joining with Roosevelt's "brain trust" leaders of the
U.S. Department of Agriculture in 1935, including the Resettlement Administration (RA) creator Rexford Tugwell and Secretary of Agriculture Henry
Wallace, Tannenbaum composed the legislation that established the FSA in
1937, looking to the Mexican Revolution and the *ejido* as a blueprint and
model for rural land reform in the United States. Reflecting Tannenbaum's
racial liberalism, the FSA made attempts to integrate black, white, and Mexican workers at FSA labor camps.[16] The first popular treatise on racial liberalism in the United States, *An American Dilemma: The Negro Problem and
Modern Democracy* (1944), cited Tannenbaum and the ideas of racial liberalism and agrarian reform that he had adapted from his experiences in Mexico. Written by Gunnar Myrdal, the book established a formulation of racial

justice in which the power of the "American Creed," or the U.S. commitment to the Enlightenment universals of liberty and equality, would eventually mean the end of racial segregation.[17]

In his dissertation, *La Industria Eléctrica en México*, Galarza, like Tannenbaum, carefully applied the ideals of the Mexican Revolution to the politics of Mexican rural development. He detailed the history, development, and economics of the electric power industry and its role in developing a capitalist economy in Mexico, to demonstrate its importance for the improvement of rural Mexico.[18] His dissertation reflected the optimism resulting from New Deal regional planning projects like the Tennessee Valley Authority (TVA), that centered on dams and electricity as a means to modernize the U.S. countryside. Galarza viewed the TVA as an inspiring developmental model that could shift U.S. diplomacy in Mexico as part of the Good Neighbor Policy. Galarza's focus on New Deal planning, industrialization, and development in Mexico was also a concern taken up by other Mexican labor activists, intellectuals, elites, artists, and politicians as the cure for Mexico's economic struggles, and as a means to wrench Mexico from land-based inequalities. The highest rungs of Mexico's political leadership, including Presidents Cárdenas and Camacho, traveled to tour the TVA, hoping to replicate its formula for agrarian transformation in Mexico. Galarza's focus on the development of the Mexican countryside from "feudalism" to industrialization in his dissertation later inflected Galarza's arguments for a Mexican labor importation program.[19]

While completing his dissertation, Galarza and his wife worked as educators at a progressive community school in Long Island, called the Gardner School. Between 1932 and 1936, they served as co-principals and then as owners of the school.[20] As a progressive educator, Galarza's support of a more inclusive democratic liberalism solidified and shaped his sense of politics. Galarza also did research for the Foreign Policy Association in New York, grounding his belief and pride in democracy and veneration for U.S. freedoms that would remain with him his entire life and form an important part of his political vision. He became involved in solidarity work with other New Deal progressives of his generation for the Loyalists engaged in fighting fascism during the Spanish Civil War (1936). He also became a strong supporter of the Abraham Lincoln Brigade, U.S. volunteers who served in the Spanish Civil War, and traveled throughout the United States giving speeches and assisting in fund-raising campaigns.. Meanwhile, Galarza's associates at the Foreign Policy Association introduced him to members of the Pan-American

Union (PAU), and he soon left New York for Washington, D.C,. to work in the division of intellectual cooperation at the PAU in 1936.

Galarza's position at the PAU presented him with an undeniable means to give voice to Mexican workers and to participate in high-level policy discussions regarding employment and civil rights. In the division of intellectual cooperation of the PAU, Galarza merged his interests in education and Latin America, writing two articles in 1939, one entitled "Problems of Education in the Western Hemisphere" and the other entitled "Educational Research in Latin America." These essays exemplified his belief in the application of New Deal science to educational policy and the industrialization of Mexico, as he focused on "better coordination and more efficient interchange of knowledge between the United States and Latin America."[21] Galarza's implied goal was the modernization of education in Latin America to aid industrialization, through the application of improved testing techniques and national standards against which to measure teaching effectiveness. He thought to promote a U.S. style of liberal democracy in Latin America through education, arguing that the principles of democracy must be practiced and "hammered into codes of conduct by the schools." The best way to ensure this was to place educators in the United States and Latin America "on a plane of mutual help and understanding," a fundamental assumption of the Good Neighbor Policy and of the PAU.

In 1940, the PAU promoted Galarza to the newly formed division of labor and social information, which involved extensive travel to Latin America. His job was to collect data and prepare reports on labor and social welfare in Latin America, including labor legislation, trade unions, wages, hours, collective bargaining, child welfare, social security, housing, and more. He took a distinct interest in labor in the United States and in Latin America at this time, publishing multiple texts for the PAU journal, *Labor Trends and Social Welfare in Latin America* (1937–1942). He also began to promote his proposal for a Mexican labor importation program at this time.[22]

In a "Summary of Proposals with Regard to the Future Importation of Workers from Mexico into the United States," sent to Oswald Stein, chief of the social security section of the International Labor Organization (ILO) in 1940, Galarza suggested the formation of a joint U.S.-Mexican government agency to function within the framework of the PAU, with the ILO as the labor recruiter. He maintained that this agency would be "an integral part of the rapidly expanding mechanism now being created to obtain greater cooperation and more friendly relations between Mexico and the United States," as part of the Good Neighbor Policy. Referring to his proposal as a program

Figure 3. Portrait of Ernesto Galarza pointing to a map of Latin America. Courtesy of Occidental College Library Special Collections.

of "rehabilitation and resettlement," Galarza saw its potential to provide jobs and housing for workers, much as the Farm Security Administration of 1937 had for white Dust Bowl migrants. Galarza also recommended that organized labor in the United States and Mexico participate from the outset and that the program have an educational purpose, to give "Mexicans a chance to learn English so that they could "understand the labor contracts which [they] sign," and "accurately interpret laws and ordinances."[23]

As historians have noted, President Roosevelt was reluctant to pursue policy on racial integration, as he claimed to be captive to the seniority of white Southerners in Congress, who occupied strategic positions on most of the Senate and House committees. His administration was racially con-servative, and it never intended to use federal welfare programs to alter race relations, as indicated by the fact that Blacks and Mexicans, the majority of agricultural workers, were not included as part of the Social Security Act, Unemployment Insurance, or the National Labor Relations Act.[24] Galarza's labor importation proposal was an attempt to extend those reforms to Mexi-can migrant workers, by providing them with the rights and guarantees that U.S. workers had accomplished as part of the New Deal. As Galarza argued, contract workers should be allowed to organize collectively as laborers, have a representative attend meetings of the joint commission, and be given an opportunity to "present grievances, to negotiate, and to bargain collectively on a fair and equitable basis."[25] With the contract, he optimistically upheld that Mexican workers would be both protected by the state and be able to join domestic labor unions to effectively organize against capitalism's inequities.

Pressured by Black civil rights protests championing the desegregation of the military and A. Philip Randolph's March on Washington Movement, President Roosevelt issued Executive Order 8802 in June 1941, institution-alizing the Fair Employment Practices Committee (FEPC). Even though its authority was limited, it was the first U.S. legislative action in support of civil rights since Reconstruction, as it required that companies with government contracts not discriminate "on the basis of race, creed, color, or national ori-gin."[26] A spokesman for the Black working class, Randolph helped convince a generation of civil rights activists that nonviolent protests and mass demon-strations were the most effective way to mobilize for social justice. Galarza followed his efforts, seeking to extend its successes to Mexican American workers. Like A. Philip Randolph, he supported trade unionism and labor organizing, and sought to end employment discrimination as part of the long civil rights movement. In a letter to the FEPC written a few months after the organization had formed, Galarza suggested that the commission consider studying the conditions of employment of Mexicans in California as part of its program. The chairman of the FEPC, Mark Etheridge, approved Galar-za's suggestion in 1941. The Mexican American civil rights organization, the League of United Latin American Citizens (LULAC), similarly pressured the FEPC in Texas toward broader civil rights legislation inclusive of Mexican Americans. In spite of their efforts, the FEPC faced numerous challenges until ultimately a unified band of Southern lawmakers dismantled it after World War II.[27]

With his efforts in the PAU and his support of the FEPC, Galarza realized the impressive opportunities that the war and an expanded state could offer communities of color. He also recognized the centrality of organized labor to civil rights, supportive as he was of the emergence of labor unions and orga-nizations, like the Congress of Industrial Organizations (CIO). As a scholar of Mexican economics, history, and government, Galarza exchanged ideas with notable Mexican officials and intellectuals of Mexico. He found inspira-tion in the Mexican government's attempts to create an activist state after the

Mexican Revolution (1910–1920), as the Mexican government reconstituted national belonging amid great economic upheaval and social conflict. Mexico's distribution of state resources to rural communities through government relief programs, as well as the efforts of New Deal officials in the United States to place farmworkers in jobs, had provided Galarza with a sense of possibility for what the U.S. federal government might do to intervene in the rural communities of the U.S. Southwest to alleviate racism, social exclusion, and economic inequalities for Mexican migrants.

Likewise, the ILO's activities in Latin America indicated a movement toward social welfare diplomacy in the Western Hemisphere, giving Galarza a unique avenue by which to appeal to leaders and policymakers from several nations for a transnational labor program. The United States had first joined the ILO in 1934. Beginning in 1936, the ILO took steps to nurture a coalition of supporters in the Americas and beyond who met and proposed a set of social rights based on labor standards as part of a New Deal for the Americas. Galarza was one of the ILO supporters involved in expanding measures of labor standards as part of a Pan-American trend. He sought to bolster workers' welfare through enhanced job opportunities in response to the crisis of the Great Depression.[28] As one among these national-level policymakers, Galarza introduced the Mexican labor program, projecting his own distinct vision of social policy in the hemisphere.

In 1941, Galarza took his proposal of an "international coalition" to carry out a long-term plan for the "resettlement, rehabilitation, and regulation" of Mexican migrants to a hearing of the U.S. House Select Committee Investigating National Defense Migration, also known as the Tolan Committee. While originally focused on the interstate movement of people seeking employment in the wake of the Great Depression of the 1930s, Galarza tasked this committee with considering the plight of Mexican migrant workers in the United States as part of the national defense moment of World War II. As Galarza stated, "The problem [of Mexican migration], is one of international good will and friendly inter-American relations as well as of agricultural economics and social welfare."[29] Through an orderly plan of state research, analysis, and legislation, Galarza argued that the labor program he proposed could extend the benefits of New Deal policies to Mexican migrant workers, whether in the United States or in Mexico. The overarching goal of the joint commission he proposed would be to provide general standards of wages, housing, and health care that would "rehabilitate" the Mexican population in the southwest, leveling the economic playing field.[30] Education was again central, as Galarza recommended English language classes and classes teaching modern farming techniques as part of the labor program, as well as the distribution of literature on modern farming methods to workers.

Galarza emphasized, however, that such a program depended on adequate state financing and setting migrants up with basic governmental health and educational services. It would also require sound policy decisions that could work to effectively govern cycles of human migration from Mexico to the United States. Galarza argued, "Methods should be developed by which the workers would be cared for in transit and standard conditions of housing and living on the job be assured them." The contract would be the means to ensure these conditions, such that "Mexican workers in the southwest [would] be enabled to receive the benefits of certain federal laws, especially those relating to wages, hours, and housing."[31]

In an enterprising fashion, Galarza engaged the themes of the immediate wartime moment, including labor shortages and the "fight for democracy" or "freedom from fascism," to defend racial equality for Mexican laborers. He emphasized the labor programs as a salve for racism, stating, "I would like to call your attention to the fact that in areas of the Southwest today there are dual wage standards and that Mexican workers today are being paid less for the same kind of work." He continued, "the [Mexican worker] is subject to very serious discrimination in the matter of seniority," as well as "segregation in many forms." This racism impacts the "productivity of labor" as a "matter of morale." If Mexican laborers were treated equally, Galarza implied, they would work harder and produce more for the war effort. He maintained that the "psychological frictions" of race were responsible for the United States' inability to procure sufficient labor for the war effort. Furthermore, the "problems of maladjustment and discrimination" have "spread beyond Mexico; they are picked up and commented upon by the enemies of the United States . . . and they build up as an example of the indifference of the people of the United States to the Mexicans."[32] Galarza appealed to the desire for United States global preeminence during the war, arguing, as other civil rights activists did, that racial discrimination limited the United States' global leadership. The labor program, he argued, would demonstrate the United States' commitment to preventing racial discrimination and secure the diplomatic reputation of the United States.

At the Tolan Committee hearings, a group of idealistic New Deal reformers took his idea of a labor program seriously, with the intent of extending the promises of the New Deal to those formerly left out: farmworkers, migrant workers, and island colonials, in the shaping of a new anti-imperial world order. That the labor programs initially emerged under the leadership of the FSA indicates that U.S. federal officials similarly thought of the labor programs as a corrective scheme that would take the New Deal beyond the color line, by granting rights to migrant farmworkers.[33]

In September 1941, after his proposal to Congress, Galarza promoted the idea of a Mexican labor importation to the Mexican ambassador Francisco Castillo Nájera, before U.S. officials had even begun discussions with Mexico regarding the bracero program. Nájera approved of Galarza's suggestion, replying "Your project for the foundation to improve the condition of Mexicans in the United States is the most constructive, practical, and farsighted step towards solving a serious problem." It would also "unquestionably contribute towards our common aim of closer ties between Mexico and the United States . . . thus we shall make Pan-Americanism a living thing."[34] Galarza was not alone in his political and social ideals, as those ideals had been framed by the hemispheric politics of welfare capitalism, Pan-Americanism, and the New Deal. The politics that Galarza and others engaged led them to make convincing arguments for state intervention in migrant laborers' lives in the years leading up to the labor program agreements, shaping policy for years to come.

The Imperialism of the Good Neighbor Policy

At his inaugural address on March 4, 1933, Franklin D. Roosevelt promoted the policy of the "Good Neighbor," stating, "In the field of world policy I would dedicate this nation to the policy of the Good Neighbor—the neighbor who . . . respects the rights of others."[35] At the seventh Pan-American convention in Montevideo, Uruguay, in December 1933, both he and his secretary of state, Cordell Hull maintained, "no state has the right to intervene in the internal or external affairs of another" and renounced armed intervention in the region. Assistant Secretary of State Sumner Welles openly admitted in a speech in 1935 that U.S actions had resulted in: "Peculiar manifestations of American foreign policy which have given special impetus to the charge against the United States that its aims have been imperialistic, that its actions have been notorious for a complete disregard of the sovereignty and independence of the republics lying within that area, and that such a policy has been in flagrant violation of the general precepts of international law." Secretary Hull further argued that the U.S. "military occupations" of Nicaragua, Haiti, and the Dominican Republic had "contributed to open animosity against the United States . . . not only have we incurred lasting enmity and resentment of the citizens of those nations in which we have intervened, but we have built up a wall of misunderstanding and prejudice between ourselves and the great republics of the South."[36] The United States' new objective, according to Welles, became the "liquidation as soon as possible of the errors committed in the past."[37]

On December 1, 1940, Vice President and former Secretary of Agriculture Henry Wallace attended the inauguration of General Ávila Camacho as president of Mexico, in an effort to express the United States' sincerity with the Good Neighbor Policy. Along with Charles Taussig and Rexford Tugwell in the Caribbean, Wallace became one of the New Deal's foremost admirers of agrarian reform and communal farming in Mexico. As part of his "good will" visit Wallace toured the agricultural fields of Mexico, and it became apparent to him that for agrarian reform and land redistribution to be successful in Mexico, *campesinos* needed farm equipment, capital, and education in modern farming techniques. In 1943, Wallace established the Mexican Agricultural Project (MAP) in partnership with the Mexican Ministry of Agriculture. The purpose of MAP was to "improve the yield of basic food crops in Mexico," and it was built upon Wallace's desire to make the Good Neighbor Policy tangible.[38] In his 1943 speech, "The Century of the Common Man," Wallace admonished the United States to assist in the development of underdeveloped countries, stating "our technical experts and industrial equipment can aid them to raise their own standards of production and of consumption." This, along with "the free exchange of goods" between the United States and Mexico, would strengthen the power of the Western Hemisphere, which he viewed as one "economic unit." Through free trade, Wallace boasted, "The United States now has her second opportunity to make the world safe for democracy."[39]

With the promises of the Good Neighbor Policy and its racial neutrality in mind, Mexican officials eventually agreed to the bracero program. As President Manuel Ávila Camacho of Mexico stated, "The differences that may exist among our countries are superseded and blended in with the mutual and lofty aspiration to establish a continental life of assured *friendship* and *reciprocal respect* in which reason shall predominate over brute force and *peaceful cooperation* over mechanized destruction."[40] According to the Mexican foreign ambassador Ezequiel Padilla, "These two forces that gnawed at the very heart

Figure 4. Henry A. Wallace shaking hands with President Manuel Avila Camacho, Mexico, 1943. Courtesy of University of Iowa Special Collections Department.

of true democracy—social injustice within the United States [i.e., racism], imperialism that destroyed the prosperity and confidence of the American peoples—show, by their common origin and simultaneous disappearance, that they are the bitter fruits of an evil system and not a product of the national consciousness of the United States."[41] As U.S. and Mexican officials turned to the Good Neighbor Policy as a model for U.S.-Latin American diplomacy, they took it for granted that the policy signaled a new type of statesmanship.[42]

In reality, the policy model set forth was not new, but had been popular throughout the Western Hemisphere since the 1880s, as Pan-Americanism (1880s–1940s). In 1890, U.S. Secretary of State James G. Blaine established the Pan-American Union (PAU), an organization of states in the Western Hemisphere designed to promote commercial trade, economic integration, and political cooperation among the United States and the countries of Latin America. The PAU took shape just after the end of the Spanish-American War and the U.S. acquisition of colonies in Puerto Rico, Guam, the Philippines, and the Virgin Islands, within the broad context of a decades-long escalation of U.S. imperialism in Latin America and the Caribbean basin. Amid a rising demand for markets, bases, mining operations, and a Panama Canal, the U.S. government continued its interventions in the region through a discourse of cooperation.

As historian Richard Cándida Smith illustrates, the PAU was the first institutional expression of a new vision of global organization that the United States vigorously promoted throughout the twentieth century. He states, "it drew upon preexisting liberal ideas that the American nations had a special place in history as the home of liberty."[43] By the 1930s, the liberalism of the PAU had already long served the purpose of expressing altruistic intentions through U.S. cultural imperialism, with government programs organized under the rubric of "cultural exchange" between liberal nation-states, promoting U.S. access to "free markets" in Latin America and the Caribbean. When Latin American officials joined in a "Pan-American identity," they tended to implement the U.S. approach to business, politics, and culture, perpetuating U.S. imperialism in Latin America and the Caribbean into the twentieth century.

Originally termed the International Union of American Republics, the PAU promoted cooperation among countries of Latin America, and encouraged agreements on various common commercial and juridical problems through a series of annual conferences. While emphasizing multilateralism, solidarity, and democracy, such conferences were designed for dispute resolution and pacification of those Latin American countries that were not interested in backing U.S. economic interests. In other words, Pan-Americanism became a means to refine U.S. efforts to exert control in Latin American by avoiding further military interventions. The PAU also made Latin America more legible to the United States for the vast public created by corporate capitalism and mass consumer culture.[44] William E. Curtis and William A. Reid, the first directors of the international bureau of the PAU, sought to stimulate and circulate knowledge about the region in the United States, for better commercial interactions between North and South. To this end, the PAU started a series of publications on Latin America and facilitated international conferences for U.S. scientists, while the Carnegie Endowment for Peace arranged goodwill tours in Latin America.

These cultural and ideological investments of the PAU led to the acquisition of new knowledge about the region even as this knowledge enabled U.S. economic expansion in Latin America through "free trade." The PAU circulated ideas about Latin America to a U.S. audience, pioneering efforts to create an "information industry" with pamphlets, handbooks, reports, and more. U.S. universities cooperated with the PAU, organizing Latin American collections, while public libraries arranged reading clubs and courses on Latin America. These institutional relationships allowed an exchange of artists, intellectuals, and musicians between Latin America and the United State, to promote closer cultural interaction between the United States and the twenty other countries in the PAU, while promoting closer cooperation and unity in politics among the American states.[45] The hemispheric liberalism espoused by the PAU allowed Washington to project its authority and influence in a new interstate system defined not by colonialism but by nominally free and sovereign nations.[46] With the PAU, the United States resolved to aid and develop the "Americas," an effort that would purportedly prevent imperial aggression.

The liberalism of the PAU functioned to mask U.S. imperialism as a benevolent enterprise and demarcated the Western Hemisphere as a sphere of influence the United States dominated. The PAU was so effective at mobilizing U.S. investments in Latin America that by 1911, Anglo-Americans owned most of Mexico's oil industry, which was the third largest petroleum producer in the world. By the late 1920s, the U.S. had established control over crucial raw materials and transit routes, gained military expertise, and invested billions of dollars in Latin America. By the 1930s, the PAU had long served the purpose of expressing altruistic intentions, while condoning U.S. access to "free" markets in Latin America and the Caribbean.

Unbeknown to its supporters at the time, the Good Neighbor Policy of the 1930s and 1940s was not new, but part of the renewed search for investment or "free trade" opportunities abroad. The Good Neighbor Policy was an innovation on the former "free trade" Pan-Americanism that had been consolidated with the PAU. The policy did not contradict imperial rule, but rather accommodated new forms of imperialism and inaugurated the expansion of U.S. trade and power over Latin America and Mexico, and it was informed by a progressive racial and economic liberalism that promoted mutual cooperation among nations in the name of free trade and free labor, while serving the needs of U.S. capital.[47]

Galarza was a staunch proponent of the Good Neighbor policy, as his research on Latin American education and modernization, and his frequent trips to Latin America, suggest.[48] Two years after the U.S. and Mexican governments initiated the bracero program, Galarza recited the binational discourse of the Good Neighbor Policy when he proclaimed the workers "are truly soldiers of the harvest, and are justly proud of the fact that they are performing an indispensable duty on the home front." As he further stated, "our communities should realize these men are more than workers. They are emissaries of good will sent to us by one of our allies—an ally whose friendship and assistance we need."[49]

Galarza went to work with the PAU in 1936, at the height of the Good Neighbor Policy. He wrote educational pamphlets on Latin American cultures and politics for a U.S. audience, contributing to the information industry created by the PAU.[50] Galarza's doctoral thesis was also rooted in ameliorating inequalities between the United States and Mexico through the development of electricity in Mexico—demonstrating his commitment to some of the material production and industrial welfare efforts of the PAU. At the same time, Galarza's efforts at the PAU were not entirely reflective of his views on labor justice in Latin America. Even as a member of the PAU, Galarza made efforts to fight for the right of labor unions across the hemisphere to unionize and to test the power of U.S. corporations, demonstrating that members of the PAU held dissenting views that did not always agree with the organization's theoretical orientation.

Earlier U.S. Interventions in Latin America and the Caribbean

While he embraced the Good Neighbor Policy, Galarza was also fully aware and critical of U.S. interventions in Latin America, which is why he eventually ended up leaving his leadership role at the Pan-American Union.[51] As a historian of Latin America, a policymaker, a labor populist, and a patriot of Mexico, he was committed to the anti-imperialist ideals of the Mexican Revolution which had denounced U.S. financial investments in Mexico. Galarza perceived in World War II and the Good Neighbor Policy a potential sea change in historic U.S. policy toward Latin America and the Caribbean, and an end to U.S. empire. Galarza's efforts in the PAU toward modernizing Mexican education, labor, and industry, and defending a labor importation program were influenced by the philosophy of Pan-Americanism that had been promoted by the PAU since the turn of the twentieth century. Yet an ideology of Pan-Americanism had fueled U.S. imperial interventions in Latin America and the Caribbean in the first place, causing population displacement and migration while also facilitating United States access to resources and markets. These earlier U.S. interventions created the condition of possibility for the Mexican and Caribbean labor importation programs, such that the labor programs signaled not an end to imperialism, but a continuation.[52]

In the 1890s, the PAU transformed the U.S. diplomatic policy laid out in the Monroe Doctrine into an ideology of "mutual cooperation" among Latin American states. Written in 1823, the Monroe Doctrine essentially stated that any European attempts to colonize Latin America would be viewed as an act of aggression toward the United States and was an explicit call for U.S. military intervention. It was a declaration of anticolonialism, as President Monroe stated, "The American continents, by the free and independent condition which they have assumed and maintain, are henceforth not to be considered as subjects for colonization by any European powers." During Latin America's national independence movements, the United States declared its opposition to potential re-colonization and to empire in Latin America.[53] While purportedly anticolonial, the Monroe Doctrine established the United States as the legitimate protector of the Western Hemisphere, paving the way for future U.S. intervention and colonization in Latin America and the Caribbean.

While the Monroe Doctrine was a unilateral call for U.S. "protection" over the entire Western Hemisphere, the U.S. did not have the military or economic strength to support such an ambitious policy, especially in the face of European colonial power.[54] This changed in 1845, when U.S. President James K. Polk called for aggressive economic expansion into the west at his inaugural address, providing the justification for the United States conquest and annexation of half of Mexico with the Mexican-American War of 1846. Polk explained that expansion was part of America's Manifest Destiny, requiring the United States to venture into Mexico.[55]

Instead of territorially expanding south into Latin America in the nineteenth century, U.S. officials and financial leaders pursued new innovative methods for hegemony by pouring finance capital into the region.[56] The U.S. minister to Mexico, Thomas Corwin (1794–1865), demonstrated this preference for economic liberalism when he argued for the United States to use the French invasion (1862–1867) as an opportunity to direct Mexico's development. To "right" the expansionist wrongs of the Polk presidency, which had led to the U.S. annexation of Mexican territory, Corwin sought to strengthen self-government and economic liberalism in Mexico by proposing an $11 million loan to Mexico to repay foreign creditors and expel the French from Mexico. Much in line with the Monroe Doctrine, he stated, "The United States are the only safe guardians of the independence and true civilization of this continent." Corwin thought his loan treaty would lay the foundation for future commercial agreements and transit concessions to U.S. railroad developers. With U.S. "aid," Mexico resisted the French occupation in 1867, restoring the republic. Mexican officials then sought to commercialize and modernize the rural Mexican landscape by making Mexico friendly to U.S. investments, a project that many Mexican leaders actively entertained for the benefit of their own liberal state-building projects.[57]

By the 1870s, U.S. imperialism had in part become a strategy of economic control, a trade in dollars for railroad construction in Latin America, as part of the pursuit for areas in which to invest, manufacture cheaply, find consumers, and exercise "free trade." In arguing for "free trade" over European colonial encroachment, U.S. officials wanted Latin America to depend on U.S. "free" markets, not "colonial" European markets. As the PAU founder, U.S. Secretary of State Blaine, stated in 1884, "while the great powers of Europe are steadily enlarging their colonial domination in Asia and Africa, it is the especial province of this country to improve and expand its trade with the nations of America."[58] In reality, U.S. practices were not a deviation from European practices, but variations on them that drew inspiration from British colonialism. U.S. westward expansion entailed colonial rule over new territories that were not only similar to but also modeled on the colonial regimes Britain had previously constructed for the thirteen colonies. Even further, by the nineteenth century, states rhetorically preferred non-territorial rule over peripheral areas creating empires of clients and subordinated allies using a discourse of "free trade" and economic liberalism, over and against European mercantilism.[59]

Mexican leadership also took part in this turn to "free trade" and economic liberalism. President Porfirio Díaz's political regime, the Porfiriato (1876–1910), signaled a new period of U.S. influence and power in Mexico, as aggressive capitalists invested in banking, technology, resource exploitation, and land ownership in Mexico. Díaz wanted to nationalize, develop, and modernize Mexico and extend its markets.[60] In 1876, Mexico's railway consisted of only 400 miles of tracks. Under Díaz's development model, the railroad rapidly expanded as he offered concessions to major railroad companies. With the development of the railroad, Mexico could become a major source of raw materials production for the United States, and of laborers.

The Porfiriato was notorious for privatizing indigenous land into large-scale landholdings, industrializing agriculture, and commercializing the *hacienda* in the rural Mexican countryside, all with the help of foreign capital. In an effort to combine privatization and industrialization, Díaz's administration expanded the abilities of outside companies to demarcate and acquire land by undoing the legal processes by which indigenous people held lands communally. By 1910, the regime had transferred 127 million acres of communal or unoccupied lands, representing half of Mexico's arable farmland, into private hands.[61] Using a discourse of modernity to justify the government sale of indigenous lands in vast quantities to powerful Mexican property holders as well as U.S. and European investors, the Mexican government changed the Mexican labor landscape. The racial assumption that indigenous farmworkers were backward and anti-modern propelled Mexico's racial project, justifying this usurpation of land. While locals contested the purchases, Mexican authorities approved the transactions and denied their complaints, forcing indigenous populations to choose between performing labor in estate agriculture and migrating elsewhere for employment.[62] The labor mobility of *campesinos* was therefore as much the product of forces internal to Mexico as it was a product of U.S. financial intervention in Mexico.

Díaz's support of U.S. financial investments in Mexico and the creation of large wealthy landowners formed an extractive economic relationship with the land that led to increased labor migrations across Mexico. Whereas these former land tracts became *haciendas*, where *hacendados* had obligations to pay wages and give *campesinos* a share of goods produced, these relations were distorted in the new system of plantations. Many indigenous subsistence farmers became landless wage earners, dislocated from their communities and forced to work for wages to purchase food under the Porfiriato. As a result, Mexican *campesinos* migrated north, to engage in other tactics to survive in the new "modern" economy created under Díaz, many working on the railroad or in the mines of northern Mexico.[63] Díaz's efforts exemplify how the project of constructing a Mexican nation-state overlapped with the U.S.-state project of financial expansion into Latin America. While the United States' financial investments were maneuvers to maintain power and control over Mexico's resources, officials of the Mexican nation-state courted these investments and engaged in their own projects of political liberalism through modernization efforts.[64] At the same time the Mexican government consolidated and centralized its own national project, it expanded its power over the rural Mexican population.

These overlapping moments in Mexican and U.S. financial projects resulted in the continued labor mobility of peasants and working-class people who sought purportedly "free labor" as a survival mechanism. While an element of choice presumably informed their movements, and labor migrants asserted agency by choosing to move for work, these financial actions often

served as the precondition for their movement.[65] During the Porfiriato, foreign investments in Mexico fostered urban development and the creation of
centers of commercial activity, leading to the internal migration of hundreds
of workers. Investments in mining in particular brought high wages and the
founding of new cities, while at the same time upending the economic life of
entire communities and creating populations that were transient, unstable,
and prone to rebelliousness. The introduction of modern farming techniques
through U.S. investments and rising cost of land also led to the destruction of
the traditional peasant economy, forcing people to move to find work in the
wage economy. In this way, nineteenth- and twentieth-century "free trade" in
Latin America and the Caribbean consisted in the power to adapt colonialism
with new forms of racialized migrant labor.[66] From 1880–1910 migration to
the southwest United States increased drastically.

By 1910, the Mexican Revolution (1910–1920) also propelled an exodus from Mexico to the United States. As the Mexican economy collapsed
under Díaz's reign, hunger and epidemics increased, leading people to take
drastic measures to survive. For everyday Mexicans, such measures often
involved fleeing the country to avoid starvation and violence or to prevent
sons and daughters from entering the deadly crossfire of civil war. The revolution resulted in the influx of more than one million Mexican immigrants
to the United States from 1910 to 1930 for work in agriculture, railroads, and
mining.[67] In the 1920s, the number of Mexicans who crossed has been cal-
culated at 100,000 each year—not including those recorded by immigration
authorities.[68]

In the United States, refugees from the Mexican Revolution inflamed an
already robust anti-immigration movement. U.S. organized labor and immigration restriction leagues worked together to prevent Mexican migration
to the United States.[69] Just as U.S. immigration restrictionists lobbied for
anti-immigration laws, U.S. agriculture and mining companies frightened
the public and Congress with threats to food production, lobbying against
immigration restriction. The opposition to Mexican migration to the United
States nevertheless led to Mexican Repatriation (1929–1939), when President
Hoover's administration, in concert with local officials and federal authorities, set out on a campaign to deport nearly 450,000 Mexicans.[70]

The Mexican government actively participated in this program of "repatriation" and resettlement, with the goal of developing the Mexican countryside.
While U.S. financial investments in Mexico had long spurred population movement northward, most Mexican policymakers did not view out-migration as

beneficial to the country. From the time of Mexico's independence in 1821, they had cast population growth as essential for economic growth and nation-building and encouraged those who had migrated to return as *repatriados*. Beginning with Mexican president Plutarco Elías Calles (1924–1928), Mexican governmental and private agencies saw in repatriation a means to develop the economy in Mexico, such that repatriation became the cornerstone of state efforts to colonize the countryside with progressive agricultural societies in northern Mexico. Intellectuals like Manuel Gamio helped to formalize this thinking, arguing that Mexicans who had worked in the United States were more valuable for the advanced production techniques and their "high cultural level." In other words, they could form a property-owning middle class in Mexico, providing jobs for a peasant class of agricultural workers in Mexico who could assist in the state project of development and rural colonization.[71]

The ideology of Mexican revolutionary nationalism shaped Mexican officials' views on repatriation in the 1920s, as they considered repatriation to be a project of state protection and material assistance, both of which were consistent with Mexican revolutionary ideals and with the Good Neighbor Policy that emerged by 1933. In the 1930s, a reconsolidated Mexican government had sought to incorporate the idealism of the revolution with the Party of the Mexican Revolution (PRI). Following President Calles's extensive land reform, President Lázaro Cárdenas (1934–1940) implemented the revolutionary land, labor, and educational reforms of the 1917 Mexican Constitution. Land redistribution constituted a centerpiece of Cárdenas's polices across Mexico, as *campesinos* received *ejidos,* or collective landholdings, instead of working for large commercial estates. Cardenista reforms also included the creation of industrial projects and structures as cooperatives, to help modernize the countryside.[72] Such actions won Cárdenas strong allegiance among the poor, seemingly demonstrating that the state could serve to protect the interests of marginalized workers in the Mexican countryside. Alongside the nationalization of U.S. oil companies in Mexico, his reforms seemed to signal the achievement of the popular demands of the Mexican Revolution. As historians have now pointed out, *cardenismo* marked the final triumph of the state over the forces of revolution, and the consolidation and continuity of capitalist development in Mexico. Even as the Cárdenas government redistributed land to rural workers and peasants, it also handed the profits of *ejidos* over to U.S. capital.[73]

The Mexican state's efforts during "Mexican Repatriation" symbolized a benevolent and patriotic attempt to bring workers back to Mexico to economically modernize and develop the countryside. Despite the inability of the

state to absorb returned migrants into the economy, Mexican officials continued to insist that Mexican citizens come back. As the Mexican government
coaxed Mexicans in the United States to voluntarily return to Mexico, the U.S.
Bureau of Immigration set out a plan of intimidation raids, propaganda in
newspapers, and related efforts to create a climate of fear to encourage Mexicans to leave the United States of their own volition in the 1930s. Local U.S.
citizens led public repatriation committees, fueling most of the campaign in
the United States. Mexican consular officials, while protesting exploitation,
cooperated with local repatriation programs, arranging with Mexican customs officials to lower duties for personal goods, and with railroads to offer
free transportation from the border to the interior. They established a Comité
Pro-Repatriación, one of several such organizations Mexican consuls helped
to establish throughout the United States in the 1930s. In essence, repatriation sanctified the nation-state, as state authorities in the U.S. and Mexico
collaborated to refuse Mexicans access to U.S. citizenship and labor.[74]

Critical of what had happened during the 1930s with Mexican Repatriation, Galarza viewed a state-led Mexican labor migration program as an
improved form of repatriation, one that valued "friendly" inter-American
relations. As Galarza stated, a Mexican labor importation program would be
"a program of repatriation" that would be "economically sound and socially
desirable," with workers being returned to Mexico after brief work stints in
the United States. He noted that the former lack of interest in cooperative
and good neighborly action during the Mexican Repatriation effort of the
1930s had been the reason for the "socially undesirable conditions" Mexican
migrants faced, including overcrowding, slum areas, depressed wage scales,
social and racial discrimination, and heavy caseloads in relief agencies during
the Great Depression.[75] Galarza discussed the need for a new form of state-led
repatriation, which would assure the welfare of the Mexican migrant through
a joint U.S.-Mexico commission that could govern their movements. The bracero program and Mexican Repatriation (1929–1936) were thus remarkably
similar and intertwined projects, in that they were both efforts on behalf of
the U.S. and Mexican governments to control and manage laborers under a
massive labor mobility scheme.[76] Both state projects also reflected a trend
toward "resettlement" that structured New Deal social welfare programs in
Mexico and the United States.

Instead of draining the Mexican economy of its working people with permanent emigration, Galarza thought a temporary emigration scheme could
force people to return and develop the Mexican economy, leading to a stronger

nation. As Galarza claimed, previous attempts at repatriation during the Great Depression had resulted in "Nothing more than the indiscriminate dumping of human beings below the border. . . . Inevitably many of these people would attempt to return to the United States, and the whole cycle [of migration] would be repeated." The new state-managed binational labor contract of World War II, Galarza argued, would be a new benevolent form of repatriation that would at least allow Mexican migrants to return with the financial ability to work the land on the newly formed *ejidos* and develop the countryside. As he noted, the repatriation that had been tried in the past failed because it did not provide northern Mexico with "the economic means for establishing the returning Mexicans on productive land."[77] The bracero program would therefore be an attempt to resolve the mistakes of earlier repatriation efforts.

Galarza found radical possibilities in the new systems of land tenure the Mexican government had spearheaded, just as the New Deal leaders of the USDA had. With the Mexican labor program, he envisioned the bracero program as a resettlement program that would allow *campesinos* on *ejidos* to bring back their earnings to Mexico to buy equipment to profitably farm land formerly held by large landholders and investors. Galarza believed that while Mexican farmers now had land, they also needed farm equipment, capital, and education in modern farming techniques, just as Vice President Wallace had concluded after his goodwill tour of Mexico. Like Wallace's MAP project created in 1943, Galarza upheld that this new program of state-led resettlement (or repatriation) would improve the yield of basic food crops and allow small-scale independent farmers to prosper in Mexico.

Wallace's undersecretary Rexford Tugwell had also praised the virtues of Cárdenas's communal farms in 1937, looking to *ejidos* for lessons that might be learned to transform the social and political economy of the U.S. countryside. Capitalizing on President Roosevelt's and Secretary of Agriculture (later Vice President) Wallace's interest in the crisis of rural poverty during the Dust Bowl, some New Dealers advocated rural rehabilitation, which had resulted in the creation of the Resettlement Administration (RA) which became the FSA in 1937. Galarza's colleague at Columbia, Tannebaum, led the initial proposal for the FSA, initially titled, "A Program to Develop a New System of Rural Land Tenure," based on new systems of land tenure in Mexico.[78] While it at first focused on families of Dust Bowl refugees by providing aid to small farmers and repurposing marginal lands, the FSA branched out by 1942 to include Mexican imported contract laborers and Japanese Americans incarcerated during "internment."

Realizing that farmworkers had been left out of the New Deal, the FSA radicalized the New Deal's focus on "economic security" by emphasizing racial equality and agrarian democracy. At its formation, the FSA welcomed the perspective of radical unions, leftist organizations, and intellectuals, with a focus on improved rights for farmworkers. The bracero program became an extension of these officials' and intellectuals' efforts to address rural poverty in Mexico and the United States, with the FSA responsible for the management of the program. Since Tugwell was the creator of the first FSA (the RA), it should come as no surprise that soon after Roosevelt appointed Tugwell as governor of Puerto Rico (1941–1946), he became one of the first to suggest the importation of Puerto Rican farmworkers to the mainland as a solution to poverty in Puerto Rico, after the bracero program began. Tugwell's "resettlement administration" solution had already become part of the U.S. government's New Deal effort to reform colonialism and manage colonial labor on a grand scale, influencing the creation of a Japanese American inmate contract labor program, a Mexican labor program, the British West Indies labor program, and the Puerto Rican labor program.

When Galarza and the USDA first proposed the bracero program to Mexican officials, many saw it as a means to continue Mexico's repatriation efforts and to develop the countryside, as workers would leave on temporary contracts that would force their return without being criminalized as "illegal," which fit with the Mexican government's own benevolent resettlement schemes. With the inception of the bracero program in 1942, President Camacho believed that unskilled rural Mexican men were racially inferior but also thought they could acquire the qualities, skills, and wages necessary for Mexico to advance socially and technologically by being exposed to labor practices in more developed countries like the United States. He thought that rural Mexican men's mastery of skills "improved the character of the Mexican people," indirectly influencing the economy of the Mexican countryside.[79] Likewise, the Mexican government framed the labor program around racial liberalism, insisting on the equality of braceros with other workers in the United States. Proof of Mexican officials' legitimate commitment to state-led racial equality occurred when the Mexican government decided to prohibit growers from contracting braceros in Texas until the state could demonstrate improved labor and social conditions for braceros.[80] With their own project of racial liberalism, the Mexican government supported further rural labor mobility through the U.S.-proposed bracero program. At the same time, the Mexican government courted financial investments from the United States under the rubric of the Good Neighbor Policy, justifying the continued influence of U.S. capital in the region.

After Camacho's presidency, the Mexican government sought foreign investment, especially from the United States, giving generous concessions to private enterprise once again. President Miguel Alemán (1946–1952), for his part, gave frequent concessions to businessmen in Mexico who often occupied prominent government positions. Through an alliance with foreign enterprise, a group of millionaires emerged, including Alemán himself. Meanwhile, policymakers ignored the ways in which their development model again pushed the Mexican population to leave. In the 1940s, the Mexican government began to withdraw support from the government-sponsored communal lands *(ejidos)* that had been constructed as part of state reform efforts after the Mexican Revolution, instead redirecting funds from *ejidos* to large commercial agricultural proprietors. In the process, they continued displacing rural Mexicans from the land, compelling them to migrate for work—this time through a state-managed contract labor program.[81]

*   *   *

In initially proposing a Mexican labor program managed by a labor contract, Galarza endeavored to extend certain rights to Mexican migrant laborers, with enormous potential for the national inclusion of Mexican workers as "legal" sojourners within the United States. His arguments for a labor importation program convinced U.S. and Mexican government officials that the labor contract could guarantee equality, rights, and general standards of wages, housing, and health care. The labor contract became a stand-in for the civil rights and freedoms of the migrant laborer, elided imperialism, and also rhetorically served as a great equalizer among workers of the Western Hemisphere.

Galarza, like other progressive officials, was confident that the U.S. and Mexican governments could manage the importation of Mexican and Caribbean laborers to the United States in an inclusionary way and improve the livelihoods of Mexican migrants. He believed that if Mexican migrant workers were given a contract, their freedom as workers within the United States would be secured because their rights would be protected by the U.S. federal government as well as the constitution established by the revolutionary Mexican government. A few months after the inception of the bracero program,

Ambassador Nájera wrote to Galarza expressing concern that Mexican workers were being "treated as just commercial transactions," not as humans. Galarza replied to Nájera that he was aware of the problem, but that he "trusts that the FSA is serious about sincerely directing the program."[82] Even as critiques of the bracero program arose, Galarza saw government agencies as a means to ensure the freedom of workers.

As the U.S.-Mexico agreement to import contract labor specified, "The term of the contract shall be agreed upon by the representatives of the two Governments with privilege of extension with the *consent of the worker* and approval of the Mexican Government."[83] The consent attributed to workers by the contract functioned above all to impose social order through personal volition, thus performing as a paradigm of the free market economy. As an implement of exchange, the contracts were to be entered into voluntarily by liberal individuals who took part in negotiating a bargain for labor (as commodity) in exchange for certain guarantees and protections. In promoting the contract as an instrument of consent, freedom, and equality, Galarza and other officials unwittingly disavowed the contract as a mechanism of imperialism and racial coercion, while also permitting U.S. economic interests to prosper on either side of the border.

Reviewing the history of U.S intervention in Mexico shows that Mexican migrants did not move freely, according to the dictates of economic liberalism or free trade. Rather, they historically moved in reaction to multiple economic and military interventions by state governments, imperial pursuits that were validated by the liberal affirmations of Pan-Americanism and also erased in multilayered processes of state-building. The contract labor programs of World War II were a continuation of this racial coercion, as they gave U.S. employers further access to "free" workers from Mexico, suiting U.S. and Mexican economic development schemes and benefiting U.S. business interests.[84]

Long before joining the PAU, Galarza had asked for the recognition of Mexicans' contributions to the agricultural and industrial expansion of the western United States, suggesting that the Mexican migrant receive "his due." As a result of his adherence to the Good Neighbor Policy, Galarza believed in the possibility of bilateral government planning and agrarian reform to alleviate inequalities. In defending the labor programs in this way, Galarza and other U.S. and Mexican officials allowed the United States greater managerial jurisdiction over workers in Mexico and the Caribbean. This rationalization

of the expansion of U.S. state power over racialized workers had violent consequences that were unforeseen by Galarza and other officials. In examining the bracero program within the context of Japanese incarceration during
World War II in the next chapter, these violent consequences can be exposed,
to further demonstrate how this particular framing of the labor programs was
productive for race and empire.

CHAPTER 3

Japanese Braceros: The Co-Constitution
of the Bracero Program and Japanese
American Incarceration

One of the first U.S. political organizations Ernesto Galarza pursued to find official support for his vision of a Mexican labor importation program was California representative John H. Tolan's congressional committee, the Select Committee to Investigate the Interstate Migration of Destitute Citizens. While the Tolan Committee had originally set out to examine the needs of Anglo-American migrant farm workers during the Dust Bowl in the 1930s, Galarza used the December 1940 and February 1941 Tolan Committee hearings to advocate for a Mexican migrant farm labor program.[1] Tolan agreed with Galarza's idea of a labor program and wanted to hold a new hearing on the subject, but became distracted by a new concern: the "internment" of Japanese American citizens. Instead of addressing Mexican labor importation during World War II, Tolan administered a series of congressional investigations regarding the "ways and means" of Japanese American expulsion in February and March 1942. Japanese American incarceration (1942–1946) provided the immediate context for the discussions of a Mexican farm labor importation program, such that the debates over both state programs were closely intertwined.[2]

Labor concerns were central to the Japanese American incarceration hearings, as witnesses expressed fear that Japanese American removal would mean a shortage of agricultural labor in California. Emphasizing the fact that many Japanese Americans were farmers and would be unable to contribute to the "war effort" if relocated, hearing participants stressed the need to employ imprisoned Japanese American labor. Their discussions reveal that as much as "military necessity" justified removing Japanese Americans from the West Coast, so it encouraged their recruitment as farm laborers onto large corporate farms in the Midwest.[3] After the hearings to discuss "evacuation," Tolan scheduled additional hearings to address Galarza's proposed Mexican labor importation program in May 1942. Nearly all witnesses agreed that Japanese American incarcerated labor, as domestic U.S. labor, should be employed before the importation of Mexican labor. They also imagined that providing Japanese American inmates with work instead of "forced idleness" would keep their morale high and contribute to their general well-being. They did not question President Roosevelt's Executive Order 9066 authorizing the removal of any or all people from broadly defined military areas as deemed "necessary or desirable," but aimed to ensure the welfare and protection of incarcerated Japanese, two thirds of whom were U.S. citizens.[4]

The Tolan Committee's focus on the use of "loyal" Japanese American labor for "re-employment" in the agricultural fields influenced the hiring of over 33,000 Japanese American contract farm workers from 1942 to 1945, making the incarceration of Japanese Americans its own guestworker program. The state organization that managed Japanese American incarceration, the War Relocation Authority (WRA), formed a "Work Corps" with the ultimate goal of Japanese American "resettlement." Upon being expelled from their homes on the Pacific coast and imprisoned in "internment centers," Japanese Americans were then "encouraged" through WRA propaganda to fill out voluntary farm labor contracts and enlist as farmworkers.[5] Those who volunteered to work, much like Mexican imported labor, signed labor contracts to top sugar beet fields in the Midwest. Mexican labor importation and state-mandated incarceration were therefore remarkably similar projects, with the state providing swift logistical action to move large numbers of Japanese American and Mexican laboring people.[6]

Since attendees included officials from the many organizations responsible for managing both Japanese American incarceration and Mexican labor importation, the hearings the Tolan Committee facilitated are one avenue through which we can disentangle the co-constitution of these two New Deal programs.[7] There was an intriguing continuity that emerged out of the debates over Mexican labor and Japanese American removal. The members of the Tolan Committee were driven by two central concerns: the care and welfare of Mexican migrants and Japanese Americans, and the belief in the power of the state to be a responsible guarantor and protector of rights. This beguiling construction of welfare and rights seemed to extend national belonging, social welfare, and state protection to Mexicans and Japanese Americans, with the U.S. government acting as the source of democratic promise. This language emerged within the context of a liberal consensus in which U.S. labor advocates and left-leaning New Deal officials believed in the power of government to alleviate social concerns and extend the benefits of democracy to all. In addressing both projects simultaneously, the Tolan Committee hearings stressed the humane, democratic, and race-neutral procedures by which Mexicans and Japanese Americans would be treated, using the same logic of racial liberalism that Galarza and others had used to imagine a Mexican labor importation program prior to World War II.

A few scholars have noted in passing how the inauguration of Japanese American incarceration contributed to a perceived labor shortage that validated the call for a Mexican labor importation program, but little has been written about the intertwined development of these two state programs and their similarities.[8] Officials employed a language of protection and voluntary free will to legitimize Japanese American incarceration and convince Mexican men to sign up for labor contracts during the bracero program. After their initiation, both programs became official attempts to "guide" inmates and labor migrants toward democracy and self-determination, with labor and prison camps initially offering self-government through community building. These programs were also sustained efforts to educate racially "backward" Mexican migrants on "modern" American social practices and analagously "Americanize" Japanese inmates at the prison camps. Last, both state projects culminated in the recruitment of "alien" labor gangs of Mexican and Japanese American men under temporary contracts for employment in U.S. fields.

Materially, some of the same tall barbed wire and chain link fences used to construct Japanese American prison camps were later used to devise bracero labor camps and bracero processing centers. Some of these fences were also dragged south and erected in border towns to prevent Mexican migrants from entering illegally during the bracero program. The geographic isolation of Mexican migrant farm labor camps matched that of Japanese prison camps, as they were both housed in fields far from towns and urban locales and kept ignorant of their surroundings.[9] Although braceros were not watched over by armed guards or dogs, they had rare means to get to a town that was over ten miles away, making their labor camps much like isolated prisons. Guestworker labor camps, as quasi-carceral sites, were complexly connected to Japanese American prison camps. They were also further interconnected in that Japanese American inmates were often hired to cook and feed braceros in the kitchens of the bracero labor camps, with the authority of the WRA.[10]

The putative goal of the Tolan Committee hearings in discussing Mexican and Japanese American inmate labor together was to set the standards of labor practice and anti-discrimination measures to prevent their exploitation, standards that could then be written into official policies and procedures. In their debates, hearing participants recommended Japanese American incarceration and a Mexican labor importation program as benevolent New Deal programs that aimed to "fight race" and reshape knowledge production about racial difference. Implicit in the Tolan Committee arguments for equality and state protection for Japanese Americans and Mexican migrants was the unquestioned support of federal power as well as a vision of how to govern historically racialized populations in a race-neutral way. In defending a Mexican labor importation program and Japanese American incarceration as progressive moves toward freedom, and looking to the government to expand its authority over workers' lives as a step in that direction, Tolan, Galarza, and other officials authorized the federal government to turn workers into subjects of state power and coercion.[11] Mass incarceration and mass labor importation came to operate hand-in-hand to mark Japanese Americans and Mexican migrants as racial subjects deemed simultaneously eligible for state protection and open to state coercion. Even further, their employment in the most grueling types of agricultural labor contributed to the relational racialization of both Japanese American inmates and Mexican migrants as "stoop" and "alien" contract labor ineligible for citizenship, making the contract a productive tool for race-making and exclusion.

The expansion of governmental power to democratically "protect" Japanese Americans and Mexicans resulted in state-endorsed racial oppression, as government officials became empowered in either case to delineate between loyal/disloyal, citizen/alien, enemy/ally, foreign/domestic, and legal/illegal. These binaries became the precondition for "rights," enabling racial coercion as a central component of U.S. national power into the postwar era. In establishing who was "in" or "outside" the nation through these two projects, officials recreated a racial order that perpetuated the intertwined logic of liberalism and empire deliberated by the theorist Uday Mehta.[12] When viewed together, they reveal that the notions of liberal freedom, equality, and inclusion often do more than accompany racially exploitative relations but in fact produce and reproduce them, reinforcing the nation-state's role in the maintenance of racial capitalism and, therefore, empire. In official efforts to enroll Japanese American inmates and Mexican migrants in labor programs, a reinvigorated logic for racial capitalism emerged that veiled and rewrote coercive and racist labor practices as protection and social welfare. Consequently, both Mexican labor importation and Japanese American incarceration served to resolve the tension between universal freedom and capitalism in the project of modern liberalism, providing a rational justification for mass government-regulated labor mobility as well as mass deportation.

The discursive overlap between national security and social welfare that emerged in the hearings played a central role in the relational racialization of Japanese American and Mexican labor. As Galarza stated at the May 22 Tolan Committee hearing: "There is a recognition of the fact that this is a *defense* problem, not only for the United States but for the hemisphere; and that if ways and means can be found to lift this problem out of its traditional form and put it on a higher level, both from the standpoint of production and of human welfare, I believe the Mexicans would be willing to recognize the need to cooperate with the United States to assure a sufficient supply of labor."[13] Galarza was aware of the ideological power this moment of national security had to effect policy change on a higher level, and he capitalized on the wartime moment to push forward his agenda. Like other labor advocates of his era, he saw possibilities in the moment of total war to use the state as an instrument of social change. While his vision may have been more progressive than that of others in the Tolan Committee, it was still reflective of a broader moment in which many labor advocates and officials were so steeped in the 1940s liberal imagination that they could not grasp its contradictions, or even endeavor to question whether expanded government power was the best means to precipitate social change at all.

The reality of racial eviction and labor program violations on the ground was not a contradiction to the U.S. project of liberal state-building. The neutral language used to justify Japanese "relocation" and "voluntary" Mexican labor importation at the Tolan Committee hearings was in itself crucial to this coercive outcome, signaling a new government-mandated code for understanding race, labor, and citizenship in the United States after World War II. This code was new precisely because it expanded government authority over laborers through a logic of race neutral state-led reform. It was therefore not simply white supremacist right-wing growers and the coalition they formed with friends in government that triggered the racial violence and exclusion caused by Japanese American incarceration and Mexican labor importation.[14] Whether conservative growers or liberal bureaucrats, leaders on both sides of the political debate sought the growth of federal authority over farm labor for their own aims.

What is crucial here is that the debates negotiated at the Tolan Committee hearings informed the principles and the official policies that were implemented by the multiple government organizations managing the labor importation programs, including the Department of Labor (USDL), the Department of Agriculture (USDA), the Farm Security Administration (FSA), the War Food Administration (WFA), and the War Manpower Commission (WMC). They also informed the policies and practices of officials of the WRA, established by executive order on March 18, 1942, to manage the forced resettlement of Japanese Americans to the rural interior of the United States. Since officials from each of these government organizations gave testimony and engaged in debates before the Tolan Committee, the Tolan Committee hearings became key sites in the formulation and exercise of government regulation at a critical moment in the development of modern liberalism.

World War II, Labor Mobilization, and the Tolan Committee Hearings

Prior to World War II, Representative John H. Tolan, a Democrat from Oakland, had long been concerned with managing and mobilizing the U.S. agricultural labor supply. Tolan had entered Congress in 1935 during the Great Depression and by April 1940 helped to create the Select Committee to Investigate the Interstate Migration of Destitute Citizens. The original Tolan Committee hearings focused on the social and economic needs of Dust Bowl refugees, but its interests began to shift by 1941 as the large-scale migration of workers to the defense industries took center stage. Tolan therefore renamed his group the Committee Investigating National Defense Migration in March 1941, with a focus on the "two million to three million people who, attracted by defense work, have gone from their home states to other states."[15] As the federal government expanded and centralized its authority over labor migrations across the United States from 1940–1943 the Tolan Committee became involved in ensuring the welfare of those labor migrants who became subject to manpower development within the context of total war.[16] By 1942, the committee met in response to the more than twenty-four separate federal agencies attempting to deal with the problems of wartime labor mobilization, with the goal of creating additional legislative authority to coordinate their programs.

With the drafting of soldiers for the war, the federal government increasingly focused on manpower mobilization for domestic resource extraction of essential materials, including food from the farms of the United States. U.S. officials, growers, and researchers at American universities all feared a shortage of labor, especially in the fields. The Lend-Lease program of 1941, in which the United States began to supply Europe with food, oil, and war materials exacerbated concerns over food production. President Franklin D. Roosevelt's New Deal cabinet therefore established a number of institutions by executive order to manage labor mobilization, including the WMC on April 18, 1942, which sought to balance the needs of agriculture, industry, and the Armed Forces. Members of the War Department, USDA, USDL, the War Production Board, Selective Service System, and the United States Civil Service worked together through the WMC to ensure effective mobilization and placement of "manpower."

The U.S. federal government also escalated its war industries and hubs, developing an expanded military state apparatus. By the war's end, millions of Americans took advantage of the war economy, with the largest movement coming from the Southern states. These geographical labor movements were related to real economic developments that government leaders actively sought as a result of the crisis of the Great Depression. At the peak of the Emergency Farm Labor Supply Programs in 1945, U.S. officials recruited and placed between 2.5 and 3 million farmworkers in the United States. The FSA (1942) and then later the WFA (1943), alongside the WMC, were responsible for farm labor migration management, with millions of government dollars allotted to each organization.[17] The WMC mobilized farmworkers wherever they could find them, initiating a Women's Land Army and a program whereby high school students could work on farms on the weekends called the Victory Farm Volunteers. They also initiated contract farm labor programs with Italian and German prisoners of war, Navajo Indians, dairy workers from Newfoundland, and they considered farm labor programs with British Honduras, Nicaragua, Guatemala, Costa Rica, and other parts of Latin America to solve the "farm labor problem."[18]

In an early effort to orchestrate the nascent governmental efforts to manage and coordinate farm labor mobilization, the Tolan Committee held several hearings related to agricultural labor and defense migration, including the series of hearings on the "evacuation" of Japanese Americans from the West Coast (February and March 1942) and a series on a Mexican labor importation program (May and June 1942). As Tolan himself noted, the committee had been concerned with Mexican farm labor migration ever since growers directed their attention to it in the committee's August 1940 congressional hearings in Chicago and Oklahoma City. In 1941, Galarza began sending Tolan letters advocating a benevolent Mexican farm labor importation program, and, in December 1941, two of Tolan's staff members were sent to Texas to investigate demands for the importation of 32,000 Mexicans for use in the cotton harvest.[19] By this time, Tolan was under great pressure from colleagues and growers, as he stated, to attend to "a growing need for an additional source of agricultural workers to assist in the preparation and harvesting of our expanded crops" under the "food for victory" program. Representative Tolan came to embrace Galarza's vision for a state-implemented labor importation program in 1941 as a wartime exigency, but it was not until May 1942 that Tolan asked Galarza to join him in a series of congressional investigations into the feasibility of the program.[20] This delay was the result of Tolan being distracted by Japanese American incarceration.

After Pearl Harbor, the "enemy alien problem" loomed large in Tolan's mind, and he soon saw that Japanese American "evacuation" would have to be considered as part of the "migration caused by the national defense program," which would be under the purview of his committee. President Roosevelt signed Executive Order 9066 on February 19, 1942, which authorized U.S. military commanders to: "Prescribe military areas in such places and of such extent as he or the appropriate Military Commander may determine, from which any or all persons may be excluded. . . . The Secretary of War is hereby authorized to provide for residents of any such area who are excluded therefrom, such transportation, food, shelter, and other accommodations as may be necessary, in the judgment of the Secretary of War or the said Military Commander."

Executive Order 9066 did not directly refer to Japanese Americans, but it provided the military authorization to expunge Japanese citizens and noncitizens from the Pacific coast. President Roosevelt had accepted the judgment of Western Command General John L. DeWitt, who argued after Pearl Harbor that Japanese imprisonment was a "military decision based on military necessity."[21] Tolan initiated the hearings within a few days after the order, stressing the potential security risk the Japanese presented: "It is possible that the entire Pacific Coast may be evacuated. They tell me back in Washington that it is not only possible but probable that the Pacific Coast will be bombed. That has come to me from men who are supposed to know," he stated.[22]

Even before President Roosevelt had signed Executive Order 9066, West Coast liberal officials clamored for an investigation into how Japanese American incarceration would take place. "The reason we are here," Tolan stated at the March 6,1942, hearing, is a result of "the many people pouring into Washington with their troubles on account of this evacuation." As he explained, "We came to the West Coast quietly, not to tell people what they should do, but to act as a sort of clearinghouse to get some ideas and some of their recommendations to bring back to Washington."[23] Few liberal witnesses at the Tolan Committee hearings from February 21 to March 12, 1942, disputed the need for Executive Order 9066, but instead expressed concern that Japanese American "removal" could mean divesting Japanese Americans of their citizenship. From the beginning, Tolan was aware of the crisis in citizenship that the removal of Japanese American would create and sought to manage it. At the beginning of the hearings, he explained, "The nation must decide and Congress must gravely consider the extent to which *citizenship*, in and of itself, is a guaranty of equal rights and privileges during time of war. Unless a clarification is forthcoming, the evacuation of the Japanese population will serve as an incident sufficiently disturbing to lower seriously the morale of vast numbers of foreign-born among our people."[24]

If citizenship presented an existential problem for "evacuation," Tolan left it up to members of the committee to debate how evacuation would take place in a manner that would not pose a challenge to citizenship, to ensure the equal rights and privileges of Japanese American citizens. He posed the question: if the incarceration of Japanese Americans was inevitable, how could it then be used to fulfill the cause of freedom and equality in a war for democracy?[25] President Roosevelt himself embodied the contradiction at the heart of this question, when he gave a post–Pearl Harbor speech entitled "We Hold These Truths: The Rights to Life, Liberty, and the Pursuit of Happiness." In this speech, Roosevelt upheld the foundational liberal ideals of the United States: "We will not, under any threat, or in the face of any danger, surrender the guarantees framed for us in the Bill of Rights."[26] Tolan Committee members therefore employed a language of liberalism in their debates, centering on the inalienable rights and protections of the individual.

A key figure in the center of the tumult was Carey McWilliams, director of the Division of Immigration and Housing (DIH) in California. McWilliams had already held a series of meetings himself to investigate Japanese American "relocation," appointing a committee of social workers and lawyers to devise a plan. Having worked closely with Representative Tolan's former House Committee on Interstate Migration from 1940 to 1941, McWilliams persuaded Tolan to hold hearings on Japanese American incarceration in the first place.[27] McWilliams felt the Tolan Committee was uniquely qualified to hold an investigation of "the alien problem on the Pacific Coast" because of its "wide experience dealing with the problem of migration, resettlement, welfare programs, and economic opportunities." As head of the DIH, McWilliams argued that his own perspective on "evacuation" was also important, since he was charged with the "direct responsibility for the providing of certain guidance and information to alien immigrants in this state; and also the general responsibility for their welfare."[28]

Like Galarza, McWilliams has been rightfully heroized for his radical efforts to improve the welfare of migrant farm workers in California—some have even deemed him the "godfather of Chicano studies" for his influential book, North from Mexico (1949).[29] McWilliams obtained a law degree from USC in 1927, and, from 1927–1938 defended striking Mexican citrus workers in Orange County under the auspices of the ACLU. He wrote Factories in the Field (1939) based on his experiences, condemning large-scale agribusiness for its "farm fascism" and its brutal suppression of nonwhite workers resulting in a "wholesale violation of civil rights." In Factories in the Field, he laid out his dream of a rational agricultural system in which state planning could lead to a "measure of stabilization" for farmworkers, arguing that the FSA migratory labor camps had shown what a program of decent housing could do to uplift farmworkers.[30] Shortly before the publication of Factories, McWilliams accepted an offer from California governor Culbert Olson to head the DIH, where he focused on improving working conditions and wages for agricultural workers. As head of the DIH, McWilliams increased the number of camp inspectors in the federal FSA migratory labor camp program and supported farmworkers' efforts to unionize.

On February 20, 1942, McWilliams sent a letter to the Tolan Committee attaching his committee's proposed plan for evacuation, included as testimony during the hearings. This highlighted the ways internment could be benevolently conducted as a "resettlement" initiative to ensure the rights of Japanese Americans. McWilliams argued that his proposal should be submitted to General DeWitt through Tolan for "approval in principle." In response, Tolan sent a February 28 telegram to President Roosevelt, forwarding McWilliams' suggestions, which influenced Roosevelt's creation of the WRA on March 18, 1942. It recommended the employment of a "coordinator for enemy alien problems" to oversee Japanese labor, "to help the movement of these evacuees in a way to maintain, as near as possible, their normal lives." He argued that this coordinator would also help them "be made self-sustaining and avoid any injustices and the consequences of prejudices against them."[31]

McWilliams supported the removal of Japanese citizens and noncitizens from their homes on the West Coast, but he found himself trying to manage the contradictions between the doctrine of U.S. liberalism and forced relocation. As he later confessed, "I was drawn into the controversy that raged around me. In fact, I became an active participant in it."[32] In order to ensure adherence to the tenets of "life, liberty, and property" specified in the U.S. Constitution, he focused on protecting the property of the incarcerated to ensure their rehabilitation after the war, recommending an alien property custodian to care for Japanese American belongings. His confidence in the liberal state made him believe it was possible that the seized property of incarcerated Japanese Americans could be protected. He further imagined that Japanese American morale could be preserved if the U.S. government emphasized "resettlement" or "Finding and encouraging suitable employment" for the "Readjustment of individuals and families." This, McWilliams stated, "Would not only give the unfortunate victims a sense of needed relief but make them feel that they are living in a country where human dignity and human values are more than mere phrases mouthed by politicians."[33]

McWilliams, like Galarza, was inspired by the concept of "resettlement" established by Rexford Tugwell with the Resettlement Administration (RA) and later the FSA, both of which were rural reform efforts designed to transform economic relations in the countryside through social and economic planning. In 1935, the RA began to establish experimental planned "resettlements" or public cooperative communities in response to the Great Depression, the largest of which was in Greenbelt, Maryland. McWilliams argued in his proposal that similar communities could be built for Japanese Americans in the "resettlement" process. The WRA and the FSA efforts to "resettle" Japanese Americans in prison camps and on farms was therefore an extension of the earlier concept of "resettlement" or planned community building made legible by Tugwell. As McWilliams stated, "The idea is resettlement plus evacuation, conceived of as an integrated plan. . . . The resettlement of resident Japanese offers an opportunity to experiment with the original Greenbelt idea on a greatly expanded scale . . . and with much better prospects of success."

As McWilliams propounded, "the evacuation program can be made to serve an important social end and need not necessarily be regarded as something inherently baneful and undesirable."[34]

In an article titled "They Saved the Crops," McWilliams also argued for a Mexican farm labor importation program. He began the essay with a quote from Galarza that "friendly, cooperative international action" has been taken by the government of the United States with regards to the exchange of goods but never with regards to the flow of working people." McWilliams continued, "most of the complications and frictions of previous migrations may be traced to that fact. In the past, such migrations were not planned, supervised, or controlled in an effective manner." McWilliams then listed the guarantees of the Mexican labor contract and extolled his belief that rural communities will learn to understand and appreciate "these visitors from the South."[35] In arguing for standards of labor practices and anti-discrimination for farmworkers, and appealing to the government on farmworkers' behalf, McWilliams and Galarza therefore both wrote perceived "aliens" into the moral-juridical plane of the United States, reshaping knowledge production about racial difference in the early 1940s.

Just as McWilliams considered a Mexican labor importation program to be a rational and scientific task of state planning that could be handled democratically for the attainment of a racially inclusive society, so he viewed Japanese American incarceration. As McWilliams stated, "In undertaking this, the most recent of its notable investigations, the committee has an unparalleled opportunity to render an important service to the Nation, not only in furtherance of its security in time of peril, but also in safeguarding those essential values which represent the finest elements of the American tradition."[36] McWilliams maintained that mass incarceration could demonstrate that the equality, freedom, and democracy constructed as part of U.S. national ethos in a "war for democracy" was a reality that could be imposed through proper government execution. He believed that Japanese expulsion was not only morally unobjectionable, but that it could be a race-neutral humanitarian government project aimed at fulfilling the ideological aims of modern liberalism. McWilliams also proclaimed that his proposal for Japanese removal would "demonstrate that democracy can work efficiently, effectively, and with consideration for the welfare of the people who brought it into being, which differentiates it from autocracy and makes it worthy of any sacrifice."[37]

A Japanese American and Mexican
Labor Importation Program

Soon after the Japanese American incarceration hearings, Tolan held another series of hearings to discuss Galarza's proposal for a Mexican labor importation program.[38] On May 8, 1942, Tolan wrote to Galarza, inviting him to these hearings while noting, "we are prepared to recommend that a joint commission be established with properly designated representatives of the two governments to sit continuously for the duration of the war to administer the importation and return of such Mexican labor whenever the actual need for this importation shall have been demonstrated."[39] As Tolan maintained, the new hearings reflected the Committee's "longstanding interest" in the question of Mexican labor importation, and he wanted to "broaden the basis for our discussion . . . beyond the question of the importation of Mexican workers." By "broadening the basis for discussion," Tolan meant discussing Mexican labor importation within the larger setting of Japanese American incarceration. Tolan argued, "Japanese Americans now being removed from the west coast should be used to supplement our agricultural labor supply, and specifically should be used in the sugar-beet industry. All of these matters are actually part of the larger problem of mobilizing labor supply for war production."[40]

Elmar Rowalt, assistant director of the WRA, attended the May 1942 hearings on Mexican labor importation, and the Tolan Committee members discussed Japanese evacuee labor together with Mexican labor, to consider which labor force would be most convenient and remedial. Panelists repeatedly stressed that Japanese labor, as domestic labor, should be primarily used to relieve wartime labor concerns before a Mexican labor importation program was even considered. As Lemuel B. Schofield, of the Immigration and Naturalization Services (INS) stated, "The INS is not opposed to the recruiting of Mexican laborers, provided Japanese labor is not available." He pointed out that approximately 120,000 incarcerated Japanese Americans were idle in large numbers, continuing, "information is such that the Japanese would volunteer in sufficient numbers to [work] . . . in the sugar beet fields."[41] Collis Stocking, assistant director of the Bureau of Employment Security, attended the hearings to report that Japanese Americans evacuated in Oregon would be made available, and that "the sugar companies were paying transportation costs from Portland Oregon, to Malheur County, Oregon, where the workers are to be used." He indicated that this was a sign that the War Relocation authorities might actually consider releasing Japanese American workers from evacuation centers to "alleviate the situation in other states."[42]

The concern of most Tolan Committee members was that the importation of Mexican labor would be detrimental to U.S. domestic wage standards and welfare programs. In contrast, they argued that Japanese American workers, as domestic workers, would be treated more fairly. Clara M. Beyer, assistant director of the Division of Labor and Social Information of the U.S. Department of Labor, argued that employing Japanese Americans would be preferable because they did not, according to Beyer, share the experience of "exploitation of Mexican workers in this country." Beyer reflected the consensus that turning to Japanese Americans instead of Mexicans could prevent further racism and inequality. She also worried that *not* employing imprisoned Japanese Americans as workers would cause "demoralization" among them.[43] She further gave preference to Japanese Americans because she thought that, as domestic workers, employing them would protect U.S. wage earners and improve work conditions, which Beyer considered the primary focus of her role at the Department of Labor.

Even though multiple government agencies had already met regarding the feasibility of a Mexican labor importation program, Tolan stressed that the point of the May 22 hearing was to "initiate a discussion of the standards which might be satisfactory to the Mexican government and which the Government of the United States . . . would be willing to guarantee." As Galarza argued, this labor importation program was a "joint effort" to establish "rational, just, and humane methods for the distribution of Mexican migrant workers to the end that both the needs of agriculture and the interests of workers might be more adequately met and protected."[44] Galarza saw the possibility of state-enforced racial equality that the hearing presented, upholding that the labor importation program was not simply "a matter of bringing workers to the Southwest, but a matter of the adjustment and the solution of certain cultural problems, problems of friction and of ill feeling that have grown up between our two peoples."[45] He concluded that he "could see no happier event than the use of Mexican workers as an instrument for the improvement of the standard of living of all agricultural labor."[46] Galarza named racism as the central problem faced by Mexican migrant workers, a problem that could be overcome through state-managed labor migrations.[47] He implied that having labor standards and wages ordained by contracted Mexican labor could resolve the problem of inequality in the United States for farmworkers.

Tolan agreed with Galarza, referring to his reservoir of experience having traveled the United States to examine the experience of Dust Bowl migrants. Galarza's thoughts, Tolan replied, "are a good deal along the lines of my own thoughts. Speaking for myself personally, I think that if Mexican laborers come into this country they should have their standards, they should have their status." Tolan, Galarza, and others at the hearing optimistically assumed that the labor importation program would be a state-mandated attempt to achieve the equality of Mexican workers, resolving the problem of racism by extending standards of treatment and worker protections that had never before been offered to Mexican migrants. Like Walter C. Laves from the Office of the Coordinator of Inter-American Affairs, they believed the importation of Mexican contract workers was not simply a strategy "for the winning of the war," but for the "building of a longer and more just social order."[48]

Hearing attendees believed, like McWilliams, that both programs could safeguard the rights and equality of Japanese Americans so as to safeguard the American liberal tradition. As Governor Olson of California stated emphatically, "Any evacuation proposed is not prompted by race hatred, prejudice or selfish business interests." He continued, "Those [Japanese] whom claim American citizenship should realize that the action we suggest is as much a protection for them as for the communities from which they are moved."[49] Louis Goldblatt, secretary-treasurer of the California State Industrial Union Council, Congress of Industrial Organization (CIO), also testified on February 21 that there should be "adequate safeguards" for the Japanese, stating that "the Government should be responsible for providing humane treatment in the course of evacuation and for the settling of Japanese where they can perform useful work for the nation."[50]

In his concluding summary of the proceedings of the February and March hearings, Tolan argued that if war and military necessity made it inevitable that Japanese Americans should be "removed," then "only under a federal program, providing for the financial assistance, protection to person and property, and an opportunity to engage in productive work, did it appear possible to minimize injustice." He maintained that this responsibility had been recognized by the federal government, as evidenced by the executive order of the president establishing the WRA on March 18, 1942. Tolan included in his final report a section titled "Resettlement of Evacuees," in which he mentioned "the serious constitutional questions that would be raised by forced detention of citizens against whom no individual charges have been lodged." He argued that the United States was therefore compelled to give "evacuees" the opportunity to "contribute to our national economy [and] the abiding principles of our democratic way of life, as opposed to the racial discrimination made by our enemies." As he argued, "Resettlement [shall be] for the purpose of insuring full preservation of citizenship rights and ultimate participation of the evacuees in normal and productive ways of living."[51]

In essence, the Tolan Committee argued that employing Japanese American inmates as farm laborers would preserve their access to full citizenship rights. Tolan suggested that Japanese Americans should have the opportunity and the right to work in a variety of activities, not exclusively determined by agricultural considerations; if engaged in agricultural or manufacturing production, they should be assured prevailing wage rates. In its final report, the Tolan Committee opposed the employment of Japanese under military guard, which would raise a "grave constitutional question on the extent to which activities of citizens may be restricted." The committee stressed the voluntary character of Japanese American labor movements, recommending that "free movement should be assured" while arguing that the government was obligated "to protect its citizens." In addition, committee members concluded that the federal government should be held responsible for providing Japanese American workers with a "reasonable standard of living and necessary community facilities," "absentee voting," and the protection of "benefit rights" under social security programs.

Even more drastically, Tolan and his committee imagined that the WRA could constructively refashion a "whole pattern of our policy" on the treatment of racial and minority groups in the postwar world, such that Japanese American "relocation" could be racially liberating for American politics.[52] They used this moment of wartime and defense to express the ideals of racial liberalism in a display of American exceptionalism. Rather than oppose the employment of either Japanese Americans or Mexican migrants as a residual labor supply, committee members argued for the potential of Japanese American incarceration and Mexican labor importation to uplift workers and ensure the benefits of U.S. democracy to all. If Japanese Americans could be kept from demoralization through farm labor employment, then so could Mexican workers, both protected by a contract and set of standards for their equal treatment. In the contract, these standards included the stipulation that the prospective employer should pay the transportation to and from work sites, provide adequate housing and prevailing wages, and recruit labor through the United States Employment Service (USES), which would determine the number of workers each farmer would be assigned. Meanwhile, organizations on board with the liberal project of incarceration, like the Japanese American Citizen League, urged all Japanese to comply: "You are not being accused of any crime. You are being removed to protect you and because there might be one of you who would be dangerous to the United States. It is your contribution to the war effort. You should be glad to make the sacrifice to prove your loyalty."[53] This language of consent and "sacrifice" continued in the WRA prison camps and shaped the Japanese farm labor program, as an official strategy to make use of Japanese American labor emerged.

A Japanese Contract Labor Program

At the same time that Tolan Committee members debated a Japanese American contract labor program and a Mexican labor importation program together on May 22, 1942, the first experimental group of fifteen Japanese Americans left the Portland Assembly Center to harvest sugar beets in southeast Oregon on May 21, 1942. At first, the program remained very small—only about 1,500 workers were recruited during the spring of 1942 due to the lack of "volunteers." Officials discovered that few Japanese Americans wished to leave their families in the process of being forced from their homes and into assembly centers, such that the WRA ended the farm labor camp in Oregon.[54] Nonetheless, the WRA released its official policy on the seasonal agricultural work program on July 20, 1942, calling it "Group Leave" because Japanese Americans were initially recruited by the WRA in large groups for employment at U.S. sugar beet companies. Farm employers had to provide transportation and housing as well as a "pledge in writing that workers' safety would be guaranteed." The employer was supposed to pay the prevailing wage, maintain adequate living quarters at no expense to the employee, and ensure that the employment of Japanese Americans would not displace local labor—but there were no enforcement provisions.[55]

Early on, the WRA released a pamphlet entitled *War Relocation Work Corps: A Circular for Enlistees and Their Families,* notifying inmates of work opportunities available through the newly established Work Corps. The pamphlet was addressed to "Americans of Japanese Ancestry" and maintained that the purpose of the Work Corps was "To help you as much as possible, to assist you in establishing new wartime homes, and to make certain that you

Figure 5. Japanese Americans at Heart Mountain registering for sugar beet labor in Wyoming, Montana, and Colorado. Photographed by Tom Parker, September 1942. Courtesy of the Bancroft Library, University of California at Berkeley.

will have ample opportunity to earn a living and contribute to the Nation's production."[56] A statement by President Roosevelt on the front cover of the pamphlet emphasized the need to "sacrifice" in time of crisis, "with full recognition and devotion [to] what this nation is, and what we owe it." According to the pamphlet, "all able-bodied women and man of age may enlist for the duration of the war. Enlistment is wholly voluntary." Officials of the WRA, like the Tolan Committee, stressed the need to "avoid any semblance of coercion, with labor being offered, not forced." As one official stated, "efforts should be made to parallel just as closely as possible, all the activities of any American community. The building and maintenance of morale is the Authority's greatest responsibility." Officials considered enlistment in the Work Corps a privilege, and a means to prove one's loyalty and offer one's services to the war effort.[57]

The policy surrounding the leave programs developed slowly and changed over time. The WRA devised the first Japanese American labor contract in April 1942, and this contract was included as part of the Tolan Committee's "Findings and Recommendations" report issued May 1942. The WRA titled the individual labor contract form "WRA-1" or "WRA Work Corps Enlistment," with the contract conveying the worker's name, sex, age, and date enlisted. The first stipulation of the contract was, in brief, "I hereby enlist in the War Relocation Authority Work Corps." The second stipulation was an "oath of loyalty," and a statement of understanding that the purpose of the labor contract was to "conserve and develop the resources of the United States, to contribute to needed agricultural and industrial production, to obtain the benefits of governmental protection while the United States is at war, and to have the full opportunity to earn a livelihood for myself and my dependents."[58]

The USES, the FSA, and the WFA worked together with the WRA to help inmates find productive jobs with the goal of providing "normal work opportunities" and enabling "loyal citizens" and "law-abiding aliens" to "make their best contribution to the war effort." Once the USES certified the need for Japanese American farmworkers, the FSA (1942) and later the WFA (1943) facilitated their recruitment and transportation. The FSA was also initially involved in the construction of the prison camps, just as it had been involved in building camps for Dust Bowl refugees. Growers sometimes hired and transported small groups of workers at the camps themselves, but they engaged larger groups through the WRA field offices or the WFA, which then transported inmates to the location where they worked.[59] By fall 1942, the WRA Work Corps, the FSA, the USES, and growers recruited a total of 10,000 Japanese American workers in prison camps on "Group Leave." A year later, that number had increased to 15,000, by which point the WRA had about fifty relocation offices with about five hundred Japanese American inmates released per week for work on what was now deemed Seasonal Leave. If internment camps were where Japanese Americans were held as prisoners, the WRA relocation offices were where they were processed for reemployment and resettlement.[60]

As part of the WRA's resettlement program, the Japanese American labor program was designed to purge and relocate Japanese American communities far from the West Coast.[61] Dillon S. Myer, director of the WRA, explained, "The resettlement of these people in normal community life is the chief objective of the WRA." He continued, "The policy of the WRA is to urge all employable residents of the centers who qualify for indefinite leave to move into outside employment as rapidly as possible." He therefore established several relocation offices in Salt Lake City, Denver, Kansas City, Chicago, Cleveland, Little Rock, and New York City, each having between two and nine branch offices in the surrounding areas. Myer believed "every loyal

American should be given the opportunity to serve this country wherever his skills make the greatest contribution." The WRA relocation offices thus acted as a clearinghouse for job listings, with offerings including mining, railroad, fruit-packing and canning, hotels, and domestic work. These offices not only helped "evacuees" with the process of "reemployment" but sought to "aid them in adjusting themselves to the communities where they relocate."[62]

From 1942 to 1943, the WFA governed "voluntary" agricultural contract workers by a set of conditions and regulations referred to as "administrative instruction no. 22" in the WFA handbook. This was a general statement of policy on the "resettlement" of Japanese Americans outside of concentration camps for work, with a focus on ensuring their loyalty to the United States as well as their equal treatment. According to the WRA's calculations, two thirds of Japanese American inmates had previously worked in agriculture, such that the effort to employ every farmer was an effort toward their well-being. As Myer concluded, "Bottling up these skills merely because they are racially related to an enemy nation would be inconsistent with American principles." The first condition in administrative instruction no. 22 required that "there must be assurance that local sentiment in the community to which the worker is to go is such that the evacuee can successfully maintain employment and residence there." The WRA advanced a plan to prevent Japanese American placement in overtly racist communities, presuming it possible that Japanese Americans could be treated equally by local residents in the farming communities to which they were sent for work. They also assumed that all Japanese American farm labor efforts would be democratic and "voluntary," with the goal of providing for the worker's welfare.[63]

The concern for the racial "adjustment" of Japanese Americans during resettlement framed the debates of the WRA from the beginning, just as it had McWilliams's proposal. Relocation officers developed race-liberal efforts to educate the racist communities in which Japanese Americans were sent to work, as relocation officers endeavored to secure the interest and support of local residents in offering Japanese Americans resettlement plans after the war had ended. Aware that racism would be a challenge in U.S. farming communities, the WRA imagined that U.S. communities could learn to "adjust" their racist tendencies and set aside their prejudice to welcome Japanese Americans, while Japanese Americans could learn to "adjust" by assimilating into American politics and culture. Hence, Americanization efforts framed life at the camps, with "Camp Councils" mirroring those at FSA labor camps, complete with a governing board managed by a white administrator. These administrators taught inmates lessons in self-government and democracy to ensure their assimilation into American society. "Adjustment," the WRA believed, would be a reversal of racial exclusion, as their Americanization would help racialized inmates to be more easily accepted in the communities to which they were "resettled."

As focused as the WRA was on ensuring the employment of inmates as a measure of racial inclusion, the FSA and WRA became increasingly concerned by an April 1943 report that racial antagonisms were impeding Japanese Americans from joining the labor program. Myer himself noted that "The process of resettlement has been impeded by fears and uncertainties . . . making them hesitant to leave the centers." The FSA noted in a report that "A survey of evacuees' attitudes shows that very few of them would be willing to accept farm work this year unless conditions are improved." According to the report, "many of the evacuees who went out to aid farmers last year were bitterly disappointed by earnings, housing, and other conditions they found. Not only did they have to do hard unpleasant work to which they were unaccustomed, but their wages and living conditions were unsatisfactory." This situation had to be ameliorated to ensure the continued employment of Japanese Americans on farms through the following fall. Highlighting the policies listed in administrative instruction no. 22, the FSA pointed out that "community sentiment" and "general antagonism to our Japanese enemy" had "definitely opposed the use of these workers" in the spring and summer of 1942. Such antagonism had caused "resentment and loss of efficiency."[64]

The WRA was aware of such concerns, leading to a January 1943 USDA Bureau of Agricultural Economics report titled *Farmers' Attitude Toward the Use of Japanese Evacuees as Farm Labor*.[65] The purpose of this report was to discover "what administrative steps may be taken to further the utilization of the manpower in relocation centers and assist in their integration into American community life." The bureau investigated racist tendencies by region, screening agricultural communities using interviews and questionnaires. They found that "Farmers' willingness to accept the Japanese evacuees as farm labor showed marked variation from one locality to another." In the sugar beet and long staple cotton regions, "most growers were so racist, it is not recommended to offer Japanese Americans permanent residence in most of these communities." While the USDA concluded that farmers in the Rocky Mountain sugar beet region accepted the use of evacuee farm labor the most frequently, those in the large-scale farming areas of the Eastern seaboard accepted them the least. The report gauged racism by growers' ability to think of Japanese Americans as "efficient or inefficient" workers, rather than as "members of a racial group." The tendency in the Rocky Mountains was to think of them as "efficient" workers, hence this was where Japanese Americans continued to be employed the most.

Since one goal of the federal government's resettlement policy was to avoid racism and "minimize the prejudice which can hamper and reduce the potential contribution of these workers," the bureau recommended the "demonstration technique" to facilitate a more general "acceptance" of the evacuees. This technique involved placing a few experienced evacuee farmworkers into several communities not likely to be subject to continuing labor shortages—to introduce Japanese American innovations in farming practices. In "demonstrating" the inmate's skills and showing them to be friendly people, the USDA imagined that farm employers would "tend to lose their habitual distrust of strange labor and begin to welcome the help of the evacuees." For the "demonstrations," the USDA recommended selecting evacuees with the most experience, with an agricultural background, a knowledge of English, and the "personality necessary to make social adjustments." These "vanguard groups" would demonstrate to agricultural communities "that the Japanese can become useful, recognized participants in community life."[66] This suggestion placed racism at the level of individual psychology, assuming that through community education and training efforts, it could be eliminated.

Despite their attempts to reduce racism and ensure that Japanese Americans had certain freedoms, including the "freedom" to labor, race and coercion lay at the heart of the Japanese American labor programs. While jobs were "offered" to inmates, these jobs were the only available escape from prison camps.[67] Even as officials managing the inmate labor program attempted to alleviate racism in local communities, they also embarked on their own racist campaign of Americanization, imposing American culture onto Japanese Americans through assimilationist education at the prison camps. While resettlement was painted as a policy of "adjustment," it was really designed to force Japanese Americans to integrate more fully into white American communities, robbing them of their traditions and identities. According to historian Mae Ngai, camp governance, the loyalty oath, the volunteer combat unit, resettlement, and Japanese citizenship renunciation were all policies of cultural assimilation implemented by the WRA. Assimilation remained the central goal of the WRA throughout its existence. As the WRA director Myer concluded, the racism against the Japanese by their white neighbors was a result of the Japanese being "all bunched up in groups" along the coast. Had they not huddled together in ethnic enclaves and instead "flung themselves across the continent," then in a generation or two they might have become part of white America. One of the aims of the WRA's resettlement plan was to break up the West Coast "ghettos" of the Japanese American community and facilitate their entry into the American mainstream through their geographical dispersal.[68]

By March 26, 1943, the WRA worked with the WFA to professionalize the recruitment of Japanese American inmate labor and create uniformity through the establishment of a new Japanese American labor contract. Conservative farm organizations, such as the American Farm Bureau Federation, had strong allies in Congress and were able to remove the FSA from its role in recruiting and managing workers.[69] With the transfer of authority over recruitment and transportation transitioning from the FSA to the WFA, the WFA put new policies into place to manage Japanese American labor. By an act approved April 29, 1943, the U.S. government appropriated $26 million to the newly established WFA in conducting the Emergency Farm Labor Supply program. The same law gave the USES responsibility for recruiting and placing interstate and foreign labor. General supervision for the Japanese American, Mexican, and Caribbean labor programs became vested in the WFA, which established an Office of Labor to have general responsibility over the interstate and foreign labor aspects of the farm labor program.[70]

The WRA and the WFA developed new regulations permitting seasonal leave for employment in agriculture under seven-month labor contracts, and they revised War Relocation instruction no. 22 on March 16, 1943, to set up "enhanced conditions" for seasonal work. The desire for equitable treatment remained in the revised instructions for seasonal work leave. As the acting director of the WFA proclaimed, "The fact that we do impose these conditions makes it important that evacuees receive the same fair treatment that is accorded other seasonal workers under similar circumstances." Although it was arguable whether other seasonal workers even received "fair treatment," the central goal of these new labor contracts was to gain maximum control over Japanese American labor by forcing inmates to stay in the field for the full duration of the work contract. According to these new contracts, "evacuees granted seasonal leave to accept employment are expected to remain outside the center for the full duration of the period of the contract."[71]

Less than a year after initiating the Japanese American labor program, WRA and WFA officials shifted from avoiding any semblance of coercion to direct imposition of force, by means of the labor contract. During the previous year of employment (1942), the WFA had found that many evacuees returned to the center to visit their families during idle periods at work. Others "took their contracts too lightly" and quit their jobs, returning to the center. Noting the challenges of administering the seasonal program, as well as ensuring the full utilization of labor in prison camps, the WRA revised the seasonal leave procedures and offered contracts that controlled the movement of workers. As the contract stated, "[the workers were] not to return to the center except for emergency visits and then only with permission from our [WRA] relocation officer. If they return without permission, their seasonal leave may be revoked." The WRA also made it a misdemeanor to leave the center without permission, punishable by fine or imprisonment or both.[72] The new labor contract forced Japanese American farm workers to stay on the job, regardless of the circumstances or their treatment.

According to the WRA's new seasonal work leave policy, revised March 1943, government-issued labor contracts were now required, and the relocation officer must determine before issuing contracts that "the racist sentiment of the local community in which they are placed is not such that the applicant for seasonal leave can successfully maintain employment there." Given that seasonal leave was now only issued by contract, inmates also had to execute form WRA-129, stating that "My alien registration number is _____ and I understand that I am required by the Department of Justice regulations to obtain a travel permit from the U.S. Attorney General before leaving and to notify the INS and the FBI of any change of address or employment." As a mechanism of coercion and surveillance, the contract transformed workers into subjects of the state, who could be hunted down and reported to the federal government if they did not comply. The contract became a device to control, manage, and monitor their mobility and their labor, with the procedures stressing punitive measures if an evacuee returned before the contract ended or for causing "disturbances or threats to safety."[73]

Far from being a program of "resettlement," the Japanese American farm labor program served to provide seasonal agricultural laborers to growers on temporary contracts. By the beginning of 1945, agricultural workers on "seasonal leave" were employed in nineteen states under labor contracts, with approximately 33,000 Japanese Americans leaving the camps for employment "resettlement."[74] The WRA found through its investigations that farming communities in the Midwest were too hostile to permanent Japanese American settlement, their racism too great a hurdle to permit Japanese American

Figure 6. Japanese farmworkers at Twin Falls County, Idaho, Farm Security Administration Workers' Camp, July 1942. Courtesy of the Library of Congress.

residence. A few farmers feared economic competition after the war if the Japanese remained in the community; others simply saw no reason for them to stay, since their farm labor requirements were largely seasonal.[75] Even though their permanent settlement was unlikely, the WRA still viewed the temporary agricultural labor program as a worthwhile effort to keep inmates "meaningfully employed."

In January 1944, Seabrook Farms in Bridgeton, New Jersey, began recruiting from the prison camps, hiring single farm laborers and a few long-term recruits in the form of married couples or families. Seabrook Farms was a highly mechanized large-scale farm that often became a permanent settlement for many Japanese American contract laborers. It received much national attention during and after the war as a showcase of modern agriculture and processing technology, particularly as it became one of the largest food suppliers to the U.S. military during World War II. Here, the WRA recruited 2,500 Japanese Americans and Japanese Peruvians from the prison camps as a resettlement measure and to relieve labor shortage fears. Internees found themselves housed in hastily constructed tar-paper barracks that consisted of shared bathing and laundry facilities that required communal living. Those Japanese Americans convinced that they were leaving the camps for freedom and more comfortable circumstances often experienced surprise, shock, and disappointment upon arrival. Their living circumstances did not differ much from life at the prison camps. As Art Shibayama noted, "It was like a barrack in camp except that we didn't have fences around us. You know, community bathrooms and laundry room. It was just like another [internment] camp." He also found the work to be intense at Seabrook Farms, where he, like many workers, labored for long hours under difficult conditions. As he stated, "I cut flowers twelve hours a day, seven days a week as a teenager."[76] Just as in the prison camps, Japanese Americans found they were often forced to do work they were unaccustomed to, with low pay, poor housing, and exploitative working conditions.[77]

While the WRA's resettlement program attempted to undo anti-Japanese racism and transform the Japanese citizenry into worthy recipients of American democracy, the program became little more than a bundle of coercive measures to force Japanese Americans into performing low-wage "stoop" labor under dire circumstances, with the goal of ensuring "maximum use of their labor in seasonal agriculture."[78] Most workers were not informed of their future working conditions and only learned of them when they arrived on the job. The work was arduous and hours were long, with some farmers refusing to pay Japanese Americans after they had finished beet topping or fruit picking. One worker noted, "The degree of friendliness of the employer decreased as the harvest neared completion." While some workers concluded, "Although it is hard, it is worth the freedom we are allowed," most described it as a shift from "complete confinement" to "partial confinement."[79] There is no doubt that the U.S. government profited from workers' coerced labor. In the field of agriculture alone, food products harvested by Japanese Americans in 1943 had a market value of over three million dollars, and were used to fulfill the subsistence needs of the prison camps and the U.S. military. The contribution to the economy and the war effort was considerable. The Utah-Idaho Sugar Company hired 3,500 Japanese laborers in 1942, increasing its production from 72,000 acres in 1941 to 89,000 acres in 1942. State officials administering the labor program considered it a success, even as it became an instrument in advancing the interests of capital for corporate farmers.[80]

Historical Legacies of White Supremacy

Beneath the platform of the WRA's and the Tolan Committee's language of state protection was the historical disdain for Japanese Americans that had characterized Asian immigrant treatment in the United States since the first entry of Chinese migrants for work in gold mines, in agricultural fields, and on the transcontinental railroad.[81] A system of migratory agricultural labor that had begun with Chinese migration continued with Japanese migration after the Chinese Exclusion Act of 1882. As discussed in Chapter 1, both state and federal governments, in collusion with growers and labor activists, continuously turned Chinese and other Asian migrants into a permanent force of cheap and temporary migrant labor through a series of exclusionary immigration acts. When U.S. nativists feared Japanese workers as a new source of labor competition after the Chinese Exclusion Act, the U.S. government initiated the Gentlemen's Agreement (1907), preventing Japanese workers from acquiring passports. The state-based Alien Land Law measures (1913) then prohibited Asian workers from owning agricultural land. These laws were passed—not to drive out Asian workers—but to force them to remain workers and not landowners, making their presence vulnerable and impermanent. In *Ozawa v. United States* (1922), the U.S. Supreme Court unquestionably asserted that Japanese persons were not "free white persons," and could not be eligible for citizenship. The Immigration Act of 1924 set up a national quota board to determine the number of immigrants permitted to enter the United States from each country, yet Asian countries were not included. Through these cases and acts, the state claimed Asian workers "aliens ineligible to citizenship," making it a challenge for them to become farm landowners themselves.[82]

When these legislative actions shrank the number of Japanese farmworkers in the 1920s and 1930s, growers began to look to Mexico for an abundant supply of labor to augment the Japanese labor supply. Agricultural employers soon realized that social, political, and economic forces combined to render Mexicans as powerless as they had the Chinese a generation before, and growers started to show a preference for Mexican farmworkers. By creating the California Farm Bureau Federation and the American Farm Bureau

Federation in 1919 and 1920, growers lobbied to prevent the application of the Immigration Act of 1924 to Mexicans, availing themselves of a large pool of Mexican labor that could be deported easily. This flexible Mexican labor supply was continually augmented by new undocumented migrant labor through a process of making Mexican migrants "illegal."[83]

For nearly a century prior to Pearl Harbor, local white vigilantes had built a foundation of racist ideologies about Asians and Mexicans in the Southwest through social isolation, overt and covert racial discrimination, racial violence, and a series of exclusionary policies and acts, culminating in the incarceration of Japanese Americans in 1942. With Executive Order 9066, the federal government yet again supported the claims of vocal white supremacist businessmen and community groups, singling out a particular group of people, excluding them on racial grounds. In fact, racial considerations structured the very argument of "military necessity." As Gen. DeWitt stated, "The Japanese race . . . is an enemy race and while many second and third generation Japanese born on U.S. soil have become 'Americanized,' the racial strains are undiluted. . . . It therefore follows that along the vital Pacific Coast over 112,000 potential enemies of Japanese extraction are at large today."[84]

While liberals at the Tolan Committee hearings emphasized that incarceration was designed to "protect" Japanese Americans as citizens, their discursive practices masked the fact that Japanese American incarceration stripped them of their citizenship, forced them into prison camps, coerced them into underpaid agricultural labor, and made them all "enemy aliens." At the Tolan Committee hearings in May and June 1942, conservative growers in attendance also stressed the importance of using both incarcerated Japanese labor and imported Mexican labor. A grower in Oregon stated, "We believe the move to allow Mexican laborers to limited entrances into this country to assist in the labor shortage should be permitted. We believe the Japanese should be not only permitted but compelled to assist in harvest operations where they will not endanger the Nation's safety."[85] The difference was that growers did not find coercion or force problematic when employing Japanese American labor, nor were they concerned with Mexican workers' rights. Unlike Tolan, Galarza, and members of the Department of Labor, growers did not frame their arguments around racial liberalism but rather organized their arguments for Mexican and imprisoned Japanese American labor through the legacy of white supremacy that had long fueled the exploitation of nonwhite farm labor in the United States.

Growers had already asserted public pressure on the president, the Tolan Committee, and the U.S. Congress for Japanese removal in the first place, racializing Japanese Americans as "enemy aliens" and a potential threat to the security of the United States. Their success in pressing for the elimination of Japanese American farmers stimulated an already robust fear of a manpower shortage on the West Coast. In response to this growing fear, California growers argued for a Mexican labor importation program to fill the "gap" in farm labor left by Japanese Americans after many had been expunged from the fields. Given the ideological connection between war and agricultural labor, the drafting of farm laborers into the military, the migration of farm laborers into the defense industries, and the fact that thousands of Japanese farm laborers had been removed from the Pacific coast, it is no surprise that others also raised concerns of a farm labor shortage.

As early as April 1942, days after the U.S. Army began to systematically force Japanese Americans to leave their homes, agricultural interests already requested the release of "evacuees" so that they could be used as farm laborers. Allan C. Devany of the Immigration and Naturalization Service (INS) stated at the hearings, "We have to give some answer to these [sugar beet] employers because they are pleading for these laborers. Not only in California but in Colorado, Idaho, Montana, and Texas, all asserting that the labor is not available." Devany further stated, "the Immigration Service is holding these applications at the present time with the growers demanding some action."[86]

Liberal government officials of the FSA disagreed that the removal of Japanese Americans from the West Coast would cause a labor shortage. Laurence Hewes Jr., regional director of the FSA, argued that the agency could place small American farmers who do not now have adequate resources [as former victims of the Dust Bowl] on former Japanese American land so that they could "make a contribution to the national food campaign."[87] Hewes stated, "I think all agricultural officials today are concerned lest the production of lands occupied by aliens, or by citizens of Japanese descent, go out of production. . . . we can't afford any situation that results in decreased production." Likening the experience of the Japanese American "evacuees" to that of the Dust Bowl migrant, Hewes pointed out that the FSA had a wealth of experience to successfully address "the problems of housing, moving people, and trying to establish some form of economic security for dispossessed people."[88] The FSA became the state organization responsible for administering the "fair disposition" of evacuated Japanese American farmland and aiding qualified farmers to take over their land and obtain operating credit. They tried to "Handle Japanese farm properties in an equitable manner and to insure continuance of agricultural production."[89]

Conservative California growers and their advocates at the hearings similarly promised that no labor shortage would arise after Japanese American removal. J. Murray Thompson, chief of the economic section of the Agricultural Adjustment Administration in California, noted that although Japanese American citizens produced about "200,000 acres of vegetables in 1940, or about 40 percent of the California vegetable acreage . . . we in agriculture will strive to maintain as much production as possible." The manager of the Associated Produce Dealers and Brokers of Los Angeles insisted that "the removal of all Japanese from Southern California will not cause any serious dislocation in the feeding of this community." Others were more blatant in their intentions. As the Grower-Shipper Vegetable Association of Salinas stated, "if all Japs were removed tomorrow, we'd never miss them in two weeks, because the white farmers can take over and produce everything the Jap grows."[90] There is no doubt California growers sought to profit from the removal of Japanese citizens from their farms. In 1941, the total value of Japanese American farm holdings in California had been estimated at nearly $100 million, their truck crops for fresh market valued at $85 million or 32 percent of the total for the entire country.[91]

At the Tolan Committee hearings, it became clear that growers, via their political associations or cooperatives, sought to eliminate Japanese American-owned farm competition. The manager of the Associated Produce Dealers and Brokers of Los Angeles maintained at the hearings: "I have talked to many wholesale growers of vegetables for the local market who have either gone out of business in the past 10 years or greatly reduced their operations due to Japanese competition. . . . A comprehensive system of associations set up for these small Japanese farmers has enabled them to regulate market supplies and reduce prices at will, to the point that the competing white grower has been forced out of production."[92] He suggested that Anglo-American growers take over Japanese American-owned farms. This language was not ignored by other witnesses at the Tolan Committee hearings. As an Oakland attorney testified, "effort should be made to determine whether there is any connection between the clamor for the dispossession of the Japanese farmers and the desire of these clamoring interests to get possession of Japanese farms and the elimination of Japanese competition."[93]

It was obvious at the hearings that many growers wanted to remove the Japanese from business ownership and entrepreneurship and to profit from their labor by placing them exclusively in dependent, low-wage agricultural work. The chief of the economic section of the Agricultural Adjustment Administration, J. Murray Thompson, suggested that "evacuees" be resettled on land near farms under military supervision. He suggested that they could then be "accessible to areas [in California] requiring agricultural labor, particularly 'stoop' labor. These evacuees could be hired in groups at the going wage."[94] T. M. Bunn of the Salinas Valley Vegetable Exchange noted that his farmers' association had spent $25,000 on a labor camp in Salinas that could be used to house Japanese "evacuee" laborers. He stated, "with this efficient Japanese help, we feel we can be of great assistance to the Government in the producing of food stuffs during the national emergency." He also noted that several farmers of his association were willing to, as he stated, "colonize farm areas in Idaho, New Mexico, and Nevada," to make use of the farmland formerly owned by removed Japanese Americans as well as Japanese American labor.[95]

Japanese American incarceration was therefore rooted in the form of conquest and colonization that had been established with settler colonialism, as state officials and growers aspired to literally remove Japanese Americans from their land and property, and then to seize it.[96] While liberal state officials envisioned building new racially inclusive societies at prison camps, growers imagined occupying and tilling Japanese American farmland, removing and replacing Japanese American farmers. Not unlike settler colonists, growers and officials removed Japanese Americans from their homes in California while criminalizing them as "aliens," so as to revoke their right to be within the invaded territory. Their elimination, like the elimination of Native Americans during westward expansion, was the primary objective of state officials and growers, whether they saw it as such or not.[97]

The continuity between the "resettlement" of Japanese Americans and the historical "resettlement" of Native Americans on reservations are many. It is important to note that WRA leaders, including the director, Dillon Myer, were veterans of the Bureau of Indian Affairs (BIA); Myer later became the director of the BIA in 1950. The WRA was largely staffed by personnel from the BIA, such that the bureaucrats governing Japanese American incarceration modeled the concentration camps on existing colonial operations. The WRA even worked with the BIA to administer two resettlement projects for Japanese

American inmates: one project in Parker, Arizona, at the Colorado River Indian Reservation, to which the WRA sent nearly 20,000 Japanese American inmates, and the other at the Gila River Reservation in southern Arizona, to which they sent about 17,000.[98] The idea was that Japanese Americans incarcerated at the Colorado River Indian reservation would "volunteer" in the "subjugation and irrigation of nearly 100,000 acres of 'hitherto wasteland,'" working on canal construction, digging of drainage ditches, and clearing the land, so that Navajo Indians from Arizona could then be employed to cultivate and harvest that land. The camp opened on June 1, 1942, as the Colorado River Relocation Center, but it later became the Poston War Relocation Center. The WFA also hired Navajo Indian as contract farm laborers, with hundreds working alongside Japanese American inmates and braceros during World War II.[99]

The mass incarceration of Japanese Americans epitomized California agribusiness leaders' endless quest for cheap labor since the 1850s. The rapid expansion of a modern business mentality among U.S. farmers in the late nineteenth century had led to an interest in organizing themselves to promote greater efficiency and control over production.[100] They formed associations devoted to advancing the economic interests of California's rural population, and these new organizations, such as the Southern California Fruit Exchange (1893), protected the interests of those invested in particular crops. By 1920, growers' cooperatives were an established feature of commercial agriculture in California. They argued that high labor costs would pose a threat to their profitability and economic well-being. The racist mentality of growers that legitimized their endless search for profits remained evident at the Tolan Committee hearings. As T. M. Bunn blatantly confessed, "Unless we can use oriental help we cannot farm these lands economically and efficiently. We are fighting this war to hold and further secure cheap labor. So if we can't secure it in California, we will commence to look elsewhere."[101]

The Results of Japanese American
and Mexican Labor Importation

The World War II Japanese American and the Mexican labor importation programs catalyzed some of the most exploitative experiences for contract farm laborers in the United States. Due to the clout of U.S. agribusiness, the U.S. Congress enforced the law weakly and purposely ignored violations of the programs, ranging from violations of basic human rights to the deliberate

recruitment of undocumented workers.[102] In spite of the protective regulations, the machinery put in place was not sufficient to assess violations and
reprimand growers who did not fulfill their side of the contract. Those few
Mexican labor inspectors and consuls that did exist noted the "illusion" of
the importation "as a force against the war and as an alliance." As one Mexican labor inspector stated, "[Growers] see it only as cheap manual labor. . . .
they prefer Mexicans because, as foreigners and rural people, many have no
experience with labor unions. The farmers have a police force that is strong,
organized, and violent."[103]

Incarcerated Japanese Americans recognized the limitations of U.S. citizenship, with many at the Tolan Committee hearings calling out "evacuation"
as a violation of their constitutional rights, especially their right to due process. They saw through the language of protection, welfare, and rights that
structured the Tolan Committee hearings, and turned these rhetorical framings on their head by pointing out the racism inherent in the forced removal
of U.S. citizens. As an outspoken critic of the expulsion, James Omura, editor
of the *Rocky Shimpo* newspaper in Denver, Colorado, stated before the committee, "Are we to be condemned merely on the basis of our racial origin? Is
citizenship such a light and transient thing that which is our inalienable right
in normal times can be torn from us in times of war?" Omura called out the
use of race to structure the very basis of the decision to "remove" Japanese
American citizens, stating that "American" should not signify a racial trait but
a national symbol.[104] Joseph Shinoda, a member of the United Citizens Federation in Los Angeles, concurred: "But when they ask a citizen who has not, up
to now, questioned any of the sanctities that we have here with our liberties,
when they ask us to evacuate, that, I say is a denial of our citizenship."[105] Tokie
Slocum, also a member of the United Citizens Federation, pleaded against
racial discrimination in an argument for his citizenship, "This possibly may
set a rather dangerous or vicious precedent for the future," he argued. "So I
just want you gentlemen to bear in mind when you legislate that this is not
to be a racial or a minority group legislation for discrimination. . . . give us a
fair deal and please after the war is over we would like to get our citizenship
back in full status."[106]

Even after their forced expulsion from the Pacific coast, many Japanese
Americans argued for the reinstatement of their constitutional rights as U.S.
citizens. They also critiqued the categories of "loyal" and "disloyal" citizens.
They looked to the U.S. Constitution for the restoration of their rights and
guarantees, demanding the freedoms and protection that it promised to all

U.S. citizens, while recognizing their exclusion from it. At the Tule Lake concentration camp, one Japanese American noted, "No we are not dual citizens. But in the first place if we are citizens, how come we are in these camps?" Another pointed out, "I'm supposed to be a citizen of the United States." Critiquing the concept that Japanese Americans raised a national security concern, he asked, "What security do we have? If this can happen now, why can't the same thing happen in five years?"[107] Japanese Americans were well aware that the language of national "military security" did not mean security for them, exposing the contradictions between race and liberal democracy. They acknowledged that U.S. "national security" considerations dismissed their rights and had nothing to do with protecting them but, rather, resulted in their exclusion from society.

Those who felt the consequences of national security looked to their own community for security, through efforts toward their own self-protection.[108] When the WRA announced its decision to close the concentration camp at Poston, Arizona, on January 2, 1946, many refused to leave, fearing the racial discrimination they would face going back to their home communities. As one man stated after incarceration had officially ended, "We'd like to sit in Tule Lake [concentration camp] for a while. We don't want to relocate. The discrimination is too bad. I see letters from the people on the outside. There are fellows in Chicago who want to come back [to camp] but who are not allowed to."[109] Japanese Americans took matters into their own hands by forming a collective organization to make demands on the WRA at its All Center Conference in Salt Lake City. Realizing that the WRA had offered them neither protection nor security, and feeling insecure toward the changes and modifications made in WRA policy, they created their own agency to shape policy.[110]

Soon after some Japanese Americans began to be released from the concentration camps, the Tolan Committee member Carey McWilliams became an outspoken critic of Japanese American incarceration, publishing an exposé entitled *Prejudice—Japanese Americans: Symbol of Racial Intolerance* (1944), when the incarceration of Japanese Americans was still a live issue. He took part in two radio debates in California, in which he took the position that the Japanese should never have been removed in the first place. As McWilliams looked back on 1942, he maintained that "instead of total mass evacuation resulting in a measure of greater calm and more vigorous concentration on the war, the opposite happened. What had been a small flame of racial prejudice became a raging fire."[111] Liberal Tolan Committee attendees at the hearings, like McWilliams, had seen the potential for constitutional error and sought to ensure that Japanese American citizenship and property rights would remain protected as they were purged from the West Coast. In the process, they reaffirmed American exceptionalism and continued to do so even after the prison camps closed, when they labeled their actions a mistake of U.S. democracy—not a product of its structural and ideological conditions under modern liberalism.

The racist and violent "firestorms" that resulted after the Tolan Committee hearings were unforeseen by Galarza and Tolan. They were the product of the enticing power of a liberal state and an unthinking adherence to a New Deal cause that was fueled by a tradition of race and labor in the West. While Galarza imagined a more inclusive vision of democracy and rights for Mexican workers, a unified band of California agribusiness leaders sought to pressure lawmakers to safeguard racial segregation and build a nation-state fit to manage capitalism. Even as Japanese Americans were promised similar rights and protections, they were excluded from citizenship as foreign "enemy aliens," disenfranchised, stripped of land and property, and then asked to return to the fields as tractable and temporary labor. Although possibilities had opened for the equal treatment of Mexican migrants, and for the Tolan Committee to resist Executive Order 9066 in Congress, mass expulsion and the re-racialization of both Mexicans and Japanese as agricultural "stoop" labor resulted instead.

Likewise, the prerogative of national security forced state officials to segregate the "loyal" from the "disloyal," the "foreign" from the "domestic," and the "legal" from the "illegal." In essence, the overlap of social welfare and national security led to a reification of race, with a belief in the tenets of racial liberalism resolving the ambiguities inherent in mass incarceration and labor importation.[112] This is not to say that Galarza, McWilliams, and others were willingly complicit or responsible for the reification of race that resulted from federal policies implemented during World War II. Unbeknown to Galarza and others, their faith in liberalism required them to look to the federal government as a source of social change, but it resulted in the proliferation of government authority and violence, with their normative vision of liberalism serving as a mask for the actual coercion that resulted. As a result, both groups of so-called "aliens" were no longer simply objects of rule with no identity or subjectivity accorded to them by the state. They were newly constituted, through a language of rights and protections, as self-reflexive subjects who could participate in their own regulation as "volunteer" agricultural workers, not coerced labor. That shift emerged out of the politics of disavowal that gained momentum during the Tolan Committee hearings, turning the bracero program and Japanese American incarceration into celebrations of U.S. democracy and freedom.

*   *   *

While government discussions regarding a Mexican labor importation program were already underway when the Tolan Committee met in May and June 1942, one could argue that that those involved in the hearings were forced to make the best of a bad situation. It could also be argued that the possibilities in the field of discourse had narrowed in time of war, with liberal witnesses at the hearings having no choice but to go along with political and military demands that were out of their control. Or that they had no ability to argue against Japanese incarceration and a Mexican labor program, when they were outflanked at the Tolan Committee hearings by anti-Japanese racists, the military, and conservative growers who coveted Japanese American land. However, it could equally be argued that, when confronted by such racist and conservative individuals and with the exigencies of total war, Tolan and others could have protested Executive Order 9066, as well as the idea of a program to manage Mexican labor. Instead, they saw both projects as a means to fulfill liberal democratic ends, and as racially progressive programs of state protection. In any case, the point here is not to stress individual accountability, but rather to show how these liberal actors and their beliefs had significant yet unintended consequences in the creation and management of these programs.

Galarza was shocked by the blatant contract violations that took place after the implementation of the bracero program and felt deeply responsible to the contract workers who participated. While he initially thought that the Mexican labor program was an example of what American democracy could achieve, he soon noted the discrepancies between the program as it was rhetorically framed and as it actually took place on the ground. On January 3, 1945, Galarza wrote a report to the Congress of Industrial Organizations (CIO) that summarized what he perceived as the "defects" of the operation of bilateral agreements for the importation of workers. He complained that the Pan-American Union had strongly emphasized the participation of organized labor, that there was no grievance machinery at the camps, and that inspectors from the Mexican government were assigned to too large a territory to be effective. Instead of the protections and mediation that Galarza believed the government could provide, exploitation, racism, and violence against Mexican workers resulted. His complaint implied that the inclusion of the PAU, ILO, and organized labor within the state management of the labor program could have responsibly resulted in the care and welfare of the workers. Galarza spent the next two decades pressuring the U.S. government to enforce the contract policies of the bracero program.[113] During his career as a labor organizer, he noted that braceros were contributing to the formation of millionaire landowners who avoided paying higher wages by "hiring braceros, freezing prices, and making a fortune off of the sweat of braceros."[114] What emerges from a critical analysis of Japanese American incarceration and the bracero program together is not the story that Galarza and Tolan had hoped would result. Yet the race-neutral language of liberal inclusion that Tolan, Galarza, and other liberals constructed at this time produced the condition of possibility for state violence and U.S. hegemony after World War II, while signaling a new rationale for federal power over "foreign" labor.

After World War II ended, the official continuation of the bracero program was contingent upon a language of state-led democracy, rights, and freedom, a language that continued to inform Galarza's arguments for the reform of the bracero program. Throughout the 1950s, Galarza continued to look to the U.S. and Mexican governments to effectively manage the migration of Mexican migrant laborers and to ensure the fulfillment of their labor contracts, keeping in mind the original intent and promise behind the Mexican labor importation program he had originally suggested. From convincingly proposing a state-sponsored labor program to crusading to reform it, Galarza remained hopeful about the U.S. federal government's capacity to enact and engender freedom, which ironically would later force him to reify racial divides between citizens and "aliens," and between those who should have rights in the United States and those who should not.

CHAPTER 4

From Civil Rights to Immigration Restriction: The Search for U.S. Labor Rights in the 1950s

"With my heart I shout a boastful cry, long live our nation and American victory," cheered Mexican contract worker J. S. Vilchis. As the first clause of his individual work agreement stipulated, "the Government of the U.S. and the Worker mutually desire that the worker be beneficially employed in the United States with a view to alleviate the present shortage of agricultural workers in that country and to cooperate in the successful prosecution of the war." Many braceros believed in this contractual obligation and made it their reason for migrating to the United States. When a contingent left for the United States on May 13, 1943, Mexican secretary of labor and social welfare Francisco Trujillo Gurría said to them: "You are soldiers of democracy, and fight with the patriotic spirit that is alive in all of Mexico. . . . *tratados exactamente igual a los trabajadores de la Union Americana/* treated exactly equal to U.S. workers." During the early years of the program, many braceros told positive stories of jubilant welcoming committees and decent treatment despite harsh labor conditions. It was not long after the initiation of the bracero program, however, that Mexican migrant workers began to take note of the differences between what they had been told about the labor programs and the reality of exploitation and contract violations on the ground. One bracero, Felix Tapia, observed, "We laborers and citizens of Mexico have come to offer our services to our sister nation when she needed us. . . . the treatment which we have received, nevertheless, all falls short of any standard of Good Neighborliness."[1]

Feeling that the state had violated the contract, many braceros abandoned their contracts when work conditions proved excessively harsh, calling into question "legal status" as a mode of state rule. Dozens of braceros confessed, "we don't care about the contract. It only means that we can't take some better job."[2] Another bracero stated, "I have been a wetback twice and I think you are more of a free man that way. This way you are honor bound to keep the contract, but the bosses do not keep their part of it."[3] For some braceros, going "illegal" without a contract was a means to exercise their freedom and the right to choose for whom they worked. By "skipping" or "jumping" their contract, they became "libres" (free men). Leaving an abusive employer for another who would potentially treat them better was one of the only means braceros had to escape the contract as a mechanism of labor coercion. In skipping their contracts, they challenged the power of the state and imagined alternative visions of "freedom" beyond state governance. Braceros were aware, however, that this vision of freedom without a contract was limiting. Deserting their contracts turned them into fugitive "aliens" or "wetbacks," racial terms that were widely and loosely used in the 1940s and 1950s to lump Mexican migrants together under an immigration regime of racialization and criminalization. As the bracero José Santos Guevara-Rodríguez maintained, "Many men deserted the fields, but they knew the compromise they would be making when they did." As he stated, "The risk was that immigration might come look for you." While braceros' rejection of the contract was a statement of resistance, the contract's power over their lives was ever present.

In 1947, Ernesto Galarza entered the fields of California as a leader of the National Farm Labor Union-American Federation of Labor (NFLU-AFL) in an attempt to unionize braceros, along with U.S. farmworkers, to ensure the rights of the labor contract.[4] From 1947 to 1952, Galarza and the NFLU became involved in extended battles in the Central and Imperial Valleys. In October 1947, they struck the eleven-thousand-acre farms of the DiGiorgio Corporation in the Central Valley and refused to work until better pay, work conditions, and a union contract were offered. Initially, Galarza and the NFLU ventured to include undocumented migrants in their unionization campaigns. After a lengthy campaign, Galarza and the NFLU became increasingly frustrated in their efforts to strike in collaboration with undocumented workers, due to growers' strategic employment of undocumented workers to break the strikes.[5] Instead of uniting with undocumented workers and braceros, Galarza and the NFLU came to see them as outsiders who stood in the way of justice for U.S. farmworkers.

At the heart of the U.S. and Mexican labor union's exclusionary practices toward undocumented workers was the labor contract. Galarza's first exposé on the bracero program, *Strangers in Our Fields: Based on a Report Regarding Compliance with the Contractual, Legal, and Civil Rights of Mexican Agricultural Workers in the United States* (1956) focused on civil rights as its subtitle suggests for, as Galarza argued in the book, "the protection of the civil rights of the bracero is an aim that is implicit in the Agreement and the work contract."[6] The "civil rights" of the farmworker in the United States became the leading focus of the NFLU at this time. The notion of "civil rights" was beginning to gain more traction in U.S. society in the 1940s, especially with the creation of President Truman's Committee on Civil Rights (1946), designed to investigate the status of civil rights in the United States and propose measures to institute them. Some labor union members had begun to say that their struggle was for racial equality and rights, recognized and regulated by the government. Galarza and the NFLU's mission, in particular, was to mobilize the federal government to enforce the bracero labor contract to protect the civil rights of both the U.S. farmworker and of the Mexican agricultural worker. As Galarza argued, "if foreign labor should be contracted, such labor should be contracted on the basis of equal conditions for all."[7]

While U.S. labor unions have fluctuated in terms of their support of civil rights in the twentieth century, there were many moments when they combined class consciousness with racial solidarity, leading to "civil rights unionism." Historian Zaragosa Vargas has shown that the labor struggles of Mexicans in the Southwest, in particular, were inseparable from the issue of civil rights in the 1940s and 1950s, forming the foundation for the later successes of the Chicana/o civil rights movement.[8] Yet historians have typically studied the bracero program separately from the long civil rights movement in the United States. Galarza's attempts to ensure the civil rights of the bracero marked an innovative approach that at first stretched beyond the racial bounds of national citizenship. While he and other farm labor activists advocated for Mexican migrant civil rights, they eventually concluded that those rights could be attained only if undocumented migrants were prevented from entering the United States to be employed as strikebreakers.

Galarza perceived both the U.S. and Mexican governments as failing in managing the bracero program, since so many undocumented workers and braceros were able to replace them as strikebreakers. Taking matters into their own hands, Galarza and the NFLU joined transnationally with Mexican labor unions, including Alianza de Braceros and the Unión de Trabajadores Agrícolas del Valle de Mexicali (UTAVM) to prevent undocumented migrants from crossing the border.⁹ Together, the NFLU and Mexican labor unions led an effort to prevent Mexican migrants from entering the United States, posting picket lines along the border and forcing truckloads of workers to turn around and go back. Instead of uniting workers across national divides, Galarza and the NFLU resorted to excluding Mexican migrant workers from the California farm labor movement in the 1950s, whether under contract as braceros or not.

By 1951, Galarza and the NFLU concluded that if they stopped the flow of undocumented Mexican migrants, growers would not be able to hire them as strikebreakers, aiding the NFLU's struggle for the civil rights of braceros and U.S. farmworkers. U.S. labor therefore came to support deportations as a means to make the freedom and equality of U.S. farmworkers and braceros a possibility. This reasoning permitted labor and civil rights activists to claim civil rights and equality for Mexican migrants, even as they participated in racializing them as "wetbacks."¹⁰ Their commitment to racial liberalism, in combination with a political culture of white supremacy, culminated in the massive deportation project known as Operation Wetback (1954), led by Joseph Swing of the INS. Operation Wetback, as it was conceived, was a state project designed to clamp down on "illegal" immigration from Mexico during the bracero program by initiating a campaign of fear, violence, deportation, and expulsion of Mexican migrant labor. With Operation Wetback, the INS, in cooperation with U.S. labor and other local, federal, and state organizations, convinced many migrants to leave "voluntarily" through self-deportation, resulting in nearly 200,000 total deportations. Operation Wetback was never entirely successful in preventing profit-seeking growers and contractors from recruiting "illegal" labor. Instead, it resulted in an increase in the recruitment of braceros and a more permanent and strategic Border Patrol presence under the guise of "national security," fortifying and refining the power of the state to control and manage Mexican workers in the United States.¹¹

Galarza, the NFLU, and members of the U.S. labor movement were convinced of the power of the state to distinguish between who had documents and who did not. They also believed that U.S. and Mexican labor unions could effectively assist the federal government in distinguishing between wetback versus bracero and legal versus illegal. Their focus on civil rights, "equality," and protection, properly ensured by the labor contract, provided the necessary condition to exclude undocumented migrants from the union. As Hank

Hasiwar, president of the NFLU, demanded in 1951, "The union insists that
the Mexican nationals should have the right to union representation and
enjoy equal standards with American workers. The union will continue to
fight for control of the flow of imported labor so as to protect American standards for all workers."[12] They therefore continued to target the enforcement
of the contract and the policing of the border in the Imperial Valley, with the
Mexican labor unions following suit.

While supportive of braceros and their civil rights accorded by the contract, the NFLU did not consider how braceros relied on the fluidity of the
line between legal and illegal to protect themselves from abusive employers
in the face of rampant disregard for their labor rights—such that any Mexican
migrant without a contract was essentially an undocumented bracero. "Skipping the contract" was one of the few means braceros had to protest contract
violations. Meanwhile, growers strategically employed both undocumented
workers and new braceros during strikes. Their employment of undocumented workers and newly imported braceros was so effective at splitting U.S.
and Mexican workers that union members could not collaborate or unionize
effectively across the lines of race and citizenship, proving it a useful "divide
and conquer" strategy.[13]

Despite braceros' alternative visions of freedom, the NFLU's discourse
of civil rights and equality effectively yielded exclusionary impulses from
the U.S. labor and civil rights movement, reproducing white supremacy and
inequality. By striving to ensure the protections and rights of workers, U.S.
and Mexican labor felt compelled to delineate who and who should not have
access to rights, leading to new forms of state subjection, administration, and
governance over Mexican migrants' lives. Organized labor's continued faith
in the federal government's ability to fulfill the principles of equality and freedom of the contract therefore resulted in a crucial slippage in which a sym-
bolic gesture of equality simultaneously fostered and obscured the unequal
treatment of noncitizens.[14] The imperative of "civil rights" in the California
farm labor movement led to the reinforcement of a racial system of immigration regulation based on a core paradox: a system founded on the principles of freedom, equality, and fairness that generated an ever larger caste
of racialized "illegal immigrants." In other words, Galarza and the NFLU
had unwittingly devised a dialectic between civil rights and undocumented
immigration in the 1950s, such that the "illegal" migrant became the necessary condition to lay claim to civil rights, and the very concept of civil rights
became the means to reify government authority and violence.

Braceros' Perspectives on Contract Rights and Freedom

The power and importance of the labor contract was central to braceros' visions of freedom, as they struggled to defend their contractual rights, even if they knew that pursuing those rights was often hopeless. Ernesto Galarza found that out for himself when he interviewed braceros at labor camps in California as part of the research for his book *Strangers in Our Fields*.[15] At the J. Cota Camp in Miramar, California, a bracero observed, "Some of the men have read the contracts but we cannot mention this to the foreman or the contractor. They yell at us and tell us that the contract is a piece of dirt. If we want to see how useless it is, just try to see somebody about it."[16] Mexican agricultural workers were quick to point out the limitations of the contract under the profiteering shadow of U.S. agribusiness, given the discordant reality of supposed contract "freedom." Braceros also devised multiple strategies to contest their lack of choice, freedom, and legal representation. In these workers' struggles, we can begin to see that there were other possibilities for "freedom" beyond the limited political logic of liberalism, which produced racial exclusion and state violence.[17]

Though contracts for the bracero program were supposed to be in English and Spanish, in some cases braceros were not given access to their contracts right away, or were not provided with a comprehensive reading or translation of the contract. Fellow braceros often read the stipulations of the contract to those who could not. Once informed of the contract guarantees, many sought to find a representative who might assist in the defense of their contract rights. Article 17 of the Individual Mexican Labor Work Agreement stipulated: "The Worker shall enjoy the right to participate with other workers in the selection of representatives who shall be recognized by the Employer as his spokesmen for the purpose of maintaining this agreement."[18] Yet when braceros tried to elect a representative to air their grievances to the foreman, contractor, or grower, that representative would be surreptitiously deported back to Mexico. According to Galarza, he found not a single camp throughout his survey for *Strangers in Our Fields* in which the workers had a spokesperson for the group. Under the threat of deportation, many workers quickly learned that it did not pay to speak out.[19]

Any time braceros voiced their opinions on program injustices, it could mean the loss of their job and a return trip to Mexico. As the contract stated, "If the government determines that the worker is unable or unwilling to work in accordance with the terms of this agreement . . . or if the worker violates any law of the U.S., this agreement may be forthwith terminated by the Government." But the government left it up to individual employers to make the decision. If a worker individually criticized the contract fallacies, either as a representative or to defend himself, he knowingly took a risk. As one bracero explained, "the way it is, you do not want to make any complaint because they want to put you on the truck right away and because either you have just a 45-day contract or you are just going to finish a contract and it is no use anyway." That did not prevent another bracero from one day reading the contract out loud to the foreman or contractor supervising his work, upon which the foreman grabbed the contract and tore it to pieces in the field.[20]

Realizing that the contract was a one-sided agreement in which the American employer had far greater power than the worker, braceros became increasingly frustrated by the whole experience of being a contract worker. They protested their lack of choice under the contract, considering that they had no say in their labor contract stipulations or in who they were employed by, making transparent the power difference between the employer and the bracero. "The field boss tells us we should get along with the farmer and not make trouble about the contract," a bracero stated, "but they tell us about the contract themselves. If we ask for transfer to [find] more work they warn us to stay right in this camp or the immigration will pick us up for violating the laws of this country." Braceros were not permitted to discuss or even mention the contract in dissent, but field bosses (foremen) used the contract to threaten and control the workers if they tried to desert or to leave for another field. A set of braceros noted on October 10, 1955, in Patterson, California, "it seems that the contracts are enforced only when the [farm] Association can get something out of it. For us the contract has had no support." Another bracero in Tracy, California, maintained, "the contract is not good for the workers because there is no authority to guarantee the clauses." Braceros thought of telling the authorities in Mexico, but many noticed that "there is no use telling these things to the government when we get back to Mexico. The thing is past, and the men have gone to many different places and you can't prove anything anyway."[21]

Nevertheless, contract workers often saw both the U.S. and Mexican governments as a nucleus of hope and protection that could afford them real practical benefits. While they had little faith in either government's ability to defend their rights, they still desperately hoped that the state would intervene. The desire to have their contract rights defended was always present, even when braceros knew representation was limited. This is evident in the many letters braceros wrote to the nearest Mexican consul responsible for addressing bracero grievances.[22] Even as many braceros wrote to consuls, others found that the name and location of the nearest consul was not always clear, nor were the consuls readily available. The amount of territory each consul covered in the United States limited their ability to assist braceros. Even further, the main purpose of the consul's role in government was to ensure the success of the bracero program, so they often ceded to grower's wishes. Nonetheless, braceros often aggregated their earnings to pay for one among them to travel to the nearest consul to file a complaint for all. In so doing, braceros expressed a collective identity that exceeded the individual identity bestowed upon them by the contract. Expressing this communal self, some braceros would walk off the job as a collective force. "Our situation did not improve so we walked out one day," a group of braceros stated, "fourteen of us asked that the association representative come to the camp. We could not get him here so we decided to walk to Salinas. We put our clothes in gunny sacks and started out. A truck picked us up and we went to the association office." Once at the office, braceros were usually asked to either return to work or return to Mexico; only occasionally did a Mexican consul come out to the office to speak with the workers and when a consul did appear, it was usually to encourage braceros to go back to work.[23]

One of the largest concerns that came up among braceros desiring to speak to a Mexican consul was their need for adequate wages as specified in their contracts. They sent wage complaints to Mexican consuls, to the United States Department of Labor (USDL), the United States Employment Service (USES), and to Ernesto Galarza at the NFLU. Their labor contracts stated, "Wages to be paid the worker shall be the same as those paid for similar work to other agricultural laborers under the same conditions within the same area, in the respective regions of destination. Piece rates shall be so set as to enable the worker of average ability to earn the prevailing wage."[24] In accordance with the agreement, the wage guarantee varied by contract depending upon region, as the USES was supposed to make wage determinations based on the average wage for domestic farm laborers. In reality, the farm associations often worked with USES to deflate wage earnings for their region, paying "piece" rates strategically to drop hourly rates. Growers and contractors skimmed from wages by taking deductions from paychecks for housing, meals, and insurance, costs that were falsely augmented.[25] Many braceros argued, "We do not know what the [wage] rate is going to be until we are on the field. Sometimes we have to wait until the end of the day or the next day. We ask the foreman but we do not like to do it because he gets mad. He is very sensitive."[26]

As an expression of their solidarity and collectivity, many braceros responded to insufficient wages by refusing to work and either directly walking off the field or performing work stoppages in the middle of the day. As early as November 1942, just three months after the inception of the program, braceros went on strike against a lettuce grower in the Imperial Valley, protesting low wages and other contract violations. In Tracy, California, a dozen braceros maintained: "Our entire gang refused to work and asked for transfer to another camp. The Big Boss (American) came and was very mad. He called us lazy SOBs and said he would send our whole camp back to Mexico." At the Benito Valdez camp in Tracy one bracero admitted, "last week the picking got so bad we decided that we should take the risk of going back to Mexico so we asked for a raise to 13 cents a box. There were three crews of 100 men all together. Nobody worked for a few hours."[27] Their collectives strikes were sometimes effective in forcing growers to pay. As one bracero stated: "Last week we all stopped work in the field. It was five days over and we had not received our wages. It happened that the rancher came on the field. . . . he said something to the contractor and we could see he was very mad. So the contractor went off in a truck and came back with some case and he paid us right there." Often braceros struck randomly and collectively on their own without the help of any national labor organization, because they realized the futility of participating in organizational efforts with U.S. and Mexican labor unions when braceros "come and go like the wind."[28]

Although the labor contract and agreements did not outlaw strikes, some braceros did not want to go on strike whether it would gain them their rights or not, because they wanted to make sure they were earning enough to send money back to Mexico for the support of their families. Many braceros were proud of *not* striking, because they felt that it was dishonorable and could result in a humiliating return trip to Mexico that would not allow them to fulfill their duty to their families and country as the Mexican government had promised. Afraid of being sent back, many braceros instead abandoned their contracts, envisioning new possibilities beyond the exclusionary border politics exacerbated by the labor contract. To braceros, desertion of the contract was a risky but fruitful means to create their own affiliations beyond the U.S. and Mexican governments.

Some braceros even argued that "we were all illegal" at one point or another and that it did not matter whether they had a contract or not, as they were not treated any differently. As bracero Jesús Garnica noted, most growers did not treat those with or without a contract differently. Rather, they distinguished between those who had years of experience or "knew how to work," and those who did not, which determined their treatment. Braceros slipped fluidly in and out of being contracted and working without a contract, such that most experienced being braceros or *libres* at one time or another. Because their work status and conditions fluctuated, the contract often became inconsequential to them, and they acknowledged and supported fellow workers that did not have a contract. Former bracero Tirso Yepes explained that when the INS came to his labor camp, "we protected them. . . . there were two illegals, and we covered them with carton boxes used for lettuce when we saw the immigration cars coming." Yet not all Mexican workers abandoned their contracts when faced with poor working conditions or mistreatment, especially when they knew that tactic was limiting and potentially dangerous.[29]

Even as many braceros criticized the "freedom" offered them by the labor contract, the elaborate scheme created by the Mexican and U.S. government to legitimize the bracero program sometimes made it seem at once an advance beyond U.S. imperialism, a path to modernity, and a means to fulfill Mexican men's gendered patriotic duty as husbands and fathers. Historians Deborah Cohen and Mireya Loza have masterfully detailed how the Mexican government developed the Bracero Program to "modernize" and discipline Mexican men around gendered notions of honor and *patria*, under the racial assumption that indigenous *campesinos* were "primitive" and "backwards." The racial and gendered logic that structured the bracero program in Mexico sought to reorganize social relations around the family and made it normal for the husband or father to cross national borders in an attempt to support those who stayed behind. The Mexican government also taught that their remittances would in turn benefit the Mexican economy, such that Mexican manhood became defined by labor and remittances from afar. In turn, these powerful discourses inflected what braceros thought, believed, and remembered about the bracero program, such that many still characterize it as problematic yet uplifting and benevolent.[30]

If braceros suffered, many believed it worthwhile because they were able to patriotically improve the economy in both Mexico and the United States as well as bring back money to their families. As one former bracero stated, "to me, [the bracero program] was kind of sad but at the same time . . . everyone gathered their cents. Like me, I would go back with five in the bag. And, [my family] would have their new pants. A sweater for my wife and pants for the children. That was beautiful."³¹ Because these discourses of modernity, patriotism, and manliness structured their memories of the bracero program, many downplayed their suffering, arguing their degradation was worth it for what they were able to gain in return. Others were not so sure. As Carmona stated, "[The bracero program] signifies pain, suffering, and great sadness because in Mexico, things may not be great and there might not be a lot of money, but we make money last. After coming as a bracero, I was able to build a house in Mexico and have more, but at what cost?" However, even Carmona believed that it was worth it overall: "The entire experience and my recollection of memories are positive because it helped me have a better lifestyle and provide my family with more opportunities."³² Because Carmona's idea of freedom lay in the ability to provide for himself and his family, it outweighed any humiliation (or lack of freedom) he might have experienced as a product of the bracero program. This also explains why some braceros avoided work stoppages or abandoning their contracts: if often they envisioned contract freedom as the ability to economically benefit themselves and their families, striking or jumping their contracts prevented them from realizing that freedom.

Many former braceros maintained that they would join the bracero program again if they could, even as they acknowledged their mistreatment. Just as they optimistically celebrated the program, they also readily pointed out, "They had you . . . well, as a hired slave. You had to live in a barracks with hundreds or thousands of people and the first days were sad [because you missed your relatives]. It was like a prison. I could not leave and had to work, and I worked hard jobs, with heavy labor that meant you could not rest once you started." As bracero Alberto de Loera further stated, "They simply rented and disposed of us and our labor as they pleased because we were just seen as rented property, rented animals. . . . We stayed because we needed the money and would go through the humiliations for our family's stability."³³ The indignity and humiliation weighed heavily on braceros and contradicted the affirmation of patriotic manhood that the bracero program symbolized. Yet many braceros continued to return to the United States even after they had completed a forty-five-day work contract, mostly out of desperation to earn an income, but also sometimes to reclaim that very sense of familial dignity and manhood that the Mexican state's modernization narrative had promised them through the bracero program.

This is not to say that braceros did not challenge nationalist narratives surrounding the program—even those braceros who accepted this narrative were also critical of it. Loza finds, in an intensive examination of bracero oral history and memory, that braceros challenged national visions of masculinity, family, and labor meant to legitimize the national contributions of these men, by engaging in a world of vice, sexual experimentation, gambling, and queer sex acts at the labor camps. While they continued to return to the United States to work as braceros, they still participated in subversive acts in which they created their own visions of "freedom" other than those offered by the U.S. and Mexican governments through the bracero program.

While the bracero program was coercive, exploitative, depressed wages, displaced domestic farmworkers, and tore apart families with disastrous consequences, it also alleviated unemployment in Mexico, becoming an important source of income that benefited some of the poorest in Mexico. Many former braceros argued that the program helped them to improve their lives, because "during that time one would go years without any way of benefiting oneself. . . . There was no work over there [in Mexico], no way to do something [to better oneself]."[34] As the bracero Apolonio Venegas said, "in Mexico you need money to even buy a pencil and that's the reason why many of us risk everything to come to another country and suffer because we are too poor to stay."[35] José Esequiel Adame Castro concluded, like many other braceros, that he was proud to have been a bracero, because he was able to help his family and the United States. To state otherwise would have been to deny that very affirmation of patriotic manhood that he had staked his hopes on when he signed up to be a bracero several times over.[36]

Galarza and the NFLU's Campaigns for Farmworker Labor Unionization

Despite their inability to secure a spokesman, a few braceros were able to find representation through the California farm labor movement when Ernesto Galarza entered the agricultural fields of the Central Valley in 1947. Within a year after the implementation of the bracero program, Galarza began to coax various state organizations to address the many violations of braceros' rights. As soon as Galarza realized that there was an insufficient effort on behalf of the federal government to investigate bracero complaints or grievances, he made multiple reports to the War Manpower Commission (WMC), the USES, the U.S. Department of State, and other governmental organizations managing the bracero program, to highlight worker mistreatment. He also contacted the American Federation of Labor (AFL), seeking to allow braceros to join U.S. labor unions as a path to contract compliance. On May 1, 1943, he wrote to William Green, president of the AFL, complaining, "I know there is a rule against accepting union members who are not citizens of the United States. Given the extraordinary circumstances of the war, the AFL should be willing to invite its member unions to reconsider this matter for making it possible for them to join." Green responded that he agreed but made no attempt to include braceros in the AFL. Galarza then looked to other avenues outside of organized labor to secure collective solidarity between U.S. farm laborers and braceros.[37]

First, Galarza reached out to the American Civil Liberties Union (ACLU) with a proposal to create an "emergency national council" that would advocate for the rights of people of Mexican origin in the United States. In May 1944, he argued this organization would provide "a defense against social and economic discrimination, in the defense and expansion of an American democratic way of life."[38] Defending democracy and liberalism, Galarza argued that the primary focus of this proposed council would be to prevent the exploitation of Mexican braceros such that "their improved status as citizens of the Americas may reflect credibility on inter-American understanding and goodwill." Unfortunately, the ACLU found his proposal lacking, asking him to "be specific about his objectives against economic and racial discrimination," to make a statement about the specific "evils" he was tackling, and to "explain how his new movement" or organization would "fit in" with the "LULAC(s) and the *Liga Obrera(s)*."[39] Established in 1929, the League of United Latin American Citizens (LULAC) sought to combat the discrimination faced by Mexican Americans in the United States, as a counterpart to the NAACP in the Southwest. In 1935, the Spanish-Speaking Labor League (Liga Obrera) represented miners in northern New Mexico and southern Colorado. Both organizations had a specific strategy and precise target community that Galarza did not have for his proposed national organization, according to the ACLU.

Instead of reworking his proposal and sending it to the ACLU again, Galarza turned to the U.S. Department of State in August 1944, informing officials of growers' contract violations and the grievances of Mexican contract workers. Unwilling to help, Joseph McGurk, acting director of the Office of American Republic Affairs of the Department of State, responded that "two years" had hardly been enough time to give the bracero program a chance. McGurk, who had been involved in the original negotiations of the U.S.-Mexican agreement, stressed the "voluntary" nature of the contract, stating, "people naturally complain but when I talked to returned nationals in Mexico, they all expressed satisfaction with their experience and wished to renew their contracts." Galarza informed McGurk that while the workers entered contracts voluntarily, they were forced to accept employment because "they are in a terrible dilemma due to uncontrolled inflation in Mexico and inadequacy of wages." He argued, "While legally they exercise free choice, the conditions in Mexico are an important element." Galarza also maintained that the consent of the contract was nullified by the fact that many men lacked adequate employment in Mexico and had no choice but to migrate. Yet McGurk found a simplistic response and solution for each and every issue Galarza found with the labor program. It was obvious from Galarza's communication with McGurk that he could expect no change in the situation through the Department of State.[40]

In 1945, Galarza tried to more explicitly link the rights of braceros to the larger African American struggle for civil rights. He contacted private African American civil rights organizations, including the American Council on Race Relations (ACCR) and the Union for Democratic Action, claiming that "investigation and action must be taken to protect the reputation of the United States as a good neighbor and to protect American labor standards from the degrading effects of sweatshop wages and working conditions."[41] The ACCR replied that it preferred to "restrict its resources to the pressing field of Negro-white relations," and both organizations denied Galarza funding. Galarza then partnered with the historian George I. Sánchez at the University of Texas, to try to convince the ACCR to become involved in Mexican American race matters in the Southwest. After the ACCR refused to help, they both withdrew their membership from the organization. As Sánchez stated, "I, too, think that they should either begin doing more to help other racial or cultural groups or else frankly admit that their concern is for the Negro. A clarification of this matter would be very helpful to many of us who, though interested in the Negro, are specializing in some other group."[42] Mexican American scholars and activists like Sánchez and Galarza understood that the Black racial experience shared common traits with their own experiences. They tried to join Black and brown civil rights struggles by reaching out to the FEPC, ACLU, ACCR, and other organizations, but there were many hindrances to a conjoined Black/brown civil rights struggle in the 1940s and 1950s.[43]

As chief of the Office of Labor of the Pan-American Union (PAU), Galarza could have tried turning to the PAU to achieve his agenda of equal rights for braceros and Mexican Americans, but he noted in correspondence with McGurk that the PAU did not have the funds. Still, in 1945, Galarza decided to use his position at the PAU to visit over twenty labor camps and conducted over 200 personal interviews with braceros to write a report on the abuses of the bracero program. He also published a booklet on behalf of the Pan-American Union, written by Robert C. Jones, revealing the racism, terrible living standards, and unbridled exploitation of the program, which he sent to the press.[44] After the war was over, Galarza wanted to make sure every last Mexican worker "had been repatriated," with the best possible atti-tude towards the United States.[45] Since that never happened, he took more measures to ensure the protection of the workers under contract, believing that the federal government could responsibly enforce contract provisions.

In 1946, Galarza resigned from the Pan-American Union in Washing-ton, D.C., and became involved in the California farm labor movement.[46] He attended a farmworker convention in 1947, where he urged Hank Hasiwar and Bill Becker of the Southern Tenant Farmers' Union (STFU), a union started in 1934 in Arkansas to fight for the rights of sharecroppers and tenant farm-ers, to organize Mexican-origin workers. Sharing his democratic and anti-discriminatory outlook, the STFU named Galarza the director of research and education for the STFU, subsequently renamed the National Farm Labor Union (NFLU) in California. H. L. Mitchell remained president of the union in its transition from STFU to NFLU. Mitchell had been radicalized by his visits to Mexico in the 1930s, where he had witnessed the land tenure reforms of the Cárdenas regime. Together, he and other U.S. and Mexican reformers imagined how best to reverse U.S. rural poverty and inequality harnessing the possibilities of the New Deal moment to refashion the countryside.

Galarza's move to the NFLU was strategic, finally allowing him a chance to tackle his concerns regarding the bracero program hands-on. Galarza sought to change the program through policy reforms that would require growers to abide by the contract stipulations. If the contract could not be enforced—that is, if the braceros' civil rights could not be enforced—he would attempt to orga-nize braceros in the fields himself.[47] When Galarza joined the organization, NFLU members had done little to combine forces with ethnic Mexicans, and resented braceros because growers used them as replacement workers during their first strikes. Because of local farmworkers' increasingly racist resentment of Mexican agricultural workers, the NFLU leaders sent Galarza in to edu-cate them against racial prejudice, and to encourage Mexicans and Mexican

Americans to join the union. In his teaching endeavors, Galarza argued that local Mexican workers deserved full inclusion in the NFLU regardless of citizenship status, emphasizing the common cause of all workers.

When Galarza began to organize Mexican workers in California as part of the union, he found that any direct organizing had to be done in complete secrecy. He observed, "we couldn't get to them. I lost track of the number of times I was thrown out of the camp talking with braceros." He gave an example of how he tried to organize three hundred braceros in one camp ten miles west of Corcoran, California: "When I got to this camp I had to walk clear around the camp to find the gate in the barbed wire fence. I waited till evening and walked in, contacted some of the men and told them the strike was coming and please don't pick the cotton." Galarza would also pick up braceros as they were walking from the fields to the camp, or from the camp to the town, offering them a ride in exchange for a few words. He stated, "the men were afraid to talk to you. If they were seen talking with you in town they were spotted and changed to either another part of the state or sent home to Mexico." Galarza found that if he went to the Department of Labor to present a grievance on behalf of a contract worker, the department requested the name, employer, and the camp of his employer, then immediately reported that worker to his employer, who then would transfer him to another camp or request that he be "repatriated."[48]

In spite of the challenges, Galarza made every attempt to include braceros and undocumented workers in NFLU strikes. The first campaign Galarza helped to initiate on behalf of farmworkers in California was the thirty-two-month strike (1947–1950) against DiGiorgio Corporation, an agribusiness giant in the Central Valley that had the largest fruit-packing plant in the nation. Galarza and the NFLU had decided to focus on the Central Valley because it was one of the nation's top producers of labor-intensive crops and because they believed its majority-white constituency would gain political empathy from powerful whites in the region.[49] While Galarza included over one hundred thirty braceros and seventy undocumented workers in the strike, those who joined him were threatened with deportation or expelled from the country. DiGiorgio also employed new braceros as strikebreakers, a tactic that Galarza was unable to prevent. Galarza recalled: "The state was literally flooded with braceros while we were on strike and before the strike and after the strike. So everywhere we went we had to contend with these workers. . . . from 1948–1959, I participated in probably twenty strikes and always that was the problem. And if there were not enough braceros in the area to satisfy the growers that had replacements, they would bring them in from Mexico. After the strike started, with permission from the Department of Labor, they had no trouble getting permits for braceros."[50]

At the end of 1946, the U.S. government extended the bracero program until 1949, maintaining the broad outlines of the program but making growers responsible for worker recruitment and transportation—instead of the government. This administrative change resulted in bracero recruitment centers being moved from the interior of Mexico to facilities closer to the border. Meanwhile, undocumented immigration skyrocketed as growers were quick to hire "mixed crews" comprised of braceros, undocumented workers, and local Anglo-American farmworkers. By 1951, increased worker desertions on account of deteriorating wages and labor conditions in the Southwest led to a rising undocumented farm labor force.[51] The U.S. government began to accommodate growers by legalizing undocumented workers in a process referred to as "drying out the wetbacks." In this process, the INS would raid the fields, arrest undocumented workers, transport them to the border, and hand them over to officials of the Department of Labor, where U.S. officials promptly processed them as braceros and transported them back to the very fields where they had been arrested. This process was conceived and executed with the participation of growers and the Border Patrol, whereby the workers were encouraged to reach a toe across the border into Mexico and then allowed to immediately legalize their status in the United States as braceros. Galarza noted that even though federal immigration officers raided DiGiorgio multiple times, the raids were "not effective in eliminating their employment. . . . They reappear at the ranch and are again hired after they are arrested."[52] This practice demonstrates that the purpose of deporting "illegal" workers was not so much to get rid of them as to compel them to become legal contract workers, bringing them back within the bounds of state power.

Galarza became increasingly frustrated in his attempts to organize braceros and undocumented workers with the NFLU, finding the union ambushed at every turn by either new braceros or by undocumented workers. According to Galarza, "illegal workers" were a "formidable card" played against the union: "They do not speak English. They are completely ignorant of any legal obligations that the employer may have with respect to them. They cannot file claims of any kind because of their illegal status. They cannot invoke the protection of the Mexican consul. They are, in short, perfect strikebreakers."[53] It became difficult for Galarza and the NFLU to stress solidarity with

Figure 7. Group photo of members of the National Farm Labor Union. Courtesy of
Occidental College Library Special Collections.

braceros and undocumented workers when they obstructed their organizing
strategies. Instead of uniting with them, Galarza began to see them as part of
the problem U.S. agricultural workers faced. In October 1948, he attended
a meeting of the Confederación Proletaria Nacional/National Proletarian
Confederation (CPN) with the goal of uniting with Mexican unions to work
out a "joint program to combat discrimination against Mexican workers in
the United States and to attack the problems arising out of legal and illegal
migration between the two countries." Preventing "illegal" migration became
central to Galarza's strategy to combat discrimination against Mexican workers and ensure the fulfillment of their labor contracts.[54]

The NFLU's Transnational Labor Organizing Strategy

In late 1949 and early 1950, Galarza fashioned a new plan for the NFLU, and
rather than target a single large grower like DiGiorgio, confronted a cluster
of farms in the Imperial Valley that comprised the Imperial Valley Farmers Association. Galarza made El Centro, California, the new home of the
NFLU's "Labor Temple" and by 1950, he began to form transnational ties

with Mexican labor unions and the NFLU in an attempt to unionize braceros before they even left Mexico.[55] For Galarza, a large group of organized Mexican contract workers was an aspiration ever since he had first imagined a Mexican labor importation program. His original proposal for a labor importation program included the farmworkers' ability to join a union in order to uplift all farmworkers in the Southwest.

In January 1951, Galarza formed an alliance with farm labor unions in Mexico. Perceiving the labor contract as a vehicle for the rights of the bracero, the unions together sought contract compliance. Without the contract, they did not believe they could defend Mexican migrants' rights, so they focused on discouraging braceros from abandoning their contracts and encouraging them to report those who did. They contended braceros "will not skip contracts but stay and fight for compliance with them." They also maintained, "it should be understood that these duly organized braceros would be both whistleblowers and vigilantes of all illegal workers in the United States."[56] Both the NFLU and the Mexican labor unions surmised that, unless the unions could prevent "illegal immigration," their efforts would be pointless. As H. L. Mitchell, president of the NFLU, stated, "We have established cordial relations with organizations of farmworkers in Mexico seeking to prevent exploitation of Mexican nationals legally in the country, as well as American citizens. Recently an agreement was made by our union in the Imperial Valley of California with the Mexicali Farm Labor Union, across the border, for joint cooperation in organization and controlling the invasion of wetbacks from the interior of Mexico."[57]

Galarza first came into contact with Mexican labor unions as a field representative of the Joint United States-Mexico Trade Union Committee, AFL (founded in 1949), a majority democratic and anti-communist U.S. labor organization. As a branch of the Inter-American Regional Organization of Workers /Organización Regional Interamericana de Trabajadores (ORIT), this trade union committee met in Mexico in 1951 to combat the negative consequences of the bracero program. In particular, they resolved to "seek the full enjoyment of the right of Mexican braceros in the United States to organize and elect a representative as their bargaining agent" promised in Article 21 of the U.S.-Mexico Labor Agreement.[58] On February 7, 1951, while attending an ORIT meeting in Mexico City, Galarza and the NFLU signed a formal agreement for mutual assistance and cooperation with the Alianza Nacional de Braceros, an affiliate of the CPN. On March 9, 1951, the NFLU concluded a similar agreement with the Union de Trabajadores Agrícolas del Valle de

Mexicali (UTAVM), an affiliate of the official Mexican labor confederation, the Confederación de Trabajadores Mexicanos (CTM).[59]

The basic tenet of the agreements between Alianza and the NFLU was "the organization of contract workers into bona fide trade unions for the purpose of the enforcement of contracts." As Galarza explained to the Alianza, "the contracts written and ratified by the governments are not complied with because the bracero lacks the collective power to make them comply."[60] The NFLU in combination with the Alianza would give braceros that collective power, by integrating them into the rank-and-file of the NFLU as dues-paying members. Another agenda of the NFLU and Alianza was to serve as a grievance agency, providing assistance to the national governments on both sides of the border to guarantee compliance with the contract. Alianza assigned a delegate to "contact the Mexican consul in Fresno and needle him on violations, to see how fast and how far the union can take over." In their efforts to become a grievance agency, they heard complaints from braceros in Mexico, who presented them with violations of the contract provisions, upon which Alianza then contacted the Mexican consuls of the region where the contract violation occurred. Unfortunately, this strategy was not very effective, as consuls maintained that braceros had to personally present their complaints to the consulate to explain them. Alianza, the UTAVM, and the NFLU also tried to be present at meetings between the U.S. and Mexican states in the negotiation of the labor contract so that contract policy could be changed. It was clear from these efforts that the unions had confidence in the state, in international cooperation, and in the capacity of the contract to guarantee individual rights and equality. They insisted that the labor unions should have a voice in the negotiations and administration of the international labor importation agreement between Mexico and the United States to ensure the civil rights of the bracero.[61]

With the United States and Mexican governments leaving the unions out of all negotiations of a renewed contract agreement, Galarza moved the NFLU to gain control over the recruitment and the importation of Mexican labor or what he termed "the alien contract labor supply." In striving to ensure contract compliance or the civil rights of the bracero, Galarza also believed that they also had to eliminate the "wetback problem."[62] To tackle illegal immigration and "properly assure compliance" of the contract, Galarza argued they had to prevent contractors on the Mexican side of the border from contracting workers "illegally." Galarza began to see the labor contractors as the source of the problem of illegal migration: "midway between the corporate farm and the labor pools of illegals stands the private labor contractor. He is the Jekyll and Hyde character who operates as a private businessman and as a corporation employee simultaneously. He is the invisible, protected link between the employer and the illegal."[63] He sought to wrest control of recruitment from these labor contractors and place labor contracting in the hands of the union, to avoid the hiring of undocumented workers.

Galarza had learned many lessons from his attempts to inclusively organize braceros, undocumented workers, and U.S. workers at DiGiorgio Corporation in the Central Valley. He realized that any attempt that the U.S. and Mexican unions made to strike with unionized braceros would be pointless if they were replaced with undocumented workers. Taking for granted the federal government's capacity to enforce such distinctions, the NFLU and the Mexican labor unions together targeted undocumented workers as the core problem faced by the labor movement. This was demonstrated by an NFLU strike in which Galarza led over 5,000 farm workers in El Centro against Imperial Valley growers, from May 24 to June 25, 1951. The strike was against "wetback labor conditions imposed upon American workers" by the Imperial Valley Farmers Association, representing 489 of the largest growers in the United States. Local growers and police responded to this labor activity with a communist smear of the NFLU and with violence.[64]

The NFLU and the UTAVM then led a roadblock to prevent Mexican migrants from entering the United States, posting picket lines along the border and forcing truckloads of workers to turn around and go back to Mexico. On May 30, 1951, the local police arrested sixteen NFLU organizers for obstructing traffic in Calexico to prevent trucks carrying undocumented workers from entering the United States. Some union members spent nearly thirty days in jail. In one case, a truckload of braceros hit a union member, William Swearingen, who had sought to stop the truck before it crossed the border; in another, a picket line of thirteen American women in Calexico barred the way of "trucks loaded with wetbacks." According to a NFLU report entitled *Wetback Strike: A Report on the Strike of Farm Workers in the Imperial Valley of California*, these roadblocks were a success, reducing the total number of "wetbacks" in the area from 5,000 to 2,000. Despite the perceived success of these roadblocks, growers used 5,000 Mexican contract workers as strikebreakers, making braceros a "developing threat for the entire labor movement."[65] The actions of Galarza, the NFLU, Alianza, and UTAVM reveal that U.S. and Mexican organized labor worked alongside Border Patrol officials and the INS to shape the politics and governance of the border. As

Galarza responded when asked if he allowed "wetbacks" into the NFLU: "they filter in but we see they get out fast."[66]

In effect, growers' hiring practices during labor strikes, as supported by local police and the U.S. federal government, pitted unionized farmworkers in the NFLU against undocumented Mexican farmworkers, leading labor leaders to contribute to the racial construction of the "wetback." While growers effectively divided workers, it was labor's faith in liberalism that led them to fall into the divisive trap set for them, occluding the possibility of a more inclusive labor and civil rights movement. Just as undocumented workers became the condition of possibility for the liberties and rights claims of U.S. farmworkers, the freedom of U.S. labor became unattainable precisely because they refused to organize across the divides that they had helped to recreate in laying claim to rights. The NFLU, in collaboration with the Mexican labor unions, created a dialectic between civil rights and undocumented immigration in the 1950s. As an NFLU report on the DiGiorgio strikes stated, "Don't be fooled by DiGiorgio falsehoods! These strikers are trying to raise wages and better working conditions for ALL farm workers regardless of race, creed, or color."[67]

Distinguishing between legal versus illegal workers did not necessarily contradict the anti-discriminatory motto of the NFLU and the Mexican labor unions. The NFLU still had the vexed goal of achieving "equal rights" for Mexican migrants, even as they tried to prevent undocumented workers from entering the United States while excluding them from the union. Their attempts to secure farmworkers' rights demonstrate how a discourse of equality and freedom could be mobilized to exclude and racialize an entire group of people as a threat to "American" standards of labor. This threat found a name in the construction of the racialized figure of the "wetback," making race essential to labor's civil rights project.

By October 1951, Galarza's organizing efforts in the Imperial Valley had failed and the NFLU's lack of progress in organizing braceros in the United States led them to exclude braceros from their unionization efforts as well. While he had originally tried to convince his fellow union members that the Mexican contract workers were not the enemy and that they could be organized, Galarza came to see both braceros and undocumented workers as an impediment to organizing U.S. agricultural workers. Rather than organizing with braceros, he began to focus on research and the collection of evidence about the bracero program, resulting in the publication of his book, *Strangers in Our Fields*. As Galarza stated upon reflection about the Imperial Valley strikes, "it was clear that unless the bracero and wetback tide was turned back, domestic farm workers' efforts to organize were doomed in advance."[68] Dividing workers along domestic and foreign lines, using a rhetoric of civil rights, Galarza and other union members split the labor movement by race and nation, obviating an effective anti-imperial, transnational, inclusive, or collective critique of the labor importation programs.

In the NFLU strikes in the Imperial and Central Valleys, braceros and undocumented workers had their hands tied; they could not express solidarity with local farmworkers by joining strikes or refusing to cross picket lines because they could be deported or forced to become undocumented. If they became undocumented, they would be excluded from the labor movement with even less ability to defend their rights. U.S. labor's refusal to unite with braceros regardless of immigration status even further weakened the rights claims of braceros. The NFLU's focus on the rights of the contract forced domestic farmworkers to see undocumented migrants only as foreign competitors and the cause of lower wages—not as part of the same farmworker class. Again, it was their faith in the ability of the state to distinguish between legal and illegal workers and to protect the rights and equality of all workers under the contract that led them to that conclusion.

Ironically, the federal government was never quite as invested in organized labor as organized labor was in the federal government. The U.S. Department of Labor (USDL) and a group of growers met secretly with the Mexican government under President Miguel Aléman to negotiate and administer an agreement to extend the bracero program. This culminated in the signing of Public Law 78 in August 1951, extending all farm labor programs with the goal of alleviating the "perceived labor shortage" resulting from the Korean War (1950–1953).[69] The NFLU and the Mexican labor unions were kept out of the negotiations. When Galarza discovered that these meetings would take place, Galarza went to Mexico City and joined with Alianza in a public meeting to binationally discuss the labor program extension with the Mexican and American flags side by side. The Mexican government reacted with an assault on Alianza, intending to prosecute the executive board of the union. State police from the Secretaria de Relaciones Exteriores (SRE)/ Secretary of Foreign Relations arrested several Mexican unionists by order of the committee negotiating the new international agreement. The police would release them only if they agreed to cancel the scheduled meeting between the NFLU and Mexican unionists. The Mexican government then posted an attack on Alianza on the front page of Mexico City's newspaper, *El Tiempo*. It also prepared legal action, filing criminal charges against officials of Alianza and attempting to make it a crime for Mexican workers to cooperate with the AFL. The Mexican government soon moved to prosecute the Mexicali union (UTAVM) as well.[70]

The Mexican government sided with growers and the U.S. government, targeting specific leaders of the UTAVM by harassing and intimidating them, and threatening their lives. In March 1951, the Mexican government arrested the UTAVM leader Ignacio Marquez and his wife in Hermosillo, Mexico at the recruiting center for Mexican nationals, and charged them with conspiracy to organize Mexican farmworkers in cooperation with the NFLU. Illegal migration threatened to drain manpower from areas where it was needed in Mexico, jeopardizing the government's project of industrialization. Even though Mexican officials were just as opposed to the illegal migration of its citizens to the United States as labor leaders were, they did not want the labor unions taking a role in the management of the labor program.[71] Galarza contacted his friends in U.S. labor in great distress, taking personal responsibility: "the reason for this threat on our friends is that the Alianza executive board stood by me 100 percent when I was in Mexico City representing the AFL in the negotiations for nationals. . . . stress my point that the Mexican Government is making a drastic move against our friends in complete agreement with the policy of the Department of State." Mitchell sent a letter to the ACLU asking for their help, concerned that Marquez in particular might be sent to prison or murdered.[72]

In an August 1953 report entitled *The Use of Mexican Contract Nationals and Its Effects on the Employment of Domestic Agricultural Workers in the Imperial Valley of California,* the NFLU observed that the objective of the bracero program under Public Law 78 of 1951 had been to "prevent the displacement of domestic workers by foreign labor" and to "protect domestic standards of employment." According to Article 8 of PL 78, "Mexican workers shall not be assigned to work in localities in which Mexicans are discriminated against because of their nationality or their ancestry." As specified by Article 9, Mexican workers "shall not be employed in the United States in any jobs for which domestic workers can be reasonably obtained or where the employment of Mexican workers would adversely affect the wages and working conditions of domestic agricultural workers in the United States." This latter stipulation was designed "to guarantee that the domestic workers shall constitute the basic labor force and the Mexican nationals a supplementary one."[73] The central problem with the bracero program, the NFLU report explained, was that braceros and undocumented workers were taking jobs from U.S. labor and its constituents in violation of Public Law 78—not that growers and federal authorities were deliberately sponsoring contract violations that often forced braceros to go "illegal." The NFLU again framed its arguments around a hostile anti-immigrant rhetoric, even as they allegedly supported the civil rights of Mexican workers accorded by the contract. The NFLU concluded in August 1953 that hiring braceros and undocumented workers had negatively impacted American "work opportunities, working conditions, wages, and income," and that the NFLU should again have its own representatives take part in the negotiation of the farm labor agreements—an aspiration that was ironically forever denied them by federal authorities.[74]

Whose Civil Rights? From the Perspective of U.S. Labor

Since civil rights meant equal protection under the law, many labor unionists in the United States stressed the "rights" of individuals to receive equal treatment as guaranteed by the Fourteenth Amendment of the U.S. Constitution. Through their actions in the late 1940s and 1950s, "civil rights" came to signify appeals to federal state authority and a confidence in the state to intervene on behalf of individual rights. In 1946, President Truman's Committee on Civil Rights prepared a report titled *To Secure These Rights*. The report affirmed that "the central theme in our American heritage is the importance of the *individual person* . . . [as well as] a basic moral principle: all men are created equal as well as free." However, "*it is government* which must referee the clashes which arise among the freedoms of citizens and protect each citizen in the enjoyment of freedom to which he is entitled." It also stated, "there is no essential conflict between freedom and government."[75] Going even further than Roosevelt's Fair Employment Practices Committee (FEPC) designed to prohibit employment discrimination, Truman's civil rights commission declared the federal government the guardian of civil rights.

In 1951, President Truman also formed a President's Commission on Migratory Labor, formally designed to check "the extent of illegal entrance of foreign workers into the United States, and the way in which Government authority may be strengthened to eliminate illegal migration." Like the NFLU, Truman's commission focused on restricting the immigration of Mexicans without a labor contract. Before this commission, Truman argued, "the importation of Mexican nationals should not be used to the disadvantage of domestic farm workers who are attempting through their own efforts, to raise their standards to equal that of workers in other industries."[76] This echoed the AFL's civil rights arguments about braceros and undocumented Mexican farmworkers, which did not emphasize racial equality between Mexican and U.S. farmworkers so much as federal intervention toward class equality between U.S. farmworkers and U.S. workers in other industries. As Walter Mason, legal representative of the AFL, stated, "American citizens employed as agricultural migrants suffer degrading and un-American conditions of work and life. The wages that are paid and conditions of labor remain below any acceptable concept of an American standard."[77] According to the AFL, it was precisely labor imported from Mexico or "un-American" labor that had resulted in the degrading conditions of U.S. farm labor in the United States. This trend toward the foreign/domestic divide structured most of the AFL's debates on Southwest farm labor and the bracero program.

The Commission on Migratory Labor likewise concluded in its investigation that foreign labor depressed domestic wages and that domestic farm labor should be considered first before the importation of foreign workers, for the well-being and equality of U.S. farmworkers. As the original agreement had stated, the U.S. government first had to certify the growers' actual need for Mexican laborers, but the limited function of the USES gave growers unlimited power to determine labor recruitment and prevailing wage rates. Growers found that if they lowered wages sufficiently, domestic labor would not be willing to work, thus creating a superficial labor shortage that would lead the USDL to certify more braceros. As growers hired Mexican workers with impunity, the Congress of Industrial Organizations (CIO), like the AFL maintained, "a dramatic fight is being waged to bring a better life to American farmworkers." Toward this end, the CIO resolved, "We call upon Congress to take all the steps needed to insure the complete elimination of wetback labor in the U.S."[78]

In seeking either racial or class equality through the state, Galarza, the NFLU, the CIO and the AFL argued that undocumented Mexican workers and braceros were causing U.S. workers to lose their rights to life, liberty, and the pursuit of happiness. Their support of civil rights and protections for domestic workers led them to confirm popular assumptions about undocumented workers as a racial menace. According to the U.S. labor movement, the "wetback menace" was a "threat to national security, a weapon leveled at American wage and working standards by large employers of cheap labor in the South and Southwest." Their language was analogous to the ideology of the "yellow peril" embraced by U.S. labor unionists of the nineteenth century. Organized labor, stressing the sheer numbers of illegal entrants to the United States, viewed illegal immigration as an unmitigated evil, flooding the domestic labor market with cheap labor. At times, unions conflated illegal and contract labor, believing employers used both to keep wages down and unions out. They argued that both were forms of unfree labor, which was essentially "un-American labor," echoing an earlier generation of labor activists. The bracero thus became a "legal slave" and a "rented slave."[79]

The CIO in Washington maintained that "depending on foreign contract labor is hardly in accord with American ideals of equality and democracy." Yet the CIO and the AFL both stated: "[we are] not opposed to the importation of a limited numbers of foreign workers if and when there is a proven need for such labor importation. If there is a genuine need for agricultural labor, the Puerto Rican, Hawaiian, and domestic labor market should be fully utilized [first] before importing foreign labor."[80] U.S. organized labor did not disapprove of the U.S. capitalist system that validated state control and coercion over U.S. colonial workers—former or present. Rather, they vindicated the U.S. imperial practice of labor extraction as long as "domestic" workers—whether from the U.S. island colonies or the mainland—were considered first. The civil rights logic of U.S. organized labor produced an enhanced focus on citizenship, and therefore sharper strategies of exclusion, that facilitated and empowered U.S. state power.

The NFLU had stressed one of the main goals of the union in its struggle against the Imperial Valley Farmers Association was to ensure "the preferential hiring of American workers, prior to the employment of any Mexican national, legally or illegally, in the United States." A CIO pamphlet in April 1952 similarly argued that recruiting braceros over domestic workers "depressed the wage levels of our fellow citizens" and "lessened the amount of work available to them." The CIO urged Truman and Congress to put into effect the major recommendations of the President's Commission on Migratory Labor, including a minimum wage for agricultural labor and a constructive program for recruiting domestic workers. The CIO declared that "so long as 'wetbacks' flock in, they are a dangerous threat to American conditions."[81] As C. J. Haggerty, secretary-treasurer of the California State Federation of Labor-AFL claimed, "the AFL is under moral obligation to protect the living standards of all who work on our soil regardless of race, color, creed, or national origin." With this in mind, he continued, "the admission of Mexican farm hands without bilateral contract protection [illegals] is a dangerous blow aimed at both the American standard of living and the welfare of the Mexican workers."[82] They viewed undocumented migrants as an obstacle to their pursuit of civil rights and protections for all workers regardless of citizenship. Labor's opposition to undocumented workers was reflected by politically conservative elements, including Democratic U.S. Senator Patrick McCarran, most notable for his fervent anti-Communist national security campaign. As McCarran stated, "I take no issue with those who would praise the contributions which have been made to our society by people of many races, of varied creeds and colors. . . . [but] today, as never before, untold millions are storming our gates for admission and those gates are cracking under the strain.[83] It is no coincidence that soon after expressing pride in the United States' multiracial heritage and supposed racial inclusivity, McCarran subsequently stressed the necessity of immigration exclusion. Liberal inclusion and racist exclusion were so intertwined that they had become two sides of the same coin. This is not to say that McCarran was a race liberal, but rather that the anti-Communist Red Scare during the Cold War fueled a juxtaposition of racial liberalism and immigration restriction. The racialized assumption of anti-Communists that the Mexican border was "virtually an open door for subversives" was definitely a common theme for right wing political officials and the press, but it was also affirmed by labor liberals' larger vision of racial liberalism and civil rights, tenets that ultimately encouraged, inspired, and even required anti-immigrant hostility.[84]

Congress passed the McCarran-Walter Act in 1952, making guestworker programs a permanent feature of immigration policy. This act changed the ninth proviso of the Immigration Act of 1917 to allow for the admission of "temporary" imported contract workers. The act also prohibited citizens' arrests of unauthorized immigrants, a measure aimed at members of the NFLU, who, as mentioned, had begun citizens' arrests of undocumented workers at the border in 1951. As Galarza admitted, "citizens arrests had been used effectively in the Imperial Valley by members of the National Farm Labor Union in 1951."[85] This was paradoxical, considering that the NFLU had arrested undocumented workers under a creed of anti-discrimination, just as McCarran excluded nonwhite foreigners from "storming our gates" while celebrating the "contributions" of varied races to the United States. The epistemological construction of racial liberalism permitted conservatives and liberals alike to racialize and exclude noncitizens. In the end, the civil and labor rights movements' emphasis on civil rights and equality impeded them from questioning border politics and national belonging as a barrier to equal treatment for all, with long-term impact. Even at the bracero program's demise in 1964, the AFL-CIO, various Chicano/a groups, and other community organizations opposed it by arguing that the program harmed low-income domestic workers.[86]

In the end, neither the United States nor Mexican union efforts to improve conditions for braceros bore fruit organizationally in the 1950s.[87] Adhering to claims of liberal freedoms invested in rights through the state contributed to the failure of their efforts to produce equality for Mexican and U.S. farmworkers. When Galarza was interviewed years later in the 1980s, he did not view the 1950s outlook of the union as exclusionary or limiting: "The strategy of our union was based upon bringing about the termination of the bracero program, and then to bring about legislation concerning wetbacks. . . . our view was not to exclude wetbacks."[88] The civil rights-led ideology and actions he and others in the labor movement supported nonetheless led to the exclusion of braceros and undocumented Mexican migrants from the civil and labor rights movements.

After the NFLU's failures in the Imperial Valley, Galarza's new strategy was to storm Congress to condemn the flow of illegal labor linked to the bracero program. Galarza argued that "illegal labor" resulted in the deterioration of wages and treatment for all farmworkers, even as it hindered the efforts of unions. At a July 12, 1954, congressional hearing titled "To Control Illegal Immigration," Galarza argued for the passage of S. 3660, a bill designed to "make the employment . . . of any alien known by an employer to have entered the United States illegally . . . unlawful." Yet Galarza also identified with undocumented migrants at the hearing, stating, "I was probably the original wetback." He acknowledged the suffering and exploitation that "border jumpers" faced and expressed concern over their well-being. As he asserted, "the illegal immigrant is . . . forced to work under conditions approaching peonage, and he is at the same time used to undermine the living standards and job security of American citizens." As a result, Galarza argued that that the only way to secure adequate standards for U.S. citizens was to prevent "illegals" from coming to the United States. Galarza referred to the close relationship between the bracero program "and wetback traffic," but reasoned that this would change if government agencies could effectively protect "national security" by preventing "illegal" immigration.[89]

At the 1954 hearing, Galarza and the NFLU listed all the ways the USDL had failed to adequately administer and manage the bracero program and the labor contract, while also calling out the department's collusion with U.S.

growers and their labor contractors. As Galarza stated, "we do not under-stand why the Department of Labor has not taken disciplinary measures with those farm labor contractors who have been found hiring wetbacks." Galarza further referred to Mexican migrants as a "tide of dispossessed and hungry millions" that could only be assuaged if both Mexico and the United States worked on a solution to improve the economies on both sides of the border.[90] While he approved of the proposed legislation to make illegal the employ-ment of an "alien," he also argued that it would not be enough, for "where will these tides of impoverished peasants turn once we have raised a dike against them?" At the hearing, Galarza again recommended his 1941 vision of a cross-border U.S.-Mexican New Deal that he believed would make it unnecessary for Mexicans to migrate to the United States illegally. This time, Galarza called his statist solution the Joint Rio Grande Valley Public Inter-national Authority. This agency, Galarza suggested, would demonstrate "our democratic sincerity," and eventually remove the need for S. 3660 as a legal intervention against undocumented migrants because it would ensure the benefits of the labor contract.[91] At the hearing, Galarza concluded that he did not want to exclude undocumented workers, but had been forced to support that position in order to ensure the rights of all workers.

Exclusion was not the only possible outcome in the debates over braceros and "rights" in the 1950s. As Galarza's early efforts to collectively organize California farmworkers together with braceros indicate, a more inclusive organizing strategy was possible. The American Committee for the Protec-tion of the Foreign Born (ACPFB), for example, linked the rights of Mexican "aliens" and braceros with the civil rights of Mexican Americans. They argued in a 1959 petition that "the difficulties faced by the bracero reflect the prob-lems faced by the average Mexican American." They refused to recognize any distinction between citizen and noncitizen, instead highlighting their shared state of insecurity resulting from discrimination, segregation, and deporta-tion. Likewise, the farm labor activist Dolores Huerta argued at a 1960 con-gressional hearing, "the level to which farm labor has sunk leaves little room for human rights or dignity." Noting the insufficient wages and ill treatment of braceros, Huerta continued, "We should let these people come in as resi-dents and be citizens instead of having a captive labor supply."[92]

By the late 1950s, some Mexican Americans began to realize the vital con-stitutional, legal, and moral stakes they held with regard to the immigration question, noting that all Mexicans feared the state or "los Federales" regard-less of citizenship status. Being aware of the racist dimensions of immigration policy encouraged them to develop a broader sense of community solidarity with noncitizens, increasingly holding their government responsible rather than holding immigrants responsible. Organizations like the ACPFB initiated a radical new basis for political organization and mobilization that not only eclipsed but criticized the federal government for its role in maintaining a system of racist exclusion. However, most Mexican American organizations, including LULAC and the G.I. Forum, continued to proudly proclaim their commitment to American ideals and values, as well as their support of strict border control and the restriction of future immigration from Mexico, up until the mid-1970s.[93]

The anti-Communist Red Scare led to a robust attack against undocumented workers as a potential security risk that culminated in Operation Wetback.[94] Yet white supremacy and Cold War politics alone do not explain this massive racial expulsion. Civil rights had become so entrenched with "nation," under the tutelage of liberal labor advocates and policymakers, that an extension of rights to anyone outside the nation was viewed as an impediment. After the bracero program had ended, César Chávez and the United Farm Workers Union (UFW), like the NFLU, faced the problem of growers routinely employing undocumented Mexican migrants to break strikes. In response, in the 1970s the UFW formed union patrols on the U.S.-Mexico border or "wet lines" where they policed a main crossing on the U.S. border, with some members violently beating people trying to cross into the United States.[95] This was no contradiction to civil rights, as the exclusion of noncitizens had become the pre-condition for the argument that domestic farmworkers should have their rights and that those rights should be protected. Another result was that domestic civil rights and immigrant rights were often disaggregated as separate issues, dissuading leading labor advocates from including undocumented Mexican migrants in their struggles, and occluding them from making a critique of national belonging through the 1970s.

*   *   *

The link between civil rights and the individual rights of the contract was so powerful that it catalyzed a new generation of guestworker labor importations in the 1950s. Because Operation Wetback increased growers' fears of a labor shortage yet again, growers looked to other sources of workers. This time, growers again considered expanding labor programs with Puerto Rico and the British West Indies, as well as the Philippines and Japan, hoping to establish new programs that were not as mired in bureaucracy or red tape as the bracero program had become. Based on the McCarran-Walter Act, growers could legally create "guestworker" programs without the auspices of wartime necessity, and without the need for formal bilateral agreements with sending countries. From 1950 to 1960, the number of braceros in the United States increased two-fold. Meanwhile, labor importation programs with Puerto Rico and British West Indies each committed a steady supply of about 12,000–14,000 every year in the 1950s.[96]

In 1956, the United States also began to slowly import Japanese workers, from 390 in 1956; 990 in 1957; 1,200 in 1958; 1,560 in 1959; to 1,830 in 1960. Starting in 1957, the U.S. government also recruited a small number of Filipinos, with about thirty Filipino contract farmworkers employed in any given month in California.[97] The Department of Labor imported these workers to the United States "for the purpose of education in American farming methods," but the workers were used to alleviate growers' fears of a labor shortage as the Mexican government increasingly threatened to end bracero labor in the early 1960s.[98] The benefit of these new Japanese and Filipino labor importation programs for growers was that when these workers were dissatisfied or mistreated, they had no means to exercise their "freedom" by returning home, as Mexican workers did.

The Japanese Agricultural Workers' Program or SAW (supplementary agricultural worker) program drew the same response that the bracero program had received from organized labor. Again, labor unions argued for the protection of "free" American labor from "unfree" foreign labor by standing against the exploitation of and discrimination against foreign workers, "regardless of race, color, creed or national origin." They also appealed to the slave/free dialectic, as an AFL-CIO member stated, "the existing Japanese farm labor importation program is a despicable form of colonial wage slavery. No program is more Un-American."[99] Galarza similarly argued that the recruitment of these new foreign workers was "a danger to organized labor." From his point of view, the Mexican labor importation program was preferable because it at least had "some semblance of legal and administrative orderliness." He further explained, "Some argue [the Japanese Labor Program] is a fine demonstration of international good will. They will receive a fine technical education in farming while here . . . we heard this before and it did not work out. A foreign contract worker is essentially an indentured worker."

Just as Galarza noted the coercion of the contract, so did workers from Japan. As a group of seventy-eight farmers "returned" to Japan stated, "We found the United States no land of liberty." As one contract farm worker, Mitsuo Sato of Nikaho, stated, "I have lived a slave's life for three years on a farm near Yuba city." Not unlike braceros, Japanese SAW workers lamented their treatment and argued for the legitimacy and implementation of their labor contracts and their rights. Galarza and other labor leaders agreed; they, too, sought the equal treatment of contract workers that their labor contracts specified. Yet they could not escape the exclusionary impulse of national belonging and rights, maintaining that the new labor programs "prevented American farmworkers from enjoying the benefits of federal legislation" on labor.[100] By the efforts of U.S. labor, foreign contract workers had become both friends and foes, "guests" and "aliens," the necessary condition for the notion of farmworker civil rights and freedom that had been catalyzed and reframed through the labor importation programs all along.

CHAPTER 5

Boricua Braceros: The New Deal and the U.S.-Puerto Rican Farm Labor Program

Soon after Mexican labor importation began in August 1942, U.S. laymen and officials, growers' farm bureau federations, and individual growers on the East Coast clamored for a Puerto Rican farm labor program on par with the Bracero Program. The large number of unemployed workers in Puerto Rico also convinced many New Deal reformers that the United States should use its military ships to transport farmworkers from Puerto Rico to meet labor needs, alleviate poverty and unemployment on the island, and strengthen the military defense of the Western Hemisphere. The U.S. governor of Puerto Rico, Rexford Tugwell (1941–1946), supported these demands for a Puerto Rican version of the bracero program as a means to achieve economic and job stability in Puerto Rico. Tugwell had long been committed to New Deal reform on the island and had founded the U.S. Resettlement Administration (RA) and its Puerto Rican version—the Puerto Rico Reconstruction Administration (PRRA)—in 1935. Preeminent in Tugwell's mind was the need to advance the island away from the legacy of slavery toward a new, more democratic form of colonialism. In a critique of plantation agriculture, Tugwell stated, "Everyone knows how and when the African tribesmen came eastward across the Atlantic. . . . it is a sheer brutal economic monopoly that exists, long established and ruthlessly maintained, coming directly down, indeed from the days of slavery, and not immensely improved in all respects since then."[1]

Tugwell and the director of the War Manpower Commission (WMC), Paul McNutt, worked together to establish a United State Employment Service (USES) on the island and a Puerto Rican farm labor program, using a contract modeled on the Mexican labor contract. This brief Puerto Rican program ended after one year in 1944, but the recruitment of Puerto Rican agricultural workers by private companies continued until 1947, when the Puerto Rican government began a transition toward purported self-rule. In 1947, Puerto Rican officials constructed a large-scale contract farm labor program as part of the Puerto Rican state project known as Manos a la Obra or Operation Bootstrap (1947–1965), to modernize and develop the island's economy. Under the careful tutelage of Puerto Rico's first elected governor, Luis Muñoz Marín, and his administration, Operation Bootstrap gained legitimacy as a democratic attempt to end colonial subordination in Puerto Rico, and a potential pathway to self-determination. Puerto Rican officials argued that the welfare of the individual Puerto Rican worker was essential to economic progress on the island, and they became intent on building a strong Puerto Rican state to protect workers' rights.

Like the Mexican labor contract and agreement, liberalism configured the Puerto Rican labor program, as it promised freedom for workers through a set of rights and regulations governing their treatment and made the migration of Puerto Ricans to the United States seem to be a state-sanctioned act of individual free will. An important difference, however, was that Mexico was a sovereign liberal nation-state and Puerto Rico was a territorial possession of the United States. Powerful anticolonial political radicalism and labor unrest on the Caribbean islands, amplified by the Great Depression and World War II, convinced U.S. and British colonial officials to embark on policies of welfare amelioration within a capitalist framework throughout the Caribbean, often to protect their economic and security interests on the islands.[2] The ideological turn toward anti-imperialism with the Good Neighbor Policy and rights consciousness or racial liberalism led U.S. officials to refashion and modernize colonial governance on the island so as to grant Puerto Rican people "freedom" while allowing the island to remain a colonial possession of the United States.

Yet the granting of self-determination to Puerto Rico through popular political elections (self-government) and later a contract labor program (in place of unilateral or private contract labor recruitment) concealed the many ways in which Puerto Rico's colonial relationship with the United States remained unchanged. The language of "bootstraps" speaks to the nature of this unchanged colonial relationship, as it placed the burden of Puerto Rico's subordinate economic position onto Puerto Ricans themselves, relieving the United States of its historical role in stunting the island's economy. If Puerto Ricans were at fault, then they should assume responsibility by "pulling themselves up by their bootstraps" and transforming their presumed lack of progress and racial backwardness through a strong work ethic that proved they were capable of self-government. The liberal universalism and extension of rights to Puerto Ricans characteristic of Operation Bootstrap thus simultaneously racialized Puerto Ricans as backward and inferior and elided the history of U.S. colonialism on the island.

By the time of Puerto Rico's newly ordained Commonwealth status as a "free associated state" in 1952, the Puerto Rican contract farm labor program was in full force, with officials encouraging the voluntary migration of contract workers using a rhetorical strategy of national "freedom" and "*patria*." The Puerto Rican government of the 1950s prompted migrants to sign contracts voluntarily as patriots of Puerto Rico, performing a civic duty to *la patria*. Puerto Rican officials upheld both liberalism and patriotism to promote the Puerto Rican farm labor program as a real contribution to democracy, in much the same way that U.S. and Mexican officials had promoted the bracero program to Mexicans during and after World War II.[3]

U.S. officials supported the Puerto Rican farm labor program as an effort toward "self-rule," and had long trained Puerto Rican officials in New Deal principles of liberal state governance. From the 1930s to the 1940s, New Deal liberalism became a normative project in Puerto Rico, as it marked the terms of what was acceptable or unacceptable in state rule. It was a new instrument of "civilization," so to speak, which could uplift formerly colonial populations by granting them a new regime of autonomous choices and self-determination. Puerto Rican governor Luis Muñoz Marín and his administration drew heavily on their New Deal training and knowledge, acquired at U.S. universities, and the earlier efforts of Governor Tugwell, to construct the 1947 Puerto Rican guestworker program.

Heading the management of the new program was Fernando Sierra Berdecía, close friend and ally of Governor Muñoz Marín and the Popular Democratic Party (PPD). In 1947, Sierra Berdecía became head of the Puerto Rican Department of Labor (PRDL); on a quest for workers' welfare he authorized the expansion of Puerto Rican government authority over workers as he focused on securing jobs for the unemployed. He maintained that the role of the Puerto Rican government was to guarantee basic rights for laborers, especially the labor migrant. To legitimize the PRDL's expanded role over Puerto Rican workers, Sierra Berdecía pointed to the problematic history of Puerto Rican contract workers being recruited by private contractors to work on farms in the United States, deceiving and exploiting workers. He argued that the lack of state management of the contract and labor migrations had resulted in such abuses, and proposed that the state should step in as an intermediary to protect Puerto Rican workers' welfare and rights.

In response to Sierra Berdecía's call for the state regulation of contract labor, the Puerto Rican government created Law 89 on May 9, 1947, "An Act to regulate contracts for workmen or employees whose services are to be used in any State of the American Union, in territories thereof, or in any foreign country."[4] The law required labor contractors to register with the PRDL and authorized the department to regulate labor contracts—giving the insular government the expanded power to intervene on behalf of workers. Sierra Berdecía also recommended the enactment of Law 25 on December 5, 1947, establishing the Bureau of Employment and Migration (BEM) to govern a contract labor program. The autonomous endeavor on behalf of the Puerto Rican government to intervene in U.S. colonial labor recruitment and prevent the exploitation of workers by U.S. employers gave the island an appearance of proceeding on a path to decolonization.

While many scholars have written in depth about the role of the U.S. empire and state power in the establishment of the Puerto Rican guestworker program, few have examined the Puerto Rican farm labor program from the perspective of the other U.S. labor programs from which it emerged or through the lens of liberalism.[5] Anthropologist Ismael García-Colón and historian Edgardo Meléndez have exposed how migration policy was at the center of nationalist government reform efforts in Puerto Rico during the late 1940s, when the Puerto Rican government took upon itself the role of protecting migrants to the United States. As García-Colón argues, the "successful insertion of Puerto Rican officials into the sphere of the U.S. federal government" to manage labor migration was a distinctive feature of Puerto Rican "modern colonialism" beginning in the 1940s.[6] It is important to view the labor programs relationally and from the ideological perspective of liberalism, because to focus on modern colonialism can obscure the processes through which the Puerto Rican government, regardless of colonial "status," engaged in an imperial project of state-building. Framing the labor programs as products of modern colonialism can thus conceal the multiple and overlapping processes of state expansion by which workers become subject to state power. It can also elide how "nation" is intimately tied to empire, and erase how these labor programs were justified and pursued as anticolonial measures.

Viewing the Puerto Rican labor program from the perspective of the other labor programs with Mexico and the British West indies reveals that the particular logic of liberalism that emerged in Puerto Rico in the 1940s and 1950s was not new but originated in New Deal efforts to create a new anti-colonial order across the hemisphere. The labor programs were indicative of this new order and can demonstrate how liberal nation-state governance was accomplished at this time. Instead of this being a history of the U.S. government co-opting or accommodating Puerto Rican elites, or of "inclusionary colonialism," Puerto Rican state officials of the PPD imagined Puerto Rico's economy and governance on their own terms and were not mere instruments of U.S. hegemony. It is therefore important to examine how Puerto Rican officials engaged with this modern form of liberalism to create their own national projects with the goal of expanding Puerto Rican state power.[7] Their efforts resulted in competing and overlapping projects of imperialism and state-building that did not rival but contested and coalesced with those emerging in the United States at the same time.

In the late 1940s and early 1950s, the ideological bedrock of New Deal liberalism and racial liberalism justified the expansion of Puerto Rican state power over contract workers as an anti-imperial and benevolent measure, obscuring the processes by which Puerto Rican workers became racialized subjects of the Puerto Rican and U.S. governments. By the 1960s, the United States labeled Puerto Rico's development model, Operation Bootstrap, a success, and used Puerto Rico as a "showcase" of democracy and economic improvement for all Caribbean islands and for Latin America, sustaining the notion that labor contract programs could provide a pathway to "freedom" on the islands throughout the remainder of the twentieth century.

The Brief World War II Puerto Rican Labor Program

The World War II Puerto Rican farm labor program emerged from the same spirit and embrace of New Deal liberalism that had inspired Ernesto Galarza to defend a Mexican labor importation program. While it lasted for only about one year, it resulted from Governor Tugwell's commitment to reforming U.S. colonialism in Puerto Rico, which took on greater significance as part of his relationship with sugar-magnate and fellow Roosevelt adviser, Charles Taussig. From 1932 to 1936, Tugwell was one of Roosevelt's top advisers in agriculture and rural life, as undersecretary to Secretary Henry Wallace of the Department of Agriculture (USDA). Tugwell was a Columbia University economist who had earned renown by the early 1930s as a prominent critic of uncon-strained capitalism and proponent of state intervention in agriculture. In the process of creating the U.S. and Puerto Rican RA, Tugwell traveled to Mexico City and met with a team of leading figures in the Mexican revolutionary rul-ing party, joining them on inspections of rural communities outside Mexico City after the Mexican Revolution. Taking what he learned in Mexico about revolutionary agrarian reform back with him to the United States and Puerto Rico, he pioneered a land reform and agricultural diversification program that had an undeniable long-term impact on the Caribbean basin.

When the RA temporary closed its U.S. office, Tugwell left his position at the USDA to become vice president of the American Molasses Company or "Grandma's Molasses," owned by Taussig and his family. In 1937, Presi-dent Roosevelt commissioned Tugwell and Taussig to go on a "fact-finding trip" in the Caribbean, visiting islands from St. Thomas to Trinidad. At this time, violent labor unrest, riots, and colonial uprisings took place across the Caribbean, especially in Saint Kitts, Barbados, Trinidad, Jamaica, and Brit-ish Guiana.[8] Upon their return, Tugwell and Taussig reported to President Roosevelt about the alarming violence, widescale poverty, unemployment, and worker abuse they had noticed throughout the Caribbean. Taussig feared that widespread unrest would prompt U.S. intervention, upsetting the diplo-matic balance in Latin American set by the Good Neighbor Policy. Taussig recommended to Roosevelt a reformist anticolonial stance, in which the United States would tacitly acknowledge its colonial past and redress it in the construction and conduct of its military presence, while cooperating with the British for economic reform on the islands. Taussig also recommended a "joint commission" designed to improve the economy and raise the islands' standard of living.[9] Like Galarza, Taussig highlighted the need for U.S. state intervention to improve local economies, ensure the welfare of Caribbean peoples, and quiet colonial upheaval. Unlike Galarza, however, Taussig owned sugar plantations in the region, making it a personal imperative for him to construct an alternative capitalist economic order on the islands that would assuage colonial unrest and protect his business interests.

In March 1941, Roosevelt followed Taussig's advice that the United States should take the lead in improving Caribbean social and economic conditions, especially given its agreement with Great Britain to build new military bases in six British Caribbean colonies in 1940. Shortly thereafter, he made Tugwell the U.S. governor of Puerto Rico. In November 1941, Roosevelt sent Taussig to the Caribbean as chair of a commission to investigate the social and political climate in the British West Indies, forced by "practical considerations, including those of humanity." Taussig made a study of the social and economic conditions of the West Indies at this time. During the survey and reports that followed, Great Britain and the United States found that they shared interests in the problems of the Caribbean, resulting in the formation of the Anglo-American Caribbean Commission (AACC) on March 9, 1942.[10] The AACC set out to reform colonial matters, so as to "encourage responsibility of the overseas people in matters of common social and economic interest." Given the raucous anticolonial surges in the Caribbean, the AACC aimed to encourage self-governance on the islands, improve labor conditions, uplift and rehabilitate the Caribbean populations, and reduce unemployment through Anglo-American aid and tutelage. As stated in a joint announcement in March 1942, the commission members would "concern themselves primarily with matters pertaining to agriculture, housing, health, education, social welfare, finance, economic and related subjects in the territories under the British and United States flags."[11]

Puerto Rican governor Rexford Tugwell became the second-ranking U.S. member of the AACC upon its creation in 1942; Taussig and Britain's colonial secretary took the helm as co-chairs.[12] Inspired by Taussig's efforts in the AACC, Tugwell attempted to imitate some of its social reform efforts in Puerto Rico. Inspired by the efforts of the AACC to establish a contract farm labor program agreement between the U.S. and Jamaica, Tugwell recommended to the WMC a "Puerto Rican Land Army" in the employ of the U.S. government, "which would be used for planting and harvesting." Tugwell was hopeful that a Puerto Rican USES could recruit a large number of Puerto Rican farmworkers in land army units at "reception centers," and then "dispatch" them to areas in the United States where they were needed to harvest crops. Tugwell argued that Puerto Ricans were U.S. citizens who should be considered for employment as agricultural workers in the United States during the war, especially in light of increasing labor shortages in the United States and the unemployment problem in Puerto Rico.[13] After his 1937 trip with Taussig and his experience as a member of the AACC, Tugwell became even more committed to colonial reform in Puerto Rico. He supported a Puerto Rican version of the bracero program during World War II as a means to achieve economic uplift and job stability in Puerto Rico.[14]

Tugwell contacted multiple state officials to create a USES office of the USDL in San Juan, requesting the application of the Wagner-Peyser Act to Puerto Rico and the "funds to provide personnel for this purpose." In 1933,

New Deal senator Robert F. Wagner had sponsored the Wagner-Peyser Act, establishing the USES as part of the Department of Labor; the resulting system of public employment offices offered employment assistance to unemployed U.S. citizens. During World War II, the USES shifted function to recruit workers to replace agricultural laborers who had entered the armed forces or industry. Tugwell wrote to Maj. Gen. James L. Collins and Lt. Gen. Somervell of the U.S. War Department, arguing "The [USES] be established in Puerto Rico before the growing unemployment problem becomes much more acute." Lt. Gen. Somervell agreed with Tugwell, writing to the WMC that a branch of the USES on the island would be a "Real contribution to the war effort in the Caribbean." He further stated, "It is anticipated that Puerto Rico will become a source from which manpower can be recruited."[15]

As Tugwell became increasingly impatient with the plodding approach of the multiple state officials he contacted, he complained to WMC chairman McNutt, "I have recently read that the WMC has agreed to import ten thousand workers from Jamaica. This is in addition to Bahamians and Mexicans already imported. Naturally, I cannot help wondering why the WMC continues to ignore the Puerto Rican labor supply [as citizen labor]." In the meantime, Tugwell encouraged the unilateral and private recruitment of Puerto Rican workers by U.S. employers to alleviate seasonal unemployment.[16] Tugwell's connections, including Maj. Gen. Collins, McNutt, and the WMC official George Cross investigated the feasibility of Puerto Rican contract labor recruitment through February 1943. As a result of the efforts of Governor Tugwell and McNutt, the WMC established a USES office in Puerto Rico in June 1943, with the principal objective of recruiting Puerto Ricans as laborers for the mainland United States. In June 1943, eighty-six Puerto Ricans arrived in Baltimore as skilled "war applicants" who were capable of paying their own transportation, albeit at a reduced rate.[17]

Besides the difficulty of transporting such a large group of workers, the citizenship status of Puerto Ricans became an impediment to the successful initiation of a Puerto Rican farm labor program. After the Jones Act of 1917 granting Puerto Ricans citizenship, they could freely enter the mainland and were broadly eligible for employment even though they were racially marked by employers as "aliens" or "foreigners." Given Puerto Ricans' unique status as citizens, many U.S. officials feared that after being brought to the United States they would not return to the island.[18] To assuage U.S. fears of Puerto Ricans staying in the United States, WMC officials wrote a "Draft of Proposed Language for Incorporation in Contract to Assure Return of Puerto

Rican Workers." The proposed language stipulated that "the worker will not transfer to other employment without the consent of the WMC" and "the Worker agrees to return to Puerto Rico upon termination of his employment." This draft language also stated that if the worker did not apply to the USES nearest to his last place of employment for return transportation to Puerto Rico within seven days of the termination of his contract, he would have to pay to the United States government a sum equal to the cost or value of his transportation to and from the United States. Puerto Rican congressman Bolivar Pagán, aware of the racial fears surrounding the threat of non-deportability of Puerto Ricans as citizen labor, also proposed a bank fund by which a portion of Puerto Ricans' earnings might be held for them in Puerto Rico, like that which had been set up for Mexican migrant workers.[19]

Despite the racial fears of Puerto Ricans staying permanently in the United States, the USES sent them. From June to December 1943, over 1,000 Puerto Rican farmworkers went to the United States under contracts that modeled the Mexican labor contract as an experimental program devised by the AACC, the WFA, and the USES. Puerto Ricans shared a similar experience to Mexican contract workers, despite their access to citizenship. The U.S. Supreme Court case *Downes v. Bidwell* (1901) had long rendered Puerto Ricans "foreign in a domestic sense."[20] Scholars have shown the importance of "alien exclusion" in defining Puerto Ricans as outside of the bounds of full citizenship through legal, cultural, and racial means, to prevent their equal incorporation into the United States. As historian Sam Erman argues, Puerto Ricans have been "almost citizens," neither citizens nor aliens, with Puerto Rico in a liminal position that is neither foreign nor domestic.[21]

While Puerto Ricans' ambiguous citizenship status did not render them as "deportable" as Mexican contract workers, the exploitation they faced led many Puerto Rican workers to return to the island in the face of hostile local communities.[22] According to the WMC, the 1943–1944 Puerto Rican contract farm labor experiment spearheaded by Tugwell was a failure because 60 percent left their contracts, with 15 percent returning to Puerto Rico. The WMC blamed Puerto Ricans for the catastrophe, but a representative had visited several camps and found unlivable housing conditions, deductions from wages, lack of medical service, lack of cleanliness, and spoiled food. The labor importation was thereafter discontinued and the Puerto Rican office of the USES closed on June 30, 1944.[23]

The 1943–1944 World War II Puerto Rican labor program emerged contemporaneously with the British West Indies labor programs and the bracero program, but it was not the first contract labor program in Puerto Rico. Since the early 1900s, U.S. colonial officials, companies, and employers (private agencies, crew leaders, and growers) had unilaterally and privately recruited and hired Puerto Rican laborers under contracts to work in the United States, without governmental interference.[24] Private contract labor recruitment had occurred in San Juan and Ponce since Puerto Rico had first become a U.S. colony, with employers attracted by the fact that the 1885 Foran Act prohibited only the employment of "foreign" contract labor, and could not be applied to Puerto Rico due to its status as a colony of the United States. Some private employers literally coerced and kidnapped Puerto Ricans onto steamships early on, with Puerto Ricans landing in places as far off as Honolulu. Others went to great lengths to migrate as contract laborers, even though they found unbearable working conditions upon arrival on the mainland or Hawai'i. Many Puerto Rican contract workers refused to tolerate working conditions and sent petitions for redress to the governor of Puerto Rico, who in turn forwarded their complaints to the Department of the Interior in Washington.[25]

U.S. officials of the short-lived World War II Puerto Rican Farm Labor Program attempted to reform U.S. colonialism on the island. The status of Puerto Rican laborers as citizens, however, proved a double-edged sword, as their citizenship status made them uniquely eligible for contract labor recruitment at the same time that it limited U.S. control over their movements. When the USES closed in Puerto Rico in 1944, private U.S. contract recruiters continued to visit the island on an individual basis to encourage workers to migrate to the mainland for work without federal assistance, as they had formerly done. Advertisements by these employers filled Puerto Rican newspapers, and many opened semi-permanent offices on the island in the early 1940s to recruit Puerto Rican labor.[26] That private U.S. recruiters were coming to the island without state management would become a major problem for the Puerto Rican government by 1947, resulting in a distinct shift in the management of Puerto Rican labor after World War II.

The New Puerto Rican Farm Labor Program

During the 1930s and 1940s, U.S. colonial officials, including Tugwell, embraced a distinct diplomatic approach to the island of Puerto Rico, seeking to educate Puerto Ricans on self-government. Tugwell's role at the AACC reinforced his push for reform of the status in which the United States held Puerto Rico as a colony, as well as for further reform of the island's economy. While Tugwell embraced the logic of "freedom" to foster the revised administration of U.S. governance in the Caribbean, he was against Puerto Rican separatism. Tugwell wanted to make sure that Congress would no longer act unilaterally toward island political officials, but also hoped to improve the laboring economy of Puerto Rico through U.S. aid and intervention, which he believed would not be possible after separation and independence. With the Atlantic Charter and conferences at Dumbarton Oaks and San Francisco denouncing colonialism, as well as the establishment of the United Nations, many U.S. and Puerto Rican officials began to envision a future beyond U.S. colonialism. As Governor Tugwell indicated in his book *Stricken Land: The Story of Puerto Rico* (1946), "We were trying to make the United Nations organization work."[27] In giving Puerto Rican officials control over the management of the economy and labor of Puerto Rico, the United States attempted to mold a self-governed Puerto Rican nation with a governing role in partnership with the United States.

Even as U.S. officials planned a farm labor importation program with Puerto Rico, President Roosevelt decided in March 1943 to recommend to Congress "an amendment to the Organic law of Puerto Rico which will permit the Puerto Rican people to elect their own governor, and will redefine the functions and powers of the Federal Government of Puerto Rico, respectively." Roosevelt established a committee with "an equal number of Puerto Ricans and continental residents," which met in Washington from July 19 to August 7, 1943. This committee included U.S. Secretary of the Interior Harold Ickes as chairman, Abe Fortas, Rexford Tugwell, Father Raymond A. McGowan, Luis Muñoz Marín, and others. The committee unanimously agreed "that the people of Puerto Rico be given an opportunity to exercise freely the powers of local government and to elect their own Governor."[28] In 1946, President Truman relieved Governor Tugwell and appointed Jésus T. Piñero as governor, the first native Puerto Rican to hold the post. In 1947, the U.S. Congress approved legislation allowing Puerto Ricans to elect their own governor. In 1949, Luis Muñoz Marín became the first democratically elected governor of Puerto Rico.

Governor Tugwell had already begun the project of centralizing state authority in Puerto Rico in the 1930s, through administrative reforms that consolidated decision-making in the hands of locals, as exemplified by

his support and partnership with Piñero, Muñoz Marín, and others in the
PRRA. The aim of the PRRA was to create a long-term plan for the economic recovery of Puerto Rico, which officials believed would calm the violent strikes and uprisings against U.S. corporations in Puerto Rico during
the Great Depression. Based on the Chardón Plan (1935) crafted by PRRA
director Carlos Chardón, Muñoz Marín, and Tugwell, the PRRA aimed
for the long-term economic recovery and industrialization of Puerto Rico.
Inspired by New Deal economic relief reforms and infrastructure, the point
of the Chardón Plan was to resolve the problem of poverty and chronic
unemployment on the island. According to first line of the Chardón Plan,
"The economic problem of Puerto Rico . . . may be reduced to the simple
term of progressive landlessness, chronic unemployment, and implacable
growth of the population."[29] Following the ideas of social scientists of the
time who argued that Puerto Rico faced a "Malthusian dilemma" in which
the population growth outpaced food production, officials began to establish eugenic practices and policies to reduce the population and to purportedly improve the economy, resulting in campaigns to sterilize Puerto Rican
women. As Tugwell's book *Stricken Land* indicates, responding to "overpop-
ulation" on the island had become the cornerstone of U.S. federal policy in
Puerto Rico by this time.[30]

While working for the PRRA, Muñoz Marín campaigned with the populist Partido Popular Democrático (PPD) in the rural areas of Puerto Rico.
As a result, he became president of the Senate of Puerto Rico in 1940, after
which he began advocating for the working class by advancing legislation for
agricultural reform, economic recovery, and industrialization. In November
1941, Tugwell appointed Teodoro Moscoso as Coordinator of Insular Affairs
on the island and as his Spanish-speaking aide. As coordinator, Moscoso
came up with the concept of the Puerto Rican Development Administration,
Fomento, in early 1942, with the goal of industrializing Puerto Rico through
a series of development projects designed to create jobs in industry.[31] Tugwell
and Muñoz Marín saw Fomento as an effective master plan for economic
development and modernization of the island. Moscoso's ideas became
reality through Operation Bootstrap by the mid-1940s, a program that also
depended on making business in Puerto Rico attractive to U.S. corporations
through lower labor costs and tax exemptions for investors.[32]

Having trained at U.S. universities with liberal New Deal reformers,
members of the PPD overlapped in social planning interests with U.S.-
appointed leaders like Governor Tugwell and possessed parallel imaginations

with the U.S. planners of the RA. As a result, these PPD leaders worked to create an expanded activist state as a vehicle for bringing economic growth, modernization, and social justice to Puerto Rico. To this end, the PPD elevated New Deal pragmatism into a guiding principle for government policy and had great faith in social science as a vehicle to bring about progress and social change. PPD officials hired economic planners, social workers, geographers, economists, sociologists, and others to empirically test theories that could improve Puerto Rican society. Central to their efforts was the control of labor migration, which functioned as a "safety valve" when state planning was unable to generate sufficient employment.[33]

By the mid-1940s, Puerto Rican government officials and advisers focused on migration planning as the central political motivation of the Muñoz Marín years. To avoid private recruiters loading planes full of Puerto Ricans for work in domestic, industrial, or farm labor in the United States, PPD members began to draft legislation to expand the authority of the PRDL and to curb the worst abuses of the private recruitment system. Many of these agents charged a fee to both the employer and the employee and took them to places where there were no jobs. Airline agencies also used the false promises of potential jobs to sell airline tickets, with Puerto Ricans unable to find work upon arrival in the United States.[34] The PPD considered developing a new labor contract for migrant laborers to guarantee available labor as well as fair and equitable working conditions, and protect workers against discrimination and abuse by unscrupulous *patronos* (employers). They touted a Puerto Rican farm labor program as a social welfare measure that would ameliorate unemployment and poverty as part of Operation Bootstrap.[35]

In Sierra Berdecía's new position as head of the Puerto Rican Department of Labor (PRDL) in 1947, he sought to promote the welfare of workers by improving their working and living conditions and securing jobs for the unemployed. He noted, "The legislature of Puerto Rico has placed upon the PRDL the responsibility of administering more than 50 laws," including, "an eight-hour workday, wage orders by a minimum wage board, a day of rest, and no discrimination against any employee . . . because of race, color, or national origin."[36] He maintained that the role of the Puerto Rican government was to guarantee basic rights for laborers, especially the labor migrant.

To legitimize an expanded role for the PRDL over migrant workers' rights, Sierra Berdecía pointed to the problematic history of Puerto Rican farmworkers migrating to Hawai'i (1900) and Arizona (1920s) under contracts that were poorly regulated, even though growers' associations had promised decent wages and excellent working conditions. The Arizona Cotton Growers Association and the Hawaiian Sugar Plantation Association arranged these programs with the Bureau of Insular Affairs of the Department of the Interior. When plantation owners in Hawai'i recruited Puerto Ricans to cut sugarcane from November 1900 to September 1901, so much abuse arose that Puerto Ricans stopped migrating to Hawai'i after less than one year of recruitment.[37] Focusing on the Arizona labor program specifically, Sierra Berdecía argued in a speech that "The labor scouts had grossly misrepresented conditions in Arizona. Workers were told that houses with 'electric lights' were furnished and that wages were high. When they discovered that they had been deceived, the workers staged a minor rebellion. Less than fifty percent remained in the field."[38] According to Sierra Berdecía, the PRDL's focus had to be on preventing another strike by acting as a regulatory intermediary in employee-employer relationships, whether in Puerto Rico or the United States. He brought notice to the problems that arose from U.S. private recruitment of Puerto Rican workers to explain why the state should step in and manage a contract labor program to prevent workers from being exploited.

To manage Puerto Rican migration to the United States and ensure the protection of workers, PPD leaders passed Law 89 in the legislature on May 9, 1947, creating a Puerto Rican contract labor program. A Puerto Rican Emigration Advisory Committee formed shortly thereafter in July 1947. Among its members were Moscoso, Muñoz Marín, Sierra Berdecía, and Clarence Senior, with Sierra Berdecía serving as chairman. They planned a two-month research trip to investigate Puerto Rican employment in the United States beginning in July 1947, with Sierra Berdecía issuing a report on November 17, 1947. Sierra Berdecía explained that the PRDL should supervise the employment of Puerto Rican workers who wished to voluntarily migrate to the United States, to aid in the problems of "adjustment" that Puerto Rican laborers faced after arriving in the United States.[39]

Muñoz Marín's administration argued that a farm labor migration program would bring "freedom" to the island, as it would assist in the development of Puerto Rico by bringing economic renovation and remittances. When Muñoz Marín became governor in 1949, he promised "development through democracy," relying on the aspiration of economic freedom instead of independence. Muñoz Marín argued that political independence would "shackle" Puerto Rico with "economic misery," and that the island should instead "search for economic conditions under which independence would be possible." As he declared, "Any status for Puerto Rico which connoted loss of

American citizenship and disassociation from the American Union meant the discontinuance of our present favorable economic conditions. . . . Our objective is to bring economic freedom, real freedom, full freedom, to the flesh and blood human beings who are our people, to the patria—the homeland and the people."[40]

In January 1949, the same month that Muñoz Marín became governor of Puerto Rico, President Truman advanced a vision of U.S. diplomacy as democratic and anti-imperial with his January 1949 "Point Four Program." This program of "technical assistance" for all developing countries brought the institutional strategy of the New Deal to U.S. diplomacy, with Puerto Rico representing an attempt, by Roosevelt's former cabinet members, to internationalize the New Deal. Puerto Rico was seen as a "training ground" or "working model" for the Point Four Program, and evidence of its "practicability." By sharing U.S. knowledge of agriculture in particular, Truman claimed, Point Four would help "The free peoples of the world, through their own efforts" to create self-sufficiency through economic production.[41] He continued, "The old imperialism—exploitation for foreign profit—has no place in our plans. What we envisage is a program of development based on the concepts of democratic fair-dealing . . . for the better use of the world's human and natural resources." Point Four was an explicitly anti-Communist program crafted during the Cold War to show developing countries that American capitalism was superior to communism. Many envisioned the Point Four program a kind of "international Works Project Administration (WPA)," designed as a self-help measure, so that "more unfortunate people could help those not so fortunate to help themselves."[42]

On July 3, 1950, President Truman declared an end to U.S. colonialism in Puerto Rico with Public Law 600, an act of Congress that enabled the people of Puerto Rico to organize a local government of their own design as well as a constitution of their own toward improved self-government. After the drafting of Puerto Rico's Constitution in 1952, Puerto Rico voted to officially become a Commonwealth or "freely associated state," a status allowing a measure of self-determination while still maintaining U.S. sovereignty over the island. As historian Laura Briggs notes, the Commonwealth status "gave the island increased self-rule in the form of a home-grown governance, but continued the U.S. military presence, the authority of the U.S. federal government, and ultimately expanded North American economic influence." Many Puerto Rican officials embraced Public Law 600 as an anticolonial measure, even though U.S. officials argued that it "would not change Puerto Rico's fundamental political, economic, and social relationship to the United States."[43] Those who sought to consolidate power within the PPD aimed to achieve national dignity and decolonization by trying to make the U.S. empire more equitable through *estado libre asociado* or "free association," not by separating from it.

After P.L. 600, Muñoz Marín expanded Operation Bootstrap as a live example of Truman's Point Four Program, deeming the island's modernization project a success. As the Puerto Rican commissioner of labor Sierra Berdecía stated in a 1957 speech, "Puerto Rico is no longer a colony. We are the Commonwealth of Puerto Rico—self-governing and freely associated with the United States." Sierra Berdecía argued that this had resulted in a "new form of democratic relationship with the United States," that "permits us maximum freedom to solve our problems." He optimistically refuted allegations that the United States was an "imperialist" and "colonial" power, concluding, "Nuestra casa es suya."[44] In line with Truman's Point Four Program, Puerto Rican officials composed a Puerto Rican farm labor program as an initiative that would eventually bring self-determination and self-rule to the island through economic self-sufficiency. Like the Mexican bracero program, the labor contract and labor program agreement was dignified as a pact of mutual aid.[45] Not only would individual Puerto Ricans sign labor contracts of their own consent, but officials marketed the labor programs to male workers as a masculine and heteronormative patriotic effort that would provide men with a means to care for their families as breadwinners.

In a propaganda display parallel to that of the Mexican bracero program, the Puerto Rican labor program became a gendered symbol of Puerto Rican cultural nationalism, enforcing masculine patriotism through a racial discourse of modernity. The imagery disseminated to male agricultural workers in Puerto Rico about the migration process often invoked the figure of the *jíbaro*, or Puerto Rican self-sufficient farmer as a symbol of the Puerto Rican nation. The *jíbaro* had long served to bolster the image of the populist PPD as that of a proud people who worked and toiled the land to earn an honest living, with the party's motto, *Pan, Tierra, y Libertad* (Bread, Land, and Liberty) highlighting its connection to the populist farmer figure.[46] Under Muñoz Marín's leadership, the male migrant farmer-peasant became part of a national Puerto Rican ethos, a symbol the Migration Division revised in its efforts to manage labor migration in the 1950s. Muñoz Marín and the PPD evoked the myth of the *jíbaro* to create a new political and racial order as the nation's standard bearer or embodiment of the Puerto Rican nation. He employed the *jíbaro*, a specifically white, mostly Spanish, folkloric image, to distinguish rural Puerto Ricans in farming communities from black Puerto Ricans, who lived mostly in coastal towns and cities—thus promoting the Puerto Rican farm labor program as a program for white workers and a project of whitening, while sublimating and managing blackness. In this way, officials of the PRDL and MD turned farm labor migrants into patriots of an island on the path to self-determination, racial modernity, and whiteness.[47]

The PPD created a complex propaganda system that included radio discourses, news coverage, and small booklets, as well as PPD spokesmen who traveled around the island speaking to rural people and delivered a gospel of social justice. Similarly, the MD delivered pamphlets, radio programs, and newspaper articles that they themselves termed "indoctrination efforts," to encourage Puerto Ricans to journey to the United States to work as farm laborers and as heroes of Puerto Rican national development. From the perspective of the MD, Puerto Rican farmworkers, now political agents, could migrate to the United States with a contract and state protection, making migration a political choice, meant to satisfy the political desires and needs of the populace while also fulfilling the ideals of *Pan, Tierra, y Libertad.*[48]

In a promotional film commissioned by the PRDL, titled *Los beneficiarios,* the PRDL stressed the importance of the labor contract, contrasting what happened to a worker if he left Puerto Rico without a contract. As a propaganda piece disseminated by the PRDL to recruit workers, the film presents the story of a man who knows no English, arrives without a contract, has no idea where to go, is unable to pay his taxi fare, and has a boss who arbitrarily decides his wages. It compares his experience with that of a different man who has a contract, and demonstrates how the PRDL helps him to find his way through the airport, sets him up with work immediately upon arrival, hands him a copy of his contract, pays for his travel and health care, helps him to meet friends at the labor supply center, and serves him Puerto Rican food. The film concludes dramatically by presenting the contract as a matter of life or death, as the worker without a contract eventually dies from a worksite accident and has no death benefit, resulting in his family in Puerto Rico living in destitution.[49] Central to the story is the irresponsibility of the worker, who abandoned his masculine duty to provide for his family as breadwinner when he left Puerto Rico without a contract.

The promises offered agricultural workers through the Puerto Rican government's indoctrination efforts proved anything but reality upon their arrival to the United States, where they faced racialization and marginalization anew. While Puerto Rican officials promised Puerto Ricans freedom through the labor contract, the labor program ultimately gave U.S. corporate farms access to cheap and vulnerable Puerto Rican labor. The efforts of liberal New Deal leaders in Puerto Rico in the 1950s to reform colonialism and racism rearticulated a system of racial labor relations that, instead of ending colonialism, coherently expanded U.S. and Puerto Rican state power and reinvigorated racial capitalism, resulting in labor coercion.

Managing Puerto Rican Labor in the 1940s

The language Puerto Rican officials employed for a Puerto Rican labor program echoed that of U.S. and Mexican officials in the construction of a Mexican labor program and a Japanese American inmate labor program. Both were touted as antiracist projects of "resettlement," designed to grant each group gainful employment. Just as the War Relocation Authority worked toward the resettlement of Japanese American inmates from prison camps to farms in pursuit of racial "adjustment," the Puerto Rican Emigration Advisory Committee (EAC) supposed that they could assist in the racial adjustment of Puerto Rican migrants to the United States, passing new laws and policies to protect Puerto Rican migrants from rampant racism in the United States. The EAC, like the Tolan Committee, likewise argued that the Puerto Rican farm labor program would assist in attenuating racism toward Puerto Rican braceros in the United States.

The Puerto Rican labor migration office, or BEM, developed a two-part labor program, one that focused on recruiting workers for low-wage temporary jobs in the urban areas of Chicago and New York, and another that focused on recruiting farm labor for the rural United States. The resulting Puerto Rican farm labor program became the second largest farm labor importation program next to the Mexican bracero program, with over 600,000 Puerto Rican workers imported to the United States between 1948–1990. The BEM had two divisions: the Puerto Rican Employment Service (PRES) in San Juan and the Migration Office in New York (later the Migration Division), with the former focusing on the recruitment and selection of workers in Puerto Rico and the latter focused on migrants' needs after arriving in the United States. In Puerto Rico, the Bureau of Employment Security (PRES) of the PRDL disseminated information about the farm labor program to recruit workers in the Puerto Rican countryside, and then provided orientation to the workers prior to leaving Puerto Rico. The Migration Division (MD) field offices gave a second orientation to Puerto Rican workers in support of their "adjustment" once they arrived in the United States. By 1958, the Migration Division had 130 staff members and a budget of $1 million annually. At its peak in 1968, it had thirteen offices throughout the United States geared toward Puerto Rican seasonal agricultural workers.[50]

While they purportedly opposed the migration of Puerto Ricans to the United States, the central task of the MD with regard to the farm labor program was "to secure employment in the States for Puerto Rican agricultural workers in order to improve individual standards of living and the general economy in Puerto Rico," as well as to "assist agricultural workers in the solution of all problems they encounter during their stay in the States."[51] To this end, the MD supervised the labor contract to ensure the minimum standards of housing, wages, and working conditions, to give orientation to workers upon their arrival, to assist in their "adjustment," and to "solve problems" arising in the social areas."[52] The MD used claim report forms to accomplish these tasks. To file a grievance or complaint against any violations of their contracts, farmworkers had to fill out a claim form and submit it to the closest regional office of the MD. An MD field officer, the equivalent of a Mexican consul in the bracero program, would then investigate the health, accident, or unemployment claim, examining housing, eating, and working arrangements at labor camps.

In 1951, the PRDL reorganized and named Clarence Senior chief and director of the MD, with the two-pronged objective of expanding the national offices of the PRDL for urban employment of Puerto Ricans in industries in New York and Chicago, and expanding its farm labor program. A member of the Socialist Party in the United States, Senior had long had an interest in Mexico in the 1930s and then Puerto Rico in the 1940s, publishing books and articles on politics in Puerto Rico and Mexico.[53] In the 1930s, Clarence Senior became a long-time Southern Tenant Farmers' Union (STFU) collaborator in the United States, and worked with H. L. Mitchell to organize Arkansas sharecroppers before the STFU moved to California and became the National Farm Labor Union (NFLU) that Ernesto Galarza came to represent. In California, Galarza, like Senior, worked alongside Mitchell to organize farmworkers in the Central and Imperial Valleys in 1948. Echoing Senior, Galarza also became involved with the Confederación de Trabajadores Mexicanos (Confederation of Mexican Workers) in the 1950s, over a decade after Senior had been invited by the union to study the progress of land reform in the Comarca Lagunera, or Laguna District of Mexico in 1936.

In 1937, Senior went with Mitchell as a representative of the STFU to the cotton-growing region of the Comarca Lagunera in the Mexican states of Coahuila and Durango, to study the program by which Mexican president Lázaro Cárdenas redistributed cotton lands from large plantations to resident laborers in the implementation of the objectives of the Mexican Revolution. The Comarca Lagunera had been the site of extensive capital investment in the late nineteenth century, as U.S., European, and Mexican investors sought to build a cotton kingdom there. When strikes posed a serious challenge to *hacendados* or landowners, the government stepped in to calm the militant workers with a state-directed plan of cooperative and collective cultivation. The Mexican government's efforts to transfer power to workers collectively at the Comarca Lagunera or "La Laguna" was a stepping-stone to commercial production by smallholders, not unlike the USDA's plans for FSA communities that later would become camps for Mexican braceros and Japanese inmates.[54] STFU union members saw the potential of Mexico's government project to transform agricultural relations in La Laguna, and hoped to transpose it onto the sharecropping regions of the U.S. South.

Senior wrote a book celebrating the success of collective farming in La Laguna titled *Democracy Comes to a Cotton Kingdom: The Story of Mexico's La Laguna* (1940) and, like many other leftist New Deal officials seeking agrarian reform in the United States, decided the U.S. government might take a lesson from the Mexican government in its handling of agricultural land reform and planning in the United States. As Senior stated in the book, "This outline is presented in the hope that those who are concerned with the problems of rural organization, cooperative production and distribution, farm credit, education, socialized medicine, economic democracy, and the freeing of 'backward' peoples may find something in the bold steps Mexico is taking to give them encouragement." He also stated of the Laguna model that "The region is one of the most thrilling spots in the world to anyone who wants to see a new world built on release from slavery."[55] Government-implemented programs of communal farming, later guestworker programs, seemed to Senior an advance away from the structural remains of colonialism and slavery, towards "freedom."

In the 1940s, Senior had served as director of the University of Puerto Rico's Social Science Research Center, where he completed a number of studies on Puerto Rican migration. He then joined the Puerto Rican Emigration Advisory Committee with Sierra Berdecía and Moscoso in 1947. An advocate of the welfare of Puerto Rican laborers, vocal in support of self-determination for Puerto Rico, and close to inner circles of the PPD in San Juan, Senior had a political interest in the protection of Puerto Ricans who migrated to the United States. As he stated in his book *Self-Determination for Puerto Rico* (1946), "the days of imperialism are numbered. . . . we must end our colonial system in Puerto Rico at the earliest possible moment. Unless we do, we stand convicted of perpetration of a fraud on all our democratic ideals."[56]

While the director of the Puerto Rican farm labor program, Clarence Senior wrote another book, *The Puerto Ricans: Strangers—Then Neighbors* (1951), in which he further castigated U.S imperialism, in an argument for the inclusion of Puerto Ricans as America's "newest neighbors" under the Good Neighbor Policy. His portrayal of the United States as a "nation of immigrants" conveniently cast race and empire as a misfortunate obstacle that could be remedied through democratic government intervention. In the history of immigration to the United States, he argued, many groups started out as strangers but became neighbors, including "the descendants of Negroes" who were "brought here by force, robbed of their cultural heritage, reduced from the status of human beings to that of chattels, and only recently, as historic time goes, partially restored to human status." Senior derided those moments in the U.S. past where racist sentiments were tied to nationalist feelings, such as during the period of immigration restriction and the eugenics movement. Senior linked these moments to the "imperialists" who considered it their duty to "carry the advantages of Anglo-Saxon civilization" to the "lesser breeds without the law." These imperialists, he argued, exerted an extremely harmful influence by offsetting the democratic forces in the country that had been opposed to the ventures that "gave the United States the colonial possessions of Puerto Rico, the Philippine Islands, Hawai'i, Guam, and the Panama Canal." Senior concluded that Americans were not at heart imperialists, but "friendly, neighborly, hospitable people," and that "the challenge of racism, xenophobia, and imperialism" could be overcome by "improving our democracy."[57]

Like Galarza had with Mexican migration, Senior examined earlier Puerto Rican migrations and concluded that they had resulted in exploitation, isolation, and disillusionment because of poor governmental supervision. The only way to change this was to have the PRDL intervene in the migration process to improve race relations. Senior was optimistic that the expansion of the Puerto Rican government in migrant labor affairs could effectively mitigate racism through anti-discrimination laws, education, and a liaison with social welfare agencies in the United States. As Senior optimistically stated, "frictions that Puerto Ricans experience in the United States are being overcome one community after another as local institutions combat people's tendencies 'to hate foreigners.' They seek to work with the newcomers as fel-low citizens."[58] This became one of the essential functions of the MD under Senior's leadership—to prevent racist friction in the United States by joining with U.S. social service organizations.

The essential instrument for protecting and racially liberating Puerto Rican migrant workers was the labor contract. As Senior argued, "It is imperative that standards be established governing the importation and use of foreign workers." Senior proclaimed the contract a source of freedom for the "for-eign" worker, as it prevented their enslavement: "Without adequate standards, [they will] continue to be brought in under conditions of virtual peonage. This not only endangers the already low standards of seasonal farm work but is an affront to the dignity of the worker as a human being." Senior considered the MD a social service institution and hired social workers as his staff, to do the humanitarian work of recruiting Puerto Rican workers and ensuring the pro-visions of the labor contract by mediating workplace abuses. If the offices of the MD functioned to prevent racism, Senior argued, the PRDL labor contract "protect[ed] the workers from [racial] abuses which have sometimes charac-terized labor relations in agriculture."[59] As Senior reported in his book *Strang-ers—Then Neighbors*, the work agreement formulated by the PRDL and the USES provided for, as he stated, "freedom from discrimination on the basis of race, color, creed, or labor union membership or activity."[60]

Even further, Senior believed that a Puerto Rican labor program could resolve the problem of racism in the United States, because Puerto Ricans could teach U.S. mainlanders how to behave in a "race-free" society. As Senior stated, "it is in the field of race relations especially that the Puerto Ricans may make a contribution—if we allow him." Like many Puerto Rican officials before him, Senior pointed to the island as a shining example of racial har-mony, stating that "Puerto Ricans of dark, light, and white skins have lived together for several centuries without serious discrimination or recrimina-tion. . . . this healthy attitude can be a model [for the United States]." As an orientation pamphlet distributed by the PRDL to migrant workers indicated, "we don't discriminate against anybody because of his race or the color of his skin. . . . we must continue practicing this wherever we live."[61] In this pam-phlet, the MD argued that Puerto Ricans could generously gift the people of the United States with their racially harmonious cultural practices. If PRDL officials silenced race and blackness in Puerto Rico, they made racism in the United States a concern that could be overcome through "correct" interper-sonal practices and government intervention.

At the same time, the MD's focus on racial adjustment turned the state management of Puerto Rican labor into a moral concern designed to create healthy, educated, and whitened Puerto Ricans. Another role of the MD was to guarantee the freedom of workers by addressing their racial "adjustment" and incorporation into the United States. According to Law 25 establishing a migration office, the Puerto Rican government intended "To provide the proper guidance with respect to opportunities for employment and the problem of *adjustment* usually encountered in an environment in which they are ethnologically alien." This law highlighted the racial and cultural differences between "alien" Puerto Ricans and U.S. citizens as something that could be resolved through proper government planning.

In other words, the MD racialized Puerto Ricans as outside U.S. white society, but also viewed them as capable of inclusion with state intervention. The MD assisted in the racial adjustment of Puerto Ricans by educating Puerto Rican migrants about American culture, educating U.S. receiving communities about Puerto Rican culture, and by assisting in the assimilation of Puerto Ricans into white U.S. culture. The MD taught English language courses in cooperation with the Puerto Rican Department of Education to "Puerto Rican adults who will engage in agricultural work in the United States." The English courses provided workers "insights into the customs and habits of the continent," so that they could make "a satisfactory personal and social adjustment to the new environment."[62] As Senior stated, "the adjustment patterns of Puerto Rican residents are following the same course as earlier waves of immigration. . . . [as they] adopt the values and aspirations typical of a white urban area." Even as Black people faced an even greater challenge in the face of this history of discrimination, "their problems would disappear," Senior argued, "as anti-discrimination laws become more effective and public opinion becomes increasingly less biased, the negro should find his relative disadvantage declining."[63] This assimilationist perspective led the PRDL to argue that racism could eventually be overcome through interaction with "white culture," as no need for racism could exist if Puerto Ricans were properly assimilated and whitened.

Senior, like most officials of the MD and PRES, focused his attention optimistically on improving democracy, casting racial and imperial domination as a U.S. problem that could be corrected. These officials upheld this logic in their information campaigns, in their attempts to ensure the provisions of the labor contract, and in their efforts to manage the recruitment of workers for the farm labor program. In the process, Puerto Rican officials made coercion

Figure 8. Puerto Rican contract farm workers being taught English. Courtesy of the Offices of the Government of Puerto Rico in the United States (OGPRUS) Records, Center for Puerto Rican Studies Library and Archives, Hunter College, City University of New York.

seem impossible because of Puerto Rican state intervention on behalf of workers. The MD's assimilationist or "adjustment" model, biased as it was by the political philosophy of racial liberalism, silenced the ways the farm labor program systemically reproduced labor coercion and race. As a result, the Puerto Rican labor program generated and elided patterns of discrimination between the Puerto Rican elite and rural populations, as the PRES recruited Puerto Ricans for contract labor on the basis of what seemed to be their existing level of modernization or "improvement." In the process, they racialized darker-skinned and Black Puerto Ricans as unmodern, employing the labor contract as a means to whiten the population and rid Puerto Rico and the United States of Blackness. The attempts of the PRES and the MD to put the ideals of liberalism into practice through the farm labor program, in effect, was productive for the racialization of Puerto Rican farm workers, and it resulted in the silencing of race and empire.

The Outcry Among Puerto Rican Contract Laborers

At the Second Annual Farm Labor Conference in San Juan in 1958, Carlos Castaña, then chief of the Farm Placement Division of the PRES, explained the four-part orientation process for Puerto Rican contract farm workers. After the applicant registered at the local office of the PRES, he stated, all applicants were interviewed and "handed informational material about work in the United States. This material includes information on such topics as living conditions, food, language, customs, religion, and life on the farm." During this first phase of orientation, the PRES advised workers to obtain a medical certification from a local public health unit, clearance with the local police, social security card, and a PRES identification card. The second phase of orientation took place at the recruitment center in Puerto Rico, where the workers' contract would be explained to them. They would be advised as to their responsibilities to the employer and to the community as a whole and also reminded of their responsibilities to the families they were leaving behind. The third phase of orientation took place at the airport, where workers were given a last-minute talk and a crew leader was chosen from among them to report directly to a local representation of the MD at the airport in the United States. The fourth part of the orientation took place in the United States, where "the Migration Specialists [field officers of the MD] took over the responsibility of guidance, of seeing to the welfare of the migrant workers, and of cooperating with local USES offices and other agencies."[64] The purpose of this very extensive orientation process was to bring the contract worker within the confines of the Puerto Rican state, to discipline and control migrants so that each knew what his responsibilities were to the state and the employer, as well as what the employer's responsibilities were.

This elaborate process of worker recruitment and orientation, according to Castaña, was designed to secure "A better adaptation in their new life in the states" and "a means for achieving a better understanding of mutual problems."[65] As Petroamerica Pagán de Colón, director of the umbrella organization for the MD and the PRES, the Bureau of Employment and Migration (BEM) indicated, "In the very process of signing an individual contract between the worker and the employer, we aim to establish a relationship between the worker and the employer." As Pagán de Colón stressed, the focus of the BEM was on educating the worker on his rights and responsibilities, educating the employer on his rights and responsibilities, and positively impacting "the relationship between the worker and the employer, on the one hand, and the worker and the local community, on the other." Pagán de Colón emphasized that "in this process each worker retains his identity as a human being and does not become a machine for the planting and harvesting of crops."[66] The BEM thus regulated social relationships between employers and employees, to protect Puerto Rican workers from abusive and unscrupulous U.S. employers.

Given that Puerto Ricans were technically U.S. citizens, U.S. employers protested the need for a labor contract, but Puerto Rican officials emphasized that the contract was necessary. Pagán de Colón emphasized that Puerto Rican workers faced a disadvantage because of their "foreign" culture and language, such that they needed the contract as well as the protection of the Puerto Rican government.[67] She stressed that there were no laws to protect agricultural workers in the United States, and that the contract was meant to ensure that Puerto Rican workers would not be discriminated against or treated inhumanely.

Págan de Colón also described the worker's choice and free will in going to the United States, as the worker could select his employer and place of employment. As she stated, "Anyone who knows our program recognizes the fact that our primary concern is with the individual, whether employer or worker. Each worker is interviewed personally in the application-taking process.... He is given the opportunity of choosing his employer and place of work."[68] This emphasis on choice was made clear from the very beginning of the formation of the Puerto Rican migration program in 1947, as officials stressed with Migration Law 25 that Puerto Rico "neither encourages nor discourages migration," creating a legal language for the freedom of Puerto Ricans to migrate of their own discretion.

This focus on choice was contradicted by the majority seasonal agricultural employment options available on the island, which was a direct consequence of the legacy of slavery and colonialism. The BEM created a complex propaganda system to encourage Puerto Ricans to migrate, falsely promising job choice, an improved quality of life in the United States, and higher wages. Most Puerto Rican officials denied that they recruited laborers. The farm placement specialist Luis F. Cuchí insisted that "although the migration program was widely publicized throughout the island ... those who migrated did it on their own free will, as they have the right to do as citizens of the United States."[69]

Upon arrival in the United States, Puerto Rican contract workers, referred to as "Boricua braceros" by the Puerto Rican press, immediately noted the difference between what they were told about the migration experience by the BEM and their lived realities. At the Second Annual Farm Labor Conference in 1958, organized by Sierra Berdecía and the PRES, Puerto Rican contract farmworkers interviewed by Pagán de Colón, Sierra Berdecía, and Frank Johnson gave their perspectives on the Puerto Rican labor program by invitation of the PRES. As one contract worker warned: "The employer sometimes forgets that he has workers. He takes them to and from work, but he does not even speak to them. He does not treat them like human beings. Sometimes the employer is too tough or standoffish." From his experience, "the employer broke the contract all the time. . . . I had one contract which was supposed to end on Nov. 22 but the employer ended it on Nov. 7. I don't know why." When officials asked if their employers had ever told them that "the contract meant nothing," all the workers responded, "not me personally, but I have heard of it from others." Another worker shared that he had once gone to Florida without a contract and "was able to find work. It was more or less the same in Florida as in the North," implying that it did not matter whether he had a contract or not. Another complained, "The people who get the higher rates are not migrants, but people from the locality. I got 65 cents where a continental got a dollar." Síerra Berdecía responded to these comments by stating, "people resent discrimination in regard to the rate of pay as well as to any other form of discrimination. We have to work on this problem. It is a human problem."[70] It is clear that Puerto Rican state officials suspected that workers were not being treated as they should have been, especially given the centrality of the question in PRDL officials' investigations: "Have your employers ever told you that the contract meant nothing?"

Puerto Rican contract workers were broadly aware of the contradictions of the contract, filling out thousands of claim forms and letters to the MD and the PRDL. They disputed payroll deductions, wage discrepancies, inadequate housing facilities, and contract violations. As one letter signed by multiple Boricua braceros to the MD indicated, "In Article II, the contract stipulates that the employer guarantees a minimum of 160 hours of work. . . . I demand that by mediation of the Department of Labor in New York that they pay us for lost time. I have a family in Puerto Rico and I have not been able to send home a single cent." This same group of workers further expounded upon the mistreatment they had suffered at the hands of U.S. employers, stating, "It seems that the general belief among Americans is that the workers of the camp are their toys that they can play with at their own whims, make false promises to, and waste their time. I have seen them . . . grab a Puerto Rican

by the neck and squeeze, then later with the help of the police kick them out
(*tirarles la maleta*) for no reason." The workers also complained that the labor
officials of Puerto Rico and the United States responsible to the workers get
paid but do absolutely nothing, and that Puerto Rican workers only matter
"when there is a rush to go to war and the crops are being lost." They also
pointed to the lack of protection and rights the state provided, even though
Puerto Ricans were U.S. citizens "under the American flag," and "born in
American territory." As this letter stated, "There are so many abuses that they
are committing against Puerto Rican citizens in the camps that eventually
one has to protest." Their letter concluded, "thirty more men have come to the
camp with very little work and mistreatment. What is going on?"[71]

Puerto Rican contract workers frequently left their places of employment
en masse, with upward of 40 percent of contract farmworkers skipping their
contracts to find better jobs than the jobs offered them by the PRES in partnership with the USES. In light of their disappointing experiences, Boricua
braceros often deserted their jobs due to the lack of fulfillment of their contract guarantees, preferring instead to "vote on the road."[72] As a PRDL *Annual
Agricultural and Food Processing Report* indicated in 1953, "An investigation
conducted by officers of our New York Migration Office revealed that in most
cases living conditions, wages, and lack of full time employment were the
causes of the workers moving out of a farm." In an excerpt from the report,
one Puerto Rican official mentioned that "two iron laundry tubs are all they
have for bathing and laundering for 14 workers; they have to chop logs for
fuel to heat the water." The workers also "complain of 60 cents wages; they
informed and we verified that the farmer employs school boys and pays them
a [higher] rate of 62.5 cents per hour." Another concern was "the inability of
the employer to offer full time employment to the workers." The BEM's solution was to lead an educational campaign targeting growers employing Puerto
Rican contract workers, but the workers' claim forms indicated that desertion
was a persistent problem that BEM's efforts were rarely able to resolve.

Given their lack of efficacy in preventing contract "jumping," BEM diverted
the blame away from the state, condemning the "unscrupulous agents of farmers" who "have no connection to the USES or the BEM," and who "took the
opportunity of this situation to coax the workers with promises of higher
wages and abundance of work to other places, causing wholesale desertions."
While the PRES worked with the MD to resolve the "illegal recruitment" of
workers, the PRES argued that agribusinessmen encouraged "skipping" as
they preferred to hire "walk-ins" so as to have a disposable labor force on hand

at all times that would not require them to meet the demands of the Puerto Rican government. While the PRES considered this "illegal," they could not ultimately stop it from happening.[73] Contract workers' complaint letters and claim forms also indicate that the BEM did little to resolve workers' claims. In one such letter, one contract worker, Alejandro Hernandez Alicea at Ciaone Brothers Farmers and Gardeners in Keyport, New Jersey, stated, "No human can live in these conditions. We pay for food and ask for our money and they don't even give us water to drink." The MD investigated and decided that his and other complaints at this employer were all due to misunderstandings, stating, "together with the farmer, we taught them how to use the heater, and make their own food."[74]

Individual claim forms and letters indicate that the workers felt that the Puerto Rican government was, in part, responsible for the issues they faced. While the PRDL faulted individual U.S. employers, it was the Puerto Rican government that controlled the movement and job prospects of workers while doing little to remedy their concerns and complaints. This was made apparent by the fact that even after eight years of contracting laborers for farm work, the BEM and the MD were still receiving repetitive claim forms from workers pointing to the same unbearable living and working conditions.[75] In another claim form, contract employees of the J. D. Noller and Sons Farms and Gardeners in Keyport, New Jersey, complained that "Living quarters were dirty, the water had to be brought in by buckets from a half of a mile away, there was no sink in the kitchen, the cooking pots were full of holes, there was no bathroom, and there was danger of fire in the rooms because of the heater." Again, the local office of the MD decided that no action should be taken because the workers had no basis for their complaints. In yet another claim, Andrés Arroyo at Curtice Brothers in Morris, New York, asserted that he had a contract but no work, stating, "I have not earned a penny to return to Puerto Rico for my children and have been charged $30 for food." He pointed out it was not the fault of Americans, but the fault of the PRDL, as Puerto Rican officials did not visit the camp to investigate the situation.[76]

In a November 1956 trip to the United States to investigate the shortcomings of the farm labor program, Muñoz Marín, Sierra Berdecía, and other farm placement personnel of the PRDL found filthy living conditions, low wages, and worker exploitation. They found the worst laboring conditions among Boricua braceros at Seabrook Farms in New Jersey, the same large-scale industrial farm that had hired Japanese American inmates under contract during the period of Japanese American incarceration. Puerto Rican contract

Figure 9. Luis Muñoz Marín visiting farmworkers in a mess hall. Courtesy of the Offices of the Government of Puerto Rico in the United States (OGPRUS) Records, Center for Puerto Rican Studies Library and Archives, Hunter College, City University of New York.

workers' treatment did not differ much from that of Japanese American contract laborers during World War II. According to PRDL, "The huts were dirty and disorderly, and full of grass. The kitchen was horrifying. It was a nauseating spectacle with a grand production of flies every time someone came close. The stove did not work well and the cook had improvised one outside in the dirt." Without a stove, there was little to stave off the intense cold in the fall and winter months, and workers also complained of frequent food-contaminated illness during seasonal heat waves. To the dismay of the PRDL, they found many workers had abandoned their work at Seabrook before their contract was complete. Yet instead of preventing Seabrook from hiring future contract workers, the visiting members of the PRDL found a solution at every turn. They argued that the problem of clothes and vehicles could be resolved through education and orientation in Puerto Rico, while the issue of housing could be fixed by encouraging farm employers to mind the "rules of order and cleanliness," and to "exercise effective vigilance to maintain the most desirable levels of health at all times." The PRDL also concluded that "a reasonable increase in wages would attract a large number of workers in Puerto Rico and also reduce the big problem of contract 'skips.'"[77]

In a report of the MD, Senior remained certain that the state could assure the rights of the workers and create order through the labor programs, and blamed the PRES for not properly orienting the workers. He pointed out that Puerto Rican workers had been promised by PRES that they would be given modern housing facilities with indoor hot water, electricity, plumbing, heating, and warm beds upon arriving in the United States. Senior argued that the PRES orientation efforts had failed and that contract workers needed to be told of the realities of having a latrine instead of a toilet, and of having to walk one hundred feet from their abodes to collect hot or cold water in the winter. Since Senior and the MD processed worker claim forms, it was in their interest to demonstrate the realities of the labor program instead of painting a rose-tinted picture. To prevent further complaints, Senior decided as director of the MD to institute another step in the orientation process: to inform workers of the lack of "modern" facilities at the labor camps once they arrived in the United States.

In spite of their negative investigations and reports, the PRES and the MD insisted upon the great benefit of the farm labor program to the Puerto Rican people throughout the 1950s. As Págan de Colón noted at a 1955 meeting, "it is encouraging that so much progress has been made in improving the living and working conditions of migrant workers." She claimed that the PRDL, through its educational program, had effectively reduced the number of complaints from workers. As the PRDL noted in a 1955 report, "the migration program has greatly helped to solve local problems of employment and [has] improved the economic conditions of many families in Puerto Rico." The Division of Statistics of the Puerto Rican Planning Board pointed out the immense contributions made by the agricultural migrant workers to the island's economy, with their total earnings amounting to over $14.5 million.

The labor contract had served as an initiative to provide for the general welfare of Puerto Rican migrants, and as a strategy to avoid the private recruitment of Puerto Rican workers. As state officials maintained, the guest-worker labor contract was fundamentally created to "avoid a labor system of virtual peonage."[78] If the avoidance of a system of peonage was a challenge even with optimistic government intervention, it seemed the supposed economic benefits of Puerto Rican contract farm labor program far outweighed the social costs.

*   *   *

In the transition from an agricultural colony under U.S. domination to a conceptually autonomous government dependent on foreign capital, industrial production, and migrant laborers' remittances, Puerto Rican officials sought to redefine and legitimize the relationship between its people and the new Puerto Rican administration. The principles of the New Deal organized their efforts in the 1940s and 1950s, with the Puerto Rican labor program emerging as a product of state officials striving for reforms and social change as an expedient to dissolve U.S. colonialism on the island. Muñoz Marín's administration in the PRDL focused on labor migration to develop the island as part of a national project, with the presumed goal of preventing U.S. colonial labor exploitation and preparing the island economically for national independence and "freedom." These Puerto Rican officials' visions overlapped with those of officials who saw the state-managed contract labor program in Mexico and the British West Indies as exemplars of democratic national progress.

The books published by Ernesto Galarza and Clarence Senior in response to the farm labor importation programs point to some of the central ideas that linked them across time and place. Whether in Galarza's *Strangers in Our Fields* (1956), or Clarence Senior in *Strangers— Then Neighbors* (1951), both books considered Puerto Ricans and Mexican contract workers as "outsiders" who could be protected from discrimination and exploitation with proper intervention and guidance from state institutions. Like Galarza, Senior envisioned Puerto Rican contract laborers as "strangers" capable of eventually being received as "neighbors" in the United States.[79] Senior and Galarza both portrayed the history of colonialism and racism in the United States as blunders, not inherent in the logic and functioning of U.S. liberalism. With proper state management, Galarza and Senior argued that imperialism and racism could be concerns of the past, clearing the path for a society based on equality and freedom so that the benefits of profits under capitalism could be distributed to all.

It is no coincidence that Galarza and Senior's ideas for agrarian reform merged in this way, as they had a shared history and interest in labor organizing as well as in applying the Mexican government's rural reform efforts to other regions. Whether as leaders of the NFLU or the MD, both Galarza and Senior expressed interest in forming an alliance with labor unions in the United States and in Latin America (or the Caribbean) to benefit agricultural workers. According to an MD report, the duties and responsibilities of the personnel of the Migration Division in the area offices were to "promote, develop, and maintain cooperative relationships with appropriate state, county, and city agencies and with private organizations and *labor unions* which are concerned with and demonstrate a sincere interest in solving and minimizing the employment problems of Puerto Rican migrants."[80] Being admittedly "pro-union," the MD tried to intervene for workers in the face of discrimination, wage theft, and exploitation, as if it were a local labor union. The MD actively encouraged U.S. unions to view Puerto Rican laborers as protected equals to U.S. workers, with the same rights; hence the interest of the AFL in the employment of Puerto Rican contract labor over Mexican contract labor to resolve the inequalities that U.S. farmworkers faced.

In some ways, the Puerto Rican farm labor program was the program Galarza had originally envisioned for Mexican migrants, as the MD was both populist and pro-union, held meetings and conferences with U.S. labor leaders, and included U.S. labor in iterations of the labor contract agreement. In the case of the bracero program, the WFA, the USDL, and the USES operated apart from U.S. labor organizations and did not share this pro-union sentiment, nor did these organizations invite the assistance of U.S. or Mexican labor organizations in the management of Mexican contract farm labor. As Galarza's frustrated efforts to secure labor union representation at all meetings between U.S. and Mexican officials regarding the bracero program indicate, unions were not welcome at the table when it came to the managed migration of Mexican labor. Yet the pro-union outlook of Puerto Rican officials managing the Puerto Rican farm labor program did not change the end result: Boricua braceros still faced some of the same challenges that Mexican braceros confronted, and suffered the same experience of racialized exploitation in U.S. fields. Even with the MD officials' efforts to ensure contract compliance, their investigations of workers' claims often favored Northeastern farm cooperatives, even as they stressed the worker's responsibility to the employer. This was in part due to their long-term desire to secure the continuation of the labor program for the economic benefit of the island on its path to eventual "freedom," but it was also due to the ideological quandary of liberalism, through which they had both silenced and facilitated systemic racism and exploitation.

In 1956, Ernesto Galarza and the Joint U.S-Mexico Trade Union Committee, which had united U.S. and Mexican labor unions, recommended to the U.S. federal government that Puerto Ricans should be brought to the United States first before any other contract laborers, as an anti-exploitation measure. The Joint Committee declared in a report: "Greater emphasis must be given to the placement and protection of U.S. farm workers, including Puerto Ricans, in preference to bringing in labor from other countries."[81] The committee shared the perception that Puerto Rican laborers were protected by their citizenship status, even though "alien exclusion" had long defined Puerto Ricans as outside the bounds of full citizenship through legal, cultural, and racial means. The assumption that Puerto Ricans, as U.S. citizens, should even sign a labor contract usually assigned to noncitizen laborers in the United States indicated that officials did not consider Puerto Ricans to be the same as "domestic" or citizen labor in the United States. Nonetheless, the Joint Committee believed that citizenship in combination with the labor contract could prevent Puerto Ricans from being underpaid or abused by employers and preclude them from being used by employers to reduce the wages of domestic U.S. farm laborers. The preferential treatment of Puerto Rican labor that emerged in the 1950s was, in part, a product of the Puerto Rican government's deliberate attempt to encourage U.S. labor leaders and employers to consider Puerto Rican labor as "domestic" in support of the expansion of the Puerto Rican contract labor program after 1947.

Galarza kept a running file of information regarding the Puerto Rican, British West Indian, and Japanese SAW programs of 1956. Like his fellow members of the U.S. section of the Joint U.S.-Mexico Trade Union Committee, Galarza saw Puerto Ricans as "domestic" laborers, not vulnerable to deportation in the same way that Mexican contract workers were, and therefore more capable of pushing for recognition of contract guarantees. The BWI program seemed a close second to Galarza, as it appeared to offer real compliance machinery to fulfill the labor contract. U.S. labor unions suggested the preferential hiring of Puerto Rican and BWI labor to safeguard Mexican workers who did not enjoy the same state protections as these groups. Milton Plumb, director of publicity of the U.S. section of the Joint U.S.-Mexico Trade Union Committee, furthered this logic of "good" and "bad" labor importation programs, or "protected" and "unprotected" labor programs. Plumb published an article in 1959 titled "What Is the Truth About the BWI Labor Program?" He argued that in 1956, the CIO gave the BWI program a clean bill of health, maintaining that the "BWI program has been given wide support by labor and liberals," "BWI contracts are strictly enforced," and "BWI Programs enhance U.S. prestige abroad." He further maintained that "because of their better education, their common language, the lack of discrimination in their homelands, and their habitual insistence, as freedom loving men, on their rights both as British subjects and individual human beings, they are better equipped to stand up for their rights than any other group of foreign workers, and they do so." Plumb's publicity campaign suggested that the Caribbean labor programs should be considered efforts "to offset the Communist penetration of the Caribbean and other Latin American areas," as well as "symbols of democracy, freedom, and human betterment."[82]

Viewing the configuration of these labor programs together provides a more comprehensive understanding of empire and state hegemony as rooted in the political and epistemological project of liberalism and nation. The labor programs were not part of a traditional history of colonial metropoles ruling over peripheral populations through conquest and dominion (the "us versus them" of most colonial histories).[83] Rather, Puerto Rican officials recruited and managed farm laborers on the island in an effort to end colonialism and as part of a locally composed system of state power, with the goal of achieving their own vision of freedom. Puerto Rican officials, perceiving the possibilities in a Puerto Rico-U.S. alliance for modernization and economic improvement on the island, did not see themselves as imperial or colonial government proxies, but as the benevolent leaders of a new anticolonial world system designed to promote and secure international cooperation, as established through the creation of the United Nations in 1945.

PPD officials also did not necessarily accept the boundaries of their colonial subordination to the United States, but, like the architects of the other guestworker labor programs, viewed the region as part of a newly emerging postcolonial world order in which Puerto Rico could play an equal role among nations through the development and modernization of their local economy. Their interpretation of liberalism in this anti-imperial New Deal moment fueled a coercive state project of managed labor migration that facilitated the expansion of U.S. and Puerto Rican state power over Puerto Rican workers' lives. The consequence of their optimism was the continuation of the Puerto Rican government's migration policy and programs until 1993, with the government serving as a labor contractor and provider of racialized labor to U.S. agricultural interests, much as the Mexican government had become with respect to the bracero program.

CHAPTER 6

Empire and Nation:
Caribbean Independence and the Labor
Programs in the British West Indies

Before progressive New Deal officials formulated a state-managed Puerto Rican labor importation program during World War II, they pursued the idea of a labor program in the British West Indies. After meeting with the West Indies National Emergency Committee (WINEC) in New York and with Walter White of the National Association for the Advancement of Colored People (NAACP), Charles W. Taussig advised Roosevelt to send him on a fact-finding commission to address issues of racial and economic unrest on the islands (November 1941). White gave Taussig a letter of introduction to show Afro-Caribbean political leaders that would encourage them to speak with Taussig frankly on his tour of the Caribbean. After his trip, Taussig recommended to Roosevelt that the United States take a reformist stance toward the region and form a "Joint Commission" to relieve poverty on the islands. Roosevelt eventually took Taussig's advice, and it led to the formation of the Anglo-American Caribbean Commission (AACC) between the United States and Great Britain on March 9, 1942.[1] The AACC became a model of regional cooperation, and was intended to address the problems shared by both colonial governments in agreement with local interests in the Caribbean.

Roosevelt's New Deal advisers on the Caribbean, Charles W. Taussig, and the U.S. governor of Puerto Rico, Rexford Tugwell, headed the AACC on the U.S. side. Aiming at the agrarian reform Tugwell and others had studied in Mexico, the AACC proposed a U.S.-British West Indies labor importation program to improve the welfare of workers and modernize the economies of

the British Caribbean islands on a purported path to freedom and independence. Bahamians began to enter the United States for employment in agriculture on March 16, 1943, followed shortly by Jamaicans on April 2, 1943,
with Barbadians and British Hondurans following soon thereafter. The agreement and labor contracts that the U.S. and British governments prepared
were modeled on the Mexican bracero program, with the same emphasis on
freedom, welfare, and good neighborly intentions.[2]

With the Good Neighbor policy, Roosevelt had renounced the U.S. government's right to unilaterally intervene in the Caribbean and the Americas,
and condemned its former militarism, but then began to expand the number
of troops in the Caribbean soon after World War II began. The formation of
new bases in the Caribbean functioned to "strengthen Caribbean security and
contribution to the war effort," during World War II, as part of the U.S.-Great
Britain Destroyers-for-Bases agreement (September 1940). The Bases Agreement provided land grants to the U.S. military to build bases in Trinidad, the
Bahamas, Jamaica, Antigua, and British Guiana. As a purported extension of
the Good Neighbor Policy to the Caribbean, the bases offered employment
and a higher wage scale than Afro-Caribbeans were accustomed to, effectively
calming and subduing the burgeoning anticolonial labor movement that had
mushroomed there in 1935–38.[3] The bases provided work to the unemployed
but upon completion, proved insufficient to quell unemployment and unrest,
such that the AACC instituted the labor programs a few years later. Deemed a
success, the British West Indies farm labor programs, alongside several other
initiatives, effectively curbed unemployment. As one 1943 U.S. report stated,
"The construction of the U.S. air and naval bases in the Caribbean, the purchase
by the United States and Great Britain of the sugar crops of most of the islands,
the arrangement of agricultural work in the United States for Caribbean laborers, and the increased production of strategic materials in certain areas have
[all] served to offset in large measure the unemployment [on the islands]."[4]

Within the context of World War II and the Good Neighbor policy, officials structured the British West Indies labor contract as a statement of Allied
friendship and benevolence. As the Bahamian Agreement stated, the program existed "for the purpose of making agricultural workers from the Bahamas available for work in the United States of America for the production
of food for the winning of the war." The Jamaican Work Agreement stated,
"The government and the worker mutually desire that the worker shall be
beneficially employed in the United States of America to alleviate the present
shortage of labor and to aid in the successful prosecution of the war." Another

version of the Agreement stated that the labor programs were "in the furtherance of the common war effort of the United Nations."[5]

When officials argued that the Caribbean labor programs made "a vital
contribution to the effort of the United Nations," the contract again became
an innovation to advance the cause of worker "freedom," even as it legitimized the expanding structure of colonial labor. It was no contradiction that
state governments labeled contract work "free labor," even though contract
workers were, quite literally, a colonial labor supply. Rather, it was part and
parcel of the realities created in this historic moment of liberalism, when state
discourses of equality, anti-imperialism, national security, agrarian reform,
and modernization erased and facilitated the very real continuities between
colonial rule and expansive liberal state governance over labor migrations.
The farm labor importation program thus became a means by which the U.S.
government was able to further its hegemony over the Caribbean, while purportedly working against the "colonial order of things."

The Caribbean labor programs, however, were rooted in the early twentieth-
century labor chains formed in the rising tropical fruit-packing and shipping
industries in the Caribbean as well as in the Panama Canal Zone. U.S. business
leaders' imperial incursions through land investments, steamship transportation, and agricultural production in Latin America and the Caribbean at the
turn of the twentieth century had resulted in cycles of British West Indian
migration to the Panama Canal Zone and to U.S.-owned farm plantations
throughout the Caribbean and Latin America by the 1920s. U.S. corporations
also hired workers from the British West Indies to cultivate and harvest sugarcane in Florida, where they had imported workers under temporary contracts
since the 1910s. These temporary contract programs were grounded in the
political and economic dynamics that had emerged post-slavery in the Caribbean, including the liberal regulatory state project to secure free labor markets
in order to fulfill labor demands.[6] The World War II state-regulated contract
labor importation programs with the British West Indies were not new, but
were rather a continuance of former "free labor" innovations in recruitment
practices that had long been established in the region.

The family history of the California Central Valley agribusiness mag-
nate Robert DiGiorgio points to some of the rich entanglements between the
early-twentieth-century U.S. empire and the 1940s guestworker programs.
As detailed in Chapter 4, DiGiorgio was the first California grower Ernesto
Galarza and the National Farm Labor Union targeted for unionization in

the late 1940s. Unbeknown to Galarza, DiGiorgio's family had built their wealth by employing British West Indian laborers on fruit plantations in the Caribbean in the early twentieth century. Robert's uncle, Joseph DiGiorgio (1874–1951), had immigrated from Italy to Baltimore, where he worked as a middleman in tropical fruit sales, founding the Baltimore Fruit Exchange in 1904. Joseph amassed a vast empire of tropical fruit harvesting and distribution and began to import British West Indian workers to his banana plantations in the Caribbean and Central America. In 1923, he partnered with the Standard Fruit Company on the Honduran coast (later Dole Foods), forming the Mexican American Fruit and Steamship Company, which became a major competitor with the United Fruit Company during the 1920s. Employing British West Indian laborers on his fruit plantations in Cuba, Jamaica, Mexico, and Nicaragua meant Joseph DiGiorgio's profits were immense. From his profits, Uncle DiGiorgio purchased nearly 40,000 acres in California's Central Valley in 1919 and in 1920 to grow grapes for wine. He founded the DiGiorgio Corporation, which became the largest grape, plum, and pear grower in the world, worth $18 million in profits in 1946. He and his nephew, Robert, sought to apply the same processes of labor and resource extraction in California that Joseph had established in the Caribbean and Central America, this time employing Mexican migrant workers who had been legitimately contracted and recruited through the state to work in California through the bracero program.[7] DiGiorgio employed so many Mexican braceros in the 1940s that Ernesto Galarza decided to target DiGiorgio's farms first during his efforts to unionize braceros.

It seems odd that any New Deal progressive or labor advocate would have wished to continue this historic cycle of exploitation through a Caribbean guestworker program, but the effort by state officials and liberals to create the labor programs was no anomaly. To New Deal leaders, the expansion of state power over labor from the Caribbean colonies through the labor contract seemed a natural and salutary response to the global inequalities that had arisen as a result of the abuses in plantation agriculture, especially in the tropical fruit business. They perceived the labor programs as essential to their agrarian reform efforts on the islands, designed to undo the historical inequalities created by enslavement, in conversation with Black civil rights organizations in the United States. The British West Indies labor programs thus point to the complex process through which colonial governance and imperial geopolitics were refashioned in the post–World War II period.[8]

The anti-imperial and race-neutral logic officials used to legitimize the labor programs was challenged and exceeded by the contract workers themselves. British West Indian contract workers, like their Mexican and Puerto Rican counterparts in the Southwest, called out the promised freedom and anti-imperialism of the labor programs as a falsehood. One group of Jamaican workers wrote to the War Food Administration (WFA), "Our willingness to work . . . marks our true character and honesty of purpose. We are still suffering daily impositions of the most Nazi-like and undemocratic nature, and we all agree on the face of the facts that [our employer] does not honor the allegations of our contract made by the U.S. government." They denounced their "rough treatment" in 1944 as the "exact replica of that practiced in Germany and Japan."⁹ Another worker wrote to the U.S. federal government, "Sir, I am a Jamaican and contracted to do war work in the United States. I am very sorry to say that we are doing slave work. . . . We leave Jamaica to work as decent citizens and to be treated as men, and not as boys or dogs." A group of workers from Barbados suggested, "Sir, my government and you all have agreed that a few hundred of us should come out from Barbados to help harvest the war food, feed the soldiers and sailors, and for the welfare of the USA, and I have done my duty. Now that it is time that I should go home I can't get out." Their words indicate that the conditions that they experienced in the United States hardly marked their attainment of liberal subjectivity or "freedom," as suggested by the labor agreement and contract. At the same time, the labor programs in the Caribbean made the United States a site of hope for workers who sought the future independence of the Caribbean islands.

By turning to the struggles of Jamaican and Bahamian workers in the 1940s and their advocates in the Black anticolonial civil rights movement, wider visions of social justice, beyond the nation-state and universal "freedom" as it is framed by "rights" and "choice," become legible. These workers and civil rights leaders participated in the intellectual production of U.S.-led independence in the Caribbean, pushing the universalist and inclusionary dimensions of the concept of the "nation-state" as far as they could to locate themselves within it. While U.S., Puerto Rican, and British West Indian colonial officials worked to build and consolidate a particular political culture that revolved around the nation-state and disavowed race and colonialism, the laborers critiqued the ironies that resulted. Meanwhile, many Black civil rights activists pointed to the hypocrisy of the U.S. nation-state, even as others became educated in a new regime of self-determination and "rights," shaping the radicalism of the Black anticolonial civil rights movement.

The Anglo-American Caribbean Commission
and the Struggle over Farmworker Freedom

In 1942, Eric Williams, scholar, activist, and future first prime minister of an independent Trinidad and Tobago (1962), set out a path for Caribbean independence through economic development, calling out sugar as both "king" and curse while arguing for U.S. expert intervention. In his 1942 book, *The Negro in the Caribbean*, he concluded that "no permanent solution can be found for the future welfare of the Caribbean which does not have as its aim and purpose the raising of the standard of living of the area, and so raise the productive capacity of the islands. . . . This is the contribution the United States can make." He argued that such a contribution would carry out the U.S. government's ideological mission to liquidate colonialism in Latin America and the Caribbean under the Good Neighbor Policy. For, as Williams argued, much as Governor Muñoz Marín would argue in Puerto Rico, that *economic* independence would lead the British West Indies on the path to *political* independence. In response to poverty on the islands, Williams stated, "some [economic] scheme, if the Good Neighbor Policy is to survive, will have to be devised."[10]

So influential was Williams's scholarship to the Anglo-American Caribbean Commission (AACC) that the group hired him on its Research Council in 1944, with Williams taking a leave from his position as assistant professor of social and political science at Howard University. As Williams stated, "Taussig, who knew all about *The Negro in the Caribbean*, decided that I was to be associated with the AACC." Taussig used Williams's scholarly work as a yardstick to establish the principal goals of the AACC, even though he at first struggled to convince other members to recruit a Black representative of the Caribbean colonies into an all-white organization.[11] In his scholarly work, including his classic book, *Capitalism and Slavery* (1944), Williams's goal was to free global Black society from all vestiges of colonial rule. He believed that U.S. economic and expert assistance, if done under the aegis of the Good Neighbor Policy, would be better than British colonialism for the islands, and that the Caribbean should look to the United States to end archaic British colonial rule and ensure that "surpluses that normally went to Europe will be consumed in the Western Hemisphere."[12]

Inspired by Williams's scholarly work, as well as the concerns of Black anticolonial civil rights activists in WINEC and the NAACP, Taussig set out to improve labor conditions, uplift the Caribbean economy, and reduce unemployment in the British West Indies. By 1943, the AACC's most important concern was to make the best possible use of Caribbean labor in the war effort. With the aim of ending colonial dependency, the AACC worked to facilitate the importation of Caribbean agricultural laborers to the United States—including the short-lived Puerto Rican labor program led by Rexford Tugwell, then the second-ranking U.S. member of the AACC next to Taussig. According to Taussig, "the one great natural resource of the Caribbean is its vast reserve of manpower." He continued, "When the West Indian was a slave the lowliest bookkeeper accounted for him on the asset side of the ledger. Now that he is a free man, he is too frequently entered on the books as an economic liability."[13] Taussig saw the labor program as a mechanism to turn the "free men" of the Caribbean into assets once again, this time in the name of freedom instead of slavery.

While the British colonial government worked with the WFA in an agreement to export workers from Jamaica to the United States, the AACC served as the agency representing the Jamaican government in the administration of the labor program. The AACC initially worked cooperatively with the WFA to ensure contract compliance for the workers.[14] In 1945 alone, the WFA employed approximately 46,000 workers (33,000 Jamaicans, 6,000 Barbadians, 1,000 British Hondurans) in thirty-eight of forty-eight states, scattered throughout some 2,000 cities, towns, and villages.[15] Official reports of the AACC highlighted the safeguards implemented by the labor programs to ensure the welfare of Caribbean labor, including a 75 percent employment guarantee, a minimum wage, and adequate housing, almost identical to the contract protections of the bracero program.

When growers violated these stipulations, and the state failed to step in to remedy the contract violations, Caribbean workers often refused to work or abandoned one labor camp to move to another in search of higher wages or better housing. As many contract workers came to the United States literate and politicized by labor unrest and union campaigns in the Caribbean in the 1930s, they also formed their own committees and threatened the federal government with violence and direct action if the government refused to guarantee the stipulations of their contracts. Because their contracts stated that workers were in the United States for the purpose of the war, the war was often the primary basis upon which workers from the British West Indies lodged complaints.

Hundreds of letters written to the WFA by Afro-Caribbean workers referred to the "war effort" or the "fight for freedom" or referred to themselves as "the soldiers of the home front," to demand immediate attention to the contract violations they suffered. As forty Bahamians at Stony Brook Camp in Dansville, New York, wrote, "we arrived at the above-mentioned camp when we expected a good deal of work. . . . a great deal of manpower hours [are] being carried out here, in a period when it is greatly needed, not only among the farmers here, but also over the globe. For the past four weeks there is not enough work to supply half of the 125 men sent here." When growers overestimated the number of workers needed, a strategy often used to ensure an adequate labor supply, Caribbean workers responded that the resulting lack of work prevented them from fulfilling their obligation to help "win the war." They pointed to the 75 percent work guarantee in their contracts. As the Bahamians at Stony Brook explained, "these forty workers maintain that the company men tried to [placate] us by saying you sent us ahead of time. But sirs, since knowing what a dreadful war is going on, [we know] our special efforts are needed." These workers further admonished the WFA: "as you know, this is not only a broke down to the war efforts, but also to our family proposition. According to governmental rules, seventy-five cents per day must go to the Bahamas government as family allowance. Should this continue, it cannot be done."[16] One of the proclaimed purposes of the labor programs, according to the AACC's campaign, was to improve local Caribbean economies through family remittances, turning working men into agents of economic progress. This was a goal the men argued was impossible to accomplish given their deliberate underemployment.

Jamaican and Bahamian workers also repeatedly referred to their contracts to insist that the government change the way they were treated. A letter signed by three Jamaicans from Moscow Hill Labor Camp in Hubbardsville, New York, wrote to President Roosevelt, "we are recruits from Jamaica as agricultural workers. According to our contract we were told we would start work on our arrival. We are now pending for a period of 8 days of which conditions are rather imperfect." A Bahamian worker, Joel Seymour, suggested in a handwritten letter from the Hebron Labor Camp in Hebron, Maryland, "our contracts read that we should have a pay day at the end of every seven days period and they are not paying us. . . . now they are taking out $7.50 per week for food and rent. [We must pay for food] we cannot enjoy and still have to pay for it, and I don't think it is legal, sir."[17] When several dozen Jamaican workers at a camp in Pinconning, Michigan, realized they would be paid thirty cents an hour instead of the prevailing wage rate, they appealed to their contract agreement for a new assignment. Thirty of these workers were summarily deported by the WFA with the approval of the AACC.

Not only did the workers suffer from lack of employment, low wages, and poor housing, they also experienced racial discrimination and Jim Crow segregation, a direct violation of contract stipulation number two of the Bahamian agreement, "Bahamians entering the United States as the result of this understanding shall not suffer discriminatory acts of any kind in accordance with Executive Order No. 8802, issued at the White House June 25, 1941." Anti-discrimination was also mentioned as stipulation 5(g) of the Jamaican agreement: "The Workers shall be entitled to freedom from discrimination in employment because of race, creed, color, or national origin, in accordance with the provisions of Executive Order No. 8802 of the President of the United States dated June 25, 1941." In Imlay City, Michigan, Jamaicans complained that they were unable to buy beer anywhere in town, the drug store fountains were closed to them, and the moving-picture theaters were open to them only two evenings each week. When they were found loitering in the streets with nowhere to go, the chief of police ordered them to leave. The police expulsion of the workers occurred even though racist local officials postulated to their defense that "pastors invited them to their churches, individuals gathered and took magazines to the camp, and a lawyer wrote for the local paper a very nice and effective defense of the Jamaicans on behalf of their non-discriminatory acceptance."[18]

In Gooding, Idaho, a violent confrontation broke out after a local white man walked up to a group of Jamaicans who were playing a guitar and singing and struck one of them for no reason.[19] The workers were also plagued by wage differentials, even though the contract promised a prevailing wage rate to prevent these workers from replacing local workers. In Ithaca, New York, Jamaicans complained of domestic workers receiving higher wages in 1944.[20] The WFA "established beyond a doubt" that "domestic help is getting fifty cents per hour and Jamaicans in the same fields are receiving forty-five cents" in Long Island, New York. The AACC discovered a similar situation at Stoughton, Wisconsin, with white men receiving ten cents more than Jamaican workers doing the same type of work. The Jamaicans working there noted that their employer told them, "if he pays us the same rate of pay he pays the white men they all would walk out on him."[21]

The AACC worked in cooperation with the WFA, and often stepped in to protect the welfare of the workers in the face of rampant racism. Jamaican workers wrote directly to Herbert MacDonald, liaison officer of the AACC in Washington, D.C., representing the Jamaican government. Macdonald had two assistant liaison officers, E. C. Carnell-Sara in Upper Darby,

Pennsylvania, and M .S. Goodman in Indianapolis. In Imlay City, Michigan, Goodman argued that "proper work with the community could have eliminated existing discrimination." Since that work had not been done, he advised that "the camp should operate a canteen so that beer and soft drinks would at least be available to Jamaicans [and] would take some of the edge from the resentment against them."[22] The AACC also investigated a complaint from a group of fifty-eight Jamaicans in Kennedyville, Maryland, alleging that camp manager Raymond Hill refused to honor their contracts, and "told us that Washington has nothing to do with his camp and that Washington does not run his camps and will not." This camp manager also told the workers that if they called the AACC, they would be "sent to jail." Carnell-Sara investigated the situation and wrote to the WFA that he had visited the camp and found, "Without a doubt this is the worst situation I have yet seen. . . . In my opinion, Mr. Hill is as near a slave driver as it is possible to get. . . . It seems that he caused three men to be jailed for what he called 'refusing to work.'" Carnell-Sara was not at all convinced, after listening to the evidence, that there really were any refusals to work, and found that Hill threatened to call the sheriff when any worker complained. Carnell-Sara suggested "the removal of every last man from this camp in the shortest time possible." The area representative of the WFA refused his suggestion, stating that it would be "an injustice to the workers and to the farmers. . . . Mr. Hill may be crude and rough but he pays them very good money, probably more than anywhere else in Maryland. The living conditions would be 100 percent better if the workers would just cooperate."[23]

While the WFA and AACC investigated some worker complaints, rarely did they address the racism and violence workers faced, instead often insisting that the workers were stretching the truth. In one case, the WFA explained, "it is true that on occasion it has been necessary to have workers arrested for committing serious misdemeanors and held pending repatriation. In all cases, every effort has been made by the [WFA's] Office of Labor to release them from civil authorities into our custody so that repatriation can be completed."[24] In its investigations of contract violations, the WFA consistently agreed with growers that most of the workers' complaints were invalid, which meant the it rarely stepped in to intervene beyond investigation. If field representatives of the WFA or AACC did intervene, it was to deport or "repatriate" the workers responsible for the complaint. While they often provided suggestions to employers to ameliorate conditions that even officials often found "unfortunate" or "terrible," there is little evidence that they followed through.

The WFA insisted that the organization existed to protect the welfare of the workers under contract, but its primary purpose was the control and management of workers' complaints, to avoid leakages about program violations to the press. Press leakages still occurred, however, as was the case when one USDA official went to a Florida labor camp in February 1944 to "show the contribution the Bahamian and Jamaican workers are making to the United Nations' cause," and instead found abysmal living and working conditions.[25] In spite of the resulting press, the director of the WFA argued, "Scrupulous pains are taken to see to it that the commitments made by the U.S. government and the Bahamas government to protect the welfare of the Bahamian workers are carried out and that all the terms of the workers' contracts with the WFA are fulfilled."[26] The proof was in the numbers, the director of the WFA explained, as "out of 4,698 Bahamians brought to the United States in 1943 by the War Food Administration for agricultural employment, only 1,505 had returned one year from the beginning of recruitment." While the WFA lauded these figures, they were hardly worth celebrating, since they indicated that nearly 32 percent of all workers had opted out or were deported within the first year. The WFA even began to flag some resistant workers on record as having "refused to work" to prevent them from returning on a new contract. As one group of eight workers stated, "we would like to be informed as to the laws which subject a worker employed by the WFA to be marked 'refused to work.'"[27]

In response to the injustices in the fields, Caribbean workers often performed work stoppages, demanding a field representative of the WFA investigate their circumstances. Workers in Port Jefferson and Deansboro, New York, went on strike as a result of low wages and poor housing, refusing to work until the WFA representative for that area was made available to the camp. The WFA report stated, "they are not working at present time and have been very destructive, tearing the telephone off the wall, throwing food in the mess hall, and plugging up the latrines in the sewage system."[28] Another WFA report indicated that a group of Jamaicans refused to work in response to their pay rates at Camp Manuel in Plymouth, Massachusetts, and local police put them in jail.

Local police and sheriff departments commonly cooperated with the WFA by housing those workers who refused to work in local jails while the WFA arranged for their deportation. At a labor camp in Sherburne, New York, all workers refused employment because of the wage rates and walked out of the camp as a group, after which the state police promptly returned them. The WFA arranged for the imprisonment of seven of the workers that it considered to be the "ringleaders" at the camp, pending deportation.[29] When several Bahamian workers at Hebron Labor Camp in Maryland refused to shovel hay because of the work conditions, which required them to stand on wagons thirteen feet from the ground with no protection on the sides, they were promptly delivered to the county jail. According to the workers, they begged to go back to work, just to be released from jail, where they had been kept for ten days. In the end, state authorities forced them to sign a paper that said they were unwilling to work in order to leave the country. As one letter from the Bloomingdale labor camp in Maryland stated, "a lot of the farmers take us for prisoners."[30] Many seasonal migrants, whether from Mexico, Puerto Rico, or the British West Indies, shared these feelings of separation and imprisonment, demonstrating how discipline and control were central to labor relations and life in the labor camps.

Another group of workers at Cool Springs Labor Supply Center in Harberson, Delaware, wrote directly to President Roosevelt, proclaiming there was "not enough work." Their letter begged for immediate investigation into their treatment, stating, "We have this war at heart; and we have volunteered to do our part to help win the war, and also to assist you in agricultural work. But may I say sir that we are not been properly represented." The letter requested a meeting with an official to hear their grievances, including a lack of edible food, no compensation for their losses after a tent fire, no way for workers to send money orders back home, no health care, and wage theft. The WFA sent out a representative, who found that only some of the workers' complaints were legitimate. The solution was to secure a camp manager with an assistant who could correct these issues by taking care of "the problem of orientation." He concluded, "complete personnel must be had if these workers are to be treated as they so desire."[31]

Realizing that the government would do very little to help them with flagrant violations of the contract program agreement, the workers made other attempts at gaining access to rights, including applying for U.S. citizenship. One farmer, Donald Delaney of Joliet, Illinois, wrote to the WFA, "a citizen of Jamaica who is temporarily staying at Joliet, Illinois on a contract with the government of the Island of Jamaica to aid in the harvesting of our crops has sought advice from me as to the possibility of obtaining American citizenship." Another letter from a farmer in Whitehall, Maryland, sought to sponsor the permanent stay of a Jamaican worker who "would like to remain in the states and learn building construction work, which would include masonry, carpentry, and bricklaying." In both cases, the WFA wrote back, "we are sorry to advise that the International Agreement with the Jamaican Government,

Figure 10. Bahamian workers at Cool Springs Labor Supply Center in Harberson, Delaware. Courtesy of Delaware Public Archives.

as well as Public Law 229, 78th Congress, under which we operate, stipulates that a recruit must returned to Jamaica at the termination of his work agreement." C. E. Herdt of the Operations Branch of the WFA noted, "during the period of their stay in the United States, they are not eligible to apply for American citizenship, and in order for them to become eligible again, it will be necessary for them to return to Jamaica and return to the United States under the regular quota."

When Afro-Caribbean contract workers tried to attain U.S. citizenship, they fought within the bounds of liberalism to gain access through the state to rights and benefits that they hoped might prevent the violence and exploitation they experienced. Other Afro-Caribbean contract workers refused to turn to the state for protection entirely, preferring instead to respond to violence with violence. As one letter signed "Farm Workers" by Jamaican workers stated: "Sir, through unbearable circumstances we are penning this letter to you. During recruitment we were told as our contract papers will verify this, that our minimum pay would be thirty cents per hour whether it be by task or hourly work [and this has not been the case]. The board and lodging conditions [are unlivable]. We are therefore requesting your quick attention as a continuance of this might bring trouble." A group of Bahamian laborers at the Cheriton, Virginia, Farm Labor Supply Center complained of lack of sufficient earnings and threatened gun violence: "There is a group of about 600 here, sir, and we decided that if the men are not transferred from Cheriton, Virginia by July 1, it will be hell here. They are planning a riot when the farmers come in the yard at morning. Lots of them have guns. . . . We are only human, we are not gods nor angels."[32] For these workers, the labor programs were not the social welfare institutions that the governments claimed, leading them to threaten the U.S. and British governments with threats of physical retribution.

Contract workers also protested the difference between their treatment in the U.S. North versus their treatment in the U.S. South. When many Jamaicans employed in the North were asked to shift to cane-cutting in Florida (where Bahamians were already employed), a riot effectively ensued. Whereas in the North, Jamaicans had sometimes received a welcome reception in local towns, they arrived in Florida to find cement-block dormitories surrounded by barbed wire, their movements controlled by local growers, the Farm Security Administration (FSA) housing authorities, and the WFA. In October 1943, ninety-three Jamaicans "refused to get off the busses," according to Herbert MacDonald, and when the WFA managed to convince them to go to the mess hall they "scraped their food on the ground and trampled it" and "abused everyone and everything in sight." The authorities immediately sent them to the local jail in Dade County where they awaited deportation. Within two weeks, the number of Jamaicans sent to Florida jails rose to seven hundred, as many refused to sign the "Jim Crow" agreement forced upon them. The WFA replaced those that were deported with new Jamaican laborers, seeking ever more passive workers.[33]

Meanwhile, the U.S. federal government explained away the labor militancy of workers as a function of their status as British colonial subjects, which made them volatile. The WFA stated, "Jamaican workers as a whole are very well educated, and are intimately familiar with and have usually committed to memory every word in the agreement as well as the employment agreement, and in addition, due to the fact that they are British subjects and British trained, they are well aware of their rights and privileges and will be constantly voicing their opinions and arguing for any cause whatsoever."[34] Due to the perceived volatility of Jamaicans, they were often kept in separate camps and fields from other contract workers. As the WFA maintained, Jamaicans had to be kept separate from Mexican braceros: "In handling Jamaicans, the administration of their problems should at all times be kept separate and distinct from the Mexican National Program just as the workers must be kept in so far as possible physically separated."[35] Even though the British West Indian, Mexican, and Puerto Rican labor programs emerged relationally, it is rare to find archival evidence of cross-racial interaction or solidarity between these contract workers, due to the ways in which the WFA disciplined and controlled workers by segregating them in labor camps and fields by color and citizenship. The segregation of workers proved a useful tactic for growers and the government to discourage solidarity among workers.

At one point, the WFA sent a group of several hundred Jamaican workers to Arizona to work alongside braceros in the fields. A report indicated that "differences of opinion occurred almost at once between these workers and Arizona growers. Considerable strong language was exchanged and some violence threatened. As a result, many dissatisfied Jamaicans were transported out of the area."[36] Jamaicans agitated at once with braceros for better working conditions, no doubt alarming Arizona growers, as it resulted in their immediate removal from the camps.

Another tactic growers used to discourage solidarity among contract workers was to play the supposed "superiority" of one group of laborers over another using preferential hiring or paying disparate wages to each group. This caused some infighting between Bahamians and Jamaicans. One WFA report referred to an investigation of Bahamian workers receiving ten cents more per hour than Jamaican workers at Blakeford Farms in Centreville, Maryland, since they seemed more willing to cooperate.[37] The citizenship of Puerto Ricans also proved a special point of contention among Caribbean contract workers, as Puerto Rican workers often felt they had to compete for jobs with British Caribbean workers who did not have U.S. citizenship, making solidarity between the two groups elusive.

Over time, growers became more and more powerful in administering the labor programs, taking over or collapsing the "benevolent" role of the state, such that the state came to do the bidding of growers. By 1955, growers refused to work with Herbert MacDonald of the AACC (now titled the Caribbean Commission), "forcing him to resign," because of his interference in the face of poor camp management and grower abuse.[38] MacDonald's successor in the Caribbean Commission proved much more cooperative with growers by ignoring the abuses of the labor program when he saw them. By the early 1960s, when the USDL sought to work with the INS to bring an agreed set of minimum standards to all guestworker contracts, it took them over two years to convince Florida growers to adjust to the contract stipulations of the Caribbean labor programs so that the federal government could "better protect" the workers. As one Department of Labor letter suggested, these growers were "influential with Senator Holland of Florida."[39] The labor programs thus resulted in state officials and growers colluding to create a cheap and expendable agricultural labor force, with the liberalism of the bracero program and the Caribbean labor importation programs both obscuring and legitimizing this outcome.

Black Anticolonial Civil Rights and the Caribbean Labor Programs

The workers were not without advocates, as Black civil rights activist organizations including the NAACP in Washington, D.C., the Bahamas Benevolent Protective Association (BBPA), and the Jamaican Progressive League (JPL) in New York intervened whenever they could to champion contract workers. By the 1940s, nearly a quarter of Harlem's population in New York was of West Indian origin, leading to the formation of these organizations. The JPL, formerly the Jamaican Benevolent Association, was an anticolonial group of Black activists that formed in 1936 to promote self-government in Jamaica and address the social welfare concerns of Jamaican communities in the United States. They also helped to create the People's National Party (PNP) on the island, devoted to universal suffrage and Jamaican independence.[40] The JPL had formed specifically to promote the independence of the British West Indies, and viewed the labor programs as a step in that direction. They therefore worked cooperatively with the WFA to manage the British West Indies labor programs in the 1940s. The JPL often received letters regarding labor contract violations directly from Jamaican or Bahamian workers and would then contact the WFA and the AACC to demand an investigation and assure workers of contract compliance in the labor programs.

On July 13, 1944, Rev. Egbert Ethelred Brown of the JPL received a letter from multiple Jamaican workers and forwarded their complaints to the WFA. As he stated, "it was reported that the sleeping quarters are so overcrowded that 100 men out of a total of 300 are forced to sleep on the floor, and that there is not sufficient work for the men so that the average weekly earnings of

each man are five dollars. There is only one toilet on the property and no facility for bathing." Brown's letter expressed the intention of securing the welfare
of the workers to ensure that the state was doing its intended job in cooperation with the WFA. As Brown stated to the WFA, "the League [JPL] will this
season continue the policy of the last of cooperating with your Department
in passing on to you complaints which have been brought to the directors, to
the end that you will be good enough to investigate such complaints, and in
the cases where it appears that real grievances exist you will take appropriate
action leading to their removal."[41]

Likewise, Origen Taylor of the Bahamas Benevolent Protective Association (BBPA) received a letter from Bahamian workers that made general
charges of the mistreatment, including being fed "slop," and being "beaten
within inches of their life if they ask questions concerning their rights as
workers under contract." Taylor wrote to the WFA expressing his concern
regarding the "cases where they were thrown into prison if they ask for their
wages" and the "cases where they have also been threatened with guns on
numerous occasions." The WFA responded to the BBPA, "an intensive investigation has been completed," and "your broad references to man-handling,
placing of workers in jail without authentic charges, and the threat of use
of firearms is exaggerated." Nonetheless, Taylor warned the WFA, "if these
conditions continue to exist after being called to your attention, we will be
forced to bring them to the attention of "higher authorities in the United
States and the Bahamas Government." The BBPA expressed concern regarding the welfare of the laborers, turning to the state to address imported
laborers' welfare and ensure the fulfillment of Caribbean workers' rights
under contract.[42]

The historical moment of World War II accelerated the anticolonial
movements led by Afro-Caribbean activists in the United States, as many saw
World War II as an effort to "free" the world from the tyranny of European
imperialism. These activists profoundly shaped Black culture, politics, and
protest, as well as the progress of Caribbean independence.[43] As the anticolonial Black civil rights activist Paul Robeson stated at a mass rally in Manhattan in 1942, World War II "is not a war for the liberation of European
nations," but "a war for the liberation of all peoples, all races, all colors anywhere in the world."[44] The leader of the National Negro Congress (NNC),
Max Yergan, likewise wrote in the *Courier*: "It must always be remembered
that the Hitlerite scourge of today has its roots in the imperialism of which
India and Africa have been the victims. Competition among the imperialist

powers for more land and peoples to exploit brought on the fascist regime." Initially reluctant to support the war because of the role of the British Empire, figures such as George Padmore, Richard B. Moore, Claudia Jones (Trinidad), C. L. R. James, Eric Williams (Trinidad), and others began to fear that if the United States did not achieve victory, it would mean the intensification of race hatred and colonialism. They also came to appreciate that the war could potentially aid their cause against British and Dutch colonialism, especially given Taussig's willing ear. They argued that the assurance of self-governance and self-determination for the Caribbean, in the words of Richard B. Moore, "is unquestionably necessary to remove this major danger of war from the Western Hemisphere," since "conflicts over colonies constitute the major source of war in the modern world."[45]

During the 1940s, when the labor programs began, both foreign- and U.S.-born Blacks in the United States together forcefully argued that their struggles against racial segregation were inextricably bound to the struggles of African and Asian peoples for independence across the globe. They articulated a common experience of racial oppression rooted in the expansion of Europe and the consequent dispersal of Black laborers throughout Europe and the New World. Many civil rights activists who fit the anticolonial paradigm confined their critique and resistance to British imperialism, neglecting the role of United States expansion.[46] In contrast, Walter White of the NAACP stated in the *Baltimore Afro-American*, "the colored people of India, China, Burma, Africa, the West Indies, the United States, and other parts of the world will continue to view skeptically assertions that this is a war for freedom and equality." Moreover, "Failure to solve this problem will inevitably mean other wars," caused by "the continuation of white imperialist exploitation of colored people."[47]

Black civil rights movement leaders called on the United States through an incipient United Nations (UN) to end colonialism and racism and support the independence of all African nations and the British West Indies. They attempted to use the UN as a forum to gain support for Black civil rights struggles in the United States, such that a delegation of Black leaders, including W. E. B. Du Bois and Richard B. Moore, attended the 1945 San Francisco Conference to demand Black self-representation. They argued that the promotion of the progressive development of the peoples of colonial territories should be directed toward "independence" or "self-government." The AACC seemed a step in that direction, but anticolonial civil rights leaders wanted self-representation and self-leadership in such organizations. During the course of the 1940s, civil rights activists put significant pressure on the U.S. state to end global colonialism as part of the "war effort."[48] The UN became a symbol of that strategy, as demonstrated by the conference in San Francisco, in which forty-six nations met and declared war on Germany and Japan.

On April 6, 1945, Du Bois organized a conference on colonialism in Harlem. Richard B. Moore gave a presentation on the approach he thought the West Indies National Council (formerly the WINEC) should project at the UN meeting in San Francisco. His opinion was that "the West Indies were a shield for the continent of America and had played an important role in the war. They have been under the control of European powers for well nigh 300 years, and have contributed very largely to the amassing of great fortune by nationals of those European powers controlling them. . . . the amount of self-government granted is negligible." He argued that race was central to the problem: "they always divided the colonies into two groups, the whites in one with 'dominion status' and the Blacks and browns in a status of 'complete subjugation and utter exploitation.'" Moore also stated that the independence of the Caribbean peoples was a necessary requisite for world peace and was required to meet the central provisions of the Atlantic Charter. "All forms of imperial rule [must] give way peacefully to the independence of all subject peoples. Will you not in this new world Charter 'proclaim liberty throughout all the land unto all the inhabitants thereof'?"[49]

Yet Moore was critical of the AACC and vacillated on whether it was benevolent or a vehicle for U.S. imperialism: "The Anglo-American Caribbean Commission has conducted broadcasts, made studies, and held conferences, but has done practically nothing to implement the rights of these people to self-government and self-determination." Moore urged several proposals at the UN conference, including "forthright recognition of the inalienable right of the Caribbean people to self-government and self-determination. . . . genuine equality of rights both in fact and in law for all peoples everywhere and full democratic citizenship rights, including universal adult suffrage, for all people." A central concern of Moore's was to rehabilitate and rebuild the economies of the Caribbean so as to overcome poverty, which he had not seen happen with the AACC.[50]

The 1935–38 labor uprisings in the Caribbean, which had emerged in response to widespread unemployment and falling wages, were central to Moore's claims. The British colonial government ruthlessly repressed the uprisings through mass shootings and arrests. The response of New York Black civil rights leaders to the uprisings indicated a turning point in Black

anticolonialism. They made appeals addressed to the British and U.S. governments, Pan-American foreign ministers, Caribbean leaders, delegates to
the adoption of the UN charter, and American political officials to demand
a Caribbean "federation," in which the islands would unite to govern themselves as one nation, thus ending colonialism on the islands.[51] In one such
declaration in July 1940, Moore stated, "the political control of the peoples
of these territories by non-American powers is now recognized to be a menace to the safety and security of all American nations. . . . Any such menace can be removed only by the integration of the West Indian peoples into
the Pan-American family of nations strictly on the basis of the right of self-
determination. Only thus will it be possible to create an enduring foundation
for genuine 'Good Neighbor' relations."[52]

One reason the U.S. and British governments had framed the labor programs as part of the effort to improve island economies in the first place was
to placate growing Afro-Caribbean civil rights leader's protest against colonialism in the Caribbean. Since agriculture was considered a war essential
industry, labor imported for that purpose would be "defense" labor, marking
the contract worker as an ally of the United Nations. This proved very effective, as Moore was able to proclaim that vital support had been rendered by
the Caribbean peoples to the war effort: "despite the debilitating hindrances
and galling yoke of colonial domination, the Caribbean peoples have loyally
and unstintingly supported the UN in the present war against Nazi barba-
rism and fascist domination. . . . they have made notable contributions to the
armed forces *and in labor power*, finance, and essential materials."[53]

The U.S. government reinforced this language, advertising that the initial 8,800 Jamaican and 4,600 Bahamian laborers, employed in the United
States in 1943, " are making a vital contribution to the cooperative effort
of the United Nations."[54] While U.S. officials lauded the program's benefits,
this description of the British West Indies labor programs was consistent
with Black civil rights leaders' belief in positive government intervention to
advance antiracism, labor protections, and eventual national independence.
In the words of Eric Williams's colleague at Howard, Ralph Bunche, the main
objective of the AACC was "to help the peoples of the Caribbean area realize
that their problems are a matter of concern and interest to Washington and
London, that they figure in the total pattern of the United Nations, and that
something is being done to solve their problems."[55]

Bunche lauded the AACC as a "contributor to the goals of the United
Nations," in an era when many African American civil rights activists saw

the UN as a forum to address issues of racial, colonial, and economic oppression, and as a site of radical hope for the global anticolonial movement. Black
activism was therefore shaped by a particular moment in which the U.S.
government came to be perceived as progressively moving toward Caribbean
independence, through the formation of a United Nations.[56] Because the federal government proclaimed that the labor programs were meant to fulfill the
benevolent mission of the UN, contract workers from the British Caribbean
seemed to be actors in the anticolonial civil rights struggle. As many argued,
the Caribbean workers made notable contribution with their labor power, as
a vital support in the formation of a UN and the eventual independence of
the islands.[57]

Other Black activists criticized the governance of the labor programs,
but not the intent of the programs. Amy Ashwood Garvey, for instance, a
Jamaican Pan-Africanist and former wife of Marcus Garvey, was concerned
specifically that Jamaican women should be included as participants in the
labor programs as "domestic workers." She wrote a number of letters in 1944
that protested the recruitment of solely male West Indian workers in the U.S.
Emergency Farm Program, asserting a gender bias in the program. Garvey
sought to "uplift" the Caribbean population by ensuring that they had access
to jobs, whether in the United States or in the Caribbean, which would benefit the Caribbean economy and ensure one of the central goals of her activism:
freedom and self-rule for the British Caribbean colonies.[58]

Some Black activists perceived in this moment of 1940s welfare capitalism the possibilities it had to end colonialism in the world, believing its
application might lead to national independence in the Caribbean.[59] As Max
Yergan of the National Negro Congress and the Council on African Affairs
noted, "Raising the living standards and well-being of the peoples of colonial
countries to a new and higher level is an indispensable condition for gaining
economic security in the postwar world. It is an indispensable condition for
avoiding right here in the United States a repetition of the wholesale unemployment and privation that we experienced in the last decade."[60] Welfare
capitalism was a necessary feature of economic expansion, Yergan argued,
since new markets abroad were required to prevent an economic collapse like
the Great Depression in the United States and around the world.

A large liberal and left faction in the United States shared Yergan's idea
that more markets were needed in the Caribbean, including U.S. Vice President Henry Wallace, who was supported by many Black activists for the Democratic ticket after President Roosevelt's death in 1945. An article from the

African-American newspaper the *Pittsburgh Courier* noted: "The only sane way out is the way visualized by such leaders as Henry Wallace and Philip Murray. It is to help industrialize the industrially backward—that is the colonial—countries on the basis of freedom and equality, and free and equal access to all raw materials and natural resources." From this perspective, the leading industrial nations should serve as anticolonial collaborators in the world, rather than rivals, and should "forgo the luxury of imperialism and accept as equal [trading] partners the peoples who are in bondage today."[61] This goal of "colonies" taking their place as independent "equals" among nations within a capitalist world system sanctified the modern nation-state as a symbol of anticolonialism.

Under "free trade" capitalism, the Jamaican and Bahamian labor programs came to be seen as a means to create economic and political independence on the islands. The sheer profit in dollars from wages alone seemed to signal the future economic independence of the islands. As the AACC stated, "the economic significance to the West Indies of this highly successful operation [the labor programs] is shown by the fact that during 1945, the workers sent back to their homes in voluntary and compulsory savings a sum amounting to approximately $20 million."[62] According to an AACC report, while Caribbean workers earned only twelve cents per hour working on the U.S. military bases on the islands, Jamaicans and Bahamians working in the United States were guaranteed a minimum wage of thirty cents per hour. The result was economic progress, as guestwork seemed to alleviate unemployment and raise wages on the islands. Another AACC report noted that "the war has brought increased money income to laborers throughout the Caribbean area. Even in Puerto Rico and Jamaica, where unemployment has previously plagued the population, wage rates have risen." A U.S. State Department report further lauded the AACC for allowing the workers "comprising 8,800 Jamaicans and 4,300 Bahamians" to make "a vital contribution to the cooperative effort of the United Nations."[63] According to the report, the labor programs had proven the benevolence of the U.S. and British governments while gifting the Caribbean with the economic capacity to take its place as a potential equal among nations in the UN.

Some African American and Caribbean diasporic elements of the civil rights movement of the 1940s were critical of U.S.-led economic development of the islands and were not interested in facilitating capitalism and "free trade" through equitable state sponsorship. The activist and scholar W. E. B. Du Bois did not see the AACC or the UN as an appropriate answer to racism or

Figure 11. Claudia Jones, Paul Robeson, Amy Ashwood Garvey, Eslanda (Essie) Robeson, 1959. Courtesy of the Schomburg Center for Research in Black Culture, New York Public Library.

colonialism. Representing the NAACP at a conference of Americans United for World Organization at the Department of State in 1944, he argued, "the emphasis on nations and states and the indifference to races, groups, or organizations indicated that the welfare and protection of colonial peoples are beyond the jurisdiction of the conference's proposed governments."[64] Du Bois knew that if there was such a global forum of nations, Black people would have little or no voice in it. Similarly, Paul Robeson told a friend that he thought President Roosevelt's reformism would have as its chief result the guarantee that capitalism would exist for another fifty years. And George Padmore of Trinidad argued that the United States would emerge from the war not as a liberating force but as the dominant imperial power, using dollar diplomacy rather than outright annexation to control the key commercial and strategic routes on the African continent and the islands of the West Indies.[65]

Claudia Jones, an early critic of U.S. involvement in the Caribbean, also recognized the ability of U.S. imperialism to camouflage or mask itself. She migrated from Trinidad to Harlem in 1924, where she later joined the CPUSA through the Young Communist League and became one of the party's leading theorists on Black women's exploitation. Jones located the heart of U.S. imperialism in the establishment of the AACC. She argued that the organization built up U.S. capitalist interests in the Caribbean as a source of cheap food and raw materials, a market for British and U.S. products, and as a "reservoir of cheap labor." The latter goal, Jones argued, continued to drive Caribbean emigration, resulting in "Anglo-American rivalry" but also collaboration, creating a relationship for exploitation. When faced with the "immense task of solving the economic problems of the West Indies," Jones found that too many national leaders of the West Indies took the view that they could "tactically bargain between the two imperialisms for greater benefits for the West Indies," by accepting "handouts" from either the British or the Americans. Jones and other key visionaries attentive to the linked dangers of capitalism and imperialism were deeply suspicious and critical of the Caribbean contract labor programs, and saw that the United States government could never offer an escape from colonialism.[66]

Caribbean Independence and the Perpetuation of Guestworker Programs

Like many Black civil rights activists engaged in the concept of Pan-Africanism, Eric Williams believed that the national independence of the islands of the Caribbean would lead to an end to colonialism and imperialism. As Williams's efforts demonstrate, he saw the nationalist project in places like Jamaica and Trinidad as an important step toward decolonization. Williams saw a federation of islands in the Caribbean as the key to independence, as a federation could grant the Caribbean sufficient economic "pull" to act as an equal among nations. Before a federation was possible, he argued, it was important that the U.S. government assist the Caribbean by reforming the island economies. When he was working for the AACC, Williams initially viewed the group as a statist solution to various economic and political problems in the Caribbean. Through his experience and research at the AACC, Williams gained considerable insight into Operation Bootstrap in Puerto Rico. In the 1950s, he began to uphold Operation Bootstrap as a model of success for encouraging the economic growth of all Caribbean islands. Williams did not find U.S. investments or aid in the Caribbean to be a problem, as long as the islands had self-representation in government. By this time, Puerto Rico, as a Commonwealth, had become a colony "liberated" through democratic revolution and industrial capitalism, with the United States government deemed a patron in a universal struggle against colonialism through "hemispheric cooperation."[67] With the PPD in Puerto Rico promoting the labor program as an object lesson in market-directed popular sovereignty, Puerto Rico became a "showcase" for what democratic capitalism could do for other Latin American and Caribbean colonies interested in adopting the Operation Bootstrap model.

By 1955, Williams began to see the Caribbean Commission as a colonial agency and quit, after which he gave several influential speeches on anticolonialism. Still, in his Woodford Square speech, "Economic Problems of Trinidad and Tobago" (July 1955), he was concerned in large part with demonstrating the relevance of Operation Bootstrap in Puerto Rico to Trinidad's development. Using Operation Bootstrap as a model, Williams formed and led a political party, the People's National Movement (PNM) in Trinidad and Tobago and then started "Operation Jobs" to restructure the economy and alleviate unemployment (1956–1966). Attacking past policies of both Britain and the United States in the Caribbean, he used the United States' Chaguaramas Base in Trinidad as a rallying point for Trinidadian nationalism in 1959. By March 1960, Williams framed the base location issue as the embodiment of national independence, such that the United States eventually "gave" the base to Trinidad.[68] His actions expressed anticolonialism even as he enticed U.S. aid and investments to improve the economy of Trinidad and Tobago as part of "Operation Jobs." While Williams exposed the military bases as vestiges of imperial rule, he was unable to view U.S. economic intervention or "free labor" and "free trade" as imperial innovations, optimistic as he was about the promises of self-representation under nationhood and national development. Williams therefore continued to seek statist solutions to economic problems on the islands throughout his term in office.

Like Puerto Rican officials, Williams did not see collaboration with the U.S. in his development campaign as a continuation of colonialism, but rather as a form of economic aid. Williams stated in his December 1960 Massa Day Done speech, "the Second World War meant the end of Massa Day," or the end of colonialism. Williams explained, "Men and women all over the world are on the march. . . . They are resolved, as we must be, that there is no more imperialism within our own society than in the society of nations." He quoted this from a book by the politician Wendell Willkie, *One World* (1940), which advocated an end to colonialism through U.S. tutelage and leadership.[69] In his speech, Williams framed national independence as antithetical to impe-rialism, as part of his campaign for the office of prime minister in Trinidad and Tobago. Williams stated, "today, with the PNM, those who were consid-ered by Massa unfit for self-government, permanently reduced to a status of inferiority, are on the verge of full control of their internal affairs and on the threshold, in their federation, of national independence." According to Wil-liams, the PNM stood for the dignity of West Indian labor, for the equality of races, interracial solidarity, economic development, education, and uplift, "without any special privilege being granted to race, colour, class, creed, national origin, or previous condition of servitude."[70] Less than one year after this speech, Williams became the first prime minister of Trinidad and Tobago (1962–1981), often referred to as the "father of the nation," as he helped to end official British colonialism on the islands.

In 1963, Williams committed Trinidad to the principles and objectives of the UN in solidarity with the Western world, in support of a trading arrange-ment that recognized the rights of less developed countries. By 1967, he courted an agreement with Canada to export legal guestworkers from Trini-dad and Tobago under temporary contracts, as a means to improve the econ-omy on the islands.[71] Williams entered politics with a personal commitment to expose colonialism and imperialism, as he did in his book *Capitalism and Slavery* (1944), which detailed the contribution of slavery to the develop-ment of British capitalism. Just as Galarza was concerned with the develop-ment of the border region of both the United States and Mexico, Williams was concerned with the Caribbean's economic development and uplift in the aftermath of slavery. He believed that crop diversification, land reform, labor relief, and a guestworker program could each spark economic growth, and eventually freedom, on the islands.[72]

In 1958, Claudia Jones wrote critically and prophetically of Williams's decision to "look to the United States for salvation, based on a one-sided esti-mate of the relative progress of Puerto Rico and on the hope of tourism from the Americas." Interestingly, Jones also followed closely the trajectory of the bracero program as well as the 1950s efforts of the American Committee for the Protection of the Foreign Born, and she remained critical of development programs that involved the United States.[73]

Just as it had in Puerto Rico, the "bootstrap" approach failed in Trini-dad, as unemployment rose from 6 percent in 1956 (at the start of Williams's leadership) to 15 percent by 1966.[74] The continuation of the labor programs was therefore needed to pacify worker unrest. By 1970, the characteristic feature of the Trinidadian and Puerto Rican economies was their highly dependent quality—dependent on foreign ownership over the economy, external trade, foreign jobs, and foreign aid resources. Meanwhile, Caribbean economies became increasingly dependent on guestworker programs, both as an added source of income and as a solution to the continued problem of unemployment.

In the case of Jamaica, Norman Manley's PNP did not challenge the administration of the guestworker programs. The Jamaican media published few disparaging accounts of the inequalities, exploitations, and contract violations, so there was little public outcry against the programs. Instead, the labor programs came to be seen as "aid programs" in which Caribbean workers were given the opportunity to earn money to take back to the islands in the form of remittances. The PNP was thus inclined to defend the labor programs, even as Jamaicans and other Caribbean workers sought out contract jobs ever more desperately. Faced with rural unemployment, many rallied for the labor programs, such that when radio stations announced that U.S. recruiters were coming on a specific day, ten men would arrive for every job available. By 1960, 40 percent of Jamaican men headed to the United States for employment.[75] Eventually, the JPL used the guestworker program to secure the patronage and votes of Jamaican workers, abandoning its anticolonial critique.[76] Backed into a corner by poverty exacerbated by U.S.-led investments and loans, the new anticolonial governments ensured that the guestworker programs remained a feature of the now independent Caribbean nations.

*   *   *

When U.S. officials adopted the anticolonial agendas of civil rights and labor activists, it became increasingly difficult for them to discern the difference between "economic aid," "social welfare," and "security" interests in the Caribbean. The pursuit of national-security assets in the U.S.-British West Indies and the creation of the AACC demonstrated this challenge well; both created political and economic stability on the islands to ensure "free trade" within a pattern of Anglo-American "collaboration" in empire. By the end of the 1940s, the United States search for national security was global in scale and sought military power and a favorable economic order as a means to protect U.S. prosperity—by keeping the Caribbean and Latin America open to U.S. investments and a source of cheap and exploitable labor. There was a consensus among political leaders of the British West Indies, Puerto Rico, and Mexico that guestworker programs were one good solution, and in some cases, the best solution to postwar unemployment, as they struggled to avoid political pressure from the unemployed. As in the case of Eric Williams and the independence of Trinidad, the result was the continuation of U.S. influence and access to Caribbean markets and resources, as well as the continued use of guestworker programs as a "safety valve" to prevent labor unrest.

During the Cold War, U.S. policy folded the British colonies into its hemispheric security arrangements and retreated from any type of "reform." The AACC or Caribbean Commission in particular retreated from its reformism on the islands, focusing instead on preventing communism from growing in the region. As the British Caribbean gained independence in the 1960s, its leaders pursued political and economic modernization through parliamentary democracy and state-sponsored capitalist development. At the same time, nationalist intellectuals and officials built and maintained a national cultural identity that would assert a distinctive way of life, ostensibly in opposition to the former colonial order.[77]

The postcolonial liberal social order that formed seemed so productive that President Kennedy's Alliance for Progress (1961) made Teodoro Moscoso, one of the central architects of Operation Bootstrap in Puerto Rico, its coordinator. Puerto Rico, a U.S. dependency, became a blueprint for U.S. development policies in the era of decolonization, in support of economic cooperation and democratic capitalism over Cuban communism. According to Moscoso, the purpose of the Alliance was to bring "economic and social development" and "reality to national aspirations" to developing countries around the principles of self-help, modernization, tax reform, and agrarian reform—not empire. As President Kennedy stated of the Alliance, "Let us once again awaken our American revolution until it guides the struggles of people everywhere—not with an imperialism of force or fear but the rule of courage and freedom and hope for the future of man."[78]

When U.S officials took on the mission of anticolonial advocacy and sanctified the nation-state through, for example, popular governance and the access to the "rights" and remittances of the contract labor programs, they obscured former colonial practices on the islands, advancing U.S. expansion and empire. The labor programs promised health, education, sustenance, security, freedom from discrimination, and greater access to political rights, even as they resulted in racialized violence, exclusion, and deportation. If the workers expressed self-governance, in the presumed agency granted to them by the labor contract, they were often automatically deported, nullifying the freedom and consent offered. National independence in the Caribbean therefore did not negate the possibility of imperial coercion via liberal devices, such as the labor contract. Instead, local nationalized state officials used liberal devices like the labor contract to describe what was once colonial labor exploitation as anticolonial, cleansing the contract of its colonial origins and perpetuating imperialism into the twenty-first century. The rhetorical self-determination and happiness promised by the contract labor programs had functioned to secure colonial labor without colonialism, even as the programs helped the British West Indies achieve what many civil rights activists in the Caribbean and the United States had desired all along—postcolonial independence.

EPILOGUE

Civil Rights for Whom?: U.S. Civil Rights and the Labor Importation Programs

In 1958, the civil rights leader A. Philip Randolph began to campaign against the bracero program and launched the National Advisory Committee on Farm Labor (NACFL) as a fact-finding agency and lobbying force, with the goal of building public awareness of the substandard living conditions of farm laborers in the United States. The organization, according to an NACFL pamphlet, desired to "help these fellow Americans attain equal protection under our laws . . . [and] create better understanding of the needs of the poorest and least protected of our working people—the farm workers."[1] Between 1959 and 1964, Randolph served as cochair of the NACFL, and held multiple hearings on farm labor and rural poverty, sending out information letters to its members in a campaign to obtain collective bargaining rights for farmworkers. Like Galarza and the National Farm Labor Union (NFLU), the NAFCL worked with the American Federation of Labor (AFL) to unionize domestic farmworkers and abolish the bracero program, arguing that braceros had been used to replace American citizen workers. The NAFCL referred to braceros as "cheap imported workers who are in a strange land, unable to speak the language, unfamiliar with American concepts of fair labor standards, and who, because they can be deported at a moment's notice, are easily intimidated."[2] Instead of organizing with braceros, Randolph and the NAFCL decided they were unwelcome in the struggle for the equal rights and protection of U.S. farmworkers.

Almost two decades earlier, on the eve of U.S. entry into World War II, Randolph had spearheaded a different campaign, this one for the civil rights of African Americans in the military, leading to the creation of the Fair Employment Practices Committee (FEPC) through Executive Order 8802. Having organized and served as the first president of the Brotherhood of Sleeping Car Porters, the first predominantly Black labor union, Randolph called on African Americans to march on Washington to demand an end to racial segregation in the U.S. military and to racial discrimination in employment in the defense industries. President Roosevelt's response, Executive Order 8802, made the promise of equal opportunity—"regardless of race, creed, color, or national origin"—a legislative order that inspired labor advocates. This order became a key stipulation in all guestworker labor contracts throughout the 1940s and 1950s, framing U.S. labor importation programs as inclusionary and race-neutral measures in dialogue with civil rights efforts.[3] Randolph's original call to end racial segregation in the U.S. military eventually extended to all defense work, even contract farm labor, and it rested on appeals to the federal government to protect American workers' civil rights. His later call to end the bracero program also rested on appeals to state power to protect American workers' civil rights, this time resulting in the exclusion of guestworkers from U.S. citizenship and from the civil rights movement.

The World War II bracero program had initially been, in part, a strategy of New Deal labor advocates to achieve the civil rights of all farmworkers in the United States—an inclusionary effort. Yet in the struggles for civil rights and social justice for farmworkers in the 1950s and 1960s, the exclusion of noncitizen workers became the necessary condition required to make the argument that U.S. farmworkers should have civil rights and that those rights should be protected. Envisioning racial equality only for workers who were citizens of the United States pushed braceros and other guestworkers out of the picture and reinforced the need for state power to deport and expunge laborers as a protective measure for U.S. labor.

By insisting on the U.S. state's capacity to grant freedom to migrant workers—either through their inclusion or exclusion—and to the colonies of the British West Indies, César Chávez, A. Philip Randolph, Ernesto Galarza, and many other civil and labor rights activists of the period helped to make Caribbean and Latin American workers subject to U.S. state power and violence. Throughout his long career, Galarza and many others attempted to reconcile liberal inclusion and state violence, never quite recognizing that one produced the other. The crux of the problem of guestworker importation programs and of national independence in the Caribbean was that they maintained the fiction of the liberal promise of freedom, thereby serving as the means through which Mexican and Caribbean workers became racialized subjects of an expanding U.S. state, within and beyond national borders.

The Mexican and Caribbean labor programs formalized the construction of the categories of "alien" or "illegal," as the labor contracts forced those who contested their circumstances or refused to work into a state of criminality or illegality and thus deportability. The migrant workers' exclusion from the nation because of their "illegality" or lack of a contract set the framework for them to be exploited, allowing agribusiness to further profit from their labor and their vulnerability. Hence, our contemporary farm labor predicament in the United States, characterized by undocumented or "illegal" surplus labor or temporarily "legal" migrant guestworkers, without much distinction in either labor or living conditions between the two. While Puerto Rican contract laborers entered the United States uniquely as U.S. citizens, their citizenship status did not negate the expansion of state violence over their lives through the labor contract; Puerto Rican contract workers were still racialized as "aliens" in the simultaneous formation of Mexican and Caribbean farm labor programs, with their recruitment as low-wage workers reinforcing their racialized status as exploitable workers, resulting in similar migration experiences. Even further, it was precisely Puerto Ricans' citizenship and their lack of deportability that slowly made Puerto Ricans less desirable as workers to agribusiness leaders, resulting in the eventual demise of the Puerto Rican farm labor program in 1993.[4]

By the 1960s, a new liberal consensus had formed against the bracero program, which led to its end on December 31, 1964.[5] As noted with the continuation of the Puerto Rican farm labor program until 1993, this did not mean labor importation schemes disappeared altogether. After the bracero program ended, employers continued to hire Mexican contract workers unhindered through H-2 labor programs, but their number was small compared to the number of men recruited during the bracero program. Instead, growers relied mostly on the recruitment of undocumented migrants to maintain wage controls and disciplinary measures over the work force. By the late 1970s and early 1980s, liberal labor advocates began to flip the rhetoric on undocumented migration, arguing for social justice for labor migrants regardless of documentation status. Appeals to curtail undocumented migrants came mostly from a conservative base by the 1980s as Republicans increasingly blamed the economic uncertainties of the U.S. job market resulting from outsourcing and globalization on undocumented migrants.[6]

In the mid-1970s, shifts in the politics of the Chicana/o movement led many to reconceptualize their relationship to Mexican migrants and they began to include undocumented migrants in their struggles. They developed a conception of community that was inclusive of both Mexican Americans and Mexican immigrants, insisting that anti-immigrant sentiments and policies translated into discriminatory measures against anyone who looked brown. By the late 1970s, the Center for Autonomous Social Action (CASA), the Committee on Chicano Rights (CCR), the National Council of La Raza (NCLR), the Mexican American Legal Defense and Education Fund (MALDEF), LULAC, the UFW, and many other organizations began to support undocumented Mexican migrants, arguing they took jobs that no one else wanted. The AFL-CIO joined with the Mexican organizations in support of undocumented migrants, but they continued to argue that contracted guestworkers would replace domestic workers, reduce wages, and bust unions. Meanwhile, farmers' lobbies insisted legislators should introduce measures to curtail undocumented migration only if they also expanded the H-2 visa category.[7]

While farm labor rights advocates in the United States continued to call out the recruitment of contract labor as the root cause of unbearable living and working conditions for U.S. farmworkers, guestworker programs from other regions, including Central America, expanded dramatically in the 1980s. In 1986, the Immigration Reform and Control Act (IRCA) became the most comprehensive reform of immigration laws since 1952, introducing employer sanctions against hiring undocumented migrants and increasing the INS enforcement budget with the goal of reducing the number of undocumented migrants who entered and resided in the United States. It also expanded the H-2 labor program into the H-2A and H-2B visa programs, with the H-2A program focusing on importing laborers from the Caribbean and Latin America for agricultural work, and the H-2B program focusing on bringing nonagricultural laborers, often for the technology sector. Notwithstanding the decision to end the bracero program, these other programs have continued into the twenty-first century, and the federal government still presents them as protective measures to secure the rights and welfare of foreign farmworkers in the United States in the face of a purported "deluge" of undocumented labor migrants.[8]

Meanwhile, many following the democratic capitalist model of development popularized with the bracero program and Operation Bootstrap in Puerto Rico still argue that guestworker programs should be perpetuated for their ability to reduce poverty and offer rights. Today, the H-2A visa is governed by both the Department of Homeland Security and the Department of Labor, "to provide agricultural employers with an orderly and timely flow of legal workers, thereby decreasing their reliance on unauthorized workers, while *protecting the rights of laborers*." According to the first stipulation of the H-2A Agricultural Clearance Order, the employer is required to provide the "same benefits, wages, and working conditions" that it does to domestic workers, and each job opportunity is "open to any U.S. worker regardless of race, color, national origin, age, sex, religion, handicap, or citizenship."[9]

Guestworker programs have been repeatedly proposed and debated since 1942 as a way to fix our broken immigration system, such that the history of these labor programs will continue to shape public debates and policy decisions. This makes it all the more imperative to reflect on how we understand these labor programs, as well as the logic that produced them. Guestworker proposals were key to IRCA in 1986 and later to proposals in the 1990s and 2000s. Since 1986, there have been major debates about whether a renewal of something like the bracero program is an acceptable compromise, with Republicans arguing for it and Democrats split. Mexican popular opinion and government leaders, including Mexican president Vicente Fox (2000–2006), have often favored such a program. Labor unions in the United States have been opposed, as has nearly every Latinx civil rights organization, but still the immigration reform debate centers on preventing undocumented immigration and providing legal pathways to work through guestworker programs. Contemporary policymakers consistently defend guestworker programs as a solution to the employment needs of U.S. businesses in response to an increasingly restrictive immigration regime. To appease big business concerns over insufficient labor, the government continues to offer contract labor and legal paths to work in the United States so that migrant workers do not "take jobs" from U.S. citizens.

Around the world, guestworker programs are still in use today to access temporary migrant labor from less developed countries for specific industries, services, government projects, and events. In 2022, the FIFA World Cup will kick off in Qatar, where two million migrant workers, mostly from Africa and Asia, are working hard under contract to build the infrastructure needed. To date, exploitation and abuse of these contract workers has been rampant, with workers exposed to forced labor, excessive hours, and unpaid wages. In November 2017, Qatar signed an agreement with the UN and the International Labor Organization (ILO) that reformed the system of contract labor or "sponsorship" put in effect, producing another liberal consensus of treaties, agreements, legal rights, and state protection. The Qatari government was given full authority to apply these rights in practice and enforce them, with a Wage Protection System (WPS), Labor Dispute Resolution Committees, and the Workers' Support and Insurance Fund. The government even announced a nondiscriminatory minimum wage for all migrant workers in Qatar, but none of these have eliminated the coercion of the contract labor system, leaving workers at the mercy of unscrupulous employers. Today, a discourse of state rights, protections, reform, and better implementation remains in place in debates over guestworker programs, fortifying the imperial practice of hiring contract laborers into the twenty-first century, even as little progress on protecting migrant workers has been made.

This drive to address the "rights" of migrant workers was rooted in the liberal formation of guestworker programs, including the bracero program, Puerto Rican labor program, and the British West Indies labor programs. The overarching goals of Galarza's "joint commission" to govern a Mexican labor importation program, the Puerto Rican Migration Division (MD), the Bureau of Employment Migration (BEM), the Anglo-American Caribbean Commission (AACC), and others were to provide general standards of wages, housing, and health care to "rehabilitate" or economically uplift the Caribbean and Mexican populations, specifically through the management of labor migration. Similarly, each program shared a language of good neighborly intentions, anti-imperialism, and bilateralism, even though Puerto Rico was a colony of the United States and the British West Indies were colonies of Great Britain. With both the Mexican and the Caribbean labor importation programs, as with Japanese American incarceration, the United States government became invested in choices, especially in the choice of the workers to serve the Allied "free" nations as an expression of democracy and good will.

As a result of the efforts of New Deal advocates across the hemisphere, the labor programs rhetorically applied liberal subjectivity to racialized subjects of the U.S. empire, as a means to aid the economic development of the Caribbean islands and Mexico, to administratively ensure the care and welfare of the workers whether in Mexico or on the islands, to fulfill the democratic goal of self-government or "self-determination," and to end colonialism. The granting of local state governance compelled former colonies in the Caribbean to embrace agendas that promoted modern liberalism, leading to overlapping state projects that encompassed multiple processes of imperialism and state-building, as seen with the contract labor importation programs. In this "transition" away from colonialism, the end of empire was defined by an assertion of local liberal policies that defined how working people would experience Commonwealth status, statehood, or independence.[10]

Each government involved endorsed the labor programs as projects of contract "freedom," obscuring the fact that coercion was central to the management of labor migration. While valuable critiques surrounding guest-worker programs have hitherto centered on denouncing imported contract farm labor as "slave" or "unfree" labor, or existing somewhere on a continuum between free and unfree labor, it is perhaps more crucial to ask how the coercion of contract labor has been maintained through the centuries since the transatlantic slave trade. Rather than define "freedom," it is critical that we demonstrate how the logic of freedom has been used to maintain capitalist racial coercion as a product of the history of human enslavement. In the case of the Japanese American inmate labor program, as in the Caribbean and Mexican labor programs, contract rights and freedoms have served as a palatable means to control and coerce Asian, Brown, and Black labor.

This book makes visible some of the intertwined logics, forces, and structures that bind the historical trajectories of guestworkers in the United States under a legal system of labor coercion. Honing in on the historical formation of the labor contract in each of these guestworker scenarios shows that U.S. guestworker programs are imperial formations, with each of the participating places and people entangled in an adaptive yet systematizing web of U.S. federal law, policymaking, and capitalist accumulation. With the turn in domestic and foreign policy in the 1940s toward addressing the long-term impacts of racial discrimination, hemispheric policymakers and labor advocates thought they could promote social change through guestworker programs. Instead, they turned Latin American and Caribbean migrant workers into subjects of state power, reinforced the logic of deportability, and racialized them as outsiders, incapable of social integration in the United States, and suitable primarily for agricultural employment.

The promoters and facilitators of the labor programs during and after World War II modified U.S. imperialism and made it conform with the modernizing ethos of racial and New Deal liberalism in the mid-twentieth century. While they did not have the goal of making overseas colonialism more efficient and effective, their commitment to anti-imperialism, racial equality, and New Deal government planning fit within a rubric of reformed liberalism; it led them to test and refine systems of labor management that were more in line with global anti-colonial and antiracist projects, thereby propagating, innovating, and authorizing empire. The framework of legal rights and inclusive nationalism through the labor programs also helped the United States to retain a moral legitimacy in global leadership.

Unlike Galarza, Randolph, and others, however, some civil rights anticolonial leaders refused to limit their visions of social justice to state-centered reforms. Stokely Carmichael, later known as Kwame Ture, for example, criticized the domesticated civil rights movement that had become focused on "individual rights" and "integration." Desegregation was not enough, he argued, because it was about the individual Black citizen rather than "the Black community." Instead of turning to the federal government for state-mandated equality, Carmichael spoke of a solidarity between Black people in the United States and Latin Americans through concrete working relationships. In a speech titled "Solidarity with Latin America" at the First Conference of the Organization of Latin American Solidarity (1967) in Cuba, he stated: "We share with you a common struggle, it becomes increasingly clear; we have a common enemy. Our enemy is white Western imperialist society. Our struggle is to overthrow this system that feeds itself and expands itself through the economic and cultural exploitation of nonwhite, non-Western peoples—of the Third World." "Anglo society has been nearly successful in keeping all of us, the oppressed of the Third World, separated and fragmented. . . ." he continued. "We recognize this as the old trick of 'divide and conquer' and we are working to see that it does not succeed this time." Carmichael called for global solidarities since "Our destiny cannot be separated from the destiny of the Spanish-speaking people in the United States and of the Americas." "Our victory will not be achieved unless they celebrate their liberation side by side with us," he concluded, "for it is not their struggle, but our struggle together."[11]

Carmichael and other radical activists were aware of the power of the U.S. state over the lives of the people of Latin America and the Caribbean, as well as the grave limitations of looking to the state for social change. For Carmichael, a state-centered approach to racial equality through state-managed desegregation was the problem, not the solution. "Integration speaks not at all to the problem of poverty, only to the problem of Blackness," he argued. "Integration today means the man who 'makes it,' leaving his Black brothers behind in the ghetto as fast as his new sports car will take him. It has no relevance to the Harlem wino or to the cotton-picker making three dollars a day."[12] Chicano/a activists of the 1970s reached a similar conclusion when it came to the struggles of Mexican Americans and those of undocumented Mexican migrants. They identified the deportation regime as a systemic and violent force targeting all ethnic Mexicans, and identified guestworker programs as a cause for that violence. As the Committee on Chicano Rights (CCR) leader Herman Baca stated in 1978, "It would create an apartheid system in the Southwest if these guestworker plans were put into effect because you need a tremendous enforcement system." While Baca, too, analogized guestworker programs to "slavery," he also saw them as a product of the larger cause of global capitalism and U.S. imperialism. Critiquing "good-willed liberals" who called "for a reshuffling without getting to the causes of the problem," Baca argued for an alternative practice of social membership, defying the logic of the nation-state by revealing its collusion with capital.[13] Carmichael's and Baca's observations compel us to reckon with the intimate historical connections between the politics of race, immigration, nation, and empire, as well as with consensus politics.

Conservatives and liberals alike advocated for the farm labor importation programs for different reasons during and after World War II, with growers mounting intensive lobbying campaigns in Washington to ensure their continuation throughout the postwar period. The bipartisan political consensus that emerged in support of guestworker programs, through the unification of welfare capitalism, turned guestworker programs into a feasible response to hemispheric economic inequality and racism. The analysis presented in this book is a reminder that effectively revising immigration politics and improving on immigrant worker conditions will not come from top-down state-led social justice measures. In order to see the world differently, we need a change in our perspectives beyond national borders, the nation-state, and the law that has shaped our thinking. We must question the logic of liberalism that brought forth labor programs in order to think about policy with greater nuance and to avoid past mistakes. Without a fundamental change in our epistemologies, guestworker programs will continue to seem like the solution to the violence of deportation and labor exploitation when, in fact, guestworker programs have historically been the catalyst for racial violence and increased deportation measures.

Any struggle for social justice for guestworkers must be conceived with the inclusion of the opinions and voices of contract workers, as Caribbean and Mexican migrant workers have engaged in countless efforts to challenge the violence of the contract over their lives, developing their own language for critiquing the logic of liberalism. For example, one bracero contested the "freedom" of the labor programs, pointing out that it was better to avoid a labor contract: "it is better to be a free worker. . . . that way you can choose your boss. This way they tell you you have to fulfill your contract before you can transfer to another job. They will not let you pick your boss. It makes us feel like we have been sold."[14] For these workers, the promises of contractual rights and "civil rights" never came to fruition. Placing the labor programs with Mexico and the Caribbean in relation to one another and in relation to different historical contexts demonstrates how liberal reformers within and outside the U.S. state erased and reproduced race and empire under the guise of civil rights and international collaboration. I do not mean to suggest that we dismiss or abandon the meanings and language of freedom, civil rights, and anticolonialism. But the history of these complexly intertwined labor programs challenges us to ask a deeper question. Civil rights and freedom, but for whom and at what costs?

NOTES

Introduction

1. Speech (Discurso) by Sr. Lic. Francisco Trujillo Gurría, Sec. del Trabajo y Provisión Social, to a contingent of Mexican workers that went to the United States on May 13, 1943, Box 17, Folder 8, Ernesto Galarza Papers, Special Collections, Stanford University Libraries (EGP); Anne Roller Issler, "Good Neighbors Lend a Hand: Our Mexican Workers," *Survey Graphic Magazine* 32, no. 10 (October 1943): 389–394, Box 24, Folder 9, EGP.

2. For the public glorification of the Jamaican guestworkers during World War II, see Cindy Hahamovitch, *No Man's Land: Jamaican Guestworkers in America and the Global History of Deportable Labor* (Princeton, NJ: Princeton University Press, 2011), 58–63.

3. Allan M. Winkler, *Homefront U.S.A.: America During World War II* (Wheeling, Ill.: Harlan Davidson, 2000), 24.

4. *A National Theme for Labor Day, 1942*, Office of War Information (OWI) Report, RG 208, Records of the Office of War Information, Box 616, U.S. National Archives (NARA).

5. This speech led to his "Point Four Program" to provide economic aid to underdeveloped countries. Harry Truman, "Truman's Inaugural Address, January 20, 1949," Harry S. Truman Library and Museum.

6. Letter to President Truman, signed by multiple braceros, May 1945, Box 17, Folder 9, EGP. The bracero program originally involved both a railroad and a farm labor importation program, although the railroad program was short-lived (1942–1945). See Erasmo Gamboa, *Bracero Railroaders: The Forgotten World War II Mexican Workers in the U.S. West* (Seattle: University of Washington Press, 2016); Barbara Driscoll, *The Tracks North: The Railroad Bracero Program of World War II* (Austin: University of Texas, 1999). Scholarship on the bracero program also includes Kitty Calavita, *Inside the State: The Bracero Program, Immigration, and the INS* (New York: Routledge, 1992); Deborah Cohen, *Braceros: Migrant Citizens and Transnational Subjects in the Postwar United States and Mexico* (Chapel Hill: University of North Carolina Press, 2011); Richard B. Craig, *The Bracero Program: Interest Groups and Foreign Policy* (Austin: University of Texas Press, 1971); Erasmo Gamboa, *Mexican Labor and World War II: Braceros in the Pacific Northwest, 1942–1947* (Austin: University of Texas Press, 1990); María Herrera-Sobek, *The Bracero Experience: Elitelore versus Folklore* (Los Angeles: UCLA Latin American Center Publications, University of California, 1979); Don Mitchell, *They Saved the Crops: Labor, Landscape, and the Struggle over Industrial Farming in Bracero-Era California* (Athens: University of Georgia Press, 2012); Ronald L. Mize, "Power (In)-Action: State and Agribusiness in the Making of the Bracero Total Institution," *Berkeley Journal of Sociology* 50 (2006): 76–119; Ana Rosas, *Abrazando el Espíritu: Bracero Families Confront the U.S.-Mexico Border* (Berkeley: University of California Press, 2014); Mireya Loza, *Defiant Braceros: How Migrant Workers Fought*

for Racial, Sexual, and Political Freedom (Chapel Hill: University of North Carolina Press, 2016); Matt Garcia, "Ambassadors in Overalls: Mexican Guest Workers and the Future of Labor," *Boom: A Journal of California* 1, no. 4 (Winter 2011): 31–44.

7. Letter from the Mexican labor inspector, 1945, Box 17, Folder 9, EGP; letter to the War Food Administration (WFA), signed by six Bahamian workers at Cheriton, Virginia, June 26, 1944; letter to President Roosevelt, August 16, 1944, RG 224 Records of the Office of Labor, War Food Administration, Entry 6, Box 17, NARA; letter to *Edward P. Morgan and the News*, American Broadcasting Network, September 26, 1958, Box 51, EGP.

8. Penny M. Von Eschen, *Race Against Empire: Black Americans and Anticolonialism, 1937–1957* (Ithaca, NY: Cornell University Press, 1997), 96–121; Howard Winant, *The World Is a Ghetto: Race and Democracy Since World War II* (New York: Basic Books, 2002); Elizabeth Borgwardt, *A New Deal for the World: America's Vision for Human Rights* (Cambridge, MA: Harvard University Press, 2005).

9. Takashi Fujitani, *Race for Empire: Koreans as Japanese and Japanese as Americans During World War II* (Berkeley: University of California Press, 2013), 25–35.

10. Jason Parker, *Brother's Keeper: The United States, Race, and Empire in the British Caribbean, 1937–1962* (Oxford: Oxford University Press, 2008), 21–23, 35; Charles Taussig, "A Four-Power Program in the Caribbean," *Foreign Affairs* (July 1946), 702–703.

11. Eric Williams, *The Negro in the Caribbean* (Washington, D.C.: Associates in Negro Folk Education, 1942); "Summary of Proposals with Regard to the Future Importation of Workers from Mexico into the United States," October 1941, Box 6, Folder 2, EGP.

12. Despite the message of racial unity, widespread segregation and racial violence were common in local U.S. communities, as embodied by the Mexican "repatriation" efforts of the 1930s and the 1943 zoot suit riots in Los Angeles. George J. Sanchez, *Becoming Mexican American: Ethnicity, Culture, and Identity in Chicano Los Angeles, 1900–1945* (Oxford: Oxford University Press).

13. On the persistence of racism in the era of racial liberalism, see Jodi Melamed, *Represent and Destroy: Rationalizing Violence in the New Racial Capitalism* (Minneapolis: University of Minnesota Press, 2011); and Eduardo Bonilla-Silva, *Racism Without Racists: Color Blind Racism and the Persistence of Racial Inequality* (Lanham, MD: Rowman & Littlefield, 2003).

14. Historians have written amply about the shift toward racial liberalism, including Simeon Man, *Soldiering Through Empire: Race and the Making of the Decolonizing Pacific* (Berkeley: University of California Press, 2018); Mary L. Dudziak, *Cold War Civil Rights: Race and the Image of American Democracy* (Princeton, NJ: Princeton University Press, 2000); Nikhil Pal Singh, *Black Is a Country: Race and the Unfinished Struggle for Democracy* (Cambridge, MA: Harvard University Press, 2004); Winant, *The World Is a Ghetto;* Carol A. Horton, *Race and the Making of American Liberalism* (New York: Oxford University Press, 2005), 121–189, and more. In defining racial liberalism, many historians mention Gunnar Myrdal's book, *An American Dilemma: The Negro Problem and Modern Democracy* (New York: Harper & Row, 1944), commissioned by the Carnegie Corporation in 1937. Thomas J. Sugrue, *Sweet Land of Liberty: The Forgotten Struggle for Civil Rights in the North* (New York: Random House, 2008), 59–63; Singh, *Black Is a Country*, 38–39.

15. Only historical analyses of the Puerto Rican farm labor program focus on the centrality of the politics of the New Deal to the Puerto Rican labor program. See, for example, Ismael García- Colón, *Colonial Migrants at the Heart of Empire* (Berkeley: University of California Press, 2020).

16. On how the New Deal failed to pursue racial equality, see Cybelle Fox, *Three Worlds of Relief: Race, Immigration, and the American Welfare State from the Progressive Era to the New Deal* (Princeton, NJ: Princeton University Press, 2012); Sugrue, *Sweet Land of Liberty,* 51–58; George Lipsitz, *The Possessive Investment in Whiteness: How White People Profit from Identity Politics* (Philadelphia: Temple University Press, 1998), 5, 38–39; Alice Kessler-Harris, *In Pursuit of Equity: Women, Men and the Quest for Economic Citizenship in 20th Century America* (New York: Oxford University Press, 2001), 16; Singh, 87. Many historians have documented the shifts in the concept of liberalism that occurred with the New Deal, but rarely mention racial liberalism. See Alan Brinkley, *The End of Reform: New Deal Liberalism in Recession and War* (New York: Vintage, 1995); Eric Foner, *The Story of American Freedom* (New York: W. W. Norton, 1994); Richard Hofstadter, *The Age of Reform* (New York: Vintage, 1955); Ira Katznelson, *Fear Itself: The New Deal and the Origins of Our Time* (New York: Liveright, 2013); Gary Gerstle and Steve Fraser, *The Rise and Fall of the New Deal Order, 1930-1980* (Princeton, NJ: Princeton University Press, 1989); Borgwardt, *A New Deal for the World.* One exception is Eric Schickler, *Racial Realignment: The Transformation of American Liberalism, 1932-1965* (Princeton, NJ: Princeton University Press, 2017), 27.

17. This stipulation is usually attributed to the Mexican government's concern over worker treatment, as the Mexican secretary of foreign affairs, Ezequiel Padilla Peñaloza, was reluctant to consider a labor importation agreement because of past exploitation and discrimination against Mexican workers. Agreement of August 4, 1942 for the Temporary Migration of Mexican Agricultural Workers to the United States as Revised on April 26, 1943, by an Exchange of Notes Between the American Embassy at Mexico City and the Mexican Ministry for Foreign Affairs, RG 224, Entry 6, Box 19, NARA.

18. Ruben Flores, *Backroads Pragmatists: Mexico's Melting Pot and Civil Rights in the United States* (Philadelphia: University of Pennsylvania Press, 2014), 15, 41, 50–51.

19. According to Tore Olsson, during the Roosevelt years nearly every key leader of the USDA visited Mexico. Tore C. Olsson, *Agrarian Crossings: Reformers and the Remaking of the U.S. and Mexican Countryside* (Princeton, NJ: Princeton University Press, 2017), 49–60, 136–146. For instance, in the first major work of racial liberalism, *An American Dilemma* (1944), Myrdal cited Tannenbaum's ideas about racial liberalism, which Tannenbaum had acquired in Mexico. For more on how racial equality became an issue of concern for the FSA, see Verónica Martínez-Matsuda, *Migrant Citizenship: Race, Rights, and Reform in the U.S. Farm Labor Camp Program* (Philadelphia: University of Pennsylvania Press, 2020).

20. Greg Grandin, *Empire's Workshop* (New York: Holt, 2006), 33; Amy Spellacy, "Mapping the Metaphor of the Good Neighbor: Geography, Globalism, and Pan-Americanism during the 1940s," *American Studies* 47 (Summer 2006): 39–66; Alan McPherson, *The Invaded: How Latin Americans Fought and Ended U.S. Occupations* (New York: Oxford University Press, 2014); Darlene Sadlier, *Americans All: Good Neighbor Cultural Diplomacy in World War II* (Austin: University of Texas Press, 2012).

21. Franklin D. Roosevelt, "The Good Neighbor Policy," August 14, 1936, FDR Presidential Library; Roosevelt-Camacho Meeting, April 20, 1943, RG 208, Entry 376, Box 436, NARA.

22. See Mary Dudziak and Nikhil Pal Singh.

23. Jodi Melamed, "The Spirit of Neo-Liberalism: from Racial Liberalism to Neoliberal Multiculturalism," *Social Text* 24, no. 4 (Winter 2006): 6.

24. Many also had a desire to migrate based on specific local and national conditions that intertwined with social systems and place. Cohen, *Braceros,* 67.

25. See Jason M. Colby, *The Business of Empire: United Fruit, Race, and U.S. Expansion in Central America* (Ithaca, NY: Cornell University Press, 2011); Julie Greene, *The Canal Builders: Making America's Empire at the Panama Canal* (New York: Penguin Press, 2009).

26. Mae Ngai, *Impossible Subjects: Illegal Aliens and the Making of Modern America* (Princeton, NJ: Princeton University Press, 2004), 94–95, 129; Lilia Fernández, "Of Immigrants and Migrants: Mexican and Puerto Rican Labor Migration in Comparative Perspective, 1942–1964," *Journal of American Ethnic History* (Spring 2010): 27. Notably, historian Gilbert Gonzalez has stressed that guestworkers are a form of colonial labor, but does so by arguing that the bracero program is just like European colonial migrations like Algerian emigrants to France, or Indian "coolies" to the British West Indies. Gilbert G. Gonzalez, *Guest Workers or Colonized Labor? Mexican Labor Migration to the United States* (Boulder, CO: Paradigm, 2006), 15–51.

27. For influence, see Lisa Lowe, *Intimacies of Four Continents* (Durham, NC: Duke University Press, 2015).

28. Michel Foucault, "Governmentality," in *The Foucault Effect*, ed. Graham Burchell, et al. (Chicago: University of Chicago Press, 1991). This definition of empire is taken from the *Oxford English Dictionary*. Moon-Ho Jung, "Empire," *Keywords for Asian American Studies*, ed. Cathy J. Schlund-Vials et al. (New York: New York University Press, 2015), 70.

29. For a more detailed definition of "the state," see Margot Canaday, *The Straight State: Sexuality and Citizenship in Twentieth-Century America* (Princeton, NJ: Princeton University Press, 2009), 4–10; Timothy Mitchell, "The Limits of the State: Beyond Statist Approaches and Their Critics," *American Political Science Review* 85 (1991): 77–96; James C. Scott, *Seeing Like a State: How Certain Schemes to Improve the Human Condition Have Failed* (New Haven, CT: Yale University Press, 1998). Also see Chantel Rodríguez, *Health on the Line: The Politics of Citizenship and the Railroad Bracero Program of World War II* (Ph.D. diss., University of Minnesota, 2013), 17–29.

30. Normalizing claims to whiteness have underscored liberalism from its inception. Lipsitz, *The Possessive Investment in Whiteness*; Lowe, *Intimacies of Four Continents*; Uday Singh Mehta, *Liberalism and Empire: A Study in Nineteenth Century British Thought* (Chicago: University of Chicago Press, 1999); Cedric Robinson, *Black Marxism: The Making of the Black Radical Tradition* (Chapel Hill: University of North Carolina University Press, 1983); Saidiya Hartman, *Scenes of Subjection: Terror, Slavery, and Self-Making in the Nineteenth Century* (Oxford: Oxford University Press, 1997); Jodi Byrd, *Transit of Empire: Indigenous Critiques of Colonialism* (Minneapolis: University of Minnesota Press, 2011); Mary Louise Pratt, *Imperial Eyes: Travel Writing and Transculturation* (New York: Routledge, 1992); Evelyn Nakano Glenn, *Unequal Freedom: How Race and Gender Shaped American Citizenship and Labor* (Cambridge, MA: Harvard University Press, 2002).

31. For more on liberal inclusion and state violence, see Chandan Reddy, *Freedom With Violence: Race, Sexuality, and the U.S. State* (Durham, NC: Duke University Press, 2011), 9; A. Naomi Paik, *Rightlessness: Testimony and Redress in U.S. Prison Camps since World War II* (Chapel Hill: University of North Carolina Press, 2016); Melamed, *Represent and Destroy*; David Campbell, *Writing Security: United States Foreign Policy and the Politics of Identity* (Minneapolis: University of Minnesota Press, 1992). Also see Walter Benjamin, "Critique of Violence," *Walter Benjamin, Selected Writings*, ed. Howard Eiland and Michael Jennings, vol. *1, 1913–1926* (Cambridge, MA: Harvard University Press, 2004); Michel Foucault, *"Society Must Be Defended": Lectures at the Collège de France, 1975–76*, ed. Mauro Bertani et al. (New York: Picador, 2003).

32. On earlier U.S. contract labor programs, see Gunther Peck, *Reinventing Free Labor: Padrones and Immigrant Workers in the North American West, 1880–1930* (New York: Cambridge University Press, 2000), and Alanis Enciso, "El primer programa bracero y el gobierno de

Mexico, 1917–1918," *Hispanic American Historical Review* 81 (May 2001). Tony Bennet, Francis Dodsworth, and Patrick Joyce, "Introduction: Liberalisms, Government, and Culture," *Cultural Studies* 21 (2007): 525–548.

33. It is important to note that federal apprehension and deportation statistics do not include the vast majority of people who were forced to leave the United States by self-deportation, due to fear campaigns led by local, state, and federal officials. Adam Goodman, *The Deportation Machine: America's Long History of Expelling Immigrants* (Princeton, NJ: Princeton University Press, 2020), 45–46, 53; Kelly Lytle Hernández, *Migra!: A History of the U.S. Border Patrol* (Berkeley: University of California Press, 2010), 120. Also see Daniel Kanstroom, *Deportation Nation: Outsiders in American History* (Cambridge, MA: Harvard University Press, 2007); Mark Reisler, *By the Sweat of Their Brow, Mexican Immigrant Labor in the United States, 1900–1940* (New York: Praeger, 1976); Kitty Calavita, *Inside the State: The Bracero Program, Immigration, and the INS* (New York: Routledge, 1992). On the state regulation of labor migrants on the East Coast, see Cindy Hahamovitch, *The Fruits of Their Labor: Atlantic Coast Farmworkers and the Making of Migrant Poverty, 1870–1945* (Chapel Hill: University of North Carolina Press, 1997).

34. By "overlapping imperial projects," I do not intend to ignore the history of U.S. hegemony in Latin America, or the historic inequalities that have structured the diplomatic relationship between, for example, Mexico and the United States. Rather, I aim to show how the logic of coloniality is perpetuated through the expansion of state-power within the state. I am indebted to Ileana Rodríguez-Silva for the phrase "overlapping imperialisms." See her book, *Silencing Race: Disentangling Blackness, Colonialism, and National Identities in Puerto Rico* (New York: Palgrave Macmillan, 2012), 136. José Vasconcelos, *The Cosmic Race/ La Raza Cosmica* (Baltimore: Johns Hopkins University Press, 1997), originally published in 1925; Christopher Boyer, *Becoming Campesinos: Politics, Identity, and Agrarian Struggle in Postrevolutionary Michoacán, 1920–1935* (Palo Alto, CA: Stanford University Press, 2003); Gilbert M. Joseph, *Everyday Forms of State Formation: Revolution and the Negotiation of Rule in Modern Mexico* (Durham, NC: Duke University Press, 1994).

35. Mark Overmeyer-Velázquez, "Good Neighbors and White Mexicans: Constructing Race and Nation on the U.S.-Mexico Border," *Journal of American Ethnic History* 33 (Fall 2013): 10–14. On state-led modernization and the bracero program, see Cohen, *Braceros.*

36. Testimony of Felix Tapia, September 27, 1945, Galarza Field Notes, Box 6, Folder 3, EGP; Testimony of two "nationals" at the Rudy Avila Camp in Patterson, California, Galarza Field Notes, Box 18, Folder 6, EGP.

37. Few historians detail the bracero program as a product of U.S. empire or colonialism. One exception is Gilbert G. Gonzalez, *Guest Workers or Colonized Labor?* Amy Kaplan and Donald Pease, *Cultures of United States Imperialism* (Durham, NC: Duke University Press, 1993).

38. Lowe, *Intimacies*, 37, 40–41.

39. Recent examples of this work include JoAnna Poblete, *Islanders in the Empire: Filipino and Puerto Rican Laborers in Hawai'i* (Urbana: University of Illinois Press, 2014); Fujitani, *Race for Empire*; Manu Karuka, *Empire's Tracks: Indigenous Nations, Chinese Workers, and the Transcontinental Railroad* (Berkeley: University of California Press, 2019); Laura Briggs, *Reproducing Empire: Race, Sex, Science, and U.S. Imperialism in Puerto Rico* (Berkeley: University of California Press, 2003); Matthew Casey, *Empire's Guestworkers: Haitian Migrants in Cuba During the Age of U.S. Occupation* (New York: Cambridge University Press, 2017); Robert McGreevey, *Borderline Citizens: The United States, Puerto Rico, and the Politics of Colonial Migration* (Ithaca, NY: Cornell University Press, 2018); García-Colón, *Colonial Migrants at the Heart of Empire*

(2020). Also see Aníbal Quijano, "Coloniality of Power, Eurocentrism, and Latin American," *International Sociology* 15 (June 2000): 215-232; Walter Mignolo, *On Decoloniality: Concepts, Analytics, Praxis* (Durham: Duke University Press, 2018).

Chapter 1

1. Henry Anderson, "Fields of Bondage: The Mexican Contract Labor System in Industrialized Agriculture" (Self-published May 1, 1963), Martinez, CA, 2; Truman E. Moore, *The Slaves We Rent* (New York: Random House, 1965); Ernesto Galarza, *Merchants of Labor: The Mexican Bracero Story, an Account of the Managed Migration of Mexican Farm Workers in California, 1942-1960* (Charlotte, NC: McNally, 1970 [1964]),16.

2. Southern Poverty Law Center, *Close to Slavery: Guestworker Programs in the United States*, A Report by the SPLC, 2005. https://www.splcenter.org/20130218/close-slavery-guestworker-programs-united-states.

3. Ngai, *Impossible Subjects*, 161. Also see Ann Stoler, "On Degrees of Sovereignty," *Public Culture* (January 2006): 125-146.

4. Much like popular representations of slavery in the historiography before the 1960s, the image of braceros produced at this time was one of a passive people who do not control their own destiny, an image which was meant to get the attention of Black activists and others involved in the civil rights movements of the 1950s and early 1960s. For an example of pre-1960s representation of slavery, see Ulrich B. Phillips, *American Negro Slavery* (New York: D. Appleton Press, 1918). For more on nineteenth century "free labor ideology," see Eric Foner, *Free Soil, Free Labor, Free Men: The Ideology of the Republican Party before the Civil War* (New York: Oxford University Press, 1970); Tomás Almaguer, *Racial Fault Lines: The Historical Origins of White Supremacy in California* (Berkeley: University of California Press, 1994), 32-37.

5. See especially Walter Johnson, "To Remake the World: Slavery, Racial Capitalism, and Justice," *Boston Review* (October 2016), with responses, and Cedric Robinson, *Black Marxism*.

6. Lisa Lowe, *Immigrant Acts: On Asian American Cultural Politics* (Durham, NC: Duke University Press, 1996), 12-14.

7. For more on how the concept of freedom has been instrumental in authorizing colonial violence and has underwritten U.S. imperial agendas, see Amy Kaplan and Donald Pease, *Cultures of United States Imperialism*; Penny Von Eschen, *Race Against Empire*; Mary Renda, *Taking Haiti: Military Occupation and the Culture of U.S. Imperialism, 1915-1940* (Chapel Hill: University of North Carolina Press, 2001). Also see Stephanie Smallwood, "Commodified Freedom: Interrogating the Limits of Anti-Slavery Ideology in the Early Republic," *Journal of the Early Republic* 24, no. 2 (Summer 2004): 289-298; and Stephanie Smallwood, "Freedom," in *Keywords for American Cultural Studies*, ed. Bruce Burgett and Glenn Hendler (New York: New York University Press, 2014), 111-115.

8. The historian Hugh Tinker concludes in his analysis that indentured servitude or coolie labor was a "new system of slavery," while David Northrup argues that it was a mostly voluntary labor supply. More recently, the historian Elliott Young states, "In between the poles of free and voluntary emigrant and slave, there was a vast complex gray zone." Hugh Tinker, *A New System of Slavery: The Export of Indian Labour Overseas, 1830-1920* (Oxford: Oxford University Press, 1974); David Northrup, *Indentured Labor in the Age of Imperialism, 1834-1922* (New York: Cambridge University Press, 1995); Elliott Young, *Alien Nation: Chinese Migration in the Americas from the Coolie Era Through World War II* (Chapel Hill: University of North Carolina Press, 2014), 22.

9. Here I am referring to the organized practices (mentalities, rationalities, and techniques) through which subjects are governed, or "the art of government" that leads to more efficient

forms of social control by enabling individuals to govern themselves. See Foucault's theory of biopolitics and governmentality in Michel Foucault, "Society Must be Defended," "The Birth of Biopolitics," "The Courage of Truth" in Foucault, *The Courage of Truth: The Government of Self and Others II, Lectures at the Collège de France 1983–1984*, ed. Frédéric Gros (New York: Palgrave Macmillan, 2011); *Society Must Be Defended: Lectures at the Collège de France, 1975–76*, ed. Mauro Bertani et al. (New York: Picador, 2003).

10. John Locke, *Second Treatise of Government* (Indianapolis, IN: Hackett, 1980 [1690]).

11. Amy Dru Stanley, *From Bondage to Contract: Wage Labor, Marriage, and the Market in the Age of Slave Emancipation* (Cambridge: Cambridge University Press, 1998), xi, 1, 4. On classical liberal thought, market relations, and contract, see Thomas C. Holt, *The Problem of Freedom: Race, Labor, and Politics in Jamaica and Britain, 1832–1938* (Baltimore: Johns Hopkins University Press, 1992).

12. Singh, *Black Is a Country*, 20; Robert J. Steinfeld, *The Invention of Free Labor: The Employment Relation in English and American Law and Culture, 1350–1870* (Chapel Hill: University of North Carolina Press, 1991); Edmund Morgan, *American Slavery, American Freedom* (New York: W. W. Norton, 1975).

13. Adam Smith, *The Wealth of Nations* (New York: Bantam Classics, 2003 [1776]), 229. Seymour Drescher, "Free Labor vs. Slave Labor: The British and Caribbean Cases," in *Terms of Labor: Slavery, Serfdom, and Free Labor*, ed. Stanley L. Engerman (Stanford: Stanford University Press, 1999), 51–59.

14. Manisha Sinha, *The Slave's Cause: A History of Abolition* (New Haven, CT: Yale University Press, 2016); Gelien Matthews, *Slave Rebellions and the British Anti-Slavery Movement* (Baton Rouge: Louisiana State University Press, 2006).

15. Tinker, *New System of Slavery*, 1–2, 16. Also see Madhavi Kale, *Fragments of Empire: Capital, Slavery, and Indian Indentured Labor Migration in the British Caribbean* (Philadelphia: University of Pennsylvania Press, 1998). It is important to note that in California, all Chinese were racialized as "coolies," whether they had a labor contract or not.

16. Lisa Lowe, *The Intimacies of Four Continents*, 74.

17. Sidney Mintz, *Sweetness and Power: The Place of Sugar in Modern History* (New York: Penguin, 1985), 61–72. Moon-Ho Jung, "Seditious Subjects: Race, State Violence, and U.S. Empire," *Journal of Asian American Studies* 14, no. 2 (June 2011): 231.

18. Tinker, *A New System of Slavery*, 73, 115, 194.

19. Robert Steinfeld, *Coercion, Contract, and Free Labor in the Nineteenth Century* (Cambridge: Cambridge University Press, 2001).

20. Hugh Tinker, *A New System of Slavery*.

21. The historian Amy Dru Stanley has developed this idea through the figure of the prostitute. Stanley, *From Bondage to Contract*, 219.

22. As the historian Moon-Ho Jung notes, "Neither free nor enslaved labor, coolies signified an ambiguous contradiction that seemed to hold the potential to advance either." Moon-Ho Jung, *Coolies and Cane: Race, Labor, and Sugar in The Age of Emancipation* (Baltimore: Johns Hopkins University Press, 2006), 6, 19, 26.

23. "An Act to Prohibit the 'Coolie Trade' by American Citizens in American Vessels," *Congressional Record*, 37th Congress, 2nd Session, February 19, 1862.

24. William S. Kiser, "A Charming Name for a Species of Slavery: Political Debate on Debt Peonage in the Southwest, 1840s–1860s," *Western Historical Quarterly* (2014): 185–87. For more on the roots of peonage in the South and the Southwest, see Pete Daniel, *In the Shadow of Slavery: Peonage in the South, 1901–1969* (Urbana: University of Illinois Press, 1972); Greg Downs

and Kate Masur, eds., *The World the Civil War Made* (Chapel Hill: University of North Carolina Press, 2015). For more on the question of coercion and contract labor in the American West, see Gunther Peck, *Reinventing Free Labor: Padrones and Immigrant Workers in the North American West, 1880–1930* (Cambridge: Cambridge University Press, 2000).

25. Lisa Lowe, "Autobiography Out of Empire: A Future Beyond Empire," *Small Axe: A Caribbean Journal of Criticism* 28 (March 2009): 98–111; Moon-Ho Jung, "Seditious Subjects," 227.

26. Nayan Shah, *Contagious Divides: Epidemics and Race in San Francisco's Chinatown* (Berkeley: University of California Press, 2001), 160–162.

27. Almaguer, *Racial Fault Lines*, 39, 48–51.

28. Edward Dallam Melillo, *Strangers on Familiar Soil: Rediscovering the Chile-California Connection* (New Haven, CT: Yale University Press, 2015), 82–83.

29. Young, 46; Lucy M. Cohen, *The Chinese in the Post-Civil War South: A People Without a History* (Baton Rouge: Louisiana State University Press, 1984), 41–42.

30. "American Emigrant Company," *New York Times*, September 6, 1863. American Emigrant Company, "Chartered for the Purpose of Procuring and Assisting Emigrants from Foreign Countries to Settle in the United States," John Williams, General Agent for Emigration (New York: Office of the Iron Age, 1865), Harvard University Library, 3–5, 10–11.

31. Andrew Gyory, *Closing the Gate: Race, Politics, and the Chinese Exclusion Act* (Chapel Hill: University of North Carolina Press, 1998), 29–33. Gyory separates "the ideals of free labor, free movement, and freedom" from whiteness and racism, and in doing so, is able to make the claim that whiteness was just one of many ideals shaping workers' sensibilities and actions in the late 1800s (alongside freedom and equality). In contrast, I contend that it is precisely the ideals of freedom and equality that allowed white supremacy and immigration restriction to flourish, as we can see through the nature of the debates over slavery and freedom. Gyory, 73.

32. See, for example, the "Truckee strategy," as detailed in Adam Goodman's *The Deportation Machine*, 9–36.

33. "'For the Equality of Men—For the Equality of Nations': Anson Burlingame and China's First Embassy to the United States, 1868," *Journal of American-East Asian Relations* 17 (2010): 20–21. Burlingame speech, New York, June 23, 1868. For more on the Burlingame-Seward Treaty and anti-Chinese hostility, see Beth Lew-Williams, *The Chinese Must Go: Violence, Exclusion, and the Making of the Alien in America* (Cambridge, MA: Harvard University Press, 2018), 27–36; Goodman, *Deportation Machine*, 12–15.

34. Goodman, *Deportation Machine*, 167–177; Charles McCain, *In Search of Equality: The Chinese Struggle Against Discrimination in Nineteenth Century America* (Berkeley: University of California Press, 1996).

35. Jung, "Seditious Subjects," 221–247.

36. Shah, *Contagious Divides*, 167–177.

37. Jung, "Seditious Subjects," 221–247.

38. The Foran Act, January 26, 1885, 23 Stat 332 U.S.C. *The Statutes at Large of the United States of America from December 1883 to March 1885* (Washington, D.C.: U.S. Government Printing Office, 1885).

39. Daniel Kanstroom, *Deportation Nation: Outsiders in American History* (Cambridge, MA: Harvard University Press, 2010), 92–93, 118–122.

40. See the Supreme Court case *United States v. Ju Toy* 198 U.S. 253 (1905); Kanstroom, *Deportation Nation*, 129; Also see Shah, *Contagious Divides*, 160. Reference to "hordes" from the U.S. Supreme Court case *Chae Chan Ping v. United States* (1889).

41. The Department of Labor came into statutory life on March 4, 1913. Department circular, Department of Labor, March 12, 1913, RG 174, General Records of the Department of Labor, Office of the Secretary, Box 144, NARA.

42. Judson MacLaury, *History of the Department of Labor, 1913–1988* (Washington, D.C.: U.S. Department of Labor, 1997).

43. This act created the Asiatic Barred Zone, prohibiting any person of Asian descent from entering the United States. It also raised the head tax to $8, imposed a $10 visa fee, instituted a literacy test, and broadened deportation rules. By this point, the government began to introduce the full-scale production of passport controls as an emergency war measure. These became the norm in regulating migration. Ngai, *Impossible Subjects,* 19–20.

44. Cindy Hahamovitch, "Creating Perfect Immigrants: Guestworkers of the World in Historical Perspective," *Labor History,* no. 44 (2003): 79; Otey M. Scruggs, "The First Mexican Farm Labor Program," *Arizona and the West,* no. 2 (Winter 1960): 324; Alanis Enciso, "El primer programa bracero y el gobierno de México, 1917–1918"; Mark Reisler, *By the Sweat of Their Brow* (New York: Praeger, 1976).

45. U.S. Congress, H.R. 10384, An Act to regulate the immigration of aliens to, and the residence of aliens in the United States, 64th Congress, 2nd Session (Washington, D.C.: U.S. Government Printing Office, 1917).

46. Scholars have referred to this 1917–1921 labor program as "the first bracero program," but it was a bureaucratically disorganized effort that lacked the transnational administration of its successor. See Chantel Rodriguez, *Health on the Line,* 3. Also see Alanis Enciso, "El primer programa bracero," and Barbara Driscoll, *The Tracks North,* 6–8. For more on the congressional emphasis on "free will," see Alexandra Filindra, "The Emergency of the 'Temporary Mexican': American Agriculture, the U.S. Congress, and the 1920 Hearings on the Temporary Admission of Illiterate Mexican Laborers," *Latin American Research Review* 49, no. 3 (2014): 91–95.

47. Tinker, *A New System of Slavery,* 284.

48. Quoted from Tinker, 343, 357.

49. As the historian Gunther Peck argues, "precisely what constituted free labor was bitterly fought over by immigrant workers, their padrones, middle-class reformers, immigration officials, and corporate employers in North America between 1880–1930." He also notes that these labor contractors or *padrones* gained power from the relative weakness of the state. Peck, 8, 20.

50. Scruggs, "The First Mexican Labor Program," 323, 325. Ngai, *Impossible Subjects,* 52; Hahamovitch, "Creating Perfect Immigrants," 80.

51. Scruggs, "The First Mexican Labor Program," 323, 325. Ngai, *Impossible Subjects,* 52; Hahamovitch, "Creating Perfect Immigrants," 80; Enciso, "El primer programa bracero."

52. Kelly Lytle Hernández, *Migra!,* 12, 26, 36, 120–121. See also Julian Lim, *Porous Borders: Multiracial Migrations and the Law in the U.S.-Mexico Borderlands* (Chapel Hill: University of North Carolina Press, 2017), 4–13.

53. S. Deborah Kang, *The INS on the Line: Making Immigration Law on the US-Mexico Border, 1917–1954* (New York: Oxford University Press, 2017), 32. Ngai, *Impossible Subjects,* 57, 60.

54. Hernández, *Migra!,* 92; Ngai, *Impossible Subjects,* 57; Goodman, *Deportation Machine,* 33–72; Kang, *The INS on the Line,* 32–45.

55. George J. Sanchez, *Becoming Mexican American: Ethnicity, Culture, and Identity in Chicano Los Angeles, 1900–1945* (Oxford: Oxford University Press), 213–214.

56. Mark Barenberg, "The Political Economy of the Wagner Act: Power, Symbol, and Workplace Cooperation," *Harvard Law Review* 106 (May 1993): 1428.

57. Lizabeth Cohen, *Making a New Deal: Industrial Workers in Chicago, 1919–1939* (Cambridge: Cambridge University Press, 1990).

58. William Forbath, *Law and the Shaping of the American Labor Movement* (Cambridge, MA: Harvard University Press, 1991), 127–148, 165.

59. Holly J. McCammon, "Legal Limits on Labor Militancy," *Social Problems* (May 1990): 206–210, 287.

60. Cohen, *Making a New Deal*, 252–253, 267–268, 287. Irving Bernstein, *The Turbulent Years: A History of the American Worker, 1933–1941* (Boston: Houghton Mifflin, 1969).

61. Cohen, *Making a New Deal*, 253.

62. Italics mine. Franklin D. Roosevelt, "Statement on Signing the National Labor Relations Act," July 5, 1935, available online from Gerhard Peters and John T. Woolley, *The American Presidency Project*, http://www.presidency.ucsb.edu/ws/?pid=14893.

63. Wagner, "Talk on Labor Relations 9–10," February 29, 1936, Wagner Papers, SF 103, Folder 36, as quoted in Barenberg, "The Political Economy of the Wagner Act," 1424.

64. U.S. Congress, National Labor Relations Board, Hearings before the Committee on Education and Labor, United States Senate, on S. 1958, a Bill to Promote Equality of Bargaining Power between Employers and Employees, to Diminish the Causes of Labor Disputes, to Create a National Labor Relations Board, and for Other Purpose. Statement of Senator Wagner, 74th Congress, 1st Session (Washington, D.C.: U.S. Government Printing Office, 1935).

65. Robert Wagner, "Company Unions: A Vast Industrial Issue," *New York Times*, March 11, 1934.

66. For more on the role of the NLRB, see Frank W. McCulloch and Tim Bornstein, *The National Labor Relations Board* (New York: Praeger, 1974).

67. Rebecca Zietlow, *Enforcing Equality: Congress, The Constitution, and the Protection of Individual Rights* (New York: New York University Press, 2006), 94; George Lipsitz, *The Possessive Investment in Whiteness*, 5–6, 216–217. Also see Margot Canaday, *Sexuality and Citizenship in Twentieth-century America* (Princeton, NJ: Princeton University Press, 2009) and Scott Kurashige, *The Shifting Grounds of Race: Black and Japanese Americans in the Making of Multiethnic Los Angeles* (Princeton, NJ: Princeton University Press, 2008).

68. To be sure, conservative growers also pressed for the labor programs, complaining anew of a labor shortage much as they had during World War I. As U.S. officials debated the efficacy of the labor contract in the early 1940s, growers again looked to Mexico for labor, in spite of the prohibition of foreign contract labor laid down in the Foran Act of 1885.

69. Otey M. Scruggs, "Evolution of the Mexican Farm Labor Agreement of 1942," *Agricultural History* 34, no. 3 (July 1960): 144–50.

70. Scruggs, *Evolution*.

71. Richard B. Craig, *The Bracero Program*, 42; Scruggs, "Evolution," 147.

72. Letter number 2309, "With Reference to the Importation of Laborers from Mexico," June 23, 1942, RG 211, Records of the War Manpower Commission, Entry 171, Box 15, NARA. Also quoted in Scruggs, "Evolution," 147.

73. Exchange of notes at Mexico, April 26, 1943, from the Minister of Foreign Affairs to the American ambassador in Mexico City. See Foreign Relations of the United States: Diplomatic Papers (hereafter Foreign Relations), vol. 7, Mexico (Washington, D.C.: U.S. Government Printing Office, 1943), 1129, https://history.state.gov/historicaldocuments/frus1944v07/ch76; Memo to Mr. Secretary from Chairman McNutt, May 14, 1943; Memo to Mr. Leo R. Warts, Assistant Director, Operations Division, WMC, From: Office of the General Counsel, Re: Exploitation of Mexican Workers, December 2, 1942, Entry 156, Box 6, NARA.

74. Verónica Martínez-Matsuda, *Migrant Citizenship*, 4–12.

75. Martínez-Matsuda, *Migrant Citizenship*.

76. Ana Minian, *Undocumented Lives: The Untold Story of Mexican Migration* (Cambridge, MA: Harvard University Press, 2018).

77. The bracero program guaranteed no hordes and no lowering of the standards of wage work in the United States, echoing some abolitionists' arguments of the nineteenth century in efforts to replace slavery with contract wage work. For more on the gendered dimensions of the bracero program, see Mireya Loza, *Defiant Braceros*; Ana Elizabeth Rosas, *Abrazando el Espíritu*; and Deborah Cohen, *Braceros*.

78. The first labor contracts lasted six months, but they later lasted only three months, then eventually only forty-five days.

79. For more detail on Mexico's drive to modernize rural Mexico through the bracero program, see Cohen, *Braceros*.

80. See Minian, *Undocumented Lives*, 18–23.

81. Craig, *The Bracero Program*, 47. Kirstein, *Anglo Over Bracero: A History of the Mexican Worker in the United States from Roosevelt to Nixon* (San Francisco: R & E Research Associates, 1977), 19, 45, 15–53; Hahamovitch, *No Man's Land*, 33.

82. Holt, *The Problem of Freedom*, 367–369; Tinker, *A New System of Slavery*, 366–375; Hahamovitch, *No Man's Land*, 23–25. Agreement for the Employment of Bahamians in the United States, RG 224, Entry 6, Box 17, NARA.

83. Otey Scruggs, "Texas and the Bracero Program, 1942-1947," *Pacific Historical Review* (1963): 251.

84. Miguel Jáquez López, interview by Laureano Martínez, May 27, 2003, in Bracero History Archive, item 214.

85. Appolonio Venegas, interview by Mario Sifuentez, May 27, 2003, in Bracero History Archive, item 395.

86. Fortino Covarrubias, interview by Mario Sifuentez, May 25, 2006, in Bracero History Archive, item 395.

Chapter 2

1. Ernesto Galarza, "Life in the United States for Mexican People: Out of the Experience of a Mexican (1929)," in *Man of Fire: Selected Writings of Ernesto Galarza*, ed. Armando Ibarra and Rodolfo Torres (Urbana: University of Illinois Press, 2013), 30, 28–29.

2. *Man of Fire*, 30.

3. U.S. House of Representatives, Select Committee to Investigate the Interstate Migration of Destitute Citizens (Tolan Committee), Resolutions to Inquire into the Migration of Destitute Citizens, To Study, Survey, and Investigate the Social and Economic Needs and the Movement of Indigent Persons Across State Lines, 76th Congress, 3rd Session, Part 10, December 11, 1940, and February 26, 1941 (Washington, D.C.: U.S. Government Printing Office), 3885; U.S. House of Representatives, Select Committee Investigating National Defense Migration (Tolan Committee), A Resolution to Inquire Further Into the Interstate Migration of Citizens, Emphasizing the Present and Potential Consequences of the Migration Caused by the National Defense Program, Pursuant to H. Res. 113, 77th Congress, 2nd Session, Part 33, May 22, June 11, 19, 1942 (Washington, D.C.: U.S. Government Printing Office), 12432–12438.

4. Tolan Committee hearings, Part 33: 12430; Ngai, *Impossible Subjects*, 161; Craig, *The Bracero Program*, 30.

238 Notes to Pages 54–60

5. While these state projects were an attempt to include people of color as part of the national project, they also disenfranchised *indios* and Blacks. See Ruben Flores, *Backroads Pragmatists*, 49.

6. For more on these research trips to Mexico by prominent New Deal officials, see Olsson, *Agrarian Crossings*.

7. Other antiracist regimes include the multiculturalism of the 1970s–1990s, and the current regime of neoliberalism. Melamed, xi.

8. Frederick Cooper, Allen F. Isaacman, Florencia C. Mallon, William Roseberry, and Steve J. Stern, *Confronting Historical Paradigms: Peasants, Labor, and the Capitalist World System in Africa and Latin America* (Madison: University of Wisconsin Press, 1993), 31.

9. Lowe, *Intimacies of Four Continents*, 102; Steve Stern, "Introduction," in *Confronting Historical Paradigms*, 31.

10. Ernesto Galarza, *Strangers in Our Fields: Based on a Report Regarding Compliance with the Contractual, Legal, and Civil Rights of Mexican Agricultural Workers in the United States* (Washington, D.C.: Fund for the Republic, 1956); *Merchants of Labor: The Mexican Bracero Story, an Account of the Managed Migration of Mexican Farm Workers in California, 1942–1960* (Charlotte, NC: McNally, 1970), originally self-published, 1964; *Spiders in the House and Workers in the Fields* (Notre Dame, IN: University of Notre Dame Press, 1970).

11. See Stephen Pitti, "Ernesto Galarza, Mexican Immigration, and Farm Labor Organizing in Postwar California," in *The Countryside in the Age of the Modern State*, ed. Catherine McNicol Stock and Robert D. Johnston (Ithaca, NY: Cornell University Press, 2001), 165. Biographies of Galarza include Richard Chabrán, "Activism and Intellectual Struggle in the Life of Ernesto Galarza, 1905–1984," *Hispanic Journal of Behavioral Sciences* 7, 2 (1985): 135–152; *Man of Fire*; Donald H. Grubbs, "Prelude to Chavez: The National Farm Labor Union in California," *Labor History* 16, 4 (May 1975); Matt Meier, "Ernesto Galarza," *The American Mosaic: The Latino American Experience* (ABC-CLIO, 2013). Also see Joan London and Henry Anderson, *So Shall Ye Reap: The Story of Cesar Chavez and the Farm Worker Movement* (New York: Thomas Y. Crowell, 1970).

12. For more on empire and meaning-making see Julian Go, *American Empire and the Politics of Meaning: Elite Political Cultures in the Philippines and Puerto Rico during U.S. Colonialism* (Durham, NC: Duke University Press, 2008), 16–18.

13. Eric Love, *Race Over Empire: Racism and U.S. Imperialism, 1865–1900* (Chapel Hill: University of North Carolina Press, 2004), 12.

14. Richard Chabran, "Activism and Intellectual Struggle in the Life of Ernesto Galarza (1905–1984)," *Hispanic Journal of Behavioral Sciences vol. 7* (1985), 135–152.

15. Ernesto Galarza, "Without Benefit of a Lobby," *Survey Graphic* (May 1931).

16. For more on Dr. Frank Tannenbaum, see Olsson, *Agrarian Crossings*, 47–59, 89–90. For more on the FSA, see Martínez-Matsuda, *Migrant Citizenship*. Galarza and Tannenbaum attended luncheons and worked in the same social circles at Columbia University. See Invitation from the "Board of Director and Editors of Survey Associates" to attend the Western Hemisphere Luncheon, Herbert H. Lehman Collections, Columbia University Libraries, New York.

17. Myrdal, *American Dilemma*, 30, 238, 320, 373.

18. Ernesto Galarza, *La Industria Eléctrica en México* (Ph.D. diss., Columbia University, 1947). Gabrielle Morris and Timothy Beard, *The Burning Light: Action and Organizing in the Mexican Community in California* (Berkeley: Regional Oral History Office, Bancroft Library, University of California, 1982), iii, 35.

19. For more on why this rhetoric of "development" became popular among Mexican intellectuals in the 1940s, see María Josefina Saldaña-Portillo, "Development and Revolution: Narratives of Liberation and Regimes of Subjectivity in the Postwar Period," in *The Revolutionary Imagination in the Americas and the Age of Development* (Durham, NC: Duke University Press, 2003). Lytle Hernández, *Migra!*, 112; Cohen, *Braceros*, 32–35. Ernesto Galarza, "Qué forma y modalidades ha tomado una industria de técnica tan avanzada como es la de la electricidad, en un país de regimen esencialment feudal en plena transición?" in *La Industria Eléctrica en México.* On Cárdenas's visit at the TVA, see Olsson, 4, 170. Also see David Ekbladh, "Mr. TVA: Grassroots Development, David Lilienthal, and the Rise and Fall of the TVA as a Symbol for U.S. Overseas Development, 1933–1973," *Diplomatic History* 26 (Summer 2001).

20. Paula Fass, "Without Design: Education Policy in the New Deal," *American Journal of Education* (1983); Arthur Zilversmit, *Changing Schools: Progressive Education Theory and Practice, 1930–1960* (Chicago: University of Chicago Press, 1993).

21. Ernesto Galarza, "Problems of Education in the Western Hemisphere," *Pan-American Union, Division of Intellectual Cooperation* (1939); "Educational Research in Latin America," *Pan-American Union, Division of Intellectual Cooperation* (1939); Matt Meier, "Ernesto Galarza;" *Survey of Research on Latin America by United States Scientists and Institutions* (Washington, D.C.: U.S. National Research Council, 1946), 87.

22. Oswald Stein of the ILO gave technical advice to Latin American officials on the introduction of social and economic reforms in Latin America countries, especially social security. These reports focus on the economic recovery and development of Latin America. See, for example, Ernesto Galarza, "Labor Trends and Social Welfare in Latin America," *Pan-American Union, Division of Labor and Social Information* (1941).

23. Ernesto Galarza, "Statement of Ernesto Galarza of the Pan-American Union before Select Committee of the House of Representatives to Investigate the Interstate Migration of Destitute Citizens," December 9, 1940; "Summary of Proposals with Regard to the Future Importation of Workers from Mexico into the United States," October 1941, Box 6, Folder 2, EGP.

24. Fox, 253–256.

25. Galarza, "Statement."

26. An anti-New Deal alliance of Northern and Southern conservatives forced the termination of the FEPC within five years, but it galvanized civil rights movement leaders and expanded their sense of the possible. Singh, 87. Sugrue, 71. Borgwardt, 138–139. For more on the FEPC, see Neil Foley, "The Politics of Race in the Fight for Fair Employment Practices," in *Quest for Equality: The Failed Promise of Black-Brown Solidarity* (Cambridge, MA: Harvard University Press, 2010), 54–93; Emilio Zamora, *Claiming Rights and Righting Wrongs: Mexican Workers and Job Politics during World War II* (College Station: Texas A&M University Press, 2009), 125–157.

27. "Memorandum for Dr. Rowe from Ernesto Galarza," October 4, 1941, Box 5, Folder 6, EGP; *Man of Fire*, xvii. Zamora, 125–157; Katznelson, *Fear Itself.*

28. Jill Jensen, "From Geneva to the Americas: The International Labor Organization and Inter-American Social Security Standards, 1936–1948," *International Labor and Working Class History* (2011): 215–240.

29. "Memorandum for Dr. Rowe from Ernesto Galarza."

30. "Memorandum for Dr. Rowe from Ernesto Galarza."

31. "Memorandum for Dr. Rowe from Ernesto Galarza."

32. Tolan Committee hearings, Part 33, 12434, 12436.

33. For more on the FSA as a "civil rights" organization, see Martínez-Matsuda, *Migrant Citizenship*.

34. Francisco Castillo Nájera, Ambassador of Mexico, to Ernesto Galarza, September 10, 1941, Box 5, Folder 11, Ernesto Galarza Papers (EGP), Stanford University Libraries, Special Collections.

35. Former U.S. presidents had also used the term, but Roosevelt implemented it. Italics added for emphasis. Franklin D. Roosevelt, *First Inaugural Address*, March 4, 1933, available online at Gerhard Peters and John T. Woolley, "The American Presidency Project," University of California, Santa Barbara.

36. In 1945, Hull received the Nobel Peace Prize for his part in organizing the United Nations. "Statement by the U.S. Secretary of State Cordell Hull at the Seventh International Conference of American States," in Thomas M. Leonard, ed. *Encyclopedia of Latin America: The Age of Globalization*, vol. 4 (New York: Facts on File, 2010).

37. Assistant Secretary of State Sumner Welles, "Good Neighbor Policy in the Caribbean: An Address by the Honorable Sumner Welles before the Institute of Public Affairs at the University of Virginia, Charlottesville, July 1935" (Washington, D.C.: U.S. Government Printing Office, 1935).

38. The Rockefeller Foundation funded MAP, which partnered with Mexico's revolutionary state to raise the yield of food crops among small farmers who had benefited from *ejidos*. Olsson, 65–70; John C. Culver and John Hyde, *American Dreamer: The Life and Times of Henry A. Wallace* (New York: W. W. Norton, 2000); Richard S. Kirkendall, *Social Scientists and Farm Politics in the Age of Roosevelt* (Columbia: University of Missouri Press, 1966).

39. This speech served as an anti-imperialist response to Henry Luce's "American Century," *Life*, February 17, 1941. Henry A. Wallace, *The Century of the Common Man* (New York: Reynal & Hitchcock, 1943); "National Affairs: Wallace to Mexico," *Time*, November 25, 1940; John Maze and Graham White, *Henry A. Wallace: His Search for a New World Order* (Chapel Hill: University of North Carolina Press, 2009). After his visit, Wallace established the Office of Foreign Agricultural Relations in the USDA in 1940. According to this agency, "any postwar plan must include adequate recognition and provision for sound agricultural development in all of the Americas." Monthly News Report, "Agriculture in the Americas," by the Office of Foreign Agricultural Relations, USDA (July 1942), RG 208, Entry 27, Box 37, NARA.

40. Henry Wallace, Ezequiel Padilla, Eduardo Salazar, *Pan-American Friendship: Speeches* (Mexico City: Department of State for Foreign Affairs (SRE), Bureau of International News Service, 1941). Also see "Mr. Roosevelt's Speech to the Board of the Pan American Union," *Bulletin of International News* 16 (April 1939): 21–23.

41. *Pan-American Friendship*, 49. Italics added.

42. For more on the Good Neighbor Policy, see McPherson, Spellacy, and Sadlier. Also see Colby, 175–198; Mary Stuckey, *The Good Neighbor: Franklin D. Roosevelt and the Rhetoric of American Power* (East Lansing: Michigan State University Press, 2013); Frederick Pike, *FDR's Good Neighbor Policy: Sixty Years of Generally Gentle Chaos* (Austin: University of Texas Press, 1995); Irwin Gellman, *Good Neighbor Diplomacy: United States Policies in Latin America, 1933–1945* (Baltimore: Johns Hopkins University Press, 1979); Bryce Wood, *The Making of the Good Neighbor Policy* (New York: Columbia University Press, 1961).

43. Richard Cándida Smith, *Improvised Continent: Pan-Americanism and Cultural Exchange* (Philadelphia: University of Pennsylvania Press, 2017), 3–5. Historians have debated what was new and old in FDR's hemispheric agenda. Most agree that the 1930s saw a switch from gunboat

diplomacy to cultural imperialism and other forms of economic leverage by government and corporate actors that was by no means "anti-imperial." This literature goes back to William Appleman Williams, *The Tragedy of American Diplomacy* (New York: W.W. Norton, 1962). Also see Walter LaFeber, *The New Empire: An Interpretation of American Expansion, 1860–1898* (Ithaca, NY: Cornell University Press, 1963); David Green, *The Containment of Latin America: A History of the Myths and Realities of the Good Neighbor Policy* (New York: Quadrangle, 1971); Justin Hart, *Empire of Ideas: The Origins of Public Diplomacy and the Transformation of U.S. Policy* (New York: Oxford University Press, 2013).

44. Matthew Frye Jacobson, *Barbarian Virtues: The United States Encounters Foreign Peoples at Home and Abroad* (New York: Hill and Wang, 2001), 41. Ricardo D. Salvatore, "The Enterprise of Knowledge: Representational Machines of Informal Empire," in *Close Encounters of Empire: Writing the Cultural History of U.S.-Latin American Relations*, ed. Gilbert M. Joseph, Catherine C. LeGrand, and Ricardo D. Salvatore (Durham, NC: Duke University Press, 1998), 93. In 1947, the name of the PAU was changed to the Organization of American States.

45. Clifford B. Casey, "Pan-American Union," *Hispanic American Historical Review* 13 (November 1933), 437–456; Javier Corrales and Richerd E. Feinberg, "Regimes of Cooperation in the Western Hemisphere: Power, Interests, and Intellectual Traditions," *International Studies Quarterly* 43 (1999): 1–36.

46. Greg Grandin, "The Liberal Traditions in the Americas: Rights, Sovereignty, and the Origins of Liberal Multilateralism," *American Historical Review* 117 (2012): 68–91; Cándida Smith, 4. Jacobson, *Barbarian Virtues*, 41–50; Mark T. Gilderhus, *Pan American Visions: Woodrow Wilson in the Western Hemisphere, 1913–1921* (Tucson: University of Arizona Press, 1986).

47. Paul A. Varg, "The Economic Side of the Good Neighbor Policy: The Reciprocal Trade Program and South America," *Pacific Historical Review* 45 (February 1976): 47–71.

48. Galarza cowrote a pamphlet for the American Red Cross entitled *American Neighbors* (1940) that aimed at educating U.S. citizens on Latin American cultures as an expression of this diplomatic vision. Ernesto Galarza, Herbert Eugene Bolton, and Delia Goetz, *American Neighbors* (Washington, D.C.: American National Red Cross, 1940).

49. Ernesto Galarza, "A Study of the Problems of Mexican Nationals in the Nine Camps of the Cucamonga, Upland, Ontario, and Chino Districts of San Bernardino, California," *Labor and Social Relations in Latin America* (Summer 1944), available in Box 17, Folder 8, EGP.

50. Ernesto Galarza, *Hacia la Paz por la escuela* (Washington, D.C.: Pan-American Union, 1936); *Stegomia, jr.: A play project for junior high school students dramatizing the contribution of the Cuban scientist, Dr. Carlos Finley, to the building of the Panama Canal and the progress of medicine through the discovery of the yellow fever germ carrier.* (Washington, D.C.: Pan American Union, 1936); "Some Truth about Hemisphere Unity," *Mexican Life* (December 1941): 17–20, 44; "Problems of Education in the Western Hemisphere"; *Labor in Latin America: A Survey by Ernesto Galarza* (Washington, D.C.: American Council on Public Affairs, 1941); "Labor Trends and Social Welfare in Latin America"; "The Latin American Universities in Step with History," *Pan-American Union Bulletin* 73 (Washington, D.C.: U.S. Government Printing Office, 1940): 677–687.

51. Galarza resigned from the PAU in 1947 when he realized that the U.S. Department of State colluded with U.S. mining businesses in Bolivia to prevent tin workers from unionizing and obtaining higher wages. Chabrán, 135–152.

52. On the "conditions of possibility" set by the logic of freedom, see Lowe, 6.

53. While the Monroe Doctrine served as an enlightened call for a diplomacy premised upon nonintervention, it also served as an explicit justification for U.S. military intervention—should

Europe attempt to colonize Latin American countries. Steven Chambers, *No God but Gain: The Untold Story of Cuban Slavery, the Monroe Doctrine, and the Making of the United States* (New York: Verso, 2015), 120-123; Message of President James Monroe at the commencement of the first session of the 18th Congress, December 2, 1823.

54. Jay Sexton, *The Monroe Doctrine: Empire and Nation in Nineteenth-century America* (New York: Hill and Wang, 2011), 5, 17, 248.

55. James K. Polk "Inaugural Address," March 4, 1845. Online at The American Presidency Project.

56. For more on U.S. investments in Latin America, see Mira Wilkins, *The Maturing of Multinational Enterprise: American Business Abroad from 1914-1970* (Cambridge, MA: Harvard University Press, 1974); Josh deWind, *Peasants Become Miners: The Evolution of Industrial Mining Systems in Peru, 1902-1974* (New York: Garland, 1987); Dan LaBotz, *Edward L. Doheny: Petroleum, Power, and Politics in the US and Mexico* (New York: Praeger, 1991); Gilbert M. Joseph, *Revolution from Without: Yucatan, Mexico, and the United States, 1880-1924* (Durham, NC: Duke University Press, 1987); Emily Rosenberg, *World War I and the Growth of the United States Predominance in Latin America* (New York: Garland, 1987).

57. Dollar diplomacy was not new in the 1900s, even though President Taft coined the phrase in 1909. Jason Mason Hart, *Empire and Revolution: The Americans in Mexico Since the Civil War* (Berkeley: University of California Press, 2006), 11-16, 22; Sexton, *Monroe Doctrine*, 143-145.

58. James G. Blaine, "Proceedings of the Eighth Republican Convention held in Chicago, Illinois," June 3, 4, 5, 6, 1884 (Chicago: Republican National Committee), 191. Quoted in Jacobson, *Barbarian Virtues.*

59. Julian Go, *Patterns of Empire: The British and American Empires, 1688 to the Present* (New York: Cambridge University Press, 2011), 25, 66.

60. For more on the process of "modernization" in Mexico, see Mark Overmyer-Velásquez, *Visions of the Emerald City: Modernity, Tradition, and the Formation of Porfirian Oaxaca, Mexico* (Durham, NC: Duke University Press, 2006); Gilbert M. Joseph and Allen Wells, *Summer of Discontent, Seasons of Upheaval: Elite Politics and Rural Insurgency in Yucatán, 1876-1915* (Palo Alto, CA: Stanford University Press, 1996); Michael Matthews, *The Civilizing Machine: A Cultural History of Mexican Railroads, 1876-1910* (Lincoln: University of Nebraska Press, 2014); Jürgen Buchenau, "The Rise and Demise of a Regional Power: The Multilateralism of Mexican Dictator Porfirio Díaz, 1876-1911," *The Latin Americanist* 63 (September 2019).

61. Olsson, 17-19. Alan Knight, *The Mexican Revolution, vol 1: Porfirians, Liberals, and Peasants* (New York: Cambridge University Press, 1986), chap. 1; William Beezley, *Mexicans in Revolution, 1910-1946: An Introduction* (Lincoln: University of Nebraska Press, 2009), 4.

62. Hart, *Empires and Revolution*, 172, 200.

63. Cohen, *Braceros*, 35-41. Christopher Boyer, *Becoming Campesinos: Politics, Identity, and Agrarian Struggle in Postrevolutionary Michoacán, 1920-1935* (Palo Alto, CA: Stanford University Press, 2003); Gilbert M. Joseph, *Everyday Forms of State Formation: Revolution and the Negotiation of Rule in Modern Mexico* (Durham, NC: Duke University Press, 1994).

64. Gilbert Gonzalez and Raul A. Fernandez, *A Century of Chicano History: Empire, Nations, and Migrations* (New York: Routledge, 2003), 30; John Mason Hart, *Revolutionary Mexico: The Coming and Process of the Mexican Revolution* (Berkeley: University of California Press, 1987). Friedrich Katz, "Labor Conditions on Haciendas in Porfirian Mexico: Trends and Tendencies," *Hispanic American Historical Review* 54 (1974): 1-47.

65. While the force of railroads alongside U.S., British, and French investments in Mexico were disruptive, a cultural familiarity with the United States also sometimes drove people to move north—out of choice. George Sánchez, *Becoming Mexican American*, 17–51.

66. For more on "free trade" as a means to adapt colonialism, see Lowe, 15.

67. For more on the Mexican Revolution, see Alan Knight, *The Mexican Revolution, vol. 1: The Mexican Revolution, vol. 2: Counter-Revolution and Reconstruction* (Omaha: University of Nebraska Press, 1990); Michael Gonzales, *The Mexican Revolution 1910-1940* (Albuquerque: University of New Mexico Press, 2002).

68. For more on Mexican out-migration in the era of the Mexican Revolution, see Sánchez, *Becoming Mexican American*, 17–51. Alexandra Délano, *Mexico and Its Diaspora in the United States: Policies of Emigration Since 1848* (New York: Cambridge University Press, 2011); Camille Guérin-Gonzalez, *Mexican Workers and American Dreams: Immigration, Repatriation and California Farm Labor, 1900-1939* (New Brunswick, NJ: Rutgers University Press, 1994); Fernando Saúl Alanís Enciso, *They Should Stay There: The Story of Mexican Migration and Repatriation During the Great Depression* (Chapel Hill: University of North Carolina Press, 2017). Also see Saskia Sassen, *The Mobility of Labor and Capital: A Study in International Investment and Labor Flow* (Cambridge: Cambridge University Press, 1988).

69. Ricardo Romo, "Responses to Mexican Immigration, 1910-1930," in *Beyond 1848: Readings in the Modern Chicano Historical Experience*, ed. Michael Raúl Ornelas (New York: Kendall/Hunt, 1993), 115–135.

70. Sanchez, *Becoming Mexican American*, 213–214; Francisco E. Balderrama and Raymond Rodriguez, *Decade of Betrayal: Mexican Repatriation in the 1930s* (Albuquerque: University of New Mexico Press, 1995); Guérin-Gonzalez, *Mexican Workers*, 77–110; Alanís Enciso, *They Should Stay There*.

71. Casey Walsh, *Building the Borderlands: A Transnational History of Irrigated Cotton Along the Mexico-Texas Border* (College Station: Texas A&M University Press, 2008), 135–137; Dennis Nodín Valdés, "Mexican Revolutionary Nationalism and Repatriation During the Great Depression," *Mexican Studies/Estudios Mexicanos* 4 (Winter 1988): 1–23; Lawrence Cardoso, *Mexican Emigration to the United States 1897-1931* (Tucson: University of Arizona Press, 1980), 148; Gabriela Arredondo, *Mexican Chicago: Race, Identity, and Nation 1916-1939* (Urbana: University of Illinois Press, 2008).

72. For example, in the borderlands region of Matamoros, the Mexican state created the Valle Bajo Río Bravo development project to increase the export of cotton. After government officials completed the building of infrastructure and irrigation for farming, they colonized the region with Mexicans repatriated from Texas in 1936-1939. Walsh, *Building the Borderlands*, 135–153.

73. Walsh, 113.

74. Valdés, "Mexican Revolutionary Nationalism," 7–11; Goodman, *Deportation Machine*, 46.

75. See Statement of Ernesto Galarza, chief of the Division of Labor and Social Information of the Pan-American Union, Before the Select Committee of the House of Representatives to Investigate the Interstate Migration of Destitute Citizens, Box 6, Folder 2, EGP, December 9, 1940. Also see Tolan Committee hearings, Statement of Ernesto Galarza, December 11, 1940, 3883–3886.

76. Minian, 17–20. Ngai, *Impossible Subjects*, 72.

77. Statement of Ernesto Galarza Before the Select Committee.

78. Tore C. Olsson, "Sharecroppers and *Campesinos*: The American South, Mexico, and the Transnational Politics of Land Reform in the Radical 1930s," *Journal of Southern History* 3 (August 2015): 630–631; Martínez-Matsuda, 6–9.

79. Cohen, *Braceros*, 31–39, 79; Rosas, *Abrazando el Espíritu*, 19.

80. Due to the intense racial discrimination faced by braceros upon their arrival in Texas in the early years of the program, Mexico banned Texas from contracting braceros until 1947. J. Durand, "The Bracero Program: A Critical Appraisal," *Migración y Desarollo* (2007), 31; Scruggs, "Texas and the Bracero Program, 1942–1947," *Pacific Historical Review* 32: 251–264.

81. Even as the P.R.I. increasingly implemented an economic order that privileged business interests and foreign investment, popular groups fought back every step of the way. See Tanalís Padilla, *Rural Resistance in the Land of Zapata: The Jaramillista Movement and the Myth of the Pax Priísta, 1940–1962* (Durham, NC: Duke University Press, 2008), 5–9; Stephen Niblo, *Mexico in the 1940s: Modernity, Politics, and Corruption* (Wilmington, DE: Scholarly Resources, 1999); Minian, 32.

82. Ambassador Nájera to Galarza, and response from Galarza, November 5, 1942, Box 5, Folder 11, EGP.

83. "Individual Work Agreement" of August 4, 1942, as amended April 26, 1943, RG 211, Records of the War Manpower Commission, Entry 171, Box 15, NARA.

84. As García-Colón states, the New Deal initiatives of the Wagner-Peyser Act, the RA, and the FSA attempted to manage the flow of these seasonal migrants, but in fact, increased the use of seasonal migrants in Northeast agriculture. García-Colón, *Colonial Migrants*, 46.

Chapter 3

1. U.S. House of Representatives, Select Committee to Investigate the Interstate Migration of Destitute Citizens (Tolan Committee), Resolutions to Inquire into the Migration of Destitute Citizens, To Study, Survey, and Investigate the Social and Economic Needs and the Movement of Indigent Persons Across State Lines, 76th Congress, 3rd Session, Part 10, Washington Hearings, December 11, 1940, and February 26, 1941 (Washington, D.C.: Government Printing Office), 3885.

2. Many historians and activists have carefully documented the euphemisms used to describe Japanese internment, including "internment," "evacuation," and "relocation"—not "incarceration." For more on the importance of terminology about Japanese American incarceration, see James Hirabayashi, "'Concentration Camp' or 'Relocation Center'—What's in a Name?" *Japanese American National Museum Quarterly* 9 (1994). U.S. House of Representatives, Select Committee Investigating National Defense Migration (Tolan Committee), 77th Congress, 1st Session, pursuant to H. Res 113, Problems of Evacuation of Enemy Aliens and Others from Prohibited Military Zones, Part 29, 30, 31, February and March 1942 (Washington, D.C.: U.S. Government Printing Office).

3. Brian Masaru Hayashi, *Democratizing the Enemy: The Japanese American Internment* (Princeton, NJ: Princeton University Press, 2004), 79.

4. Franklin Roosevelt, Executive Order 9066: Authorizing the Secretary of War to Prescribe Military Areas, February 19, 1942, *Documents from the National Archives: Internment of Japanese Americans* (Dubuque, IA: Kendall/Hunt, 1989), 9–10.

5. Just as some braceros signed a contract in hopes of contributing to the war effort, there were occasions when internees also asked to work outside of the prison camps to escape the boredom and earn a small amount of money.

6. Regarding these ten thousand "volunteers," see Roger Daniels, *Concentration Camps USA: Japanese Americans and World War II* (New York: Rinehart and Winston, 1972), 101. *War Relocation Work Corps* (Washington, D.C.: War Relocation Authority, 1942), RG 224, Records of the Office of Labor, War Food Administration, Entry 1, NARA.

7. Although the Tolan Committee hearings may not reveal the full range of political opinion or the actual negotiations over the bracero program, they constitute a key source of formal political discourse on the programs.

8. They include Adrian Cruz, "Labour Militancy Deferred: Racial State Interventions and the California Farm Worker Struggle," *Race & Class* 56 (July 2014), 43–58; Takashi Fujitani, *Race for Empire: Koreans as Japanese and Japanese as Americans During World War II* (Berkeley: University of California Press, 2011), 81; Lori Flores, *Grounds for Dreaming: Mexican Americans, Mexican Immigrants, and the California Farmworker Movement* (New Haven, CT: Yale University Press, 2016), 41. Flores notes, "Along with the military draft, Japanese internment created the wartime labor shortage that justified in many political and agribusiness leaders' minds the need for a Bracero Program."

9. Kelly Lytle Hernández, *Migra!*, 123; Amy C. Offner, *Sorting Out the Mixed Economy: The Rise and Fall of Welfare and Developmental States in the Americas* (Princeton, NJ: Princeton University Press, 2019), 222; John Thomas, *One Hundred Years of Solitude, Struggle, and Violence Along the U.S.-Mexico Border: An Oral History* (London: Cambridge Scholars, 2018), 64.

10. Narrative Report, July 12, 1944, RG 224, Entry 6, Box 22, NARA.

11. In the agreement and individual contract, the worker entered into the contract with the "employer," which was the United States government as represented by the WMC. "Agreement Between the United States and Mexico," August 4, 1942, RG 211, Box 2–3, NARA.

12. Uday Singh Mehta, *Liberalism and Empire*; Mehta, "Liberal Strategies of Exclusion," *Politics & Society* (1990).

13. Tolan Committee hearings, Part 33: 12433–36.

14. Most historians of the bracero program and the Caribbean labor programs have argued that these were state-led labor contracting systems in which the state colluded with conservative growers to ensure access to a cheap and exploitable agricultural labor supply. It was much more complicated than that.

15. Select Committee Investigating National Defense Migration, A Resolution to Inquire Further into the Interstate Migration of Citizens, Emphasizing the Present and Potential Consequences of the Migration Caused by the National Defense Program, Part 23, St. Louis hearings, November 26 and 27, 1941, p. 8696.

16. James N. Gregory, *The Southern Diaspora: How the Great Migrations of Black and White Southerners Transformed America* (Chapel Hill: University of North Carolina Press, 2005). For more on total war mobilization during World War II, see John J. Corson, *Manpower for Victory: Total Mobilization for Total War* (New York: Farrar & Rinehart, 1943); Ronald Takaki, *Double Victory: A Multicultural History of America in World War II* (Boston: Little, Brown, 2000). See also RG 16, Records of the Office of the Secretary of Agriculture, including the records of the Office for Agricultural War Relations; RG 174, General Records of the Department of Labor (DOL); RG 211, Records of the War Manpower Commission (WMC) at NARA.

17. The Farm Labor Program included: the Recruitment and Placement Division, the Women's Land Army division, the Victory Farm Volunteers division, and the Labor Utilization division. Preliminary Inventory Number 51, Records of the Office of Labor of the WFA, NARA.

18. During the war, the U.S. government interned nearly 380,000 German prisoners of war (POW), who they often contracted for labor to a variety of private industries, including, mining, railroads, farming, and logging. Barbara Schmitter Heister, "The 'Other Braceros': Temporary Labor and German Prisoners of War in the United States, 1943–1946," *Social Science History* 31, no. 2 (Summer 2007): 239–271. On the use of POW labor as well as the potential Costa Rican farm labor program, see RG 224, Entry 1, Box 15–16; on the proposed Central American labor programs, see Rufus Holman to Paul McNutt, December 14, 1943, RG 211, Entry 164, Box 4; on the short-lived Newfoundland labor program, see Records of the Office of Labor, General Correspondence, RG 224, Entry 6, Box 17–19, NARA.

19. Tolan Committee hearings, Part 33, p. 12413.

20. Senator John H. Tolan to Ernesto Galarza, May 8, 1942, Box 5, Folder 6, Ernesto Galarza Papers (EGP), Special Collections, Stanford University Libraries.

21. Federal government officials and military commanders strongly emphasized "military necessity," a phrase justifying the removal of all West Coast Japanese in 1942. They used the term broadly, incorporating military planning involving Western Hemispheric defense and boosting civilian morale for the war effort. Hayashi, 76.

22. Many decision-makers were well aware that Japanese Americans posed no security threat. See Peter Irons, *Justice at War: The Story of Japanese American Internment Cases* (Berkeley: University of California Press, 1983). Also see Hayashi, 6. Select Committee to Investigate the Interstate Migration of Destitute Citizens, Resolution to Inquire Further into the Interstate Migration of Citizens, Emphasizing the Present and Potential Consequences of the Migration Caused by the National Defense Program, Parts 29, 20, 31: Problems of Evacuation of Enemy Aliens and Others from Prohibited Military Zones, February 21 and 23, 1942, 11053.

23. Tolan Committee hearings, Part 31, 11629.

24. John H. Tolan, House Report No. 1911 and 2124, *Report of the Select Committee Investigating National Defense Migration, House of Representatives, On the Need for a Single Procurement Agency to Effect All-out War from Military Areas,* March 19, 1942 and May 13, 1942, p. 11.

25. *Report of the Select Committee.* At the same time, the hearings served as a platform for those advocating the removal of Japanese Americans from the West Coast. Politically powerful officials at the hearings, including the mayors of San Francisco, Portland, Los Angeles, and Seattle, and agribusiness groups had an obvious and acknowledged economic interest in the removal of Japanese Americans at the hearings.

26. Franklin D. Roosevelt, "We Hold These Truths: The Rights to Life, Liberty and the Pursuit of Happiness," radio stations from Washington, D.C., December 15, 1941, in *Vital Speeches of the Day* 8, no. 6 (1942).

27. As McWilliams himself stated, "On January 26, 1942, I wrote to your committee . . . [and] urged that you undertake the present investigation." Tolan Committee hearings, Part 31, 11788–94.

28. Hearings, Part 31. Peter Richardson, *American Prophet: The Life and Work of Carey McWilliams* (Ann Arbor: University of Michigan Press, 2005), 107; Carey McWilliams, *Prejudice,* viii.

29. He was called this by Matt S. Meier in the second edition of *North from Mexico* (1990), because McWilliams's work was an invaluable reference for activists in the Chicano movement of the 1960s and 1970s. Richardson, *American Prophet,* 158; Carey McWilliams, *North from Mexico* (Westport, CT: Greenwood Press, 1948).

30. Richardson, 60; Carey McWilliams, *Factories in the Field: The Story of Migratory Farm Labor in California* (Boston: Little, Brown, 1939); Don Mitchell, *They Saved the Crops: Labor,*

Landscape, and the Struggle Over Industrial Farming (Athens: University of Georgia Press, 2012), 27–28.

31. Hearings, Part 31, 11632–11635.

32. Defending McWilliams, some argue he was "forced" to try to put "the best face" on the already decided policy of Japanese incarceration. Richardson, *American Prophet*, 105–109. Carey McWilliams, *The Education of Carey McWilliams* (New York: Simon & Schuster, 1979), 101; McWilliams, *Factories in the Field*.

33. On July 6, 1942, Roosevelt issued Executive Orders 9095, creating the Office of Alien Property Custodian. Tolan Committee hearings, Part 31, 11790–11792. McWilliams attended the hearings in San Francisco on March 6, 7, and 12, 1942.

34. Carey McWilliams, "Japanese Evacuation: Policy and Perspectives," *Common Ground* (Summer 1942), 65–72. Richardson, 108–109.

35. Carey McWilliams, "They Saved the Crops," *The Inter-American* (August 1943), Box 24, Folder 8, EGP.

36. Tolan Committee hearings, "Findings and Recommendations on Evacuation of Enemy Aliens and Others from Prohibited Military Zones," *Fourth Interim Report of the Select Committee Investigating National Defense Migration*, House of Representatives, 77th Congress, 2nd Session, May 1942 (Washington, D.C.: U.S. Government Printing Office, 1942), 17, 18.

37. "Findings and Recommendations."

38. Memo from Galarza, Re: "A brief elaboration of my suggestion to Rep. Tolan that his Committee consider the advisability of establishing a Joint International United States-Mexican commission on migration." Box 5, Folder 6, EGP. Also see Tolan to Galarza, May 8, 1942.

39. Tolan to Galarza.

40. Tolan to Galarza.

41. Tolan Committee Hearings, Part 33, 12457–8.

42. Tolan Committee hearings, Part 33, 12423–4.

43. Hearings, 12426, 12429.

44. Memo from Galarza.

45. Tolan Committee hearings, Part 33, May 22, June 11, 19, 1942, 12433.

46. Tolan Committee hearings, Part 33, 12452.

47. Hearings, 12434–12435.

48. Hearings, 12438.

49. McWilliams, *Prejudice*, 119; Tolan Committee hearings, Part 30, 11624. Other committee members restated Olson's words, including George Gleason, Part 31, 11626–11627.

50. Tolan Committee hearings, Part 29, 21 February 21, 1942: 11187–11189.

51. Tolan Committee, "Findings and Recommendations," 17–18.

52. Tolan Committee, "Findings and Recommendations," 12, 18–19.

53. Quoted from Page Smith, *Democracy on Trial: The Japanese American Evacuation and Relocation in World War II* (New York: Simon & Schuster, 1995), 146.

54. Sandra C. Taylor, "Leaving the Concentration Camps: Japanese American Resettlement in Utah and the Intermountain West," *Pacific Historical Review* 60, no. 2 (May 1991).

55. Report of the Commission on Wartime Relocation and Internment of Civilians, *Personal Justice Denied* (Washington, D.C.: U.S. Government Printing Office, 1982), 182. Daniels, 101; Taylor, 181–182.

56. Milton Eisenhower, "War Relocation Work Corps: A Circular for Enlistees and Their Families," War Relocation Authority (Washington, D.C.: U.S. Government Printing Office,

1942). Milton Eisenhower, a proponent of the New Deal, was the original director of the WRA, but he resigned after less than three months.

57. "The Japanese Question in the United States," a compilation of memos by Lt. Commander Kenneth D. Ringle, RG 208, Entry 84, Box 9, NARA.

58. Tolan Committee, "Findings and Recommendations," 207–208.

59. Taylor, 181; Abe Fortas to Paul McNutt, July 18, 1944, RG 211, Entry 171, Box 17, NARA; USDA, Memo No. 975–935, Re: The Administration of the Farm Labor Program, March 13, 1943, RG 224, Entry 1, Box 15, NARA. On occasion, Japanese American inmates would be housed at FSA camps with braceros, Mexican Americans, African Americans, and guestworkers from the Caribbean. For more on the FSA's role during Japanese American incarceration, see Martínez-Matsuda, *Migrant Citizenship*, 93, 211–216.

60. By 1943 the director of the WRA, Dillon Myer, decided to change the name of the policy from "group leave" to "seasonal work leave," because "we found that the people who go out in agricultural work often can't find housing to establish themselves throughout the whole year. They go out in April or May and come back about the middle of December to the center." See Testimony of Dillon S. Myer, U.S. Congress, Investigation of Un-American Propaganda Activities in the United States, 78th Congress, 1st Session (Washington, D.C.: U.S. Government Printing Office, 1943–1944), 9626.

61. The first leave programs centered on higher education, allowing students to attend college at approved universities with the goal of permanent resettlement.

62. Newspaper clipping, Dillon S. Myer, "Relocating a Farm Population," *Extension Service Review* (July 1943), RG 224, Entry 1, Box 24, NARA.

63. War Relocation Authority, administrative instruction no. 22, July 20, 1942, "Report of the Subcommittee on Japanese War Relocation Centers to the Committee on Military Affairs," U.S. Senate, May 7, 1943 (Washington, D.C.: U.S. Government Printing Office, 1943), 212–223.

64. Farm Security Administration, Labor Division, "The Use of Japanese Evacuees as Farm Laborers," April 1943, RG 224, Entry 1, Box 15.

65. USDA, Bureau of Agricultural Economics, "Farmers' Attitude Toward the Use of Japanese Evacuees as Farm Labor," January 30, 1943, RG 224, Entry 1, Box 15, NARA.

66. "Farmers' Attitude," 19–20.

67. Valerie Matsumoto, "Japanese American Women during World War II," *Frontiers: A Journal of Women Studies* (1984).

68. Myer quoted from Richard Drinnon, *Keeper of Concentration Camps: Dillon S. Myer and American Racism* (Berkeley: University of California Press, 1989), 267; Taylor, 2–4; Yuka Tsuchiya, "Meet the 'New Neighbors': Seabrook Farms and Visual Narratives of Japanese American Success in America's Cultural Diplomacy in the 1940s and 1950s," in *The Years of Cultural Cold War: Asia and the United States*, ed. Yuka Tsuchiya and Toshihiko Kishi (Tokyo: Kokusai-Shoin, 2009), 19; Ngai, *Impossible Subjects*, 201. Assimilation has long been a master narrative of American immigration in the United States, starting with sociologist Robert Park and others at the University of Chicago in the first half of the twentieth century. For more on the vexed relationship between assimilation and racialization, see Catherine S. Ramírez, *Assimilation: An Alternative History* (Berkeley: University of California Press, 2020).

69. Craig, *The Bracero Program*, 47; Kirstein, *Anglo Over Bracero: A History of the Mexican Worker in the United States from Roosevelt to Nixon* (San Francisco: R&E Research Associates, 1977), 19, 45, 15–53.

70. The county extension agent was a key figure in the intercounty movement of laborers with the authority to approve or disapprove such movements. A county extension agent also

reported annually on farm labor activities within each county. See Preliminary Inventory No. 51, Records of the Office of Labor of the WFA, RG 224, Records of the Office of Labor, War Food Administration, NARA.

71. Administrative notice, Leland Barrowitz, Re: Attached is a revision of the WRA Handbook Section on Seasonal Release, No. 82; WRA Handbook: Seasonal Work Leave, 60.3, February 16, 1944, Supersedes Issuance of 27 October 1943, RG 224, Entry 6, Box 20, NARA.

72. War Relocation Authority, administrative instruction no. 22, 42.

73. WRA Handbook: Seasonal Work Leave, 60.3, February 16, 1944, Supersedes Issuance of 27 October 1943, RG 224, Entry 6, Box 20, NARA.

74. Paul V. McNutt to Harold C., re: "utilization in agricultural production of groups confined in camps or institutions," March 8, 1943, RG 211, Entry 171, Box 17, NARA.

75. "Farmers' Attitude."

76. Interview with Art Shibayama by Alice Ito, October 26, 2003, Densho Visual History Collection.

77. During World War II, the U.S. government lobbied neighboring Latin American countries to round up and deport "dangerous" aliens from Axis countries to the United States. The U.S. government paid for the travel and incarceration expense of the 2,253 persons of Japanese ancestry who were deported by more than ten Latin American countries from 1942–1944. Tetsuden Kashima, *Judgment Without Trial: Japanese American Imprisonment During World War II* (Seattle: University of Washington Press, 2004), 102–103; Tsuchiya, 4, 24.

78. Letter to Bruton from the WFA, March 17, 1944, RG 224, Entry 6, Box 20, NARA. Tsuchiya, 4.

79. Taylor, 184; Matsumoto, 9; Mitziko Sawada, "After the Camps: Seabrook Farms, New Jersey, and the Resettlement of Japanese Americans 1944–47," *Amerasia* 13, no. 2 (1986–1987): 117–136.

80. Daniels, 101; Timothy J. Lukes and Gary Y. Okihiro, *Japanese Legacy: Farming and Community Life in California's Santa Clara Valley*, Local History Studies, Vol. 31 (Cupertino: California History Center, 1985), 7.

81. Cletus E. Daniel, *Bitter Harvest: A History of California Farmworkers, 1870–1941* (Berkeley: University of California Press, 1981), 64, 259. On race and Japanese American incarceration, see Jacobus tenBroek, Edward N. Barnhart, and Floyd W. Matson, *Prejudice, War and the Constitution* (Berkeley: University of California Press, 1970); Daniels, *Concentration Camps USA*; Richard Drinnon, *Keeper of Concentration* Camps; Greg Robinson, *By Order of the President: FDR and the Internment of Japanese Americans* (Cambridge, MA: Harvard University Press, 2009); Hayashi, *Democratizing the Enemy.*

82. Yuji Ichioka, *Issei: The World of the First Generation of Japanese Immigrants, 1885–1924* (New York: Free Press, 1990); Yuji Ichioka, *Before Internment: Essays in Prewar Japanese American History,* ed. Gordon Chang and Eiichiro Azuma (Palo Alto: Stanford University Press, 2006); Eiichiro Azuma, *Between Two Empires: Race, History, and Transnationalism in Japanese America* (Oxford: Oxford University Press, 2005).

83. Daniel, *Bitter Harvest,* 68; Ngai, *Impossible Subjects*; Joon Kim, "California's Agribusiness and the Farm Labor Question: The Transition from Asian to Mexican Labor, 1919–1939," *Aztlan: A Journal of Chicano Studies* 37, no. 2 (Fall 2012).

84. *Final Report: Japanese Evacuation from the West Coast, 1942,* Headquarters Western Defense Command and Fourth Army, Office of the Commanding General, Presidio of San Francisco, California (Washington, D.C.: U.S. Government Printing Office, 1943), as found at The Virtual Museum of the City of San Francisco.

85. John C. Duckwall to Oregon District House of Representatives, Tolan Committee Hearings, Part 33, 12532.

86. Hearings, Part 33, 12449–12451.

87. Hearings, Part 31, 11657.

88. Hewes and the FSA were later involved in relocating Japanese Americans and making sure that the lands they owned were kept in production by substitute operators. Laurence I. Hewes Jr. to Remsen Byrd [Bird], May 23, 1942, Special Collections, Occidental College, Los Angeles. In the field offices, three teams composed of representatives of the FSA, the Federal Security Agency, and the Federal Reserve Bank were available to assist evacuees to "settle their affairs." Tolan Committee, "Findings and Recommendations," 4.

89. Tolan Committee, "Findings and Recommendations," 4.

90. Tolan Committee Hearings, Part 29, 11007, 11194–11195; Part 31, 11681; Statement by Austin E. Anson of the Shipper-Grower Association, *Saturday Evening Post*, May 9, 1942.

91. Tolan Committee hearings, Part 29, 11194.

92. Tolan Committee hearings, Part 29, 11007.

93. Statement by Clarence E. Rust, "On Enemy Evacuation," Tolan Committee hearings, Exhibit 9, Part 29, 11254.

94. Tolan Committee Hearings, Part 29, 11195.

95. Tolan Committee hearings, Exhibit 26, Part 30, 11284–11285.

96. Iyko Day argues that Japanese internment was part of a broader settler colonial inheritance that is embedded in Western liberal democracy. Iyko Day, "Alien Intimacies: The Coloniality of Japanese Internment in Australia, Canada, and the United States," *Amerasia* 36 (2010). Also see *Alien Capital: Asian Racialization and the Logic of Settler Colonial Capitalism* (Durham, NC: Duke University Press, 2016).

97. For more on settler colonialism in general, see Jodi Byrd, *The Transit of Empire: Indigenous Critiques of Empire* (Minneapolis: University of Minnesota Press, 2011); Lisa Lowe, *The Intimacies of Four Continents*; Audra Simpson, "Settlement's Secret," *Cultural Anthropology* 26 (2011); Patrick Wolfe, "Settler Colonialism and the Elimination of the Native," *Journal of Genocide Studies* 8 (December 2006); Kelly Lytle Hernández, *City of Inmates: Conquest, Rebellion, and the Rise of Human Caging in Los Angeles, 1771–1965* (Chapel Hill: University of North Carolina Press, 2017).

98. Tolan Committee, "Findings and Recommendations," 209–214. For more on Myer, see Drinnon, *Keeper of Concentration Camps*.

99. Those sources that do exist indicate that the Navajo contract labor program was small. In July 1944, the WFA recruited 22,000 braceros, 3,000 or more Japanese, and 300 Navajo Indians to work in agriculture in the Pacific Northwest region. *Monthly Narrative Report*, July 12, 1944, RG 224, Entry 6, Box 22, NARA.

100. See McWilliams, *Factories in the Field*, Daniel, *Bitter Harvest*, and Devra Weber, *Dark Sweat, White Gold: California Cotton, Farmworkers, and the New Deal, 1919–1939* (Berkeley: University of California Press, 1994), among others. In David Vaught's book, *Cultivating California: Growers, Specialty Crops, and Labor, 1870–1920* (1999), racial capitalism is ignored in his romantic portrayal of the "horticulturalists."

101. Tolan Committee hearings, Exhibit 26, Part 30, 11284–11285.

102. Senator Carl Hayden to U.S. Secretary of Agriculture, August 22, 1942, RG 211, Records of the War Manpower Commission, Entry 171, Box 14, NARA.

103. Andrés Duarte, New York Mexican labor inspector, to the Secretary of Labor and Social Provisions in Mexico, "Sobre la permanencia de nuestros braceros en esta zona después de la terminación de sus contratos . . ." November 7, 1944, Box 17, Folder 9, EGP.

104. Tolan Committee hearings, Part 29, 11229–11232.

105. Tolan Committee hearings, Part 29, 11705–11709.

106. Part 29, 11720.

107. For other responses from incarcerated Japanese Americans that did not hinge on citizenship, see Fujitani, *Race for Empire* (2010). These quotes are from Dorothy Swaine Thomas and Richard S. Nishimoto, *The Spoilage* (Berkeley: University of California Press, 1969), 97.

108. Thomas and Nishimoto, 91.

109. Thomas and Nishimoto, 93.

110. Thomas and Nishimoto, 200–207.

111. McWilliams, *Prejudice*, viii, 3.

112. For influence, see David Campbell, *Writing Security: United States Foreign Policy and the Politics of Identity* (Minneapolis: University of Minnesota Press, 1998).

113. This led to his later activist work organizing with the National Farm Labor Union (NFLU) and his many published texts on the bracero program. See, for example, Ernesto Galarza, *Strangers in Our Fields: Based on a Report Regarding Compliance with the Contractual, Legal, and Civil Rights of Mexican Agricultural Workers in the United States* (Washington, D.C.: Fund for the Republic, 1956).

114. Ernesto Galarza to José Hernández Serrano, February 3, 1950, Box 19, Folder 6, EGP.

Chapter 4

1. "Versos" dedicados a Mexico y Los Estados Unidos, by J. S. Vilchis, Box 17, Folder 9, Ernesto Galarza Papers, Special Collections, Stanford University Libraries (EGP); see also the agreement of August 4, 1942, for the Temporary Migration of Mexican Agricultural Workers to the United States as revised on April 26, 1943, by an exchange of notes between the American Embassy at Mexico City and the Mexican Ministry for Foreign Affairs, RG 224, Box 19, NARA. Also see the front page of Pacific Lines, *Southern Pacific Bulletin* (October 1943), Box 17, Folder 8, EGP. Speech (discurso) by Sr. Lic. Francisco Trujillo Gurría, Sec. del Trabajo y Provision Social, to a contingent of Mexican workers heading to the United States on May 13, 1943, Box 17, Folder 8, EGP.

2. According to Deborah Cohen, "the most powerful weapon that most braceros had was their feet—they left." Cohen, *Braceros,* 140. Also see Report by Ernesto Galarza, October 1, 1955, Box 3, Folder 1, EGP.

3. Interview at Camp McCallum in Salinas, California, October 4, 1955; interview with twelve braceros in Tracy, California, October 7, 1955, Box 18, Folder 6, EGP.

4. After 1951, Galarza renamed the NFLU the National Agricultural Workers Union (NAWU). H. L. Mitchell, president of the union, had previously led the Southern Tenant Farmers' Union (STFU). The STFU first formed in Arkansas in 1934 to fight for the rights of sharecroppers and tenant farmers. Mitchell transferred his headquarters from Memphis to Washington, D.C., and his union affiliated with the AFL in 1946. William Green, president of the AFL, authorized the NFLU campaign to organize farmworkers in Louisiana and California. Hank Hasiwar started the union in California, with Galarza joining him in the early stages of the thirty-two-month NFLU strike against DiGiorgio. After 1954, Galarza covered the state alone. Anne Loftis, "Strangers in Our Fields: The NFLU Fights the Bracero Program," Box 3, Folder 1, Anne Loftis Papers, 1953–1978, Stanford University Libraries.

5. "California Sends 150 Back to Mexico," *New York Times,* 1947, Box 18, Folder 1, EGP. For more on Galarza and the NFLU strike against DiGiorgio farms in California, see Galarza, *Spiders in the House and Workers in the Field.*

6. Galarza, *Strangers in Our Fields*, 15.

7. Framing its arguments around racial liberalism and "equal rights," the President's Committee on Civil Rights argued that the promise of freedom and equality were part of the American heritage. The Report of the President's Committee on Civil Rights, *To Secure These Rights*, Harry S. Truman Presidential Library and Museum. House of Representatives, Committee on Education and Labor, Special Investigating Subcommittee, Investigation of Labor-Management Relations, 81st Congress, 2nd Session, 601–616. See Extension of Remarks of Hon. John F. Shelley, May 22, 1950. Shelley, a Democrat and "friend of labor," presented Galarza's analysis. Also available in Box 35, Folder 6, EGP.

8. Zaragosa Vargas, *Civil Rights Are Labor Rights: Mexican American Workers in Twentieth Century America* (Princeton, NJ: Princeton University Press, 2007); Robert Korstad, *Civil Rights Unionism: Tobacco Workers and the Struggle for Democracy in the Mid-Twentieth Century South* (Chapel Hill: University of North Carolina Press, 2003). Also see Michael Honey, *Southern Labor and Black Civil Rights* (Urbana: University of Illinois Press, 1992) and Robin D. G. Kelley, *Hammer and Hoe: Alabama Communists During the Great Depression* (Chapel Hill: University of North Carolina Press, 1990).

9. Mireya Loza as well found that Galarza and the unions invoked patriotic narratives that chastised the undocumented. Loza, *Defiant Braceros*, 100–133. Also see Ngai, *Impossible Subjects*, 161–166.

10. "Wetback" was not yet viewed as a racial term by liberal labor advocates, but was seen as a "commonsense" label for those migrating without a contract.

11. Goodman notes that between 1927 and 1964, voluntary departures outnumbered formal deportation nine to one, representing more than 90 percent of expulsions. These "self-deportations" had more to do with government planning, force, and coercion than with migrants' autonomous decisions. Goodman, *Deportation Machine*, 38, 71–72. For more on Operation Wetback, see Kelly Lytle Hernández, "The Crimes and Consequences of Illegal Immigration: A Cross-Border Examination of Operation Wetback, 1943–1954," *Western Historical Quarterly* (Winter 2006): 421–444. Also see Lytle Hernández, *Migra!*; Julian Samora, *Los Mojados: The Wetback Story* (Notre Dame, IN: University of Notre Dame Press, 1971); Juan Ramon García, *Operation Wetback: The Mass Deportation of Undocumented Mexican Workers in 1954* (Westport, CT: Greenwood Press, 1980).

12. Hank Hasiwar, "Darkness in the Valley of Plenty," *The American Federationist* (June 1951), Box 43, Folder 10, EGP.

13. For more on how "race management" works in managerial thought and practice, see David Roediger and Elizabeth Esch, *The Production of Difference: Race and the Management of Labor in U.S. History* (New York: Oxford University Press, 2012).

14. Mae Ngai refers to this "crucial slippage" when she constructs a genealogy of President Kennedy's book, *A Nation of Immigrants* (1958), to show how liberalism's commitment to formal equality directly contributed to the rise of the notion of illegal immigration. See Ngai, "A Nation of Immigrants: Cold War and the Civil Rights Origins of Illegal Immigration" (April 2010), Paper Number 28 (unpublished talk).

15. Galarza spent time in particular at Camp McCallum, a thirty-two-acre bracero camp seven miles outside of Salinas in the Monterey Bay area, which was previously a military base. Many guestworker labor camps were former military bases, as were the Japanese American internment camps. For more information on Camp McCallum, see Lori Flores, *Grounds for Dreaming: Mexican Americans, Mexican Immigrants, and the California Farm Worker Movement*

(New Haven, CT: Yale University Press, 2016); Carol McKibben, *Beyond Cannery Row: Sicilian Women, Immigration, and Community in Monterey, California, 1915–99* (Urbana: University of Illinois Press, 2006), and *Racial Beachhead: Diversity and Democracy in a Military Town* (Palo Alto, CA: Stanford University Press, 2011).

16. Bracero interviews by Ernesto Galarza, October 20, 1955, Box 18, Folder 6, EGP. Also see *Strangers in Our Fields*, 18.

17. Lowe, *The Intimacies of Four Continents*, 175.

18. This stipulation was written into all varying editions of the Individual Work Agreement. See Individual Work Agreement of August 4, 1942, as amended April 26, 1943, RG 211, Records of the War Manpower Commission, Entry 171, Box 15, NARA.

19. See *Strangers in Our Fields*.

20. Galarza interview with nine nationals, Joe Perez Camp, Terminous, California, October 20, 1955, Box 18, Folder 6, EGP; interview with eight braceros at the Julian Ramírez Camp, Tracy, California, October 14, 1955, Box 18, Folder 6, EGP.

21. Galarza interview with five braceros at the Gondo Camp in Watsonville, California, October 1, 1955, Box 18, Folder 6, EGP; interview with two braceros at the Rudy Avila Camp in Patterson, California, October 10, 1955, Box 18, Folder 6, EGP; Galarza's interview notes from Tracy and Patterson, California, October 7–10, 1955; interview with twelve braceros in Tracy, California, October 7, 1955, Box 18, Folder 6, EGP.

22. Braceros often contacted Mexican consulates immediately after their arrival. Between 1948 and 1953, braceros filed at least 400 complaints with their consul, indicating that they also often turned to the government for social justice. Julie Weise, *Corazón de Dixie: Mexicanos in the U.S. South Since 1910* (Chapel Hill: University of North Carolina Press, 2015), 97–99.

23. Interview with eight nationals at Camp Soledad, no date, Box 18, Folder 6, EGP. Ernesto Galarza handwritten field notes, Box 18, Folder 6, EGP.

24. Mexican Labor Work Agreement/*Convenio de Trabajo para Trabajadores Mexicanos*, c. 1951, Box 19, Folder 2, EGP. The same clause remained in the Standard Work Contract, as amended after Public Law 78 had been instituted in July 1951. See "Individual Work Agreement" of August 4, 1942, details above.

25. As a group of braceros declared, "We figured out that in our camp we had over 100 men last month and that the camp got about $1,300 every week for board." Box 18, Folder 6, EGP.

26. Interview by Ernesto Galarza with three braceros at the Juan Lucio Camp in Manteca, California, October 14, 1955; interview with two braceros at the D'Arrigo Company in Coyote, California, October 10, 1955, Box 18, Folder 6, EGP.

27. Police forced them back to work. Ngai, *Impossible Subjects*, 145. Interview by Ernesto Galarza with twelve braceros in Tracy, October 7, 1955, Box 18, Folder 6, EGP; interview with two braceros at the Rudy Avila Camp in Patterson, California, October 10, 1955, Box 18, Folder 6, EGP; interview with one bracero, November 9, 1955, Box 18, Folder 6, EGP.

28. Galarza interview with eight braceros at the Julian Ramirez Camp in Tracey, California, October 14,1955, Box 18, Folder 6, EGP; interview with eight nationals, Merced Camp, October 13, 1955, Box 18, Folder 6, EGP. For more on bracero labor strikes, see Weise, *Corazón de Dixie*, 95–97.

29. Tirso Yepes interview; Ngai, *Impossible Subjects*, 133; Jesús Garnica, interview by Mireya Loza for Bracero History Archive, May 22, 2006, item 291.

30. Deborah Cohen, *Braceros*; Loza, *Defiant Braceros*.

31. Antonio V. Perez Herrera, interview by Marina Kalashnikova for Bracero History Archive January 11, 2008, item 747.

32. José Carmona, in Bracero History Archive, item 3294.

33. Alberto de Loera, interview by Violeta Domínguez for Bracero History Archive, September 4, 2003, item 93.

34. Elizabeth Mandeel, "The Bracero Program, 1942–1964," *American International Journal of Contemporary Research* (January 2014), 181. Pedro L. Lechuga, interview for Bracero History Archive by Ivonne Méndez, January 12, 2008, item 724.

35. Apolonio Venegas, interview by Anais Acosta for Bracero History Archive, May 26, 2006, item 394. Also see interview with Alberto Montes González, July 27, 2005, item 136.

36. José Esequiel Adame Castro, interview by Marina Kalashnikova for Bracero History Archive, January 6. 2008, item 655.

37. Ernesto Galarza to William Green, May 1, 1943, Box 5 Folder 6, EGP. Also see Galarza, *Strangers,* 15.

38. Ernesto Galarza, "Plan," addressed to the ACLU, May 31, 1944, and ACLU to Galarza, June 6, 1944, Box 5, Folder 7, EGP; New York City meeting minutes, Box 5, Folder 9, EGP.

39. ACLU to Galarza, June 6, 1944, Box 5, Folder 7, EGP.

40. Ernesto Galarza, memo, September 6, 1944 and report to Dr. Leo Rowe (president of the Pan- American Union) referring to a conversation with the Department of State about conditions in camps for Mexican nationals, Box 5, Folder 7, EGP.

41. Edwin Embree of the American Council on Race Relations to Galarza, March 24 1945, Box 5, Folder 8, EGP.

42. George I. Sánchez Papers, Box 16, Folder 13, University of Texas, Austin. Quoted from Maggie Rivas-Rodriguez, *Texas Mexican Americans and Postwar Civil Rights* (Austin: University of Texas Press, 2015), 143.

43. One key hindrance was that Mexican Americans' arguments for civil rights in the 1940s often revolved around claims to "whiteness" as a legacy of the Treaty of Guadalupe Hidalgo in 1848. As a result, Mexican Americans and Blacks adopted legal strategies that rested on assumptions that reveal fundamental differences about what it meant to be Black or Mexican American in the post-World War II era. Sometimes Black-brown solidarity worked and sometimes it did not. See Lauren Araiza, *To March for Others: The Black Freedom Struggle and the United Farm Workers* (Philadelphia: University of Pennsylvania Press, 2013); Neil Foley, *Quest for Equality: The Failed Promise of Black-Brown Solidarity* (Cambridge, MA: Harvard University Press, 2010); Lisa Ramos, "Not Similar Enough: Mexican American and African American Civil Rights Struggles in the 1940s," in *The Struggle in Black and Brown: African American and Mexican American Relations during the Civil Rights Era,* ed. Brian D. Behnken (Lincoln: University of Nebraska Press, 2011).

44. Robert C. Jones, *Braceros Mexicanos en Los Estado Unidos,* Division of Labor and Social Information, Pan-American Union (1946). Also see a newspaper article by Sidney Wise that refers to this pamphlet. Sidney Wise, "Distinciones Raciales, Mala Vivienda y una Explotacion Desenfrenada de Los Braceros," August 3, 1945, Box 24, Folder 10, EGP.

45. Galarza letter to, September 10, 1945, Box 5, Folder 9, EGP.

46. Richard Chabrán, "Activism and Intellectual Struggle in the Life of Ernesto Galarza, 1905–1984," *Hispanic Journal of Behavioral Sciences 7,* no. 2 (1985): 135–152.

47. Dionicio N. Valdés, *Organized Agriculture and the Labor Movement Before the UFW: Puerto Rico, Hawai'i, California* (Austin: University of Texas Press, 2011), 195.

48. Interviews with Ernesto Galarza, *The Burning Light: Action and Organizing in the Mexican Community in California* (Berkeley: Regional Oral History Office, Bancroft Library, University of California, 1982), 16; Galarza, *Strangers,* 72–73.

49. Grubbs, 458; Valdés, 181.

50. Growers hired new braceros when other braceros went on strike. In response, Galarza, through affiliates in Mexico, successfully pressured the Mexican government to remove 150 braceros used as strikebreakers by DiGiorgio in 1947. "California Sends 150 Back to Mexico," *New York Times,* 1947, Box 18, Folder 1, EGP. Galarza, *Burning Light,* 16.

51. Gabrielle E. Clark, "Coercion and Contract at the Margins: Deportable Labor and the Laws of Employment Termination Under U.S. Capitalism (1942–2015)," *Law & Social Inquiry* (2016), 8. Calavita, *Inside the State.*

52. Ernesto Galarza, "Poverty in the Valley of Plenty: A Report on the DiGiorgio Strike," May 14, 1948, Box 35, Folder 3, EGP. See also Ngai, *Impossible Subjects,* 153.

53. Galarza, "Narrative." Mandeel, 173–174.

54. Press release, October 18, 1948, Box 23, Folder 4, EGP.

55. See C. J. Haggerty, secretary-treasurer of the California State Federation of Labor to Galarza, May 26, 1950, Box 17, Folder 11, EGP. Also see letter from A. J. Clark, secretary of the Central Labor Union of Monterey County, AFL, to Hank Hasiwar, NFLU, January 14, 1951, Box 19, Folder 6, EGP. For more on the DiGiorgio strike, see Deborah Cohen, *Braceros,* 145–160. Also see Galarza, *Spiders in the House,* and Mitchell, *They Saved the Crops,* 120–130.

56. José Hernández Serrano, president of Alianza, to Galarza, June 8, 1951, Box 19, Folder 6, EGP; Hernández to Galarza, December 19, 1949, and February 3, 1950, Box 19, Folder 6, EGP.

57. H. L. Mitchell to George Rundquist of the ACLU, April 5, 1951, Box 19, Folder 6, EGP.

58. For eight years, the ORIT was the dominant international trade union group in the hemisphere. "Resolution of the Conference on the Points of the Agenda," International Conference of the Trade Unions of Mexico and the United States Convened by the ORIT, Mexico, D.F., December 14–16, 1953, Box 21, Folder 10, EGP. Also see Deborah Cohen, *Braceros,* 164; Ngai, 161. Robert J. Alexander, "Labor and Inter-American Relations," *Annals of the American Academy of Political and Social Science* (March 1961): 41–53.

59. The agreement between NFLU and the UTAVM was almost identical to their agreement with Alianza. Report, *Basic Points of the Agreement signed by the NFLU and the Union de Trabajadores Agricolas del Valle de Mexicali on March 2, 1951,* March 9, 1951, Box 19, Folder 6, EGP. Press release from the NFLU-AFL, March 13, 1951, Box 19, Folder 6, EGP.

60. NFLU report; Galarza to José Hernández Serrano, October 21, 1950, Box 19, Folder 6, EGP.

61. Local 284, Soledad, to Galarza, May 26, 1951, Box 19, Folder 6, EGP; José Hernández Serrano to Galarza, June 8, 1951, Box 19, Folder 6, EGP. See correspondence between Serrano and Galarza, November 10, 1943, March 31, 1950, February 16, 1951, Box 19, Folder 6, EGP. Consul Ricardo Castro Sainz to José Hernández Serrano, no date, Box 19, Folder 6, EGP.

62. Galarza, *Spiders,* 77–78. Alianza de Braceros to H. L. Mitchell, president of the NFLU December 19, 1949, Box 19, Folder 6, EGP; Hernández Serrano to Galarza, December 19, 1949, and February 3, 1950, Box 19, Folder 6, EGP.

63. As of September 1950, there was a bracero recruitment center at Mexicali. See "Warren Is Asked to Aid Mex Labor Recruiting," *Sacramento Bee,* September 19, 1950, Box 42, Folder 10, EGP; Statement by Ernesto Galarza, c. 1951, Box 24, Folder 4, EGP.

64. Galarza to Jose Hernández Serrano, February 3, 1950, Box 19, Folder 6, EGP; Galarza to A. J. Clark, head of local union 284 in Soledad, Salinas, and Monterey, February 15, 1951, Box 19, Folder 6, EGP; A. J. Clark to Hank Hasiwar, January 14, 1951, Box 19, Folder 6, EGP.

65. *Wetback Strike: A Report on the Strike of Farm Workers in the Imperial Valley of California;* News release, May 31, 1951, Box 45, Folder 1, EGP; Ernesto Galarza, Poverty in the Valley of Plenty, May 14, 1948, Box 35, Folder 3, EGP.

66. "To Control Illegal Immigration," Hearings before the Subcommittee on Immigration and Naturalization, of the Committee on the Judiciary, U.S. Senate, 83rd Congress, 2nd Session on S. 3660 and S. 3661, July 12, 13, 14, 1954 (Washington, D.C.: U.S. Government Printing Office), 70.

67. Ernesto Galarza, "Poverty in the Valley of Plenty: A Report on the DiGiorgio Strike," May 14, 1948, Box 35, Folder 3, EGP, 3, 6–8.

68. Galarza, *Spiders,* 77–78. Loza, 126–133.

69. Agreement Between Governments of United States and Mexico Concerning Migrant Labor, Public Law 78, 82nd Congress, U.S. Department of Labor, Box 19, Folder 2, EGP.

70. The Mexican government accused UTAVM and Alianza of engaging in illegal contracting or giving out contracts to braceros without permission from the government. Galarza believed these were cover-up charges because the Mexican government wanted to avoid coverage of U.S. labor's critiques of the program and did not want U.S. labor involved in the 1951 agreement negotiations. Brotherhood of Maintenance Way Employees to the President, July 5, 1951, Box 19, Folder 6, EGP. Also see Valdés, 220.

71. Hernandez (2006), 421–444. Mandeel, 174.

72. H. L. Mitchell to George Rundquist of the ACLU, April 5, 1951, EGP; Ernesto Galarza to Serafino, "Re: Article on Page One of *Tiempo* Magazine in Mexico City on February 23, 1951," March 8, 1951, Box 19, Folder 6, EGP; Report, *The Agreement with the Union de Trabajadores Agricolas del Valle de Mexicali of March 2, 1951,*March 9, 1951, Box 19, Folder 6, EGP; NFLU press release, March 14, 1951, Box 19, Folder 6, EGP; Valdés, *Organized Agriculture,* 220.

73. Public Law 78, U.S. Department of Labor, Box 19, Folder 2, EGP.

74. Galarza reconstituted the NFLU as the NAWU in 1952. By 1956, he launched a publicity campaign to reveal the corrupt administration of the bracero program by writing the book *Strangers in Our Fields.* NAWU-AFL, "The Use of Mexican Contract National and Its Effects on the Employment of Domestic Agricultural Workers in the Imperial Valley of California," August 1953, Box 43, Folder 4, EGP.

75. *To Secure These Rights: The Report of the President's Committee on Civil Rights* (New York: Simon and Schuster, 1947).

76. From 1950 to 1952, President Truman remained committed to expanding the New Deal and established the President's Commission on Migratory Labor in 1950. The commission held public hearings across the country that stressed the need to end the process of "drying out the wetbacks," and argued for public hearings to determine wage rates rather than allowing growers associations to determine them. The power of growers' interests and conservatives in Congress prevented any significant reform. See Maurice J. Tobin, secretary of the U.S. Department of Labor, "The Recommendations of the President's Commission on Migratory Labor," April 1952.

77. Statement by Walter Mason on the proposal to extend the Mexican contract labor program, June 12, 1953, Box 19, Folder 9, EGP.

78. Galarza to the President's Commission on Migratory Labor, December 1, 1950, RG 174, Entry 52, Box 3, NARA; Resolution adopted by the 16th CIO Constitutional Convention,

December 1954, Box 21, Folder 6, EGP; CIO Aids Farm Labor, Pamphlet 205 (April 1952), RG 174, Entry 52, Box 4, NARA; Mitchell, *They Saved the Crops,* 194.

79. The AFL-CIO's leadership promoted the view that unauthorized migration was hurting all workers until the 1970s. It was primarily leftist labor unions and Mexican American organizations that demanded sanctions against employers who knowingly hired unauthorized migrants up until the late 1970s, when conservatives began to adopt this view. "Wetback Menace," *The Teamster* (March 1954), Box 50, Folder 8, EGP; Valdés, 160. Minian, 60, 185–186.

80. Statement of Walter J. Mason on the views of the AFL on HR 2955 (Yorty bill) and HR 3048 (Poage bill), c. 1951, RG 174, Entry 52, Box 3, NARA.

81. *CIO Aids Farm Labor,* reprinted from April 1952, *Economic Outlook,* RG 174, Entry 52, Box 4; H. L. Mitchell to Michael J. Gavin, Secretary of Labor, June 25, 1951, RG 174, Entry 52, Box 2, NARA.

82. C. J. Haggerty, secretary-treasurer, California State Federation of Labor, AFL, Mexican Farm Labor Statement, *Weekly News Letter,* January 29, 1954, Box 19, Folder 6, E.G.P;

83. Pat(rick) McCarran, "The Background of the McCarran-Walter Act," *Congressional Record,* March 2, 1953, 1518.

84. See newspaper clippings, Box 50, Folder 8, EGP. Titles include "Governor Warren Indicates that Subversives are Coming Through the Mexico-U.S. Border Like a Sieve," December 21, 1951; "Communists are Entering the U.S. Under the Guise of Farmworkers," *Daily News,* February 19, 1951. In 1954, Benjamin Habberton, the acting INS commissioner, warned that more than 100 Communists crossed the border daily. See "Commies Cross Border Patrol Daily, Officers Warn," *El Paso Herald-Post,* c. 1954; "Wetback Menace."

85. Ernesto Galarza, *Merchants of Labor,* 62. Also see Cindy Hahamovitch, "Keeping the Unskilled Out: Why Hart-Celler Didn't Matter to Workers," *Labor: Studies in Working-Class Histories of the Americas* 12, no. 3 (2015): 25.

86. Clark, "Coercion and Contract," 8.

87. According to Valdés, neither country's labor federation put meaningful financial or political resources into their union organizing campaigns. Valdés, *Organized Agriculture,* 163; Cohen, *Braceros,* 141.

88. Galarza oral history interview, *Burning Light,* 16.

89. "To Control Illegal Immigration," hearings before the Subcommittee on Immigration and Naturalization of the Committee on the Judiciary, 63–64.

90. As an example, in 1889, the Supreme Court referred to the Chinese as among the "vast hordes of [foreign] people crowding in upon us." From the U.S. Supreme Court case *Chae Chan Ping v. United States* (Chinese Exclusion Case), 1889.

91. "To Control Illegal Immigration," 66-75.

92. Huerta represented the Community Service Organization (CSO). Hearing of the Senate Fact Finding Committee on Labor and Welfare, California State Legislature, Sacramento, California, June 15, 1960, Box 30, Folder 1, EGP. David G. Gutiérrez, *Walls and Mirrors: Mexican Americans, Mexican Immigration, and the Politics of Ethnicity* (Berkeley: University of California Press, 1995), 174-205.

93. Gutiérrez, *Walls and Mirrors,* 174–176; "Sin Fronteras?:' Chicanos, Mexican Americans, and the Emergence of the Contemporary Mexican Immigration Debate, 1968–1978," *Journal of American Ethnic History* 10, no. 4 (1991); Minian, 188.

94. Valdés, *Organized Agriculture,* 238.

95. Frank Bardacke, *Trampling Out the Vintage: Cesar Chavez and the Two Souls of the United Farm Workers* (New York: Verso, 2012).

96. Ernesto Galarza, statement before the Special House Judiciary Subcommittee on Japanese Labor Program in California, on behalf of the NAWU, AFL-CIO, c. 1957, Box 17, Folder 6, EGP; War Manpower Commission, *Annual Peak Employment of Foreign Nationals Employed in Temporary Agricultural Jobs in the United States, 1951–1960*, Records of the War Manpower Commission, RG 211, Entry 25, Box 2, NARA.

97. War Manpower Commission, *Annual Peak Employment of Foreign Nationals Employed in Temporary Agricultural Jobs in the United States, 1951–1960*, Records of the War Manpower Commission, RG 211, Entry 25, Box 2, NARA.

98. Carlos Romulo, Embassy of the Philippines, to Secretary of Labor Arthur Goldberg, July 16, 1961, RG 174, Entry 25, Box 7, NARA. For more on this Japanese labor importation program, see Mireya Loza, "The Japanese Agricultural Workers' Program: Race, Labor, and Cold War Diplomacy in the Fields, 1956–1965," *Pacific Historical Review* 86 (2017): 661–690.

99. California State Federation of Labor, "Asian Contract Laborers, 1950–1961," statement submitted to the House of Representatives on April 23, 1957, Box 17, Folder 6, EGP. Also see Andrew J. Biemiller, Director of the Department of Legislation (AFL-CIO), Statement before the Special House Judiciary, Subcommittee on Japanese Labor Program in California, May 16, 1957, Box 19, Folder 9, EGP.

100. Ernesto Galarza (NAWU, AFL-CIO), Statement before the Special House Judiciary Subcommittee on Japanese Labor Program in California, May 16, 1957, Box 17, Folder 6, EGP; *Sacramento Bee*, October 20, 1959.

Chapter 5

1. Rexford Tugwell, *Stricken Land: The Story of Puerto Rico* (New York: Doubleday, 1947), 492. With the PRRA, Tugwell and other U.S. state officials hoped to give Puerto Ricans practical experience in Anglo-style institutions to prepare the island for democratic state governance. For more on the historic process of U.S. political education and tutelage in Puerto Rico, see Julian Go, "Chains of Empire, Projects of State: Political Education and U.S. Colonial Rule in Puerto Rico and the Philippines," *Comparative Studies in Society and History* 42 (April 2000): 333–362.

2. Rafael Cox-Alomar, "Revisiting the Transatlantic Triangle: The Decolonisation of the British Caribbean in Light of the Anglo-American Special Relationship," *Diplomacy and Statecraft* 15 (2004).

3. Carmen Teresa Whalen, *From Puerto Rico to Philadelphia: Puerto Rican Workers and Postwar Economies* (Philadelphia: Temple University Press, 2001), 64–68; also see Deborah Cohen, *Braceros*.

4. Jesus T. Piñero, A Proclamation by the Governor of Puerto Rico, Administrative Bulletin No. 1077, Office of the Executive Secretary, San Juan, Puerto Rico, April 12, 1948.

5. One exception would be Lilia Fernández, "Of Immigrants and Migrants," 6–39. Scholarship on the Puerto Rican contract labor program includes: Edwin Maldonado, "Contract Labor and the Origins of Puerto Rican Communities in the United States," *Center for Migration Studies of New York* (1979); Jorge Duany, "A Transnational Colonial Migration: Puerto Rico's Farm Labor Program," in *Blurred Borders: Transnational Migration Between the Hispanic Caribbean and the United States* (Chapel Hill: University of North Carolina Press, 2011); Michael Lapp, "Managing Migration: The Migration Division of Puerto Rico and Puerto Ricans in New York

City, 1948–1968" (Ph.D. diss., Johns Hopkins University, 1990); Whalen, "Contract Labor: The State-Sponsored Migration," in *From Puerto Rico to Philadelphia*.

6. Edgardo Meléndez, *Sponsored Migration: The State and Puerto Rican Postwar Migration to the United States* (Columbus: Ohio State University Press, 2017); and García-Colón, *Colonial Migrants*.

7. See Ileana Rodríguez-Silva, *Silencing Race*, 88, 136; Gervasio Luis García, "I Am the Other: Puerto Rico in the Eyes of North Americans, 1898," *Journal of American History* 87 (June 2000): 39–64. Many Puerto Rican scholars have attempted to go beyond instrumentalist interpretations of the Partido Popular Democrático (PPD), including, for example, Quintero Rivera, "El papel del Estado en el modelo puertorriqueño de crecimiento económico; base clasista del proyecto desarrollista del 40" (paper presented at the Third Central American Congress of Sociology, Tegucigalpa, Honduras, 1978); Rivera, for example, sees the PPD's goal as a project aimed at constituting their own free nation-state. Cited from Emilio Pantojas-Garcia, "Puerto Rican Populism Revisited: The PPD during the 1940s," *Journal of Latin American Studies* 21 (October 1989): 521–523.

8. A total of 479 were injured, and 40 to 50 people had been killed. Political uprisings also occurred in Puerto Rico over independence, resulting in 26 deaths and serious injuries. Charles Taussig, "A Four-Power Program in the Caribbean," *Foreign Affairs* 24 (July 1946): 699. For more on Tugwell, see Michael Namorato, *Rexford G. Tugwell: A Biography* (New York: Praeger, 1988); Bernard Sternsher, *Rexford Tugwell and the New Deal* (New Brunswick, NJ: Rutgers University Press, 1964).

9. Thomas Howard, *Franklin Roosevelt and the Formation of the Modern World* (New York: Routledge, 2003); Tugwell, *The Stricken Land*, 35, 64.

10. Parker, *Brother's Keeper*, 21–23, 35; Taussig, "A Four-Power Program," 702–703.

11. Anglo-American Caribbean Committee, *St. Petersburg Times*, March 10, 1942.

12. In 1941, Tugwell accepted an appointment as chancellor of the University of Puerto Rico, and within the year became governor of Puerto Rico. After his appointment to a leadership role at the AACC, Tugwell had to deal with a backlash in Puerto Rico from those who saw the organization as a diabolical "Plan Caribe" or "Plan Taussig" that would submerge the island in a federation dominated by the British West Indies. Michael Janeway, "The Wartime Quartet: Muñoz Marin, Tugwell, Ickes, and FDR," in *Island at War: Puerto Rico in the Crucible of the Second World War*, ed. Jorge Rodríguez Beruff and José L. Bolívar Fresneda (Jackson: University Press of Mississippi, 2015), 93–95.

13. Tugwell to Paul V. McNutt of the WMC, April 19, 1943, RG 211, Entry 171, Box 15, NARA.

14. As noted in a 1944 foreign policy report, "The AACC in combination with the WFA created an experimental labor importation program with Puerto Rico in 1943 to alleviate unemployment there, which was short-lived but later more successful under 'Operation Bootstrap.'" Olive Holmes, "Anglo-American Caribbean Commission—Pattern for Colonial Cooperation," *Foreign Policy Association Policy Reports* 20, no. 19 (1944).

15. In 1935, Somervell had been appointed head of the Works Project Administration in New York City, working with local politicians and labor leaders to uphold the rights of workers and unions. Lt. Gen. Somervell to Paul V. McNutt, RG 211, Entry 171, Box 15, NARA.

16. Tugwell to Maj. Gen. James L. Collins, Commanding General, Headquarters Puerto Rican Department, San Juan, Puerto Rico, September 4, 1942; Tugwell to Paul McNutt, April 19, 1943, RG 211, Entry 171, Box 15, NARA.

17. McNutt named Winston Riley the director of the new USES office, who was formerly the director of the Vocational Guidance Program in the Department of Education in Puerto

Rico. McNutt to the Secretary of War, March 26, 1943; Newspaper clipping, "Director Outlines Objectives of New Employment Office: Winston Riley tells Plans for Recruiting Workers for U.S.," *The World Journal,* San Juan, June 26, 1943; A. W. Motley, Bureau of Placement, Department of Labor, to Glenn E. Brockway, February 12, 1943; McNutt to June 15, 1943; McNutt to Chavez, June 29, 1943, RG 211, Entry 171, Box 15, NARA. J. S. Russell, memo to Lt. Col. J. L. Taylor, Subject: Puerto Rican Labor, June 11, 1943, RG 224, Entry 1, Box 15. U.S. Senator Dennis Chavez to Paul V. McNutt, June 5, 1943; Santiago Iglesias Jr., Acting Commissioner of Labor in Puerto Rico, to McNutt, November 5, 1942, RG 211, Entry 171, Box 14, NARA.

18. Senator Rufus Holman to McNutt, December 14, 1943, RG 211, Entry 171, Box 14, NARA.

19. "Draft of Proposed Language for Incorporation in Contract to Assure Return of Puerto Rican Workers," RG 211, Entry 171, Box 14, NARA; J. S. Russell, memo to Lt. Col. J. L. Taylor, June 11, 1943, RG 224, Entry 1, Box 15, NARA. The Mexican government used Wells Fargo Bank to place 10 percent of braceros' wages in a savings account. Thousands of braceros are still waiting to be reimbursed, in their struggle for recovery of those stolen funds. See Loza, *Defiant Braceros*, 137–49.

20. See the Supreme Court case *Downes v. Bidwell,* 182 U.S. 244 (1901).

21. Sam Erman, *Almost Citizens: Puerto Rico, the U.S. Constitution, and Empire* (New York: Cambridge University Press, 2019). For an extended discussion of Puerto Ricans' citizenship status, see *CENTRO: Journal of the Center for Puerto Rican Studies* 25, no. 1, including Pedro Caban, "The Puerto Rican Colonial Matrix: The Etiology of Citizenship—An Introduction"; Charles Venator Santiago, "Extending Citizenship to Puerto Rico: Inclusive Exclusion," and Edgardo Meléndez, "Citizenship and the Alien Exclusion in the Insular Cases: Puerto Ricans in the Periphery of American Empire," *CENTRO Journal* 25 (Spring 2013). Also see José Cabranes, "Citizenship and the American Empire: Notes on the Legislative History of the United States Citizenship of Puerto Ricans," *University of Pennsylvania Law Review* 127, no. 2 (December 1978): 391–489.

22. Fernández, 8.

23. Another Puerto Rican contract labor experiment occurred in 1946, when a private Chicago employment agency, in agreement with the insular Department of Labor, established an office on the island to recruit domestic and foundry workers to Chicago on one-year contracts. The abuses that resulted made the news in Puerto Rico and the United States. Edwin Maldonado, "Contract Labor," 111–115.

24. Michael Lapp, "Managing Migration," 35.

25. McGreevey, 51–54, 122–123.

26. Eileen Findlay, *We Are Left Without a Father Here: Masculinity, Domesticity, and Migration in Postwar Puerto Rico* (Durham, NC: Duke University Press, 2014),104.

27. Tugwell, xvii.

28. The chairman of the committee, Harold Ickes, was one of the lead figures implementing President Roosevelt's New Deal initiatives in the United States. President Franklin D. Roosevelt to Harold L. Ickes, Secretary of the Interior, March 8, 1943, RG 224, Entry 1, Box 23, NARA.

29. Stuart Chase, *Operation Bootstrap in Puerto Rico: Report of Progress* (National Planning Association, 1951), 5. The National Planning Administration conducted this study with funds provided by the Economic Development Administration of the Puerto Rican government. Carlos E. Chardón, *Report of the Puerto Rico Policy Commission: Chardón Report,* June 14, 1934. Maldonado, 36.

30. Briggs, 83–87. Tugwell, *Stricken Land.*

31. Whalen, *From Puerto Rico to Philadelphia,* 28–29.

32. A. W. Maldonado, *Teodoro Moscoso and Puerto Rico's Operation Bootstrap* (Gainesville: University Press of Florida, 1997); Deborah Berman Santana, "Puerto Rico's Operation Bootstrap: Colonial Roots of a Persistent Model for 'Third World' Development," *Revísta Geográfica* 124 (January–December 1998): 87–116.

33. Scholars have noted that the initial economic achievements of Operation Bootstrap and the commonwealth arrangement would have been much less impressive without Puerto Rico's ability to exile its surplus laborers and political dissidents. See Marisol LeBrón, *Policing Life and Death: Race, Violence, and Resistance in Puerto Rico* (Berkeley: University of California Press, 2019), 8.

34. Maldonado, "Contract Labor," 113.

35. Lapp, 29–30. Chloé S. Georas and Ramon Grosfoguel, "Latino Caribbean Diasporas in New York," in *Mambo Montage* (New York: Columbia University Press, 2001), 107.

36. Fernando Sierra Berdecía, "Protecting 686,000 PR Workers," in *El Diario de Puerto Rico,* January 3, 1949, Reel 118, Ephemeral Publications, 1946–1993, Box 2836, Folder 1; Box 2838, Folder 4, Offices of the Government of Puerto Rico in the United States (OGPRUS) Records.

37. While Berdecía does not mention it, another instance was when the USDL hired twelve thousand Puerto Ricans for employment on the railroads or in construction in Navy and Army yards in the U.S. South during World War I. McGreevey, *Borderline Citizens,* 51–54, 122–123; Poblete, 27–46.

38. Fernando Sierra Berdecía, "Puerto Rican Emigration: Reality and Public Policy" (speech at the 9th Convention on Social Orientation of Puerto Rico), Reel 118, Ephemeral Publications, 1946–1993, Box 2836, Folder 1, Box 2838, Folder 4, OGPRUS.

39. Lapp, 49; Meléndez, 64–66.

40. Luis Muñoz Marín, "Development Through Democracy," in "Puerto Rico, A Study in Democratic Development," *Annals of the American Academy of Political Science,* vol. 285 (January 1953): 1–8.

41. Harry Truman, "Inaugural Address, January 20, 1949," Harry S. Truman Library and Museum.

42. Chase, *Operation Bootstrap,* 55.

43. Briggs, 112; U.S. House of Representatives, Report No. 2275, *Providing for the Organization of a Constitutional Government in Puerto Rico,* 81st Congress, 2nd Session (Washington, D.C.: U.S. Government Printing Office), June 19, 1950, p. 3.

44. For more on the impossibility of the PPD's decision, see Alyosha Goldstein, "The Attributes of Sovereignty," in *Imagining Our Americas: Toward a Transnational Frame,* ed. Heidi Tinsman and Sandhya Shukla (Durham, NC: Duke University Press, 2007), 331–333. Sierra Berdecía (speech at the Convention of the International Association of Personnel in Employment Security, Miami Beach, June 25, 1957), OGPRUS, Box 2898, Folder 10. For more on how gender defined the PPD's political project in postwar Puerto Rico, see Findlay, *We Are Left Without a Father.*

45. Rodríguez-Silva, 88.

46. Nathaniel Cordova, "In His Image and Likeness: The Puerto Rican Jíbaro as Political Icon, *Centro Journal* 17 (Fall 2005), 176–181; Darlene Dávila, *Sponsored Identities: Cultural Politics in Puerto Rico* (Philadelphia: Temple University Press, 1997), 29.

47. For influence, see Lebrón, *Policing Life and Death,* 11–14.

48. Cordova, 173, 180–181. Also see Lillian Guerra, *Popular Expression and National Identity in Puerto Rico: The Struggle for Self, Community, and Nation* (Gainesville: University

Press of Florida, 1998). While Guerra views the *jibarista* discourse as a result of the guilty conscience of those Puerto Rican officials who collaborated with the U.S. colonial system, I see it as a political response to the progressive and nationalist ideals they thought this collaboration embodied.

49. PRDL, *Los beneficiarios* (1952, Viguié News Films), Migration Division Short Films, Film #6, OGPRUS.

50. Between 1948 and 1990 the program recruited 421,238 Puerto Ricans to work in farm labor on the U.S. mainland. Duany, "A Transnational Colonial Migration," 88–90.

51. "Puerto Rican Farm Program of the Migration Division" [c. 1962], Box 2961, Folder 3, OGPRUS.

52. Report, *Recruitment of Puerto Rican Workers for Agriculture*, U.S. Department of Labor, January 2, 1964, Box 2960, Folder 28, OGPRUS.

53. Clarence Senior, *Mexico in Transition* (Milwaukee: Milwaukee Housing Council, 1938); Clarence Senior, *Democracy Comes to a Cotton Kingdom*; Clarence Senior, *Self Determination for Puerto Rico* (New York: Post War World Council, 1946); Clarence Senior, *The Puerto Rican Migrant in St. Croix* (San Juan: University of Puerto Rico, 1947); and more.

54. See Olsson, 60, 127–136; Mikael D. Wolfe, *Watering the Revolution: An Environmental and Technological History of Agrarian Reform in Mexico* (Durham, NC: Duke University Press, 2017); Jocelyn Olcott, *Revolutionary Women in Post-revolutionary Mexico* (Durham, NC: Duke University Press, 2005), 123–129; and Cohen, *Braceros*, 37–38.

55. Senior to J. R. Butler, May 23, 1939, quoted in Olsson, 2.

56. Senior, *Self-Determination*, 8.

57. This book had two different titles: Clarence Senior, *Strangers then Neighbors: From Pilgrims to Puerto Ricans* (1951) was retitled *The Puerto Ricans: Strangers—Then Neighbors* (New York: Freedom Books, 1952), 18, 26.

58. Senior, *Strangers*.

59. It is no coincidence that the Migration Division's archives are housed at the Silberman School of Social Work at Hunter College in New York. For more on the linkages among social work, migration, and Puerto Rican labor, see Emma Amador, "Linked Histories of Welfare, Labor, and Puerto Rican Migration," *Modern American History* (July 2019). Law Establishing the Employment and Migration Bureau, No. 25, approved December 5,1947, Reel 118, Ephemeral Publications, 1946–1993, Boxes 2836–2838, OGPRUS; Senior, *Strangers*, 3–4, 100.

60. Senior, *Strangers*, 7–8, 110–111.

61. Senior, *Strangers*, 110.

62. Report, *English Course for Agricultural Workers* (October 1960), *English Lesson Plans* (1960–62), Box 2958, Folder 15, OGPRUS. These English classes were meant to "help them help themselves during their stay on farms." Box 2960, Folder 26, OGPRUS.

63. Senior, *Strangers*, 34–35, 93.

64. Carlos Castaño, chief, Farm Placement Division, Bureau of Employment Security, "Orientation Program in Puerto Rico," Second Annual Farm Labor Conference, San Juan, Puerto Rico, January 1958, Box 2961, Folder 13, pp. 7–8, OGPRUS.

65. Castaño, p. 4.

66. Petro A. Pagán de Colón, director, Bureau of Employment Security, PRDL, "Opening and Closing Remarks," PRDL Second Annual Farm Labor Conference, January 7–8, 1958, Box 2961, Folder 13, OGPRUS.

67. Meléndez, *Sponsored Migration*, 85.

68. Petro A. Pagán de Colón, director, Bureau of Employment Security, PRDL, Second Annual Farm Labor Conference, "Opening and Closing Remarks," January 7–8, 1958, Box 2961, Folder 13, OGPRUS.

69. *Puerto Rico Post-Season Farm Labor Report* (1952), PRDL, Farm Placement Division, OGPRUS, Box 3248, Annual Farm Labor Reports.

70. Second Annual Farm Labor Conference, Summary of Proceedings, January 7–8, 1958, Box 2961, Folder 13, 24–29, OGPRUS.

71. Letter signed by Miguel Casiano, Bartolo Santiago, Manuel Rivero, and others from the Richmond Hill Camp in Lyons, New York, June 28, 1958, Farm Labor Program, Claims and Complaints, 1951–1959, Box 392, Folders 1–4, OGPRUS.

72. Casiano stated that the farmers treated them very poorly: "Lo amenazas votarlo a la carretera." Claim form from Miguel Casiano at Marion Labor Camp in 1958, Farm Labor Program, Claims and Complaints, 1951–1959, Box 392, Folders 1–4, OGPRUS.

73. Annual Agricultural and Food Processing Report, Puerto Rico, (1953), Administration, Annual Farm Labor Reports, 1952–1966, Box 3248, OGPRUS.

74. Claim filed by Alejandro Hernandez Alicea and others, Ciaone Brothers Farmers and Gardeners in Keyport, New Jersey, March 28, 1957, Farm Labor Program, Claims and Complaints, 1951–1959, Box 392, Folders 4, OGPRUS.

75. Sometimes the MD was successful in protecting farm workers by ensuring unpaid wages owed to workers were paid by the employer, which happened often when the worker left the place of employment before the contract expired.

76. Claim filed by Belen Ildefonso Morales, J. D. Noller and Sons Farms and Gardeners, Keyport, New Jersey, April 1, 1957; claim filed by Andrés Arroyo, Curtice Brothers Growers, Morris, New York, July 7, 1958, Farm Labor Program, Claims and Complaints, 1951–1959, Box 392, Folders 1–4, OGPRUS.

77. Memo from the PRDL, [no date], Box 2961, Folder 5, OGPRUS.

78. Proceedings, Bulletin 186, Workmen's Compensation Problems, U.S. Department of Labor (Washington, D.C.: U.S Government Printing Office, 1955); PRDL *Annual Agricultural and Food Processing Report*, 1955, Box 3248, OGPRUS.

79. Senior, *Strangers,* 26.

80. *1951 Migration Division Report*, Reel 120, Box 2775 and Box 2776, OGPRUS.

81. The Joint Committee gave second preference to contract laborers from the British West Indies, who had been transported for farm work to the Eastern United States since April 1943. "Statement of the U.S. section, Joint U.S.-Mexico Trade Union Committee on the Importance of Japanese, Chinese, Filipino and Other Agricultural Workers into Areas Supplied by the Mexican Contract Labor Program," June 28, 1956, Box 17, Folder 6, Ernesto Galarza Papers [EGP].

82. Milton Plumb, "What Is the Truth About the British West Indies Labor Program?" June 12, 1959, Box 17, Folder 6, EGP; "Statement of the U.S. section, Joint U.S.-Mexico Trade Union Committee," EGP.

83. Briggs, *Reproducing Empire,* 16–17; Ann Stoler, "Making Empire Respectable: The Politics of Race and Sexual Morality in Twentieth-Century Colonial Cultures," *American Ethnologist* 16, no. 4 (1989).

Chapter 6

1. WINEC (later the West Indies National Council) attempted to use the security crisis to lobby for American support of West Indian rights and interests, including self-government.

Parker, *Brother's Keeper,* 27–33; Howard Johnson, "The Anglo-American Caribbean Commission and the Extension of American Influence in the British Caribbean, 1942–1945," *Journal of Commonwealth and Comparative Politics* 22 (1984): 180–203.

2. While there were some minor differences in the agreements between islands, for the most part they retained the basic provisions of the bracero program agreement. Unlike the Mexican labor importation agreement, there was no formal diplomatic exchange of notes between governments, but a series of memoranda drawn up by representatives of both the U.S. and British governments.

3. The collapse in the price of sugar, together with greater restrictions on immigration in the late 1920s and 1930s, produced pressure on wages and employment throughout the British Caribbean. Between 1935 and 1938, there were several strikes, disputes, and riots in St. Kitts, St. Lucia, British Guiana, and St. Vincent (1935), Tobago, Trinidad, and Barbados (1937), and Jamaica (1938). Olive Holmes, "Anglo-American Caribbean Commission," 242; Parker, *Brother's Keeper,* 21–23, 35; Charles Taussig, "A Four-Power Program in the Caribbean," 702–703; Nigel O. Bolland, *On the March: Labour Rebellions in the British Caribbean, 1934–39* (Kingston: Ian Randle, 1995); Greg Grandin, *Empire's Workshop,* 34; Harvey Neptune, *Caliban and the Yankees: Trinidad and the United States Occupation* (Chapel Hill: University of North Carolina Press, 2007).

4. U.S. Department of State, *The Caribbean Islands and the War: A Record of Progress in Facing Stern Realities* (Washington, D.C.: U.S. Government Printing Office, 1943), 1, 38.

5. Original Agreement between the United States and Jamaican Government, April 5, 1943, RG 224, Records of the Office of Labor, War Food Administration, Entry 6, Box 18, NARA; Work Agreement (Jamaican Workers) revised March 21, 1945, RG 174, General Records of the Department of Labor, Entry 25, Box 7, NARA; Agreement for the Employment of Bahamians in the United States, March 16, 1943, RG 224, Records of the Office of Labor, War Food Administration, Entry 6, Box 18, NARA.

6. See Jason M. Colby, *The Business of Empire*; Gabrielle E. Clark, "From the Panama Canal to Post-Fordism: Producing Temporary Labor Migrants Within and Beyond Agriculture in the United States (1904–2013)," *Antipode* (2016).

7. "The Di Giorgio Fruit Corp. Completes Huge New Banana Line-Up," *The Chicago Packer,* March 10, 1928; *The Di Giorgio Story,* pamphlet by Di Giorgio Fruit Corporation, San Francisco, California (1959); Steve Stoll, *The Fruits of Natural Advantage: Making the Industrial Countryside in California* (Berkeley: University of California Press, 1998), 60–61; Curtis Marez, *Farmworker Futurism: Speculative Technologies of Resistance* (Minneapolis: University of Minnesota Press, 2015), 53–56.

8. The islands involved in the British West Indies Labor programs included Jamaica, Barbados, and the Bahamas, as well as British Honduras (now Belize). Scholarship on the World War II labor programs in the British West Indies includes Cindy Hahamovitch, *No Man's Land*; David Griffith, *American Guestworkers: Jamaicans and Mexicans in the U.S. Labor Market* (University Park: Pennsylvania State University Press, 2006); David Griffith, "Peasants in Reserve: Temporary West Indian Labor in the U.S. Farm Labor Market," *International Migration Review* 40 (1986): 875–898: Joyce C. Vialet, *The West Indies (BWI) Temporary Alien Labor Program: 1943–1977: A Study* (Washington, D.C.: U.S. Government Printing Office, 1978); Immanuel Ness, *Guestworkers and Resistance to U.S. Corporate Despotism* (Urbana: University of Illinois Press, 2011).

9. James Edward Watt at Camp Ritta in Clewiston, Florida, to the War Food Administration, Office of Labor, no date; Barbados Workers at Fort Eustis in Livingston, Virginia, August 11, 1944; A. F. Simmonds at Kennedyville Camp in Maryland, August 1944, National Archives and

Records Administration, RG 224, Records of the Office of Labor, War Food Administration, Entry 6, Box 17, NARA.

10. Eric E. Williams, *The Negro in the Caribbean* (Washington, D.C.: Associates in Negro Folk Education, 1942), 26, 108–109.

11. Eric E. Williams, *Inward Hunger: The Education of a Prime Minister* (London: André Deutsch, 1969), 81; Tony Martin, "Eric Williams and the Anglo-American Caribbean Commission: Trinidad's Future Nationalist Leader as Aspiring Imperial Bureaucrat, 1942–1944," *Journal of African American History* 88, no. 3 (Summer 2003): 274–290.

12. *Negro in the Caribbean*, 26, 108–109.

13. Taussig, "Four-Power," 708.

14. *The Caribbean Islands and the War*.

15. *The Caribbean Islands and the War*; Anglo-American Caribbean Commission, *Report of the Anglo-American Caribbean Commission to the Governments of the US and Great Britain for the Years 1942-1943* (Washington, D.C.: U.S. Government Printing Office, 1943), 23; *Report of the Anglo-American Caribbean Commission to the Governments of the US and Great Britain for the Year 1945* (Washington, D.C.: U.S. Government Printing Office, 1945), 13.

16. Nine Jamaicans at Somers, Connecticut, May 22, 1944, to the WFA; Forty Bahamians (Eustace Johnson, Leroy Curry, Edward McPhee, et al.) from Stony Brook Camp in Dansville, New York, August 17, 1944, to the WFA, from RG 224, Records of the Office of Labor, War Food Administration, Entry 6, Box 17, NARA.

17. Joel Seymour of Hebron, Maryland, Labor Camp to Washington Labor Officer of the Bahamas Agricultural Workers, RG 224, Records of the Office of Labor, War Food Administration, Entry 6, Box 17, NARA.

18. E. R. Crusbee to G. A. Woodruff, September 1943, RG 224, Records of the Office of Labor, War Food Administration, Entry 6, Box 17, NARA.

19. Newspaper clipping, "Saturday Night Race Riot Termed as 'Unfortunate,'" August 19, 1943, RG 224, Records of the Office of Labor, War Food Administration, Entry 6, Box 17, NARA.

20. Nelson Hopper to Howard Preston, October 21, 1944, RG 224 Records of the Office of Labor, War Food Administration, Entry 6, Box 17, NARA.

21. E. R. Ormsbee to M. E. Hays, September 1943; Jamaican workers at Stoughton, Wisconsin, to Herbert MacDonald, August 13, 1943, RG 224, Records of the Office of Labor, War Food Administration, Entry 6, Box 17, NARA.

22. M. S. Goodman to Herbert MacDonald, September 14, 1943, RG 224, Records of the Office of Labor, War Food Administration, Entry 6, Box 17, NARA.

23. See *Report of the Office of the Liaison Officer, Representing the Jamaican Government, Re: Kennedyville, Maryland*, August 28, 1944, RG 224, Records of the Office of Labor, War Food Administration, Entry 6, Box 17, NARA. Also see response from William N. Ensor, Area Representative of the WFA, September 6, 1944, RG 224, Records of the Office of Labor, War Food Administration, Entry 6, Box 17, NARA.

24. Howard A. Preston to Director of Labor, 1944, RG 224, Entry 6, Box 17, NARA.

25. Article from the *Nassau Tribune*, February 24, 1944; Philip Bruton to his Royal Highness, the Duke of Windsor, governor of the Bahamas Islands, March 31, 1944, RG 224, Records of the Office of Labor, War Food Administration, Entry 6, Box 17, NARA.

26. "Bahamians in Florida: the following letter has been received by us for publication: WFA, Wash," *Nassau Tribune*, March 31, 1944, RG 224, Records of the Office of Labor, War Food Administration, Entry 6, Box 17, NARA. (Letter from Philip Bruton.)

27. Letter from eight workers at Lyndonville Labor Center in Orleans County, New York, July 9, 1944, RG 224, Records of the Office of Labor, War Food Administration, Entry 6, Box 17, NARA.

28. Reports on Port Jefferson and Deansboro Farm Labor Camps, July 25, 1944, RG 224, Records of the Office of Labor, War Food Administration, Entry 6, Box 17, NARA.

29. M. E. Hays to the Director of Labor of the WFA in Philadelphia, July 11, 1944, RG 224, Records of the Office of Labor, War Food Administration, Entry 6, Box 17, NARA.

30. Letter from Bahamian workers, September 11, 1944, RG 224, Records of the Office of Labor, War Food Administration, Entry 6, Box 17, NARA.

31. Howard Preston to the Office of Labor, September 23, 1944; Jamaican "Committee" at Cool Springs Camp to President Roosevelt, August 18, 1944, RG 224, Entry 6, Box 17, NARA.

32. Letter from James Buchanan, Bahamian worker at Cheriton, Virginia, camp, June 26, 1944, RG 224, Records of the Office of Labor, War Food Administration, Entry 6, Box 17, NARA.

33. *Daily Gleaner,* November 6, 1943; *Pittsburgh Courier,* October 26, 1943; *Palm Beach Post,* October 9 and 15–16, 1943, quoted in Hahamovitch, *No Man's Land,* 73–74.

34. In a few instances, Mexican braceros worked on the same farms as Jamaicans, but were kept in separate camps. Their letters of complaint had to be kept separate because they went to different reporting offices, one in Berkeley and one in Philadelphia. Report by William A. Anglim, chief of operations of the WFA, May 24, 1945, RG 174, General Records of the Department of Labor, Box 7, Entry 25, NARA.

35. Report by William A. Anglim.

36. Wallace M. Chapman, medical report, Southwestern Division, October 1944, RG 224, Entry 6, Box 22, NARA.

37. Letter, August 5, 1944, RG 224, Records of the Office of Labor, War Food Administration, Entry 6, Box 17, NARA.

38. Note: After the war, the AACC became the Caribbean Commission (CC) in 1946 when France and the Netherlands joined the organization.

39. David E. Christian to Jerry R. Holleman, February 24 , March 28, 1961, RG 211, Records of the War Manpower Commission, Entry 25, Box 2, NARA.

40. Philip Kasinitz, *Caribbean New York: Black Immigrants and the Politics of Race* (Ithaca, NY: Cornell University Press, 1992); W. Burghardt Turner and Joyce Moore Turner, *Richard B. Moore, Caribbean Militant in Harlem: Collected Writings 1920–1974* (Bloomington: Indiana University Press, 1988); Winston James, *Holding Aloft the Banner of Ethiopia: Caribbean Radicalism in Early Twentieth Century America* (New York: Verso, 1999).

41. Ethelred Brown to C. E. Herdt, July 13, 1944, RG 224, Records of the Office of Labor, War Food Administration, Entry 6, Box 17, NARA.

42. Origen Taylor to Marvin Jones, December 8, 1944. Howard Preston to the Director of Labor, October 27, 1944, RG 224, Entry 6, Box 17, NARA.

43. See James, *Holding Aloft the Banner.*

44. The transcript of Robeson's speech is in the Robeson Archives at Howard University, quoted in Martin Bauml Duberman, *Paul Robeson* (New York: Knopf, 1988), 266.

45. Turner and Turner, *Richard B. Moore,* 76. Richard B. Moore, "Declaration of Rights of the Caribbean Peoples to Self-Determination and Self-Government," quoted in Turner and Turner, 263.

46. Carole Boyce Davies, Meredith Gadsby, et al., eds., *Decolonizing the Academy: African Diaspora Studies* (Trenton, NJ: Africa World Press, 2003), 48.

47. "FDR, Churchill Asked to Consider Color Problems," *Baltimore Afro-American*, August 28, 1943, 9, quoted in Von Eschen, 42.

48. Von Eschen, 7, 75–84; Turner and Turner, 79–80.

49. Speech by Richard B. Moore, April 6. 1945, Turner and Turner, 79–80.

50. Turner and Turner, 271–278.

51. Eric D. Duke, *Building a Nation: Caribbean Federation in the Black Diaspora* (Gainesville: University Press of Florida, 2015).

52. Richard B. Moore, "Declaration of Rights of the Caribbean Peoples to Self-Determination and Self-Government," submitted to the Pan-American Foreign Ministers' conference in Havana Cuba (July 1940), quoted in Turner and Turner, 263.

53. Moore, "Declaration of Rights," 263.

54. *The Caribbean Islands and the War.*

55. Ralph J. Bunche, "The Anglo-American Caribbean Commission: An Experiment in Regional Cooperation," Ninth Conference of the Institute of Pacific Relations, January 1945.

56. Black radicals maintained that colonized peoples ought to have representation in international bodies if dependent areas would be administered under a trusteeship or League of Nations-style mandate system, to ensure their security on the path to independence. Von Eschen, *Race against Empire*, 77; Carol Anderson, *Eyes Off the Prize: The United Nations and the African American Struggle for Human Rights, 1944-1955* (Cambridge: Cambridge University Press, 2003).

57. Richard B. Moore, "Appeal to the United Nations Conference on International Organization on Behalf of Caribbean Peoples," May 25, 1945, West Indies National Council, in Turner and Turner, 271. It is also important to note that the vision of the UN was contested by many Black civil rights activists, as a delegation of members of the NAACP at Dumbarton Oaks in 1944 suggests.

58. Amy Ashwood Garvey was a member of the Council on African Affairs (CAA), working with Black public figures like C. L. R. James, Paul Robeson, W. E. B. Du Bois, and George Padmore. Rhoda Reddock, "The First Mrs. Garvey and Others: Pan-Africanism and Feminism in the Early 20th Century British Colonial Caribbean," *Feminist Africa* 19 (September 2014): 69.

59. Duberman, *Paul Robeson,* 243–248.

60. John Robert Badger quoting Max Yergan, "World View: Correct Policy for Africa," *Chicago Defender,* July 29, 1944, quoted in Von Eschen, 71. Yergan also argued that since the world economy was severely distorted by the political and economic exploitation of colonial peoples, "such markets can only be created by raising the purchasing power in those dependent areas where millions have hitherto known little but poverty and want."

61. Kumar Goshal, "As an Indian sees it: Collaboration, Not Rivalry, Key to Post-War World," *Pittsburgh Courier,* July 1, 1944, quoted in Von Eschen, 71.

62. Anglo-American Caribbean Commission, *Report, 1942-1943,*" 13.

63. *The Caribbean Islands and the War,* 38–41.

64. "Dumbarton Oaks Proposals Exclude Colonies—Du Bois," *Baltimore Afro-American,* October 28, 1944, quoted in Von Eschen, 77.

65. Quotes from Duberman, 255, 258. Also see George Padmore, "The Second World War and the Darker Races," *Crisis* 45, no. 11 (1939), quoted in Von Eschen, 42.

66. Claudia Jones, "American Imperialism and the British West Indies," *Public Affairs* (April 1958), Box 3, Claudia Jones Memorial Collection, Schomburg Center for Research in Black Culture, New York.

67. Alyosha Goldstein, "The Attributes of Sovereignty: The Cold War, Colonialism, and Community Education in Puerto Rico," in *Imagining Our Americas*, ed. Shukla and Tinsman, 313–318.

68. This base had emerged as part of the Bases-for-Destroyers deal the United States signed with Great Britain in 1940. Ken Boodhoo, *The Life of Eric Williams* (Kingston: Ian Randle, 2002), 102, 112–113; Tanya L. Shields, *Inward Hunger: How Eric Williams Fails Postcolonial History* (Oxford: University of Mississippi, 2015).

69. Wendell Willkie was the Republican candidate running against Roosevelt in 1940. His best-selling book, *One World*, advocated the end of colonialism, with the United States' leadership rallying and unifying people across the globe. The Atlantic Charter codified his ideas. Wendell Willkie, *One World* (New York: Simon & Schuster, 1943).

70. Eric Williams, "Massa Day Done," in *Eric E. Williams Speaks: Essays on Colonialism and Independence*, ed. Selwyn Reginald Cudjoe (Wellesley, MA: Calaloux, 1993), 253–254.

71. Canada began to import guestworkers from Jamaica in 1966. Boodhoo, 15, 121. Selwyn Ryan, *Eric Williams: The Myth and the Man* (Kingston: University of the West Indies Press, 2009), 340–341; Judith-Ann Walker, *Development Administration in the Caribbean: Independent Jamaica and Trinidad & Tobago* (New York: Palgrave Macmillan, 2002), 21. Laura Hernández, "The Constitutional Limits of Supply and Demand: Why a Successful Guestworker Program Must Include a Path to Citizenship," *Stanford Journal of Civil Rights and Civil Liberties* (June 2014): 267.

72. E. Franklin Frazier and Eric Eustace Williams, *The Economic Future of the Caribbean*, Seventh Annual Conference of the Division of Social Sciences (Washington, D.C.: Howard University Press, 1944).

73. Claudia Jones, "American Imperialism"; American Committee for the Protection of Foreign Born in New York, "Our Badge of Infamy: A Petition to the United Nations on the Treatment of the Mexican Immigrant, April 1959," Schomburg Center, Box 3, Claudia Jones Memorial Collection.

74. Franklin and Williams, 58.

75. Hahamovitch, *No Man's Land*, 101–102.

76. Hahamovitch, 191–193.

77. Deborah Thomas, *Modern Blackness: Nationalism, Globalization, and the Politics of Culture in Jamaica* (Durham, NC: Duke University Press, 2004), 4.

78. Speech by Teodoro Moscoso (World Affairs Conference, Marquette University, Milwaukee, Wisconsin, September 29, 1962), John F. Kennedy Presidential Library and Museum Archives; Speech by President John F. Kennedy, "On the Alliance for Progress, 1961," *Department of State Bulletin* 44, no. 1136 (April 3, 1961), 471–474; Michael E. Latham, "Ideology, Social Science, and Destiny: Modernization and the Kennedy-Era Alliance for Progress," *Diplomatic History* 22 (April 1998): 199–229; A. W. Maldonado, *Teodoro Moscoso and Puerto Rico's Operation Bootstrap*, 173–175.

Epilogue

1. "Farm Labor Organizing, 1905–1967: A Brief History," National Advisory Committee on Farm Labor (July 1967).

2. NAFCL Information Letter #19, April 1962; Statement of Frederick Van Dyke of the NAFCL, March 7. 1961; Letter from Fay Bennett, secretary of the NAFCL, October 26, 1961; NAFCL pamphlet, *PL-78 How it Works*, Myer Feldman to A. Philip Randolph, RG 211, Records of the War Manpower Commission, Entry 25, Box 2, NARA.

3. Cornelius Bynum, *A. Philip Randolph and the Struggle for Civil Rights* (Urbana: University of Illinois Press, 2010); Herbert Garfinkel, *When Negroes March: The March on Washington Movement in the Organizational Politics for FEPC* (New York: Atheneum, 1969); Merl Elwyn Reed, *Seedtime for the Modern Civil Rights Movement: The President's Committee on Fair Employment Practice, 1941–1946* (Baton Rouge: Louisiana State University Press, 1991).

4. Fernández, "Of Immigrants and Migrants," 8; Ismael García-Colón, "'We Like Mexican Laborers Better': Citizenship and Immigration Policies in the Formation of Puerto Rican Farm Labor in the United States," *CENTRO Journal* (Summer 2017).

5. Galarza's work was instrumental in establishing this civil rights consensus, leading up to the much-publicized November 1960 CBS documentary "Harvest of Shame." This film convinced President Kennedy and many others that braceros were adversely affecting the wages, working conditions, and employment opportunities of our own agricultural workers, leading to the "end" of the program. *Harvest of Shame* (CBS Productions, 1960). See Lori Flores, *Grounds for Dreaming*, 143–146.

6. Ana Raquel Minian's book *Undocumented Lives* demonstrates that the Mexican government actively supported the migration of Mexican men to the United States during the 1970s, even as U.S. authorities pursued more aggressive anti-immigrant measures.

7. Minian, 185–226; Jimmy Patiño, *Raza Sí, Migra No: Chicano Movement Struggles for Immigrant Rights in San Diego* (Chapel Hill: University of North Carolina Press, 2017), 1–2.

8. IRCA also established the new Seasonal Agricultural Worker (SAW) program, in which migrants who could prove that they had been in the U.S. for a minimum of ninety days during the year ending on May 1, 1986, were offered a path to legal residency. IRCA's policies structured immigration reform proposals for the next thirty years following its passage. Minian, 207.

9. Rules governing labor disputes, meals, housing, rates of pay, transportation, and the three-quarter work guarantee, still remain central components of the labor contract. U.S. Department of Homeland Security, "Changes to Requirements Affecting H-2A Nonimmigrants," 73 *Federal Register* 76891, December 18, 2008; Congressional Research Service, "H2A and H2B Temporary Worker Visas: Policy and Related Issues," June 29, 2020; U.S. Department of Labor, H2-A Agricultural Clearance Order, FORM ETA-790A, Expiration August 31, 2022.

10. This is not to say that pursuing national independence meant an equal power relationship between imperial centers. After all, national independence and bilateralism have often meant political and economic dependence justified through a logic of anti-imperialism, as we can see early on with the U.S. Platt Amendment in Cuba in 1901, and later with the Good Neighbor Policy in 1933. These two U.S. state policies hardly signaled the end of empire. Juan Gonzalez, *Harvest of Empire: A History of Latinos in America* (New York: Penguin, 2000), 63–64; Colby, 61. Also see Louis Pérez, *Cuba Under the Platt Amendment, 1902–1934* (Pittsburgh: University of Pittsburgh Press, 1986).

11. Stokely Carmichael, "Toward Black Liberation" (September 1966) and "Solidarity with Latin America" (July 1967) in *Stokely Speaks: From Black Power to Pan-Africanism* (Chicago: Lawrence Hill, 2007 [1971]), 35, 101, 104.

12. Stokely Carmichael, "What We Want," *New York Review of Books* 7 (September 1966), in *Stokely Speaks*, 5–6.

13. Letter dated April 5, 1978, Box 30, Folder 6, Herman Baca Papers, University of California, San Diego, quoted in Patiño, 228–245.

14. Galarza interview at Camp McCallum in Salinas, California, October 4, 1955, Box 18, Folder 6, Ernesto Galarza Papers (EGP), Special Collections, Stanford University Libraries.

BIBLIOGRAPHY OF PRIMARY SOURCES

Manuscript and Archival Collections

College Park, Maryland
U.S. National Archives and Records Administration (NARA)
RG 11, General Records of the United States Government
RG 16, Records of the Office of the Secretary of Agriculture, including records of the Office for Agricultural War Relations
RG 96, Records of the Farmers Home Administration, including records of the Farm Security Administration and the Resettlement Administration (FSA)
RG 174, General Records of the Department of Labor (DOL)
RG 183, Records of the U.S. Employment Service (USES)
RG 224, Records of the Office of Labor, War Food Administration (WFA)
RG 211, Records of the War Manpower Commission (WMC)
RG 208, Records of the Office of War Information (OWI)
RG 233, Records of the United States House of Representatives
Records of the Department of State relating to the internal affairs of Mexico, 1940–1949; 1950–1959 (Decimal File 812)

Los Angeles, California
Occidental College Special Collections

Mexico City, Mexico
Archivo General de la Nación (AGN) Galería 3: Presidentes Miguel Alemán Valdés, Manuel Ávila Camacho, Adolfo López Mateos, Adolfo Ruiz Cortines

Stanford, California
Special Collections and University Archives, Stanford University. Ernesto Galarza Papers (EGP), Anne Loftis Papers

Washington, D.C.
Organization of American States (formerly the Pan-American Union)
Columbus Memorial Library Publications and Lectures by Ernesto Galarza

New York, New York
Hunter College, City University of New York, CENTRO de Estudios Puertorriqueños

Records of the Offices of the Government of Puerto Rico in the United States (OGPRUS)
Schomburg Center for Research in Black Culture

New York Public Library
Claudia Jones Memorial Collection

Government Publications

Anglo-American Caribbean Commission. *Report of the Anglo-American Caribbean Commission to the Governments of the United States and Great Britain for the Years 1942–1943*. Washington, D.C.: United States Government Printing Office, 1943.

Anglo-American Caribbean Commission. *Report of the West Indian Conference Held in Barbados*. Washington, D.C.: United States Government Printing Office, 1944.

Eisenhower, Milton. "War Relocation Work Corps: A Circular for Enlistees and Their Families," War Relocation Authority. Washington, D.C.: United States Government Printing Office, 1942.

President's Commission on Migratory Labor. *Report of the President's Commission on Migratory Labor*, by Maurice J. Tobin, secretary, U.S. Department of Labor, and William L. Connolly, director, Bureau of Labor Standards. Washington, D.C.: U.S. Department of Labor, April 1952.

President's Committee on Civil Rights. *To Secure These Rights: The Report of Harry S. Truman's Committee on Civil Rights*. Washington, D.C.: United States Government Printing Office, 1947.

U.S. Department of Agriculture. *Termination of the Bracero Program: Some Effects on Farm Labor and Migrant Housing Needs*, by Robert C. McElroy and Earle E. Gavett. *Agricultural Economic Report No. 77*. Washington, D.C.: United States Government Printing Office, 1965.

U.S. Department of State. *The Caribbean Islands and the War: A Record of Progress in Facing Stern Realities*. Washington, D.C.: United States Government Printing Office, 1943.

U.S. House of Representatives. Committee on Education and Labor. *National Labor Relations Board, Hearings before the Committee on Education and Labor, United States Senate, on S. 1958, a Bill to Promote Equality of Bargaining Power between Employers and Employees, to Diminish the Causes of Labor Disputes, to Create a National Labor Relations Board, and for Other Purpose*. Statement of Senator Wagner, 74th Congress, 1st Session. Washington, D.C.: United States Government Printing Office, 1935.

U.S. House of Representatives. Committee on the Judiciary. *To Control Illegal Migration: Hearings Before the Subcommittee on Immigration and Naturalization of the Committee on the Judiciary, on S. 3660 and S. 3661*. Statement of Ernesto Galarza. 83rd Congress, 2nd Session, July 12, 13, and 14, 1954. Washington, D.C.: United States Government Printing Office, 1954.

U.S. House of Representatives, House Report 1911. *Fourth Interim Report of the Select Committee Investigating National Defense Migration. Findings and Recommendations on Evacuation of Enemy Aliens and Others From Prohibited Military Zones*. Select Committee Investigating National Defense Migration. 77th Congress, 2nd session. March 19, 1942. Washington, D.C.: United States Government Printing Office, 1942.

U.S. House of Representatives, House Report 2124. *Final Report of the Select Committee Investigating National Defense Migration*. Select Committee Investigating National Defense Migration. 77th Congress, 2nd session. Washington, D.C.: United States Government Printing Office, 1942.

U.S. House of Representatives. Select Committee to Investigate the Interstate Migration of Destitute Citizens (Tolan Committee). *Resolutions to Inquire into the Migration of Destitute Citizens, to Study, Survey, and Investigate the Social and Economic Needs and the Movement of*

Indigent Persons Across State Lines, 76th Congress, 3rd Session, Part 10, Washington hearings, December 11, 1940, and February 26, 1941. Washington, D.C.: United States Government Printing Office, 1941.

U.S. House of Representatives. Select Committee Investigating National Defense Migration (Tolan Committee). *A Resolution to Inquire Further into the Interstate Migration of Citizens, Emphasizing the Present and Potential Consequences of the Migration Caused by the National Defense Program, Pursuant to H. Res. 113,* 77th Congress, 2nd Session. Part 29, San Francisco hearings: Problems of Evacuation of Enemy Aliens and Others from Prohibited Military Zones. 77th Congress, 2nd Session, February 21, 23, 1942. Washington, D.C.: United States Government Printing Office, 1942.

U.S. House of Representatives. Select Committee Investigating National Defense Migration (Tolan Committee). *A Resolution to Inquire Further into the Interstate Migration of Citizens, Emphasizing the Present and Potential Consequences of the Migration Caused by the National Defense Program, Pursuant to H. Res. 113,* 77th Congress, 2nd Session, Part 30, February 26, 28, and March 2, 1942; Part 31, February 26, 28, and March 2, 1942; Part 33, May 22, June 11, 19, 1942. Washington, D.C.: United States Government Printing Office, 1942.

U.S. House of Representatives. Subcommittee on Labor and Labor Management Relations. *Migratory Labor: Hearings Before the Subcommittee on Labor and Labor Management Relations of the Committee on Labor and Public Welfare,* 82nd Congress, 2nd Session. February 5, 6, 7, 11, 14, 15, 27, 28, 29 and March 27, 28, 1952. Washington, D.C.: United States Government Printing Office, 1952.

Supreme Court Cases

Chae Chan Ping v. United States 130 U.S. 581 (1889).
Downes v. Bidwell 182 U.S. 244 (1901).
Plessy v. Ferguson 163 U.S. 537 (1896).
United States v. Ju Toy 198 U.S. 253 (1905).

Periodicals

Chicago Packer
Daily News
Life
New York Times
Rocky Shimpo
Sacramento Bee
Saturday Evening Post
St. Petersburg Times
Survey Graphic: Magazine of Social Interpretation
The Teamster
El Tiempo (Mexico)
Time

Presidential Speeches

Adams, John Quincy. "Speech to the U.S. House of Representatives on Foreign Policy," July 4, 1821. Miller Center, University of Virginia,.

Kennedy, John F. "On the Alliance for Progress, 1961." *Department of State Bulletin* 44, no. 1136 (April 3, 1961).

Monroe, James. "Seventh Annual Message" (Monroe Doctrine), December 2,1823. Miller Center, University of Virginia. http://millercenter.org/president/monroe/speeches/speech -3604.

Polk, James K. "Inaugural Address," March 4, 1845. Avalon Project, Yale Law School. http:// avalon.law.yale.edu/19th_century/polk.asp

Roosevelt, Franklin D. "First Inaugural Address," March 4, 1933. American Presidency Project.

———. "The Good Neighbor Policy," August 1936. Franklin D. Roosevelt Presidential Library.

———. "Statement on Signing the National Labor Relations Act," July 5, 1935. American Presidency Project.

———. "United Effort for a Better World: Interdependence of All Nations," radio broadcast from Monterrey, Mexico, April 20, 1943. In *Vital Speeches of the Day* 4.

———. "We Hold These Truths: The Rights to Life, Liberty and the Pursuit of Happiness," December 15, 1941. In *Vital Speeches of the Day* 6.

Roosevelt, Theodore. "Corollary to the Monroe Doctrine," Annual Message Before Congress. December 6, 1904. https://www.ourdocuments.gov/doc.php?doc=56.

Truman, Harry S. "First Inaugural Address," January 20, 1949. Harry S. Truman Library and Museum.

Supplemental Primary Sources

Allen, Devere. *The Caribbean: Laboratory of World Cooperation*. New York: League for Industrial Democracy, 1943.

Anderson, Henry P. *The Bracero Program in California, with Particular Reference to Health Status, Attitudes, and Practices*. Berkeley: School of Public Health, University of California, 1961.

———. "Fields of Bondage: The Mexican Contract Labor System in Industrialized Agriculture," mimeographed typescript, 1963.

Austin, Augustine A. NAACP 1940–55. General Office File. Leagues—Anglo-American Caribbean Commission, 1946–51. Papers of the NAACP. Part 14, Race Relations in the International Arena, 1940–1955. Frederick, MD: University Publications of America, 1992.

Beezley, William. *Mexicans in Revolution, 1910–1946: An Introduction*. Lincoln: University of Nebraska Press, 2009.

Bell, Wendell, ed. *The Democratic Revolution in the West Indies: Studies in Nationalism, Leadership, and the Belief in Progress*. Cambridge, MA: Schenkman, 1967.

Bunche, Ralph J. "The Anglo-American Caribbean Commission: An Experiment in Regional Cooperation." The American Council of the Institute of Pacific Relations for the 9th conference of the Institute of Pacific Relations, January 1945. Washington, D.C.: United States Government Printing Office, 1945.

"The Caribbean Islands and the War: Extracts from a Survey of the Aims and Accomplishments of the Anglo-American Caribbean Commission Published by the U.S. Government." *Canada-West Indies Magazine* (1944): 9–14.

Carmichael, Stokely. *Stokely Speaks: From Black Power to Pan-Africanism*. Chicago: Lawrence Hill Books, 2007 [1971].

Chase, Stuart. *Operation Bootstrap in Puerto Rico: Report of Progress*. Washington, D.C.: National Planning Association, 1951.

"Conference on a Post-war Program for West Indies, Anglo-American Caribbean Commission, Barbados, March 21–30, 1944." *Monthly Labor Review* 59 (1944): 110.

Corson, John J. *Manpower for Victory: Total Mobilization for Total War.* New York: Farrar & Rinehart, 1943.

De Iturbide, A. "Mexican Haciendas: The Peon System." *North American Review* (April 1899).

Durand, J. "The Bracero Program: A Critical Appraisal." *Migración y Desarollo* (2007).

Franklin, Frazier E., and Eric Eustace Williams, *The Economic Future of the Caribbean,* Seventh Annual Conference of the Division of Social Sciences. Washington, D.C.: Howard University Press, 1944.

Galarza, Ernesto. *Educational Trends in Latin America.* Washington, D.C.: Pan-American Union, Division of Intellectual Cooperation, 1937.

———. *Farm Workers and Agri-business in California, 1947–1960.* Notre Dame, IN: University of Notre Dame Press, 1977.

———. *Labor Trends and Social Welfare in Latin America.* Washington, D.C.: Pan-American Union, Division of Labor and Social Information, 1941.

———. *Merchants of Labor: The Mexican Bracero Story: An Account of the Managed Migration of Mexican Farm Workers in California, 1942–1960.* Santa Barbara, CA: McNally & Loftin, 1964.

———. *Spiders in the House and Workers in the Field.* Notre Dame, IN: University of Notre Dame Press, 1971.

———. *Strangers in Our Fields: Based on a Report Regarding Compliance with the Contractual, Legal and Civil Rights of Mexican Agricultural Contract Labor in the United States Made Possible through A Grant-in-Aid from the Fund for the Republic,* 2nd ed. Washington, D.C.: Fund for the Republic, 1956.

Galarza, Ernesto, Herbert Eugene Bolton, and Delia Goetz. *American Neighbors.* Washington, D.C.: American National Red Cross, 1940.

Galarza, Ernesto, Gabrielle S. Morris, and Timothy Beard. *The Burning Light: Action and Organizing in the Mexican Community in California.* Berkeley: Regional Oral History Office, Bancroft Library, University of California, 1982.

Green, Philip Leonard. *Pan American Progress.* New York: Hastings House, 1942.

Hansen, Millard. "Training and Research in Puerto Rico." *Annals of the American Academy of Political and Social Science* 285 (January 1953): 110–115.

Henderson, Julia. "Foreign Labour in the United States During the War." *International Labour Review* 609 (1945): 609–630.

Holmes, Olive. *Anglo-American Caribbean Commission; Pattern for Colonial Cooperation. Foreign Policy Reports* 20, no. 19. New York: Foreign Policy Association, 1944.

Jones, Robert C. *Los Braceros Mexicanos en Los Estado Unidos.* Washington, D.C.: Pan-American Union, Division of Labor and Social Information, 1946.

———. *Mexican War Workers in the United States: The Mexico-United States Manpower Recruiting Program and Operation, 1942–1944.* Washington, D.C.: Pan-American Union, Division of Labor and Social Information, 1945.

Kennedy, John F. *A Nation of Immigrants.* New York: Harper and Row, 1964.

Kersten, Andrew E. and David Lucander, eds. *For Jobs and Freedom: Selected Speeches and Writings of A. Philip Randolph.* Amherst: University of Massachusetts Press, 2014.

Locke, John. *Second Treatise of Government.* Indianapolis: Hackett, 1980 [1690].

Lockey, Joseph Byrne. *Essays in Pan-Americanism.* Berkeley: University of California Press, 1939.

McWilliams, Carey. *Factories in the Field: The Story of Migratory Farm Labor in California.* Boston: Little, Brown, 1939.

——. *North from Mexico*. Westport, CT: Greenwood Press, 1948.

——. *Prejudice—Japanese Americans: Symbol of Racial Intolerance*. Hamden, CT: Archon, 1971 [1944].

——. *What About Our Japanese-Americans?* New York: Public Affairs Committee, 1944.

Meyers, Robin, ed. *Poverty on the Land in a Land of Plenty*. New York: National Advisory Committee on Farm Labor, 1965.

Moore, Truman. *The Slaves We Rent*. New York: Random House, 1965.

Muñoz Marín, Luis. "Puerto Rico, A Study in Democratic Development." *Annals of the American Academy of Political Science* (January 1953).

Myrdal, Gunnar. *An American Dilemma: The Negro Problem and Modern Democracy*. New York: Harper & Brothers, 1944.

National Advisory Committee on Farm Labor. *Case for the Domestic Farm Worker*. New York: National Advisory Committee on Farm Labor, 1965.

Padilla, Ezequiel. *Free Men of America*. Chicago: Ziff-Davis, 1943.

Patterson, Ernest Minor, ed. *The United Nations and the Future*. Annals of the American Academy of Political and Social Science. Philadelphia: American Academy of Political and Social Science, 1943.

Phillips, Ulrich B. *American Negro Slavery*. New York: D. Appleton, 1918.

Rasmussen, Wayne D. *A History of the Emergency Farm Labor Supply Program, 1943–47*. Washington, D.C.: U.S. Department of Agriculture, Bureau of Agricultural Economics, 1951.

Republican Congressional Committee. *Republican Text Book for the Campaign of 1898*. Philadelphia: Dunlap, 1898.

Senior, Clarence. *Democracy Comes to a Cotton Kingdom: The Story of Mexico's La Laguna*. Mexico City: Centro de Estudios Pedagogicos e Hispanoamericanos, 1940.

——. *Mexico in Transition*. Milwaukee, WI: Milwaukee Housing Council, 1938.

——. *The Puerto Rican Migrant in St. Croix*. San Juan: University of Puerto Rico, 1947.

——. *Self Determination for Puerto Rico*. New York: Post War World Council, 1946.

——. *Strangers then Neighbors: From Pilgrims to Puerto Ricans*. New York: Freedom Books, 1951.

Smith, Adam. *The Wealth of Nations*. New York: Bantam Classics, 2003 [1776].

Taussig, Charles. "A Four-Power Program in the Caribbean," *Foreign Affairs* 24 (July 1946).

Tugwell, Rexford. *Stricken Land: The Story of Puerto Rico*. New York: Doubleday, 1947.

Vasconcelos, José. *The Cosmic Race/La Raza Cosmica*. Baltimore: Johns Hopkins University Press, 1997 [1925].

Wallace, Henry, Ezequiel Padilla, and Eduardo Salazar, eds. *Pan-American Friendship: Speeches*. Mexico Department of State for Foreign Affairs, Bureau of International News Service, 1941.

Williams, Eric E. *Capitalism and Slavery*. Chapel Hill: University of North Carolina Press, 1944.

——. *Eric E. Williams Speaks: Essays on Colonialism and Independence*. Edited by Selwyn Reginald Cudjoe. Wellesley, MA: Calaloux, 1993.

——. *Inward Hunger: The Education of a Prime Minister*. London: André Deutsch, 1969.

——. *The Negro in the Caribbean*. Washington, D.C.: Associates in Negro Folk Education, 1942.

Willkie, Wendell. *One World*. New York: Simon & Schuster, 1943.

Zeidenfelt, Alex, "Political and Constitutional Development in Jamaica." *Journal of Politics* 14, no. 3 (August 1952): 512–540.

INDEX

Agreement: U.S.–British West Indies, 48, 159, 188–89, 194, 197, 199; U.S.–Mexico, 9, 44–45, 53, 80, 125–27, 138, 144–45; U.S.–Puerto Rico, 168, 174
agriculture, 9–10, 48, 50, 89, 101, 107–8, 153, 157, 158, 167, 191, 208; growers' associations, 45, 112, 114, 127, 165; in Mexico, 43, 67, 73–75, 172
Alemán Valdés, Miguel (Mexican president, 1946–52), 79, 142
Alianza de Braceros, 122, 138–40, 142–43. *See also* Unión de Trabajadores Agrícolas del valle de Mexicali (UTAVM)
Alien Land Laws (1913), 109
American Civil Liberties Union (ACLU), 92, 132–33, 143
American Emigrant Company (AEC), 28
American Farm Bureau Federation, 109
American Federation of Labor (AFL), 30, 38, 132, 142–44, 146, 184, 218; CIO and, 145, 146, 148, 151, 220; NFLU and, 121
American Molasses Company, 158
Anderson, Henry, 19
Anglo-American Caribbean Commission (AACC), 4, 159, 161–62, 188–89, 193–96, 211, 214–15, 222
Anti-Coolie Act (1862), 30
anti-imperialism, 7, 46, 56, 154, 192, 222–23
Anti-Peonage Act (1867), 28
Atlantic Charter, 163, 206

Bahamas Benevolent Protective Association (BBPA), 203–4
bracero program, 2, 9, 12–17, 20–21, 35, 41, 45, 48, 50, 56–57, 65–69, 76–78, 80–82, 85, 118–53, 159, 162, 168, 171, 184, 187, 191, 194, 203, 213, 217–22; as adjustment, 65, 96; citizenship, 87, 135, 146–47, 149;

drying out the wetbacks, 136; gender, 46, 129, 131; as resettlement, 77; as repatriation, 77; resistance, 120–21, 125–31; termination, 2, 220; World War I program, 11, 33–37, 41, 44, 48
British West Indies farm labor programs, 2–4, 10, 24, 42, 150, 157, 159, 184, 188–211, 216, 222; citizenship, 199–200, 202, 206, 218; imprisonment, 198–99, 204; independence, 17, 189, 192–93, 203–16; resistance, 194–202
Burlingame, Anson, 29
Burlingame-Seward Treaty, 29

capitalism, 2, 7, 8, 20, 24, 42, 55, 62, 65, 68, 86, 116, 157, 167, 184, 209–13, 215
Cárdenas, Lázaro (Mexican president, 1934–40), 54, 59, 60, 75, 77, 134, 172
Carmichael, Stokely, 224
Chae Chan Ping v. United States (1889), 32
Chardón Plan (1935), 164
Chávez, César, 56, 150, 219
Chicana/o movement, 122, 148, 219–20, 224
Chinese contract workers. *See* coolies
Chinese Exclusion Act (1882), 21, 30, 31, 108
citizenship, 14, 15, 22, 45, 49, 54, 76, 86, 87, 91, 97–98, 104, 108–10, 115, 117, 122, 124, 135, 147, 149, 160–62, 167, 186, 199–202, 206, 218–21
civil rights movement, 6, 15, 16, 63, 122, 124, 141, 192, 205, 209, 218, 224
Colorado River Indian Reservation, 113
Columbia University, 7, 59, 158
Comarca Lagunera, 172
Communist Party (CPUSA), 37
Confederación de Trabajadores Mexicanos (CTM), 139

ACKNOWLEDGMENTS

As I sit down to write these acknowledgments, I am overwhelmed with gratitude for the numerous people who have helped make writing this book possible. I would not have had the opportunity to write without the generous and gracious support and commitment of many institutions, colleagues, and friends. It was their assistance, care, and support that sustained me and gave me the strength and confidence I needed to persevere.

When I was still in community college, I worked full-time while taking classes and never thought graduate school could be a possibility. I pursued it anyway because of the support and mentorship of dozens of professors and educators at several institutions along the way, who persuaded me to take a chance and make it happen. Though they are not all listed here, I hope they know how appreciated they are. In particular I would like to thank the historian and prolific writer George Cotkin at Cal Poly San Luis Obispo, who saw great potential in me and inspired my intellectual trajectory early on. He and his wife, photographer Marta Peluso, were always supportive, and George commented on early chapters of the dissertation in its fledgling state. At Cal Poly, I would also like to thank Andrew Morris, Matthew Hopper, and Pulitzer Prize-winner Victor Valle for their mentorship and encouragement. Thank you for advocating for me and urging me to keep exploring my capacity as a scholar when I first started out.

The initial research for this project began at the University of Washington, Seattle, where I benefited from the guidance and support of an array of extraordinarily talented scholars. First, I wish to thank Moon-Ho Jung, Ileana Rodriguez-Silva, James Gregory, and Adam Warren for their unceasing mentorship and support from the inception of this project. Moon expanded my perception of what this book could be and pushed me every day to better articulate the political stakes of my project. Jim exerted a steady, critical, indispensable influence on my thinking and writing. Ileana and Adam were both enthusiastic role models and advocates of my work, and emboldened me every step of the way. I will always remember their steadfast support.

I am thankful for the Woodrow Wilson Foundation's Charlotte W. New-combe Doctoral Fellowship for the financial support needed to complete my research on this project. Grants and funding from the Simpson Center for the Study of the Humanities, the Center for the Study of the Pacific Northwest, and the Hanauer Dissertation Fellowship at the University of Washington also made it possible for me to conduct additional archival research in Washington D.C., Mexico City, California, and New York. Quintard Taylor and Jim Gregory also helped this project along by extending funding opportunities via my con-tributions to both of their public history digital projects: The BlackPast.org and the Seattle Civil Rights and Labor History Project. Fellows of a Society of Schol-ars workshop at the University of Washington's Simpson Center, led by Alys Weinbaum and Stephanie Smallwood, read original chapters of the dissertation as I eked out its twists and turns, providing insightful comments. Stephanie Smallwood read an early version of the first chapter of this book, and her advice and scholarship was a source of inspiration. I am also indebted to Michelle Habell-Pallán for her substantial guidance throughout my graduate career. I was fortunate to have met up with Adam Warren and Gabriella Soto Laveaga for a historic tour of downtown Mexico City while completing research there. I would like to thank them as well as the Tepoztlán Institute for creating space for conversations around transnational labor migrations and empire.

At Yale University, a postdoctoral fellowship at the Center for the Study of Race, Indigeneity, and Transnational Migration (RITM) allowed me to pro-cess the transformation of my Ph.D. dissertation into a book and facilitated the production of the manuscript. I would like to thank Stephen Pitti, who provided crucial interventions at the final stage of my revisions and made this a better book. I am grateful to Mary Lui, for taking time away from her own important scholarship to comment on some of my chapters. I would also like to thank Alicia Camacho-Schmidt, Anne Eller, Daphne Brooks, and Albert Laguna for meeting and welcoming me, and hashing over some critical points over coffee or lunch. I cherish the time spent with Damian Vergara Braca-montes, Iliana Yamileth Rodriguez, and Aleshia Barajas, as well as Yale under-graduate students Cathy Calderón, Angie Diaz, Larissa Martinez, and more, without whose company I would have had few opportunities for respite.

At San Francisco State University (SFSU), the highlight of my experi-ence was the support I received from Tomas Almaguer, in what was the first and still remains the only College of Ethnic Studies in the country. There, I received funding from the Office of Research and Sponsored Programs (ORSP) to collect additional sources and finish editing my manuscript. While amassing and organizing information from bracero oral histories, I had the excellent help and intellectual companionship of two Latinx Studies students, Stephanie Berrospe and Jasmin Vargas, who provided thoughtful and critical analyses as they helped me to collect sources. In my Latinx history classes at SFSU, my students taught me just as much as I taught them about immigration law and history. Their insights and personal experiences with U.S. immigration policies and our shared familial relationships with former braceros transformed my own perspective on guestworker programs.

The librarians, archivists, and other staff who helped me find the documents on which this study is based were extremely generous with their time. Special thanks to all those I encountered in the Special Collections Departments of Stanford University Libraries, the Bancroft Library at the University of California, Berkeley, el Archivo General de la Nacíon, México, and the National Archives and Records Administration in College Park, Maryland, and Washington, D.C. I would also like to send many thanks to the library and archives of the Center for Puerto Rican Studies (Centro), housed at Hunter College-CUNY in New York City, especially to Senior Archivist Pedro Juan Hernández, and to other members of the Centro library for assisting with my research there.

Robert Lockhart, my editor at the University of Pennsylvania Press, diligently and enthusiastically held my hand through the editing process. I would like to share a tremendous rush of gratitude to Bob for his openness, generosity, and professional acumen. I would also like to thank the anonymous readers at the University of Pennsylvania Press, who offered deeply substantive remarks that assisted in the revision of my manuscript. This book also owes its existence to several colleagues and friends. At the University of Washington, Quin'Nita Cobbins, Aaron Modica, Shruti Patel, Melanie Hernández, Jennifer Rose Webster, Oscar Rosales-Castañeda, Michael Aguirre, and others encouraged me to keep my perspective and write. At San Francisco State University, Melissa Guzman, Tisa Carillo, Jessica Hernández, and Leslie Quintanilla were my co-conspirators over many drinks and meals—gracías, mujeres fuertes.

Finally, I would like to thank my family and my parents in Anaheim, California, Michael and Karen Quintana, who taught me from an early age to work hard and never give up, nearly to a fault, as they—even today—refuse to rest. My ultimate gratitude goes to my life partner and greatest friend, Eric Chavez, for his dedication, love, and tireless support as I worked on this project. As for our precocious daughters, Aurelia Amaia Chavez and Lucía Luna Chavez, I thank them for their sweet joy and curiosity, reminding me what life is all about.

www.ingramcontent.com/pod-product-compliance
Lightning Source LLC
Chambersburg PA
CBHW021151160426

42812CB00078B/495